Economic Welfare, International Business and Global Institutional Change

The Locke Institute

Founded in 1989, The Locke Institute is an independent, non-partisan, educational and research organization. The Institute is named for John Locke (1632–1704), philosopher and political theorist, who based his theory of society on natural law which required that the ultimate source of political sovereignty was with the individual. Individuals are possessed of inalienable rights variously defined by Locke as 'life, health, liberty and possession', or, more directly, 'life, liberty and property'. It is the function of the state to uphold these rights since individuals would not enter into a political society unless they believed that it would protect their lives, liberties and properties.

The Locke Institute seeks to engender a greater understanding of the concept of natural rights, its implications for constitutional democracy and for economic organization in modern society. The Institute encourages high-quality research utilizing in particular modern theories of property rights, public choice, law and economics, and the new institutional economics as a basis for a more profound understanding of important and controversial issues in political economy. To this end, it commissions books, monographs and shorter studies involving substantive scholarship written for a wide audience, organizes major conferences on fundamental topics in political economy, and supports independent research. The Institute maintains a publishing relationship with Edward Elgar Publishing. It also publishes its own monograph series.

In order to maintain independence, The Locke Institute accepts no government funding. Funding for the Institute is solicited from private foundations, corporations and individuals. In addition, the Institute raises funds from the sale of publications and from conference fees. The Institute is incorporated in the State of Virginia, USA, and enjoys non-profit, tax-exempt status under section 501(c)3 of the United States Internal Revenue Code.

Officers of the Institute are listed above. Please direct all enquiries to the address given below.

4084 University Drive, Suite 103, Fairfax, Virginia 22030, US
Tel. (703) 383 6952 Fax (703) 352 9747
email: locke@thelockeinstitute.org
http://.The LockeInstitute.org

Economic Welfare, International Business and Global Institutional Change

Edited by

Ram Mudambi

Associate Professor, Fox School of Business, Temple University, US and Reader in International Business, University of Reading, UK

Pietro Navarra

Associate Professor of Economics, University of Messina, Italy and Research Associate, CPNSS, London School of Economics, UK

Giuseppe Sobbrio

Professor of Public Economics, University of Messina, Italy

THE LOCKE INSTITUTE

Edward Elgar

Cheltenham, UK • Northampton, MA, USA

Published by
Edward Elgar Publishing Limited
Glensanda House
Montpellier Parade
Cheltenham
Glos GL50 1UA
UK

Edward Elgar Publishing, Inc.
136 West Street
Suite 202
Northampton
Massachusetts 01060
USA

A catalogue record for this book
is available from the British Library

Library of Congress Cataloguing in Publication Data

Economic welfare, international business and global institutional change / edited by Ram Mudambi, Pietro Navarra, Giuseppe Sobbrio.
p. cm.
Includes index.
1. Comparative economics. 2. Comparative government. 3. Globalization—Economic aspects. 4. International business enterprises. I. Mudambi, Ram, 1954– II. Navarra, Pietro. III. Sobbrio, Giuseppe.

HB90 .E276 2003
330.9—dc21

2002034701

ISBN 1 84376 188 2

Typeset by Cambrian Typesetters, Frimley, Surrey
Printed and bound in Great Britain by MPG Books Ltd, Bodmin, Cornwall

Dedication

R.M.
To Sitaram Shastri Athalye

P.N.
To Salvatore Navarra

G.S.
To Giusy

Contents

Contributors

Fabrizio Balassone Banca d'Italia, Italy

Peter Bernholz University of Basel, Switzerland

John Cantwell University of Reading, UK and Rutgers University, USA

Bo Carlsson Case Western Reserve University, USA

Matthew Dobra George Mason University, USA

Thráinn Eggertsson University of Iceland, Iceland and New York University, USA

Silvia Fedeli Università di Roma 'La Sapienza', Italy

Francesco Forte Università di Roma 'La Sapienza', Italy

Daniele Franco Banca d'Italia, Italy

Bruno S. Frey University of Zurich, Switzerland

Bernard Grofman University of California, USA

Ram Mudambi Temple University, USA and University of Reading, UK

Pietro Navarra Università di Messina, Italy and CPNSS, London School of Economics, UK

Martin Ricketts University of Buckingham, UK

Charles K. Rowley George Mason University, USA

Eli M. Salzberger University of Haifa, Israel

Friedrich Schneider University of Linz, Austria

Giuseppe Sobbrio Università di Messina, Italy

Robert Stockwell University of California, USA

Alois Stutzer University of Zurich, Switzerland

Stefan Voigt Ruhr-University Bochum, Germany

Foreword

Institutions are crucial in shaping society and economy. Nevertheless, standard economics has tended to neglect both how institutions evolve and in what way they affect behaviour. In contrast, political economists have made important progress in analysing them in recent years.

This book is in the tradition of a broadly understood political economy, but contains contributions from various viewpoints. This is essential because institutions are varied and complex, and therefore it would not be just to use only one approach. The authors come from many different countries and represent many disciplines as well as ideologies. Their contributions are summarized and brought into perspective by a useful introductory chapter by the three editors. A wide range of issues is treated and new aspects are introduced. Thus, for example, when studying the interaction between institutions and economic development, not only the traditional indicator of national product is used, but also a step is made towards measuring welfare via self-reported individual satisfaction, or happiness. The same commendable openness is visible when the effects of institutions on global business and transition issues are studied.

Numerous insights emerge. A particularly important one relates to competing institutional forms. In most cases, they are not imposed from above, but rather emerge as the result of an open discourse and revealed efficiency. The book also throws light on the relationship between various institutions, in particular between the market and the state. It is strongly argued that the establishment of law and order, and an effective guarantee of property rights, must precede the introduction of the price system; if done in reverse order, failure and injustice result. Without a doubt, readers, whatever their own particular standpoint, will be able to derive considerable benefit from this collection.

Bruno S. Frey
April 2002

Acknowledgements

Early versions of many of the chapters in this volume were presented at the international conference on *The Political Economy of Institutional Development: Institutional Design in Periods of Rapid Change* held at the University of Messina in September, 2000. The conference was organized by the Department of Economics and Finance of the University of Messina with the support of the Association of Public Sector Economics (Italy), the ISMA Centre of the University of Reading (UK) and the John Locke Institute (USA).

The idea of organizing the conference and editing a book of collected papers has had a long gestation period. We conceived the project during the receptions and inter-session breaks of the 1999 European Public Choice Meetings in Lisbon and the 2000 North American Public Choice Meetings in Charleston, South Carolina. We owe debts to many people who provided valuable insights at various stages of the project. We wish to express our sincere gratitude to a number of senior academic colleagues who contributed with their helpful advice and guidance, although none of them should be blamed for the shortcomings of our analysis. These include Francesco Forte, Bruno S. Frey, Bernard Grofman, Arye Hillman, Charles K. Rowley and Friedrich Schneider.

We would like to thank the illustrious contributors who were generous with both their time and their wisdom. We would also like to express deep appreciation to many conference participants who served as moderators and discussants and whose ideas are incorporated in the revised versions of the chapters included in this volume. In this connection we would like to mention Roberto Artoni, Sebastiano Bavetta, Domenico Da Empoli, Valentino Dardanoni, Maria Laura Di Tommaso, Giuseppe Eusepi, Emma Galli, Manfred Holler, Kai A. Konrad, Michele Limosani, Isidoro Mazza, Patrick McNutt, Fabio Padovano, Joan Rossellò Villalonga, Massimo Salzano and Heinrich Urpsrung.

Other people, beside the authors and discussants, have made important contributions to the project. Graduate students and administrative employees of the Department of Economics and Finance of the University of Messina helped with the logistics. Giuseppe Armaleo, Lara Gitto, Teresa Grillo and Dario Maimone Ansaldo Patti put in extra hours providing crucial administrative support. We are pleased to acknowledge the Department of Social and Decision Sciences at Carnegie Mellon University for providing logistical support for the preparation of this volume during Pietro Navarra's stay in Pittsburgh as Fulbright Research Scholar.

We would like to thank Piero Orteca and the Bonino-Pulejo Foundation for the generous financial support that made the conference possible. Other institutions that have sponsored our work include the National Research Council of Italy, the Bank of Italy, the University of Messina and both the Municipality and the Province of Messina.

Dymphna Evans of Edward Elgar was very patient with the endless delays that inevitably accompany a project with numerous contributors. We would like to thank her as well as Edward Elgar, for their support.

Ram Mudambi, Pietro Navarra and Giuseppe Sobbrio

1. Perspectives on global institutional change

Ram Mudambi, Pietro Navarra and Giuseppe Sobbrio

> I am not an advocate for frequent changes in laws and constitutions. *But laws and institutions go hand in hand with the progress of the human mind.* As that becomes more developed, more enlightened, *as new discoveries are made, new truths discovered and manners and opinions change*, with the change of circumstances, *institutions must advance also* to keep pace with the times. We might as well require a man to wear still the coat which fitted him when a boy as *civilized society to remain ever under the regimen of their barbarous ancestors.* (Thomas Jefferson)

1. INTRODUCTION

While the circumstances in which humanity finds itself are constantly changing, the great truths stand the test of time. The above quote from Jefferson is as relevant today as it was when it was written over two centuries ago. Jefferson understood the importance of making laws and institutions that are both supportive of a healthy polity and economy as well as being adaptable to change and development. The creation, preservation and transformation of political institutions and their impact on societal interactions is the subject matter of this volume. Individuals are shaped by and act through structures, organizations and institutions. Therefore, both individual choices and social outcomes cannot be explained without some reference to the larger social institutional context in which their actions take place.

Economic historians studying the global shift from stagnation to growth during the twentieth century have pointed out that today there are relatively few areas in which misery persists and where material living conditions have deteriorated (Kahn, 1979; Maddison, 1991; World Bank, 1993). In general, virtually everywhere on earth people are better fed, clad, housed and educated than their forebears. However, if we observe the distribution of this unprecedented long-term growth, we notice that countries that were more developed at the beginning of the twentieth century still rank amongst the wealthiest nations, while countries that were poorer one hundred years ago still lag behind. There are some remarkable positive exceptions: Japan, the city economies of Hong Kong and Singapore, the East Asian market economies like Korea, Taiwan and, to a lesser extent, Malaysia, have significantly improved their relative share of the world's wealth. As far as statistics can be trusted, China, Indonesia and Thailand are making strides in this direction as well. On the other hand there are some negative exceptions as well. Recent evidence suggests that many of the formerly communist countries underwent a slowdown in growth and then an absolute economic decline following the fall of the Berlin Wall.

These brief considerations highlight the fact that global economic progress in the twentieth century, while generally encouraging, was not continuous and uniform. This raises questions about the fundamental causes for such heterogeneous and discontinuous international experiences. Many studies on the determinants of sustained economic growth have appeared in the literature, and more and more explanatory factors have been drawn upon in order to come to grips with this complex phenomenon.[1] In this framework, the study of the impact of social and political institutions on economic prosperity has undergone unprecedented development during recent decades. Much of the work focusses on causal relationships between economic development and various kinds of institutions, which are defined as the sets of rules and procedures by which transactions are conducted in markets and through other social organizations, including the government.[2] Following in the footsteps of scholars such as Olson (1996) and North (1994), the study of economic development is increasingly linked to an understanding of how institutions develop in order to permit increasingly complex exchanges to take place in markets and societies.

In this view, institutions are understood as a framework creating the incentive structure of a society whereby individuals and organizations coordinate their actions. Because the incentive structure of institutions is the focus of analysis, it is common practice to assign uniformly self-interested motivations to all agents (Brennan and Buchanan, 1985). This leads to the use of an approach commonly known as rational choice theory. The rational choice explanation of social interaction can be defined as social science by economic means and consists of the application of economic methodology to understand both economic and non-economic behaviors.[3] This approach shares with neoclassical economics the central role played by individuals and the need to provide solid micro-foundations for macro-level phenomena. However, it departs from neoclassical economics in considering individuals' actions to be embedded within an institutional structure, which at the same time creates and controls economic and social life. Central to this research agenda is the fact that institutions lay down the rules of the game that determine the incentives and constraints that individuals and groups face when they save, invest, produce, trade, cooperate, coerce and otherwise interact in the process of specialization and exchange from which social and economic development arise.[4]

Following North (1990) and Furubotn and Richter (1991), institutions can be understood as rules or constraints that channel individuals' actions in specific directions. They can be formal or informal, depending on their genesis. Formal institutions are designed externally and are imposed on a community from above by political action. They are made explicit by legislation and regulations and are formally enforced by an external authority such as the government or, more generally, the state.[5] Examples of this type of institution are civil law, the form of government and the electoral system. On the other hand, as analyzed by Young (1998), informal institutions evolve spontaneously from human experience. They develop gradually and tend to appeal to voluntary coordination amongst the members of a society. They tend to be flexible and the sanctions for their violation are not spelled out since they occur spontaneously. Examples of informal institutions are ethical manners, culture, conventions and customs.[6]

Although institutions are considered relatively stable, they are not eternal and immutable. There can be three basic ways in which they might arise and change over time: by accident, by planned and conscious action or spontaneously through an evolutionary process of social selection.[7] The resurgence of interest in institutional change is linked to several events that have shaken economic and political systems in many parts of the world.

The breakdown of state socialism across Central and Eastern Europe and the end of the Cold War led to an animated debate over the design of a set of market-augmented governmental and legal institutions capable of promoting economic recovery in former communist economies.[8] The institutional reconstruction following the fall of the Berlin Wall had far-reaching effects, perhaps none so important as the philosophical blow it dealt to the position of those advocating, in one way or another, a large role for the state in the economy. In this framework, institutional design has been carried out in the face of obstacles and 'path dependencies' created by the structures and attitudes that still persist from the previous communist regimes. The main lesson from the recent experiences in such transition economies seems to be that governments, because of their limited capacity to initiate and coordinate human actions, have to keep their institutional design simple. In other words, they must concentrate on fostering and protecting a good set of basic rules under which human interaction takes place.

A second event that led to a renewed interest in institutional reform is related to the transformation of the nation-states of Western Europe. The emergence of the European Union (EU) as an autonomous agent with serious power over its constituent members created a flurry of scientific interest in issues dealing with the development of federal monetary and fiscal institutions. Questions regarding the role of the European Parliament, the independence of the European Central Bank and the construction of a federal Europe are of central concern in the design of a European constitution.

By the same token, institutional awareness is also penetrating the policy advice emerging from international organizations like the International Monetary Fund, the World Bank and the like. The importance of institutional change to economic development and prosperity can be in the experience of the fast-growing East Asian countries that reshaped institutions to rely increasingly on individual initiative and openness. Further, many observers have emphasized that the East Asian institutional crisis of 1997–98 highlighted particular institutional weaknesses and the differential impact of the crisis in various countries had much to do with the institutions in place. For example, the crisis was considerably milder in Taiwan, where an open market system was much more willing to allow firms to fail. On the other hand, the crisis was more severe in Korea, where a relatively more closed system attempted to protect large firms by bailing them out. The need for international institutions able to face these new challenges and react promptly to major worldwide financial crises led to a large literature focusing on the design of more powerful and effective international economic institutions.

The past two decades have witnessed a growing trend toward economic openness. The fading of borders between independent economic systems promoted the free movement of firms, capital and labor across regions, and encouraged states and countries to exploit differences in opportunities and returns. This process, generally known as globalization, produces many winners as well as many losers, at least in the short term, and poses serious threat to traditional values, beliefs and institutions. Globalization has led to a spectacular rise in the international exchange of goods and services. Growing international competition has multiplied the number of viable locations for business facilities. If a location loses its competitiveness, firms move their operations, together with their capital and technical and organizational knowledge to locations where the conditions for business are more favorable.

In this context, legal, political and administrative institutions tend to be internationally immobile assets whose costs determine the international attractiveness of a location. They affect the capacity of firms to interact and therefore the relative transaction and coordination costs of production and innovation. To a considerable extent, such an internationally competitive environment also embodies competition between institutional systems: some of them have proved successful in achieving growth by promoting competition and openness, others have lost out and are beginning to emulate the institutions of the successful countries.[9] However, open markets, unrestricted capital flows and the activities of multinational corporations can be perceived as weakening the power of national groups. Such groups often influence governments and interfere with international trade, capital flows, migration and technological change. Confronted with this threat, some business scholars have questioned the possibility of large-scale institutional change in the present world economic environment. In their analyses it has become more and more important to integrate institutions explicitly into theory so as to design appropriate incentive structures in which all aspects of international business flourish and contribute to the creation of wealth and prosperity.

2. THEMES AND STRUCTURE OF THE BOOK

We analyze institutional change and its political, social and economic consequences under three headings. First, we collect several perspectives on the relationship between institutions and economic growth and welfare. These range from the examination of economic growth in developed and developing countries to the analysis of non-pecuniary dimensions of human welfare. Second we put together views on the role played by institutions on global business. These include chapters on innovation, entrepreneurship, corporate governance and foreign direct investment. Third, we focus on the actual process of transition from one institutional framework to another. Here we include analyses of optimal federalism, rent-seeking and economic crises. The book, therefore, is structured in three parts focussing on growth and welfare, business activity and transition.

As the reader will discover for him/herself, the authors of the chapters contained in this volume took rather different approaches to interpret the economic, social and political consequences of institutional change. This implies that the chapters in this book are wide-ranging as they consider diverse and often interrelated aspects of institutional change. Contributors come from both sides of the Atlantic, are specialized in different disciplines and are influenced by different ideological and doctrinal inclinations. Despite the variety of the contributions, overall we are gratified at the unity which the book displays. The contents of the various chapters cover much ground but all make a contribution in analyzing one or the other of issues raised earlier in this introduction. New questions are addressed and provocative answers are given. To provide a brief overview of the themes treated in the volume, let us consider the issues analyzed in each of the three parts into which it is subdivided.

Part I: Institutions, Economic Growth and Individual Welfare

In Chapter 2, Peter Bernholz investigates the institutional prerequisites for viable economic development. The new economic historians like Douglass

North and Eric Jones, but also even earlier the French sociologist Jean Baechler, put forward the hypothesis that the political, military and economic competition among many or at least several independent political units have been held responsible for the rise of the Western World. They promoted innovation, efficiency and growth, but also the flourishing of arts and the development of effective legal and political systems. The validity of this point of view, however, has still to be tested for political and economic competition in non-Western societies. If we think, for instance, of India, there were certainly many competing entities through most of its history, but development stagnated after having reached a certain level. In his work Bernholz wonders whether this can be related to ideological or religious factors as those embodied in the caste system. He further questions whether Confucianism had similar consequences to the path toward development in China. These and similar questions are addressed to investigate whether, together with political and economic institutions, ideological neutrality can be considered also as an important pre-condition for viable economic development.

In Chapter 3 Francesco Forte and Silvia Fedeli examine the effects produced by institutional change on the long-run path of the real deficit–GDP ratio in Italy. In their view the institutional change that took place in the 1990s is seen as a reaction to macroeconomic conditions characterized by high budget deficits and low economic growth. In particular, they focus on the distribution of electoral power among the political parties in the Italian Parliament. They analyze whether the variation in the distribution of political power in the national legislature, together with both the change in the system of representation and the fiscal discipline imposed by the European Union, determined a shift in the path of the deficit–GDP ratio. Forte and Fedeli argue that the general view whereby proportional representation electoral systems are associated with high deficits due to their tendency to generate short-lived governments does not apply to Italy. They point out that focussing on the electoral system change is unduly restrictive to explain the deficit path in a country that experienced such diverse deficits and debt trends under the same electoral rules. The main political variable that seems to affect the permissiveness of fiscal policies in Italy is the balance of power among the three main political parties coupled with the fiscal restrictions due to the participation in the European Monetary Union. According to Forte and Fedeli, these two facts explain the variation in the collusive fiscal behavior implemented by the major government and opposition parties.

In Chapter 4 Alois Stutzer and Bruno Frey describe institutions of initiatives and referenda as vehicles for enhancing individual welfare. Their study moves from the fact that comparative institutional analysis sees institutions only in terms of their contribution to human welfare (usually measured with income) and neglects the effects they produce in the decision-making process.

In other words, standard utility analysis considers only the outcomes of different mechanisms of decision making without taking into account the procedural utility embodied in their process. Stutzer and Frey consider citizens' participation possibilities in politics as a possible source of procedural utility. They argue that nationals enjoy both outcome and process utility, while foreigners are excluded from political decision making and therefore cannot enjoy the respective procedural utility. In this chapter Stutzer and Frey estimate a microeconometric happiness function with 1992 data for Switzerland. Utility is assumed to be measurable by individually reported subjective well-being as well as by people's reported belief in political influence. They show that self-reported subjective well-being is the higher the more extended direct political participation rights are and the more decentralized the political system is. Their findings are interpreted in such a way to draw important implications for institutional development and change.

In Chapter 5 Bernard Grofman and Robert Stockwell review the literature dealing with the institutional approaches to mitigating ethnic conflicts in plural societies. A critical weakness of traditional plural society theory is that it is concentrated only on explaining political instability leading toward the collapse of democratic rule. However, not all plural societies fail. What are the institutional requirements needed for democratic success? Grofman and Stockwell propose a fourfold classification: building institutional fences between different ethnic communities through mechanisms, implementing power-sharing mechanisms at the elite level, designing electoral institutions that have the potential for voting across ethnic lines and the election of candidates with perceived obligations wider than their own ethnic group, minimizing the importance of ethnicity for political life and for social and economic opportunity. In their study Grofman and Stockman link their views to the foundations of constitutional political economy laid out in Buchanan and Tullock (1962) and to Grofman's (2000) perspective on institutions as problem solvers.

Fabrizio Balassone and Daniele Franco, in Chapter 6, conclude the first part of the book. They examine the effect of the budgetary rules imposed by the European Monetary Union (EMU) and the process of increasing the degree of decentralization currently being undergone in several of the EMU member nations. Specifically, in their work Balassone and Franco describe the difficulty of reconciling full achievement of the allocative advantages of fiscal decentralization with full exploitation of the scope for countercyclical policy action offered by compliance with the Stability and Growth Pact. They stress the lack of reference to local governments in the Union documents establishing budgetary discipline. This, together with reforms aiming at increasing fiscal decentralization, determines an asymmetry between the budgetary responsibilities assigned to the central governments and those assigned at regional and local level. Although the operations implemented at all levels of government are relevant to compliance with the EMU regulations, in fact it is the central government that is granted responsibility for compliance and for paying any penalties in the event of violation. Without suitable regulations, local governments have the possibility to accumulate debt free-riding on the back of central government. Therefore, a potential conflict is envisaged between the constraints placed on national public finances and the financial flexibility allowed to decentralized public bodies.

Part II: Institutions and Business Activity

John Cantwell opens the second part of the book which is dedicated to chapters concerning the way institutions can impact on business activities. He analyzes the changing nature of innovation in businesses over the post-World War II period and discusses the connection between market power and innovation. In Chapter 7, Cantwell revisits and recasts the Schumpeterian theory of profit and growth through innovation with the explicit reference to the changing institutional form of innovation during the twentieth century. This chapter is structured into three sections. Section 2 sets out an evolutionary or institutional account of how profits are created through innovation, which is contrasted with the standard interpretation of Schumpeter's theory found in the literature. In this context Cantwell argues that the standard interpretation does not do justice to Schumpeter's theory, but that the original theory requires adaptation in any case to better reflect the means by which capitalist institutions have promoted innovation during and beyond the twentieth century. The remainder of the chapter illustrates and elaborates upon arguments through evidence on the changing form of innovation in the major industrialized countries during a first phase roughly from 1900 to 1970 (Section 3) and a more recent phase from around 1970 onwards (Section 4).

In Chapter 8 Bo Carlsson examines the role of institutions in explaining the differences in performance with respect to entrepreneurship and growth in two industry clusters respectively in Sweden and Ohio. He studies the effect of four types of institutional factors: the science base and the mechanisms of technology transfer; the density of networks and the role of business support services and companies in related industries; the entrepreneurial climate, especially the availability of finance; the policy environment and other infrastructure. His major findings consist of the fact that the science base plays a role in the two clusters and that the regions differ in the absorption of new technology, partly due to differences in the size and structure of firms. Moreover, bridging institutions have contributed significantly to connectivity of networks in Ohio and the greater availability of venture capital and entrepreneurial management skills makes the Ohio environment for entrepreneurship more supportive than that in Sweden.

In Chapter 9 Martin Ricketts presents a magisterial survey of the institutions of corporate governance in capitalist economies. He argues that the ways of corporate governance are multifarious. Further, these ways are in open competition with one another. They compete not merely internationally, as in the competition between the 'Anglo-Saxon', German and Japanese models of capitalism, but also within the confines of a given economy. People can choose the governance structures within which they pursue their economic well-being. A world of mobile capital and labor enables people to migrate to those jurisdictions that provide the institutions (legal frameworks, public services, tax instruments, and so on) that best serve their interests. Similarly, within a given jurisdiction, a basically permissive legal environment will allow people to create the range of institutions that confer on them the greatest net advantage on their estimation. In this framework, Ricketts proposes a 'competing institutions' perspective that suggests an evolutionary and experimental approach to the economic environment rather than a 'constructivist' and centrally planned one. He argues that this approach implies that a market economy selects the form of its participating institutions in addition to more conventionally studied matters such as the composition of output, the technology used in the production and the relative rewards of factors of production.

The final chapter of the second part is by Ram Mudambi, Pietro Navarra and Giuseppe Sobbrio. They empirically test whether the political orientation of a region produces any impact on the investment location decisions of multinational corporations (MNCs). The literature on political risk has mainly been concerned with identifying factors underlying observable government policies towards MNCs. However, such analysis ignores the subtler aspects of the location's business culture and its overall attitude towards MNC investors. These attitudes may be summarized by the political culture in the location, reflected in the political orientation of the government. These can have tangible effects on an MNC's investment location decision even if no policy pronouncements are made explicitly. Moving from this consideration, Mudambi et al. investigate whether the political tradition in a given area can influence foreign direct investment (FDI) decisions. This question is addressed with regard to different regions within a single country. The country they examine is Italy, which exhibits one of the highest levels of variation with regard to the political culture of its geographical regions. Mudambi et al. find that political culture, as represented by the pattern of support for political parties at different points on the political spectrum, is not a primary variable in the MNC investment location decision. However, it does have a significant residual impact. Thus, in choosing between locations on a shortlist, where economic and financial location factors are roughly similar, political culture can have a determining influence. In the case of Italy, a Center-right orientation is conducive to FDI by MNCs, while a Center-left orientation is not. A Far-left orientation is found to have a very negative effect on FDI.

Part III: Institutional Transition

The chapters composing the third part of the volume share the point of view that institution building is at the heart of the social and economic transformation in those countries undergoing a transition process. The perspectives included in Part III range from an historical case study of England to current examples of institutional change. In Chapter 11 Charles Rowley and Matthew Dobra discuss a historical case study of institutional transformation from which can be drawn inferences for modern day constitutional adjustments in transition countries from conditions of autocracy. They use the tools of constitutional political economy to analyze the evolution of constitutional arrangements in seventeenth-century England. Those arrangements were at the heart of the process leading to the economic development and growth associated with the Industrial Revolution. They demonstrate that the path from the Restoration in 1660 to the Glorious Revolution of 1688 can be understood as the unforeseen outcome of consistently rational decision making by all actors involved in this institutional transformation. Further, they argue that the enduring nature of the constitutional settlement following the Revolution was a consequence of a discrete change from low to high transaction costs for constitutional change. All along in their arguments Rowley and Dobra contest the conclusions pointed out by North and Weingast (1989) arguing that in their paper it is not explained how and why the Glorious Revolution came to pass, whether it was a part of an ongoing evolutionary process or an act of constitutional constructivism, whether it was a revolution or a *coup d'état* or a function of threatened foreign invasion.

Thraínn Eggertsson is interested in the political forces affecting the institutional environment of economic decision making that influence economic performance in poor countries. In Chapter 12 he observes the fact that economic performance in developing countries was roughly comparable until the trade shocks of the 1970s. After these events economic growth in those countries collapsed. Eggertsson interprets this phenomenon in the light of what in his study is indicated as the political rationality of inefficient economic systems. He focusses on the disastrous effects produced by rent-seeking practices, a malaise in poverty-stricken economies seeking institutional transition. Finally, the neglected role of competing social models in theories of economic performance is also analyzed. In this regard Eggertsson dedicates an interesting discussion to the frequent long life of social institutions that, at least in retrospect, failed to promote economic growth.

In Chapter 13 Friedrich Schneider suggests structural reforms to existing international financial institutions in the wake of the economic crises that have recently exploded in Asia. The Asian financial and economic crises resulted in a contraction of output, employment and in some countries in a sharp increase of poverty. In the light of this experience, economists, politicians and other public officials argued the ineffective or even counterproductive intervention of the International Monetary Fund (IMF). Schneider jumps in on this debate and proposes the design of a more powerful and effective new international monetary institution. He uses the tools of constitutional political economy to point out some important elements that should be required for such a new institution to function effectively. The policies proposed are expected to be successful only if this monetary institution is truly independent, especially from its major donors. In assisting countries with financial problems it should act as an independent central bank. This new organizational structure would allow it to control monetary policy and to provide instruments to intervene in the country's fiscal policies so that its goals can be more effectively achieved.

Eli Salzberger and Stefan Voigt, in Chapter 14, examine the issue of the constitutional delegation of powers. The last ten years have been a period of rapid change for the countries of Central and Eastern Europe. Almost all of them either passed entirely new constitutions or substantially modified them. This is a unique situation where the constitutional delegation of powers can be performed almost simultaneously with post-constitutional delegation. In their work Salzberger and Voigt analyze such delegation choices across eight countries. They portray the main differences among these countries with regard to the delegation, trace their origin – what effects do the legacies of the past have? – and analyze their effects. They ask, amongst other questions, what are the ramifications of a quasi-simultaneous constitutional and post-constitutional choice? Have constitutional rules been chosen in anticipation of the necessary compatibility with the rules of international organizations that one wants to be a member of? Has membership in international organizations led to a boost in credibility of those governments concerned? This chapter constitutes the last chapter of both the third part of the book and of the entire volume.

3. POLITICS, BUSINESS AND HUMAN WELL-BEING: WHAT CAN BE LEARNED FROM INSTITUTIONAL CHANGE?

In the light of the new challenges associated with a changing economic and social global environment, new political and economic institutions are being brought into being. The results have been mixed, ranging from stunning success to virtual societal collapse. As we move into the new millennium, this raises crucial questions for social scientists. Is it possible to highlight 'success factors' of the states that have managed to implement successful institutional transformation, and equally to isolate the 'pathogenic factors' that have characterized failures in institutional reform?

Our effort in addressing these issues is also an effort to talk about the shape of the future. In other words, it is an attempt to make predictions concerning what is both possible and good. Such an enterprise requires a combination of positive and normative analysis. Thus, material prosperity is useful shorthand for individual well-being, in that it has the virtue of being relatively easy from the standpoint of measurement and comparison. The material effects of institutions can therefore be studied from a positive viewpoint. However, beyond a fairly low threshold, individual well-being is more strongly affected by non-material products of institutions such as opportunity, freedom and relationships. Measurement and comparison of these outcomes necessarily involves normative analysis. In each of the three parts of this book, we have attempted to ensure that analyses from both perspectives are presented.

The institutional foundations of prosperity comprise both political and business institutions as well as the interplay between the two. We have attempted to provide as complete a treatment as possible. This has necessarily required us to call upon the expertise of scholars from a number of different disciplines, ranging from constitutional political economy, through technology management, economic organization, public economics and public choice. While these scholars have diverse approaches, they share a common interest in institutional transition and design. And it is reassuring to find, as is the case with good analysis generally, that some consistent conclusions emerge. What can be learned for the interdisciplinary perspective we have adopted in collecting the chapters comprising this volume?

Political institutions have profound effects on economic outcomes ranging from entrepreneurship to macroeconomic debts and deficits. When the citizenry wields political power, both individual well-being and business effectiveness are enhanced. Protection of individual property rights is amongst the strongest forces guaranteeing the emergence and maintenance of economic welfare. A competitive institutional environment with outcome-based survival leads to institutional flexibility that selects against poor outcomes. However, there is a difference between institutional flexibility (transition in the small) and institutional overhaul (transition in the large). In the latter case, institutional design must precede market reform, since markets cannot function without some fundamental working institutions – law and order and guaranteed property rights. Finally, we must never forget that there are some agents who gain from unfavorable institutional environments. Poverty is just as much the outcome of rational choice as prosperity.

Understanding institutional change and its political, social and economic consequences belongs to the class of achievements that recede as one advances and becomes aware of the multiplicity of the perspectives involved. Synthesizing the best of these different perspectives should be a task of the greatest importance in the coming years for economists, political scientists and all those professionals interested in institutional evolution. The result will be a new and broader understanding of both the process and the effects of institutional change that can offer better guidance in the great debates over the institutional prerequisites for spreading successfully development and growth throughout the world. We hope that readers of this volume will come to the same conclusion.

NOTES

1. For a review of the literature on the determinants of economic growth see Barro and Sala-i-Martin (1999).
2. As argued by Mueller (2000), institutions, such as constitutions, campaign finance laws, and the norms of political parties, all shape political processes and the resulting actions of government. Given the incentives embodied in these institutions, interest groups endeavor to shift the balance of power their way, seeking influence and control over policy mechanisms, the development of new laws and regulations, and the allocation of resources. A proper understanding of the evolution of political institutions, their impact on economic development, and the impediments to political reform is required in order to design projects to help recipient countries improve their institutions of governance.
3. Harsanyi (1969) and Becker (1976) suggest that people's behavior can largely be explained in terms of economic gain and social acceptance.
4. However, it is important to note that self-interest, narrowly defined, does not explain all human behavior or social outcomes. Many institutions, especially informal ones, affect interactions of individuals with markets and governments. Much economic life takes place outside the official sanctions of the state, or precedes legal and political development. These microeconomic phenomena, however, are of great macroeconomic importance, because in many countries they affect a large part of the population. Knack and Keefer (1997) present evidence that 'social capital' matters for measurable economic performance, using indicators of trust and civic norms from the World Values Survey for a sample of 29 market economies. The authors find trust and civic norms are stronger in nations with higher and more equal incomes, with institutions that restrain predatory actions of chief executives, and with better-educated and ethnically homogenous populations. Mudambi and Navarra (2002) measure the impact that the political culture of different geographical areas in Italy has on the foreign direct investment decisions of multinational corporations. They find evidence that political tradition is a significant variable in explaining the investment decisions of multinationals.
5. The external imposition and enforcement of institutions by agents selected by the political process and acting from outside the society is known as the 'protective function of the state' (Buchanan, 1975).
6. This distinction resembles the one between rules of organizations and rules of conduct (Hayek, 1973). The former are seen as designing the internal structure of organizations to serve their purposes, while the latter are viewed as coordinating the interactions of the members of a social group. The contrast between internal and external rules proposed by Kasper and Streit (1999) is similar.
7. 'Hegel has captured the dual aspect of institutions (of being doubtless man-made, but of being at the same time also naturelike and often as impossible to change as the law of gravity) by the term "second nature". A popular though deeply misleading mechanical metaphor for the

stability of institutions is the notion of "inertia". To account for the stability of institutions, it is much more helpful to rely on biological rather than mechanical analogies, and to compare institutions to "identical reproduction" rather than "inertia" . . . A less metaphorical understanding of the stability of institutions is "path dependency". Path dependency is a mechanism of identical reproduction of institutions due to either or both of the two features mentioned above' (Offe, 1996).

8. Olson (2000) suggests that the 'market-augmented government' is the appropriate path to prosperity. The reliable enforcement of private contracts and the protection of individual property rights depend on a government strong enough to guarantee those rights, yet strong enough not to undermine them. He examines this view with particular emphasis on the Soviet Union and its successor states, pointing out that the practical implementation of these principles in the creation of prosperity remains elusive.
9. The findings of Olson (1996) regarding the inter-country competition among institutional systems are interesting. He shows that the low-income countries of the Second and Third Worlds are poor not so much because of their lack of physical and human capital, but rather because of their institutions. Poor governance structures prevent them from obtaining colossal gains from foreign investment and advanced technologies. De Soto (2000) also concludes that poor countries' incomes are far below their potential due to poor institutional structures. In contrast to Olson, he suggests that foreign investment would be unnecessary if poor countries were able to unlock their fixed capital through guaranteeing property rights. He points out that in Egypt the poor have accumulated wealth that is worth 55 times as much as the sum of all foreign direct investment ever recorded there, including that spent on building the Suez Canal and the Aswan Dam. However, such countries have yet to establish and normalize the invisible network of laws that turns these assets from 'dead' into 'liquid' capital.

REFERENCES

Barro, R.J. and X. Sala-i-Martin (1999), *Economic Growth*, Cambridge: MIT Press.

Becker, G.S. (1976), *The Economic Approach to Human Behavior*, Chicago: University of Chicago Press.

Brennan, G. and J.M. Buchanan (1985), *The Reason of Rules*, Cambridge: Cambridge University Press.

Buchanan, J.M. (1975), *The Limits of Liberty: Between Anarchy and Leviathan*, Chicago: University of Chicago Press.

Buchanan, J.M. and G. Tullock (1962), *The Calculus of Consent: Logical Foundations of Constitutional Democracy*, Ann Arbor: Michigan University Press.

De Soto, H. (2000), *The Mystery of Capital: Why Capitalism Triumphs in the West and Fails Everywhere Else*, New York: Basic Books.

Furubotn, E. and R. Richter (1991), *The New Institutional Economics*, College Station: Texas A&M University Press.

Grofman, B. (2000), 'Arendt Lijphart and the New Institutionalism', in M.M. Crepaz, T. Koelble and D. Wilsford (eds), *Democracy and Institutions: The Life Work of Arendt Lijphart*, Ann Arbor: Michigan University Press.

Hayek, F.A. (1973), *Law, Legislation and Liberty, Vol.1, Rules and Order*, Chicago: University of Chicago Press.

Kahn, H. (1979), *World Economic Development: 1979 and Beyond*, London: Croom Helm and Boulder, CO: Westview Press.

Kasper, W. and M.E. Streit (1999), *Institutional Economics: Social Order and Public Policy*, Cheltenham: Edward Elgar.

Knack, S. and P. Keefer (1997), 'Does social capital have an economic payoff?', *Quarterly Journal of Economics*, **68**, 134–51.

Maddison, A. (1991), *Dynamic Forces in Capitalist Development*, Oxford: Oxford University Press.

Mudambi, R. and P. Navarra (2002), 'Political culture and foreign direct investment: The case of Italy', *Economics of Governance*, forthcoming.

Mueller, D.C. (2000), *Constitutional Democracy*, Oxford: Oxford University Press.

North, D.C. (1990), *Institutions, Institutional Change and Economic Performance*, New York: Cambridge University Press.

North, D.C. (1994), 'The Evolution of Efficient Markets', in J.J. James and M. Thomas (eds), *Capitalism in Context*, Chicago: University of Chicago Press.

North, D.C. and B.R. Weingast (1989), 'Constitution and commitment: the evolution of institution governing public choice in seventeenth century England', *Journal of Economic History*, **49** (4), 803–32.

Offe, C. (1996), 'Designing Institutions in East European Transitions', in Robert E. Goodin (ed.), *The Theory of Institutional Design*, Cambridge: Cambridge University Press.

Olson, M. (1996), 'Big bills left on the sidewalk: Why some nations are rich and others poor', *Journal of Economic Perspectives*, **10**, 3–24.

Olson, M. (2000), *Power and Prosperity: Outgrowing Communist and Capitalist Dictatorships*, New York: Basic Books.

Young, H.P. (1998), *Individual Strategy and Social Structure: An Evolutionary Theory of Institutions*, Princeton: Princeton University Press.

World Bank (1993), *The East Asian Miracle: Economic Growth an Public Policy*, Oxford: Oxford University Press.

PART I

Institutions, Economic Growth and Individual Welfare

2. Competition of political–economic systems and ideological neutrality as conditions for viable economic development

Peter Bernholz

1. WESTERN CIVILIZATION AND CAPITALISM

Present Western civilization has developed out of a medieval society strongly characterized by the supreme values of Christianity and by some influences stemming from Greek–Roman antiquity. It is not without reason that several crusades against Muslims and Slavs and persecutions of heretics like the Cathars took place during this period. Emperor Henry IV had to bow to Pope Gregory VII with bare feet in the snow at Canossa in 1077 after he had lost his power because of excommunication.

However, there existed one important characteristic of Western Europe which set it apart during the Middle Ages: secular and spiritual power were never combined and there existed strong military and foreign policy competition among many more or less independent princes and (free) cities. And this seems to have made a decisive difference. We know now that secure property rights, a reliable and enforceable contract law, generally the rule of law, not too high taxes, not too many regulations and stable money are preconditions for efficiency, innovation and economic growth. But how did it happen that these conditions were introduced in Europe? Why should the ruling elite in an autocracy agree to strong and secure property rights, to minimal state intervention, to a strong limitation of taxes, and thus of its own powers to command and to take away goods at their own discretion? It seems that the 'New Economic Historians' have tried with a certain success to answer these questions (North and Thomas, 1973; North, 1981; Jones, 1981). They have stressed that 'European disunity has been our good luck'. Feudalism with its many power centres developed during the Middle Ages and a split opened up between religious and secular powers. A strong rivalry arose among the many rulers to extend and preserve their powers by foreign policy and military endeavours. This forced them to become interested in the well-being and loyalty of their subjects and in economic development to secure a greater tax base and thus stronger armies. However, economic development itself depended on establishing adequate property rights, a reliable legal system, free markets and limited taxes. As a consequence, those states were successful in this fierce foreign policy and military competition in the long run who, by chance, design or imitation, made the greatest progress in introducing such institutions. Thus competition among states forced on unwilling rulers a limitation of domestic powers. And there seems to be evidence that such competition has been working with similar effects in other historical periods, in which quite a number of independent states were present (Bernholz et al., 1998).

The development of competing legal systems, of the rule of law and of property rights was helped not only by interstate competition but also by the increasing separation of church and state, the preventing of a theocracy (Berman, 1983). For the separation of church and state prevented the enforcement of supreme values except in cases in which secular and spiritual powers had parallel interests. Later the split in the Christian Church between Catholicism and Protestantism weakened further the power of the established church. Bloody but indecisive religious wars like the Thirty Years War led to a stalemate. This, together with the economic benefits which could be reaped by tolerant princes from allowing the immigration of productive believers of suppressed denominations like the Huguenots or Mennonites, led in time to freedom of religion (Bernholz, 1995) and the removal of regulations of economic life stemming from supreme values. Because of these developments limited government and a pluralistic society arose in Europe as a pre-democratic achievement. First capitalism and later democracy were their progeny.

However, capitalism, once made possible by institutional reforms, follows its own laws. As Schumpeter has stressed, the economic development made possible by free markets and safe property rights follows its own route of creative destruction. The profit motive and the threat of bankruptcy brought about by more successful competitors drives entrepreneurs to raise efficiency and to innovate through process and especially product innovation.

Probably the first who correctly perceived this chain of events were Marx and Engels in the *Communist Manifesto* of 1848:

> The Bourgeoisie has created more abundant and colossal means of production in its class dominance of less than one hundred years than all preceding generations taken together. Subjugation of the forces of nature, machinery, the use of chemistry in industry and agriculture, cultivation of whole continents, making navigable the rivers, whole populations stamped out of the ground . . .
>
> The incessant restructuring of production, the revolution without end of all conditions of society, the eternal insecurity and movement is characteristic . . . for the Bourgeoisie. All fixed and trusted relationships with their retinue of old perceptions and ideas honoured by tradition are dissolved, those which are newly formed age before they can ossify . . .

> The need for a steadily increasing outlet for their products chases the Bourgeoisie around the whole globe. . . . She has removed the ground from under the feet of national industry, to the great dismay of reactionaries. The age-old national industries have been destroyed and are still destroyed each day. They are crowded out by new industries, whose introduction becomes a question of vital importance to all civilized nations. They are replaced by industries no longer using domestic raw materials, but raw materials from the remotest regions, and whose products are not only consumed within the country, but at the same time on all continents. . . .
>
> The Bourgeoisie drags, by the rapid improvement of all instruments of production, the infinitely easier communication, all nations, even the most barbaric into civilization.
>
> The cheap prices of her goods are the heavy artillery with which she shoots into the ground all Chinese walls . . . The Bourgeoisie forces all nations to accept her mode of production, if they do not want to perish; she forces them to introduce themselves to the so-called civilization. (my translation)

Later, Joseph Schumpeter took a great step in explaining the reasons in his *Theorie der wirtschaftlichen Entwicklung (1912)* (*Theory of Economic Development*). He explained that mostly new entrepreneurs were enticed again and again by expected profits to found new firms or to restructure existing ones to produce new products or to introduce path-breaking and cost-saving new production processes. These innovations provide new possibilities to suppliers and customers, but put pressure on competitors with now inferior products or outdated production processes. The latter have to adjust and also to produce better and new products or introduce the new superior processes in order to prevent losses or even bankruptcy. Thus the competition by imitators follows the creative innovation by leading entrepreneurs. The process is driven by expected profits and threatening losses. It is encouraged by the possibility, available in capitalist systems, of financing new firms substantially by borrowing, so that inventors who are talented as entrepreneurs can buy the necessary inputs or, if this is not the case, sell their inventions to innovative entrepreneurs.

New products are only successful if they either satisfy a potential demand of consumers or if, as a means of production, they serve to produce cheaper or better consumers' goods. It should also be noted that important innovations lead to a substantial economic restructuring, to translocations and sectoral unemployment, since workers in the old industries are often not capable of filling jobs in the new sectors because of inadequate capabilities. Moreover, only the innovations mentioned allow growth of the population and (or) rising per capita incomes. Finally, it has to be mentioned that innovations can, of course, also take place in foreign countries. If the institutional framework there is superior, since for example property rights are safer, the legal system more reliable, taxes and unnecessary regulations less burdensome, then the domestic industries will experience the threat of increasing unemployment and the pressure on profits because of foreign competition.

It is advisable to sketch in more detail the main traits of this capitalist development process. Let us imagine a country with a closed economy, in which the food supply of the population is barely, and in which the provision of clothing and housing is scarcely, secured. In this situation a rise of productivity in agriculture is a precondition for any economic growth, since the other sectors of the economy comprise at most 10 per cent of the labour force. A substantial increase of agricultural productivity through process innovation would then allow a much greater supply of food. But without an increase of the population the demand for victuals because of the implied rising of per capita incomes would be rather limited, though some provisions, which are new or could not be afforded until now by most people, may enjoy a greater demand. But on the whole consumers will be much more interested in more and better clothing and housing. As a consequence a sectoral crisis will develop in agriculture, since it has to pay nearly the same wages as in the now expanding textile and building industries, which are looking for new hands, and since the demand for its products is growing more slowly. The 'flight' to the cities begins, the share of agriculture in the labour force and in GDP declines. And the problems stemming from these developments will be the more pronounced, the quicker the step of innovations in agriculture.

After this development there exist several important sectors of the economy, so that a further increase of wealth can take place through innovations in a few or in all of the existing industries, or through the development of new industries. Again the resulting rise of per capita income will be spent not mainly on food, textiles and housing, but on new goods like motor cars, radios, refrigerators and television sets. The consequence is sectoral stagnation of the textile industry, which has to reduce its labour costs through process innovation, because of below average growth of demand and since it has to pay about the same wages as other sectors. Its share in GDP shrinks. Similarly, further economic growth will bring about stagnation for the automobile and television industries, since demand will now grow stronger than per capita income for new goods and services like computers, health care and tourism.

A precondition for the developments sketched are ongoing process and product innovations by creative entrepreneurs. Only new products fulfilling the needs and wishes of consumers can keep the process of economic growth going. And this growth will not proceed at a constant speed, since there will be periods with less and others with more path-breaking innovations. Also, whole regions may decline if their economic structure is dominated by aging industries. One may think of Lorraine, the Saarland, Wallonie or West Virginia as examples. Other regions flourish because of newly expanding industries, like California formerly with the aircraft industry and now with the computer industry of the Silicon Valley. The share of agriculture recedes all the time, that of industry and retail trade first increases and then declines, whereas the service industry grows all the time.

The economic development of the West, of which capitalist economic growth during the last 150–250 years since 1750/1850 has been the latest outcome, had far-reaching consequences for Western civilization. It has already been mentioned that it was a precondition for the evolution of democracy, for it seems to be well established that prosperous nations are more likely to be governed democratically than poor ones (Bollen and Jackman, 1985; Lipset et al., 1993; Burkhart and Lewis-Beck, 1994; Weede, 1996a). And we have seen that prosperity is a consequence of free market economies with safe property rights.

But this is only part of the story. The consequences of restructuring and globalization extend to the very life of society. This follows from the changing pattern of consumption and of the kinds of employment available to the greater part of the population. The working hours needed for producing the increasing wealth decline and available leisure time rises. Tourism and travel to foreign countries are among the most rapidly increasing service industries. All this changes by necessity the outlook and behaviour of people who now become acquainted with different lifestyles and foreign cultures.

And there are other changes. Adolph Wagner had already formulated the *Gesetz der wachsenden Staatsausgaben* (*Law of Increasing Government Expenditures*), and the share of these expenditures in GDP is increasing. This is feasible in democracies since the disposable income can still rise because of economic growth. The rise of government expenditures is at least partly a political consequence of the restructuring of the economy. For in the aging industries jobs are destroyed, whereas new ones are created in the newly developing sectors of the economy. Given the speed of this development, there will not only be pressure on profits and wages but also unemployment in the old industries, since the people laid off are often not capable of, or willing to, take up a job in the new sectors. Given these conditions, politicians can gain votes by helping the 'endangered' industries with regulations restricting competition and with subsidies and by supporting the unemployed.

Increasing wealth also allows longer formal education, which is itself a precondition for further economic growth. Infant mortality and number of children decline and the average expected life span increases. This leads to a growing population until the smaller number of children overcompensates the other factors. An overaging of the population is then a further consequence of economic growth, which leads to additional social and political problems.

The restructuring of the economy with the declining importance of agriculture and the crafts brings about the demise of the large family. With increased real incomes and job opportunities it becomes possible for individuals to care for themselves and to follow their own inclinations independent of their families, that is to 'realize themselves'. This is especially true for women. As a consequence, even the small family unit of husband, wife and children is more and more questioned. The divorce rate rises. The number of children decreases, since the upbringing of children is labour-intensive and implies a substantial financial burden for parents. But human beings need care and help during several periods of life, namely as children, in case of severe illness and often during old age. But since the supporting structure of the large or even small family is now missing, innovative politicians are motivated to step in. Thus obligatory health insurance and old-age pension systems, mostly managed by government bureaucracies, and subsidies for children are introduced. Thus the welfare state is, besides outright redistribution which is often combined with these systems, partly a political reaction to changes brought about by capitalist development.

The consequences are, on the one hand, greater personal freedom of individuals from restrictions imposed by family and society, but on the other hand, increasing power of government and of an impersonal bureaucracy limiting personal freedom. The increasing share of government expenditures in gross national product and more and more regulations lead to burdens finally perceived as unbearable, especially since they weaken efficiency and innovativeness, and thus lower the growth rate of the gross national product (Bernholz, 1986, 1990; Marlow, 1986; Peden and Bradley, 1989; Weede, 1986, 1990; Tanzi and Schuknecht, 1997). Finally a crisis of the welfare state results.

All these developments happened in the West and obviously had a strong impact on Western civilization. The opportunities afforded by rising wealth and by more and more goods to individuals, the greater mobility and the acquaintance with other cultures and belief systems, the demise of the large and partly of the small family brought about a weakening of Christianity, of its hold on people and the influence of its moral precepts. A secularization took place and a preoccupation arose to pursue one's own career, to seek money, to seek personal fulfilment and to enjoy the many goods afforded in this world.

This evolution does not imply, however, that the development of the market economy with private property only destroyed moral and ethical rules and the bonds of family and society. Quite the contrary, it created at the same time its own rules and its more impersonal bonds. Work discipline, industry, creativity, saving and the mutual respect for property rights were all encouraged by this system, as were trust and reliability among trading partners, creditors and debtors, and the employees of firms and other organizations. Each individual was now bound and supported by, on the whole, reliable, but often impersonal and anonymous market relationships. Laws and institutions safeguarding the sanctity of contracts, the inviolability of property rights and the stability of money were introduced. Democracies developing in the wake of the economic development of the West were characterized by the introduction of the separation of government powers, the rule of law, independent courts and by parties competing for the favour of voters. These and other developments led to an abolishment of autocratic regimes, to a limitation of corruption and of arbitrary government intervention.

2. THE ORIGIN OF CIVILIZATIONS AND THEIR NORMS AND IDEOLOGIES

Let us now turn to the problem whether and to what degree different cultures or civilizations with their norms and ideologies have influenced and are influencing economic development. This is especially important, given the limitations of traditional economics and in view of such recent publications as the two volumes on *Culture, Social Norms and Economics* (1997), edited by Mark Casson, and *The Clash of Civilizations* (1996) by Samuel Huntington. It is interesting to note that the latter has been translated in German as *Kampf der Kulturen*.

In analysing these relationships I think that it may be useful to discuss not the development and the importance of specific cultural norms for specific economic policies, but to turn instead to a somewhat broader subject: namely, the relationships between cultures, understood as *Kulturkreise* or *civilizations*, and economic regimes, and to understand in this undertaking *Kulturkreise* or civilizations as more or less extended groups of people sharing an extensive and more or less integrated set of norms, institutions and organizations based on a common *Weltanschauung*, or *belief system*. Examples of such civilizations are today the East Asian–Chinese, the Hindu, the Buddhist, the Islamic, the Western and perhaps the Latin-American civilizations. To these we may add the civilizations Communism and National Socialism tried to create, especially since the communist regime lasted for more than seventy years. And in earlier history other civilizations like the Egyptian, the Sumerian–Accadian–Babylonian, the Jewish, the Graeco-Roman, the Aztec, Inca and Maya civilizations were important. On the other hand, I do not include here so-called primitive cultures as civilizations.

It is thus my task in the following to try to analyse the influence of such civilizations on political–economic regimes and vice versa. But before doing so we have to discuss some of the more important characteristics of such civilizations, of the Western civilization and, related to it, of an evolving capitalist free market regime and of democracy.

Most work in the social sciences on norms and their consequences has taken either certain norms as given, to study their consequences, or tried to explain the evolution of norms by using the assumption of rationally interacting individuals.

This is especially true for scholars applying economic or game-theoretic approaches. In this literature either the consequences of norms for economic or political behaviour or their evolution as a consequence of rational behaviour or the survival of the fittest have been analysed.

Though I appreciate the importance of this work, there exists another dimension of the development of whole sets of norms, institutions and organizations which are characteristic of civilizations. First, it seems that the sets of norms of most of these civilizations were created, invented and innovated by one individual or by only a few people, by pioneers, leaders, innovators, founders, holy men or prophets. Chinese culture would not exist without Confucius, Mencius and Lao-tse; Buddhist culture without the Buddha; Jewish culture without Moses; Christianity without Christ and Paul; Islam without Muhammad; Communism without Marx and Engels; National Socialism without Hitler. The same seems to be true for the Aztecs and Incas (Conrad and Demarest, 1988).

Second, the further development of these norms and their embodiment in corresponding institutions and organizations was also usually the work of outstanding innovators who acted as (re-) interpreters of the belief system and as builders of organizations. Ambrose, Augustine, Thomas Aquinas, popes like Gregory the Great, Gregory VII and Innocent III, Luther and Calvin are examples for the Christian civilization; Lenin, Stalin and Mao for Communism. But even Hinduism may have undergone such innovations by important people, as witnessed by the Upanishads, attached as philosophical secret writings to the Vedas, and the development of the caste system. As a historic person we know of the reformer Shankara, whose work around 800 AD was probably decisive for the revitalization of Hinduism and the decline of Buddhism in India.

Third, several of these civilizations were built on others, responded to them or interpenetrated each other. Buddhism succeeded to enter China and Japan, Christianity was built on the Jewish civilization, Islam on both. Communism and Nazism were secular religions (Maier and Schaefer, 1998) developing out of certain traits of Western civilization. This demonstrates also, that even the great founders and innovators of civilizations built on ideas or norms which they found in the society in which they grew up. Even if their innovations contradicted or broke with the existing norms and institutions, like those of Buddha did with those of Hinduism, they were dependent on them.

What is the importance of these statements for our subject? They prove that we have to doubt that the comprehensive sets of norms characteristic of civilizations were developed by rational interaction. Though I do not deny that some norms in these bundles of norms may be explained in such a way, this is certainly not true for many others, and especially not for their core. For they were introduced as part of a *Weltanschauung*, a belief system, an *ideology*, by the founders and their followers and contained statements about the nature of the whole physical and social world, the universe, the beyond or hereafter (Topitsch, 1958). They were not only interested in the benefit of people in the present world, but in the distant future or in the heavens. The normative system created by Communism strove to encourage or enforce behaviour bringing about paradise on earth, that of Christianity and Islam to guarantee salvation, that of Buddhism to break the cycle of birth and rebirth, that of the Egyptians to secure eternal life and that of the Aztecs to guarantee the further functioning of the sun and thus the survival of earthly existence. Given such broad belief systems and world views, and the aims originally motivating them, it should not be surprising that many of the norms and institutions, and of the specific organizations created did not imply a rational response to the mundane problems of individuals and resulted in a more or less distorted view of reality. As a consequence, they often led to a deterioration of the earthly lot of their followers and (or) victims. In other words, they often implied and led to political–economic regimes which condemned their societies to stagnation, or even to poverty and suffering. We shall return to this subject in Section 4. But before, we have to point out some other possible consequences of such systems.

3. IDEOCRACY AND TOTALITARIANISM AS POSSIBLE CONSEQUENCES

Ideologies on which civilizations are built contain usually a set of *supreme values* which have to be preferred by all adherents of the *Weltanschauung* to everything else, since they are considered to be *absolute truths* (I follow here the more comprehensive analysis in Bernholz, 1993, 1997; for an independent similar approach see Piekalkiewicz and Penn, 1995). This, however, often implies a tendency towards spreading these values and the behaviour they prescribe to all potential believers by peaceful means or by force. As a consequence, if the supreme values contain expansionary aims, like the task to convert or to dominate all people in the world, a *totalitarian regime* may develop.

We assert that ideologies containing a *Weltanschauung* (world view) with supreme values, which, according to this creed, have to be lexicographically preferred to all other human aims, are a necessary but not a sufficient condition for the development of totalitarian regimes. It is thus hypothesized that *no totalitarian regime has existed without some ideology playing a decisive role.* Note that respective to our theory, religions are also considered to be ideologies.[1] But ideology *per se* is not sufficient to bring about such a regime.

Three other factors have to be added to make the emergence of a totalitarian regime probable: First, *an organization* supporting the ideology has to be established with a leader or leadership having the monopoly to interpret its content. Second, *the secular power of a state has to be 'conquered' and spiritual and secular leadership to be integrated* in the hands of the same person or group. Third, such a takeover of secular power is only probable if the society in the respective state is undergoing *a deep crisis*. Finally, if the supreme values contain only limited aims a *mature ideocracy*, for example a theocracy, may arise even then under certain conditions, as shown below.

The development thus proceeds as follows. First, an ideology with a *Weltanschauung* containing supreme values is founded or revived by a charismatic leader or leadership with a small group of possibly also charismatic followers (apostles, old guard). To reach a greater mass of potential believers, the world view and aims have to appeal to many people and seemingly to solve the problems perceived by them. Otherwise the ideology would not be widely accepted in its competition with other creeds. The ideology is driven ahead by the urgent need felt by believers to realize its supreme values, which are superordinated to all other aims and contain important promises for a better life in this or in the world to come. If its goals can only be reached by turning all people into believers, or by using their services or goods, then the ideology has to strive for secular power to force its will on resisting parts of the population. To succeed in this endeavour, a strong leadership, having the monopoly right to interpret the creed, and an organization are necessary. Also, the chances of obtaining control of a government only become favourable if an economic or political crisis deeply dissatisfies broad segments of the population, who now look to new solutions for their plight. The drive for joining spiritual and secular power may also be helped if secular political leaders perceive the potential of the ideological movement for gaining and maintaining government power, and thus join it for their own personal purposes. After spiritual and secular power have been combined, an *ideocracy* will be established. This may be a *mature ideocracy*, like a theocracy, or a *totalitarian* regime.

Ideocracy need not but can be a totalitarian regime. Here we will thus differentiate between totalitarianism and mature ideocracies as subspecies. *What then, are mature ideocracies?* In a mature ideocracy the goals of the ideological movement have been broadly reached, whereas this is not true for a totalitarian regime. Good examples of mature ideocracies are the Puritan state in Massachusetts (Morgan, 1958) and the Jesuit state in Paraguay (Ezran, 1989), both founded at the beginning of the seventeenth century. Further examples may be Tibet under the Dalai Lama and Pharaonic Egypt, though in those cases I have not looked closely enough at the evidence.

Why, then, and *under which conditions do ideological movements not turn into totalitarian regimes when they have combined spiritual and secular power?* The answer to these questions can be found if the interplay of *two relevant factors* is taken into account; namely *the substantive content of the supreme values and the obstacles to their implementation.* For assume that the combination of spiritual and secular power takes place under conditions such that no obstacles remain to the immediate implementation of these values during and from this very moment, then the new ideocratic regime needs no application of force to subjugate, force into migration or eliminate unwilling people or to obtain the people and goods necessary for the implementation of its belief system.

4. THE INFLUENCE OF IDEOLOGIES ON POLITICAL–ECONOMIC REGIMES

Mature ideocracies and totalitarian regimes are cases of civilizations characterized by ideologies. With the passing of time the norms prescribed by the supreme value systems are often applied less strictly, are not enforced with adequate sanctions, or are weakened by exemptions. But this does not imply that they are not believed and followed by a great majority of the population. It follows that they can be of great relevance for the political and economic regime and also that these consequences may be most obvious if we analyse ideocracies.

Let us look thus at some of these ideocracies. Nazism and Communism deeply influenced the political and economic regime. The economy was turned into a government-directed or a centrally planned system, respectively, combined under Communism with state property of all means of production. This change was demanded by the supreme values of their ideologies, since otherwise the abhorrent plutocratic or capitalistic regime with their *Zinsknechtschaft* (interest servitude) or *exploitation of the proletariat* would have remained. Politically the *Führerprinzip* (principle of leadership by one leader) and the *Dictatorship of the Proletariat* with a Politbureau and a leading Secretary General were introduced by Hitler and Lenin to secure the implementation of the supreme values implied in the Nazi and communist ideologies. In other communist regimes like in China, North Korea, Vietnam and Cambodia similar structures and rules were introduced. In Cambodia money was forbidden (this was also an aim in the Soviet Union in the early 1920s), the people driven out of the cities and a kind of a government command agriculture introduced.

In the Jesuit state in Paraguay the Jesuit priests introduced a regime of *ora et labora* (work and pray), where the different tasks were stricly planned and allocated by them. The access of traders to the missions was limited. Two Jesuit priests were in charge and command of each mission. They themselves had to follow the commands of their superior.

After the successful revolution against the Shah in Iran the political regime was dominated by the mullahs: women had to veil from head to foot, boys and girls were separated in school and the taking of interest was forbidden. The Taliban in Afghanistan introduced the same rules, they even forbade women to work and introduced the strict Islamic law, the Sharia.

The Catholic Church never succeeded in Western Europe to introduce an ideocracy. But it succeeded for a long time with its command not to take interest (though hidden forms could not be prevented) and the persecution of heretics. Later, the Münster Anabaptists forbade the use of money and confiscated precious metals during their short-lived totalitarian regime in Münster during the first half of the sixteenth century.

Hinduism has been a tolerant religion most of the time during its history. It was rare that it even grasped secular power and created a theocracy. Still, this religion demanded a strict division of the population into castes, a retirement from worldly concerns at least in later life, forbade the killing of cows and so on and thus in many ways hindered economic activities and the mobility of the population.

These are all examples in which market economies and private property were either abolished, severely restricted or at least limited and discouraged. But sometimes the supreme values of ideologies contain rules which are beneficial to free markets, private property and economic development. Thus Max Weber (1904/05) put forward the hypothesis that Calvinist Christianity promoted capitalistic development because of its religious ideas. People could only find out whether they were predestined to be saved from hell by their success on earth. At the same time they had to live frugally and not engage in sinful luxury. Thus they worked hard, saved and accumulated wealth, which they invested in productive firms instead of spending it on jewellery, rich clothing and luxurious housing. It has to be added, however, that Catholics were driven out of Calvinist Geneva and that Calvin erected a totalitarian regime (Zweig, 1936/83) in this city. And though the Puritans in Massachusetts built up a democracy it was restricted to true believers.

What can we learn from these examples for the influence of civilizations with supreme value ideologies on the political–economic regime? Obviously, that in most cases there are rules contained in the supreme value ideologies which hinder, restrict or prevent free markets and private property, thus allowing less efficiency and innovation. As a consequence, economic development is either retarded or even prevented. The debacle of the economic regimes in communist states is now obvious everywhere, and many of their leaders have sought to change their economic regime by economic reforms in the direction of free markets and private property since the late 1970s. Such moves, of course, presupposed a reinterpretation of ideologies. In China, private ownership of land is still not allowed, for being 'capitalist'. But thirty-year leases were introduced which can even be bequeathed. When I stayed in China in

1992 I read that since Karl Marx had invested in the stock exchange, stock exchanges were compatible with Socialism.

North Korea has now been suffering from famines for years, Cubans are victims of poverty, India is still hampered by the caste system, the development in Islamic countries is slow, and the Nazi regime was already leading to serious difficulties in the German economy (Bresciani-Turoni 1948).

5. A CLASH OF CIVILIZATIONS?

We have seen that civilizations dominated by supreme values may prevent or retard economic development, and that the evolution of a market economy with private property transformed Western civilization from a backward society dominated by supreme Christian values into a secularized society with its own rules and institutions. But a capitalist system has a strong tendency to spread to ever greater parts of the world, to 'globalize'. We can measure the increasing globalization by the rising share of exports in gross domestic product (Figure 2.1). As we can see from the figure, globalization took place for the developing economies of Western Europe, Great Britain and the USA during the whole period from 1820 to 1992, with the exception of the disruptions caused by the

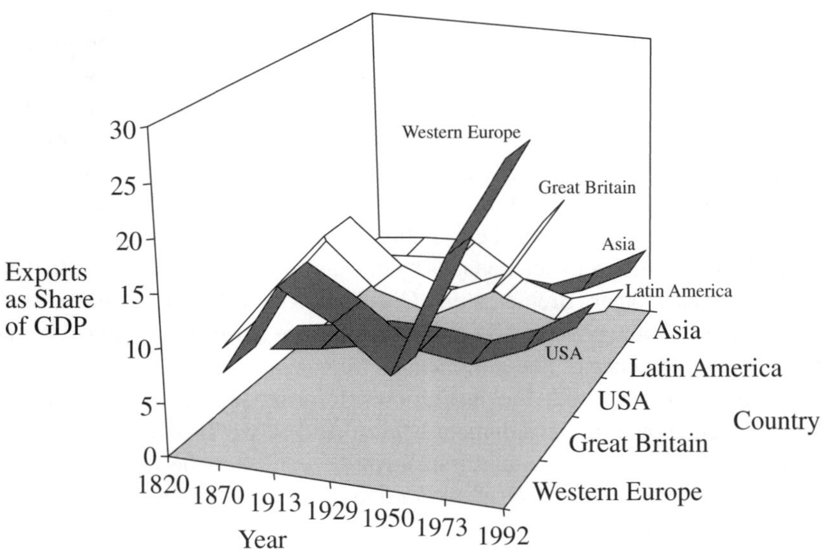

Figure 2.1 Development of export shares in gross domestic product, 1820–1992

two World Wars and the Great Depression with their exchange controls, import limitations and return to bilateral trade.

Let us note that the level of the share of exports and GDP of the USA is only lower because of the size of the country. But it, too, increased fourfold during this period. We observe also that the return to increasing globalization came later for Asia and Latin America because economic reforms were introduced only some time after the end of World War II.

The tendency to globalize is on one hand a consequence of the benefits of an ever increasing division of labour supported by decreasing transportation and communication costs. On the other hand it is made possible because of the success of free market regimes to supply more and more goods and services to the population. This fact motivates first, an effort to imitate the institutions allowing economic growth. But second, rising wealth also implies greater revenues for governments and thus potentially greater resources for military spending. Thus the governments of countries lagging in economic development are disadvantaged and may feel threatened in military and foreign policy competition. This provides another motivation to try economic reforms in the direction of free markets and safe private property rights.

But today, as in the past, the effort to introduce free market and private property institutions in non-Western civilizations may lead to conflicts with the values dominating them. Because of this the reforms may remain inadequate and falter. This can lead to crises strengthening an interpretation of the traditional belief system, which is even more hostile to a free market regime. In this case growth of per capita incomes may be retarded, be prevented or even become negative. As a consequence the respective states remain relatively weak and have scarcely a chance to become democracies. This also has important consequences for the question of peace or war. It seems to be proven by now that democracies are very improbable to wage war against each other (Bremer, 1992; Maoz and Russett, 1992, 1993; Ray, 1995; Russett, 1993, 1995; Weede, 1996b). This is, however, not true for their relationship with autocracies, since they do not prepare adequately to deter attacks by the latter. Finally, autocracies often go to war with each other (Bremer, 1992; Oneal and Ray, 1996; Oneal and Russett 1997). Thus not only poverty, corruption and absence of rule of law, but also war may be a consequence of not introducing a free market regime.

If, on the other hand, the institutional reforms succeed to a sufficient degree, then economic development begins. And as we have seen, economic growth will in time weaken and transform the values of the respective civilization conflicting with a well-working free market regime. In time more and more market-conforming institutions, legal systems and rules of behaviour have to be introduced to sustain the growth process. I have thus always doubted that there is a special and perhaps even superior path of combining capitalist development with Confucian or Japanese traditional values. The recent economic crisis in Japan and several South-East Asian countries seems to support this hypothesis. Only those values of the traditional cultures can and will be maintained which are not hindering or which are even furthering free markets, reliable legal and normative systems and safe private property.

Conglomerates preferentially treated like in South Korea, or life-long employment and support by the same firm like in Japan, are not among such institutions, since they limit and distort competition or cannot be maintained against the forces of restructuring, characteristic of the development process. Also a network of extended family and friendship relationships as in China cannot adequately substitute a reliable and enforceable legal system when the economy becomes more and more complex. Planning and collaboration by firms with MITI in Japan to further growth must raise problems as soon as the catch-up process approaches its end and firms are forced to innovate themselves in hitherto unknown directions.

One may sympathize – and I certainly do – with the efforts of Lee Kuan Yew in Singapore to prevent Western degeneration, or with Islamic movements condemning the loose morals and the secular and materialistic spirit of Western society. But it is very doubtful whether a theocracy with a legal system informed by the Sharia will ever allow economic development with all its benefits, as long as Islam is not interpreted in an adequate spirit, which seems to be possible (Weede, 1998). And it remains to be seen whether the efforts of Lee and his followers can withstand the onslaught of capitalism on their values when Singapore once realizes fully-fledged democracy as capitalism's progeny. This may be regrettable, but the positive question is whether and how the degenerations related with capitalism can be prevented without ending or severely hindering economic growth. For this problem there seems to be no solution in sight.

NOTE

1. These statements should not be interpreted to mean that the author denies the truth or dignity of religious values. But the Supreme Values of religions could be absolutely true and still imply the dangers referred to in the chapter because of specific interpretations by some of their leaders and of critical events in given historical periods.

REFERENCES

Berman, Harold J. (1983), *Law and Revolution*, Cambridge, MA/London: Harvard University Press.

Bernholz, Peter (1986), 'Growth of government, economic growth and individual freedom', *Journal of Institutional and Theoretical Economics (Zeitschrift für die Gesamte Staatswissenschaft)*, **142**, 661–83.

Bernholz, Peter (1990), 'The Completion of the Internal Market: Opportunities and Dangers from an Institutional Perspective', Centre for Economic Policy Studies (ed.), *Papers from CEPS Macroeconomic Policy Group*, CEPS Paper No. 42: Brussels.

Bernholz, Peter (1993), 'Necessary Conditions for Totalitarianism: Supreme Values, Power and Personal Interests', in Gérard Radnitzky and Hardy Bouillon (eds), *Government: Servant or Master?*, Amsterdam and Atlanta: Rodopi, pp. 267–312.

Bernholz, Peter (1995), 'Supreme Values, Tolerance and the Constitution of Liberty', in Gérard Radnitzky and Hardy Bouillon (eds), *Values and the Social Order*, Vol. 1. Aldershot: Avebury Ashgate, pp. 235–50.

Bernholz, Peter (1997), 'Ideology, sects, state and totalitarianism: a general theory', *Forum für osteuropäische Ideen- und Zeitgeschichte*, **1** (1), 51–84. Also in Hans Maier and Michael Schaefer (eds), *Totalitarismus und Politische Religionen*, Paderborn, München, Wien, Zürich: Schoeningh, pp. 271–98.

Bernholz, Peter, Manfred E. Streit and Roland Vaubel (eds) (1998), *Political Competition, Innovation and Growth*, Berlin, Heidelberg, New York: Springer.

Bollen, K.A. and R. Jackman (1985), 'Economic and non-economic determinants of democracy in the 1960s', *Research in Political Sociology*, **1**, 27–48.

Bremer, S.A. (1992), 'Dangerous dyads: interstate war, 1816–1965', *Journal of Conflict Resolution*, **36**, 309–41.

Bresciani-Turoni, Costantino (1948), *Einführung in die Wirtschaftspolitik*, Bern: Francke.

Burkhart, R.E. and M.S. Lewis-Beck (1994), 'Contemporary democracy: the economic development thesis', *American Economic Review*, **88**, 903–10.

Casson, Mark (1997), *Culture, Social Norms and Economics*, Two Volumes, The International Library of Critical Writings in Economics, Cheltenham, UK, and Northampton, MA, USA: Edward Elgar.

Conrad, Geoffrey W. and Arthur A. Demarest (1988), *Religion and Empire*, Cambridge and New York: Cambridge University Press.

Ezran, Maurice (1989), *Une colonisation douce: Les missions du Paraguay*, Paris: Editions L'Harmattan.

Huntington, Samuel P. (1966), *The Clash of Civilizations and the Remaking of World Order*, New York: Simon & Schuster.

Jones, Eric L. (1981), *The European Miracle*, Cambridge: Cambridge University Press.

Lipset, Seymour M., K.R. Scong and J.C. Torres (1993), 'A comparative analysis of the social requisites of democracy', *International Social Science Journal*, **136**, 155–75.

Maier, Hans and Michael Schaefer (eds), *Totalitarismus und Politische Religionen*, Paderborn, München, Wien, Zürich: Schoeningh, pp. 271–98.

Maoz, Z. and B.M. Russett (1992), 'Alliance, contiguity, wealth and political stability: is the lack of conflict among democracies an artifact?', *International Interaction*, **17**, 245–67.

Maoz, Z. and B.M. Russett (1993), 'Normative and structural causes of democratic peace, 1946–86', *American Political Science Review*, **87**, 624–38.

Marlow, Michael L. (1986), 'Private sector shrinkage and the growth of industrialized economies', *Public Choice*, **49** (2), 143–54.

Marx, Karl and Friedrich Engels (1848/1970), *Das Kommunistische Manifest*, Berlin: Dietz Verlag.

Morgan, Edmund S. (1958), *The Puritan Dilemma. The Story of John Winthrop*, New York: Harper Collins.

North, Douglass C. (1981), *Structure and Change in Economic History*, New York: W.W. Norton & Co.

North, Douglass C. and Robert P. Thomas (1973), *The Rise of the Western World: A New Economic History*, Cambridge, MA: Cambridge University Press.

Oneal, J.R. and J.L. Ray (1996), 'New Tests for Democratic Peace Testing for Interdependence, 1950–1985', Paper Presented at the Annual Meeting of the International Studies Association, 16–20 April, San Diego, CA.

Oneal, J.R. and B.M. Russett (1997), 'The classical liberals were right: democracy, interdependence and conflict, 1950–1985', *International Studies Quarterly*, **41**, 267–93.

Peden, Edgar A. and Michael D. Bradley (1989), 'Government size, productivity, and economic growth: the post-war experience', *Public Choice*, **61**, 229–45.

Piekalkiewicz, Jaroslaw and Alfred W. Penn (1995), *Politics of Ideocracy*, Albany, NY: State University of New York Press.

Ray, J.L. (1995), *Democracy and International Conflict*, Columbia: University of South Carolina Press.

Russett, Bruce M. (1993), *Grasping the Democratic Peace*, Princeton, NJ: Princeton University Press.

Russett, Bruce M. (1995), 'The democratic peace: and yet it moves', *International Security*, **19**, 164–75.

Schumpeter, Joseph A. (1912, 1934, 1949), *Theory of Economic Development*, Cambridge, MA: Harvard University Press.

Tanzi, Vito and Ludger Schuknecht (1997), 'Reforming government: an overview of recent experience', *European Journal of Political Economy*, **13** (3), 395–417.

Topitsch, Ernst (1958), *Vom Ursprung und Ende der Metaphysik. Eine Studie zur Weltanschauungskritik*, Wien.

Weber, Max (1904/05, 1972), 'Die Protestantische Ethik und der Geist des Kapitalismus', in *Gesammelte Aufsaetze zur Religionssoziologie*, Tuebingen: Mohr. (English: *The Protestant Ethic and the Spirit of Capitalism* (1930).)

Weede, Erich (1986), 'Catch-up, distributional coalitions and governments as determinants of economic growth or decline in industrialized societies', *British Journal of Sociology*, **37**, 194–220.

Weede, Erich (1990), *Wirtschaft, Staat, Gesellschaft*, Tuebingen: J.C.B. Mohr.

Weede, Erich (1996a), *Economic Development, Social Order and World Politics*, Boulder, CO: Lynne Rienner.

Weede, Erich (1996b), 'Correspondence: democratization and the danger of war', *International Security*, **14**, 180–83.

Weede, Erich (1998), 'Islam and the West: how likely is a clash of these civilizations?', *International Review of Sociology*, **8** (2), 183–95.

Zweig, Stefan (1936/1983), *Castellio gegen Calvin oder Ein Gewissen gegen die Gewalt*, Frankfurt/Main: Fischer.

3. The impact of the electoral system and of other political institutions on public debt and government finances in Italy*

Silvia Fedeli and Francesco Forte

1. THE BACKGROUND

In the economic and political literature there is an overemphasis on the impact of the electoral institutions on public debt and government's finances. This literature[1] is pervaded by the thesis that proportional electoral systems are the main cause of excessive public deficits and debts whereas uninominal systems bring smaller indebtedness. One of the factors leading to this conclusion is 'fragmentation': the numerousness of parties in the government coalition (a supposedly typical feature of the proportional electoral system) determines an increase of the size of the public debt, via the fragmentation of governance. Indeed according to Alesina and Perotti (1994) 'proportional, representational electoral systems typically create multiparty systems and coalition governments; on the contrary, majoritarian systems lead to single party governments'. Another factor explaining causal relations between proportional representation systems and high budgetary deficits and debts has been identified in the short life of governments. According to Alesina and Perotti (1994) 'Governments' durability is lower in representational systems characterised by coalition governments. Therefore one can suggest a relationship between the type of electoral system and the level of debt. This observation certainly fits the cases of Belgium, Ireland and Italy, the three countries with the largest debt/GNP ratios in the OECD'.[2] To sum up, a proportional electoral system by favouring the absence of a leading party implies higher fragmentation of governments and short-lived governments, thus making it more difficult to reach an agreement on fiscal governance and determining a longer delay to the

* We wish to thank Alberto Bagnai, Douglas Hibbs, Flavio Padrini, Ottavio Ricchi, Alessandro Trotto and the participants of the European Public Choice meeting in Paris, 2001. All the remaining errors are of our own making.

actions required to change a dangerous debt's growth path into a virtuous cycle. However, the absence of a leading party is inherent to the proportional system only if there is not a dominant party and if the role of the leader of the coalition is contemplated. But even in a uninominal electoral system the institution of the leader may be absent, as in Italy in the (long) period after the First World War.

Short-lived governments have different origins and characteristics with different impacts on the horizon of the decisional process. In the theory by Roubini and Sachs (1989a and 1989b),[3] a short-lived government leads to deficit and debts because it is the short horizon of the effects that matters to it and that induces it to make short-sighted policies and/or via deficit spending it pre-empts the possibilities of subsequent governments of making important deficits and debts to pursue their own different policies. The implication of this twofold causation of deficits and debts is that government instability matters when the governments are dominated by different parties or blocs of parties and/or coincide with short legislatures. Indeed, short-sighted policies that do not fit the medium-term perspectives of the parties in power will be unacceptable to them. In the case of Italy, from April 1948 to April 1994, there were only two unusually short legislatures: the first from July 1976 to June 1979 and the second from April 1992 to April 1994. In all the legislatures of the two decades from 1948 to 1968, as noted by La Palombara (1988), there has been a substantial political continuity, with the Democratic Christian party (DC) always as a solidly leading party. Thus, the 'Roubini and Sachs law' might be relevant for the subsequent 25 years when the DC weakened. And one may argue that *many* of the short governments succeeding to each other in this period imply political discontinuity. Nevertheless, an econometric analysis to test the correlation between political discontinuity and high deficits and debts requires a type of preliminary research on the factors characterising the substantial political discontinuity in Italy that if carried out, to the best of our knowledge, has never been related to fiscal variables.

According to the subsequent extended 'law of debts caused by short governments' (Grilli et al., 1991), short-lived governments cause debt growth, no matter whether an expression of political discontinuity or not: also instability caused by political fragmentation of coalitions of parties prevents long-run programmes. Actually, in the Italian case, the internal division of the DC party was one of the main reasons for the number of government crises, with one DC premier succeeding himself or, if unsuccessful, leaving room for a different DC premier either of the same or of another wing, '*corrente*', or to run a 'transitory' government (see Chiancone, 1993; Forte, 2001). And Alesina and Perotti (1994)[4] argue that this situation, while it may not be important in calm periods, becomes crucial in critical situations such as, typically, that of the oil shock of the early 1970s. But the 'extended theory' of the effects of short governments on debts and deficits, for the Italian case, seems to ask for statistical evidence.

2. UNDER THE ITALIAN PROPORTIONAL ELECTORAL SYSTEM DEFICITS AND DEBTS BEHAVED DIFFERENTLY IN DIFFERENT PERIODS: IN SEARCH OF OTHER INSTITUTIONAL EXPLANATORY VARIABLES

In Italy an almost pure proportional representation electoral system existed from the post-war period to 1994. However, the ratios of deficits and debts on GDP behaved very differently through time, as one can clearly see from Figures 3.1 and 3.2 which give the ratios to GDP of the central government debt (CGD) and of the nominal and real total deficit (CGRD) of the central government from the 1960s to 1994. Clearly one can notice different epochs for the first ratio, that, *to a certain extent*, also capture the behaviour through time of the second. Indeed, it is known that from the 1950s to the beginning of the 1960s – from when our research begins – a period of high voting power for the DC,

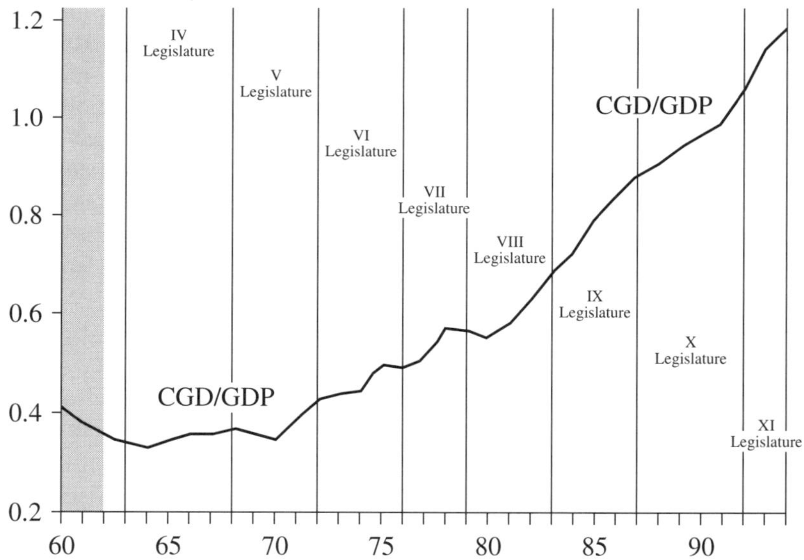

Note: [a]The shaded area from 1960 to 1962 indicates a break in the data set that becomes coherent afterwards.

Figure 3.1 Ratio between the central government debt and GDP[a]

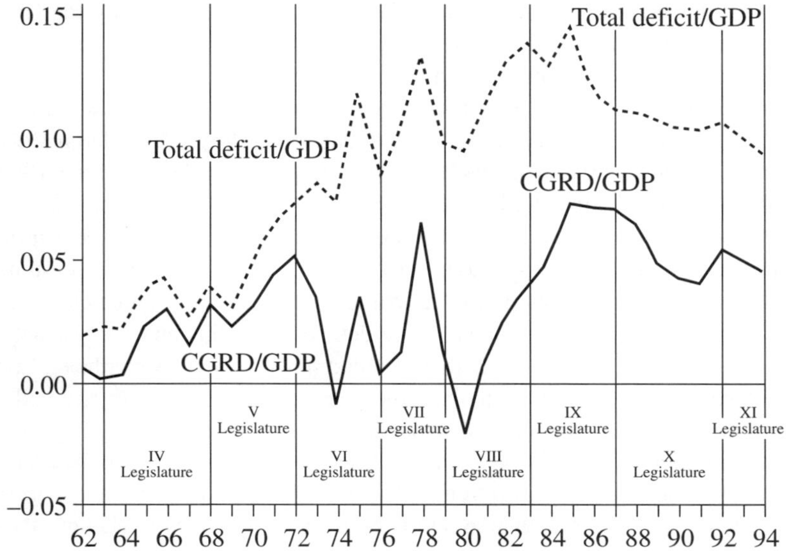

Figure 3.2 Ratios of total deficits (real and nominal) to GDP

the ratio of central government debt to GDP (CGD/GDP) had declined from nearly 50 per cent to about 40 per cent. In the 1960s, still a period of high voting power for the DC, the decline of CGD/GDP continued in alternate phases and in 1970 this ratio was 34 per cent. From the 1970s to 1982 when a collusive democracy dominated the CGD/GDP rose to about 60 per cent by a Ponzi system of financing the service of the debt with new debt, eased by the fact that the interest rate was for most of the period a 'political' rate much lower than the GDP rate of growth. From the 1980s, and mainly after the divorce between the Central Bank and the Treasury, the CGD/GDP had a great increase, as did the CGRD/GDP: the interest rate became a market rate and real GDP growth was lower than it. A primary budget surplus would have been necessary to stabilise or reduce it, but the changes in this sense began only in 1988. In 1991, with a reduced CGRD/GDP an increasing surplus in the primary balance/GDP ratio emerged. Finally, in 1995 the CGD/GDP began to decline. As it shall be seen, the fiscal adjustment made from 1988 to 1994, during the two last legislatures elected with the proportional system, was constrained by the perspective of the economic and monetary unification of Europe.

Coalitions were a predominant characteristic of the Italian governments in the periods of fiscal orthodoxy that lasted with some oscillation nearly to the end of the 1960s, as well as in the periods of high CGD/GDP that dominated during the subsequent twenty years. It also characterised the period of fiscal adjustment, initiated in 1988 on the basis of the 'plan of financial recovery' by the Goria Government that successfully programmed the surplus in the primary budget for 1992. The Goria Government lasted only from July 1987 to March 1988. Five other short-lived coalition governments were, then, involved in the realisation of this plan: De Mita (April 1988–May 1989), Andreotti (July 1989–March 1991), Andreotti (April 1991–April 1992) in the X Legislature; Amato (June 1992–April 1993) and Ciampi (April 1993–April 1994) in the XI.[5]

It may well be that by cross-section analyses (among countries), one can find statistical evidence that proportional electoral systems – with their presumed predisposition to the proliferation of parties,[6] the related fragmentation and short-lived governments – generate more deficits and debts and are less apt to control perverse fiscal situations than a uninominal system. Nevertheless, one cannot explain why, in Italy, with the same proportional electoral system[7] and an almost unchanged number of parties, the deficit and debt ratios to GDP behaved as they did. Mainly it is difficult to explain the virtuous path leading to the decline of the same ratios in the period from 1988 to 1994, *under six (different) governments.* Our main thesis is that some of the relevant variables explaining these different phases of deficits and debts can be found in the distribution of political powers of the main parties and in the changes that different distributions of power determined in the set of institutional variables. As for the latter, for the period from 1974 to the early 1980s, we refer to the change in the decision-making rules in the Chamber of Deputies as a consequence of the deterioration of the voting power of the Democratic Christian party (DC) with the increase of that of the communists (PCI) and the socialists (PSI), which also implied the development of new structures of welfare state in the areas of pensions and healthcare together with an originally weak tax reform, the increased extension of the public interventions in real and monetary economy (factors strictly related to the worsened ratio of voting power of the DC to that of the PCI). The period of fiscal adjustment was mainly stimulated by another variable partly endogenous to the distribution of power: the political commitment to the Single European Act of 1986, consequent to the new rules of the 'game of a single European market'.

3. THE CORRELATION BETWEEN THE CHANGES OF VOTING WEIGHTS AND THE CGD/GDP RATIO GIVE A BLURRED PICTURE

The relation between the upward cycle of the CGD/GDP ratio and the deterioration of the DC's parliamentary situation emerges on the basis of the simplest statistical (negative) correlation[8] found between the voting 'weights' of the DC (as resulting from the number of seats in each Chamber of the Parliament over the total) and the CGD/GDP ratio from the IV to the XI Legislatures, that is from 1963 to 1994, as reported in Table 3.1.[9]

Table 3.1 Statistical correlation betweeen the CGD/GDP and the relative voting weight of the main opposition and government parties in the Chamber of Deputies and in the Senate (1963–94)

Main opposition and government's parties	Statistical correlation between CGD/GDP and the relative voting weight of the parties	
	Chamber of Deputies	Senate
Democratic Christian party (DC)	–0.888300	–0.801578
Communist party (PCI)	–0.388819	0.201183
Liberal party (PLI)	–0.597917	–0.749977
Republican party (PRI)	0.841031	0.869358
Social Democratic party (PSDI)	–0.122114	–0.251591
Socialist party (PSI)	0.561167	0.563467

Source: Data: IMF-International Monetary Fund, IFS-International Financial Statistics.

The results show a strong correlation between the reduction of the DC party's (always the relative majority party of the ruling coalition since the 1st Legislature) share of seats in the Parliament (its voting weight) and CGD/GDP. But there is not a significant unambiguous correlation between the relative weights of the PCI (always the main opposition party) and the CGD/GDP ratio, which is important if one considers the institutional changes and practices initiated with the weakening of the DC party (see below). As for the other parties often belonging to the governing coalition, a relevant correlation cannot be found between the debt/GDP ratio and PSI voting share, even if its role in the government coalition coincides with public spending growth activated by structural reforms promoted by it, such as the creation of the national pension system of 1969, the introduction of the regions with their own finances in January 1970 and the institution of the national health-care service in January 1980. As for the voting share of the minor governing parties, a significant and correctly signed correlation is found for the PLI, but almost no correlation is found between the PSDI (Social Democratic party) and the CGD/GDP and a high positive correlation results for the small Republican party (PRI), which is quite counterintuitive, considering that this party was committed to fiscal discipline as well as the PLI. Thus even if one may argue that the simple statistical correlation between DC loss of voting share and the CGD/GDP ratio might demonstrate the perverse effects of the loss of parliamentary weight of the leading party, the picture emerging from Table 3.1 is blurred.

One may question our reference to the *central government debt* ratio to GDP, because normally, according to the Italian budgetary rules, the Parliament (before the Maastricht parameters of fiscal discipline) had to decide over the *deficit* ratio to GDP which is affected by a number of factors, such as the issuance on the market of public debt (rather than referring to the Central Bank) to finance the service of previous debts and the height of the interest rates due on the debt stock, and the effect of inflation on that stock. Let us, therefore, consider the ratio to GDP of the *real total deficit*: that is, the total deficit of the central government in real terms, CGRD, obtained by subtracting from the nominal deficit the reduction of the value of the stock of debt due to the increase of prices, that is CGRD/GDP = [(*CGD* × *rate of inflation*) + *Total Deficit*]/*GDP*. In this way one may capture the fiscal perspective facing the central government and the members of parliament when deciding on the budget, by considering the effect of the planned deficit on the financial credit resources thus available for the market economy at the expected inflation rate within the given balance of payments constraint.[10] Table 3.2 shows the relation between the share of seats (that is, the voting weight) of the main governing parties and the main opposition party and the ratio between CGRD and GDP.

The direction of the results found in Table 3.2 for the relation between DC (and PSI) and the CGD/GDP ratio is, by and large, confirmed. Also the signs for the other governing parties considered are confirmed, although relevant correlation is never found. For the PRI voting weight again we observe an unexpected positive relation with the ratio of deflated deficit and GDP. As for the main opposition party, if compared with the previous results, the PCI role remains quite ambiguous.

Apparently, the correlation found between deficits and debts and the voting weight of a given party, taken as the basic indicator of the proportional representation electoral system, seems not to confirm the basic claims of the existing

Table 3.2 Statistical correlation between CGRD/GDP and the relative voting weight (share of seats) of the main opposition and government parties in the Chamber of Deputies and in the Senate

Political parties	Statistical correlation between CGRD/GDP and the voting weight of the main political parties	
	Chamber of Deputies	Senate
DC	–0.600853	–0.587924
PCI	–0.296239	–0.079273
PLI	–0.236005	–0.276962
PRI	0.584731	0.496323
PSDI	–0.201734	–0.258745
PSI	0.494846	0.520248

Source: IMF-International Monetary Fund, IFS-International Financial Statistics.

literature. One might argue that this indicator does not reflect the effective power in the Parliament of a political party that depends on the distribution of voting weight amongst the others.

4. VOTING POWER INDICES ARE NEEDED TO CAPTURE THE CONSEQUENCES OF THE CHANGES OF VOTING SHARES OF THE VARIOUS PARTIES IN THE PARLIAMENTARY GAMES: THE SHAPLEY–SHUBIK INDEX OF VOTING POWER

When a big party loses a part of its seats, other parties might acquire a stronger position, even if their voting shares are also diminished, because their votes become more relevant to a winning coalition. Small/medium parties might even become the determinants to form a majority large enough to make a given issue pass in the Parliament. Or, as opposition parties, they may be able to play a more effective policy.

In order to properly deal with the above features of a parliamentary system, it seems to us that instead of naively relying on the voting weights of the various parties, one should consider the parties' voting powers as determined by the Shapley–Shubik (S–S) index, which measures the probability of any given voter of belonging to a winning coalition.

Following the game-theoretic approach underlying the Shapley–Shubik index of voting power (see Shapley and Shubik, 1954), we interpret the political groups represented (elected) in each Chamber of the Parliament as the players of a 'game to stay in power' and assume that any political group – the players of the game – may combine opportunistically with any other, even disregarding their ideological differences. The notion of power of a player refers to his ability to be the 'last decisive' or marginal ('pivot') player of a winning coalition over all the possible coalitions.

The Shapley–Shubik index of voting power measures the chances of any party or player of being the pivotal member of a winning coalition as follows. Consider an n-players co-operative game defined by means of a characteristic function,$\mathbf{v}$: $\mathbf{A} \rightarrow (0,1)$, where $\mathbf{A}$ is the set of all 2^n subsets of the set of players N, $(1, \ldots, n)$ and $\mathbf{v}$ assigns to each subset $A \in \mathbf{A}$ the value 1 if A is a winning coalition and 0 if it is a losing coalition.[11] The Shapley–Shubik power index, $S\text{–}S(i)$, for a player i can be defined as

$$S\text{–}S(i) = \frac{\sum\limits_{i \in C, C \subset N} (c-1)!(n-c)!}{n!} [v(C) - v(C - \{i\})]$$

where the summation is taken over all coalitions C (consisting of c members), which i belongs to and '!' denotes factorial. A crucial role in the computation of this index is played by the permutations of players. We need to count for all 2^n coalitions the number of permutations of the remaining $n - c$ members, that is only those cases in which $[v(C) - v(C - \{i\})] \neq 0$, that is, i is pivotal (his participation, as the last coming player, can change a losing coalition into a winning coalition). In this sense, $S–S(i)$ may be interpreted to represent both the possibility of measuring a player's power or 'value' by the abstract probability that he is the pivotal member of a winning coalition and what a player should expect to receive, on average, under the assumption that his reward corresponds to his marginal contribution.

One would object that it is unrealistic to assume that a priori any coalition is possible, because there are ideologically idiosyncratic parties, but, indeed, in the 1970s, the DC institutionalised in various ways an agreement with the communists. Moreover, two important institutional factors relating to the functioning of the Italian Parliament must be considered to explain the relevance of the change in the equilibrium of voting powers as captured by the Shapley–Shubik index. Article 67 of the Italian Constitution states that every member of Parliament represents the Nation and exerts his functions without agency constraint with the electors. According to the dominant interpretation this principle allows the members of parliament to vote disregarding their political (parliamentary) group: a possibility that emphasises the risks of losing power for a majority with a narrow margin over the majority quota – a feature quite independent of the type of electoral system. Another important feature was, until August 1988, the secret ballot which allowed the formation of parliamentary coalitions different from that officially supporting the government in charge and rendering it very difficult to rule. The secret ballot principle, again unrelated to the type of electoral system, originated the practice of the so-called 'snipers'.

5. THE SHAPLEY–SHUBIK INDEX OF VOTING POWER AND THE PRESUMED FRAGMENTATION OF THE ITALIAN PARLIAMENT FROM THE IV TO THE XI LEGISLATURES

Given the number of seats and, thus, the voting weights of each party represented in the Parliament in each legislature and for each Chamber, the Shapley–Shubik indices have been worked out and reported in Figures 3.3–3.6 and in Appendix 3.2 (Tables 3.A1 to 3.A9).

Unlike the conventional view of fragmentation as likely derived from the simple consideration of the voting weights of the various parties elected from the pure proportional system, the Shapley–Shubik indices of voting power of the various Italian parties show a clear cut between the power of the three main parties and the others. Indeed, the DC (the main governing party), the PCI (the main opposition party) and the PSI (the 'swing' party), for all the periods considered, held in each Chamber a voting power higher than 70 per cent with the remaining power shared amongst the other parties. This cleavage does not emerge by simply looking at the share of seats of each political group represented in the Parliament. Notice also that, perhaps unexpectedly, the Communist party – in spite of its voting weight, even more than twice the voting weights of PSI over all the periods considered – held almost always the same voting power as the PSI (the swing party).[12] Of the three small parties – PSDI, PRI and PLI – that belonged to a number of government coalitions,[13] the PSDI was the least important because for some periods it merged its parliamentary group with the PSI. On the other hand, the importance of the PRI emerges after 1980, mainly in the Senate, whereas it had almost no power before and where, in that period, it seemed to be the only party able to absorb the changes of powers in the DC party and in the PSI. As for the PLI, it was relevant at the beginning of the period considered in the Chamber of Deputies, where it appeared to compensate for the reduced voting power of the DC, whereas in the Senate, the PLI was able to get seats only in some legislatures, because its voting power was always rather minimal.

Figures 3.3 and 3.4 represent diagrammatically the three main parties' voting weights and voting powers, showing a small degree of fragmentation of

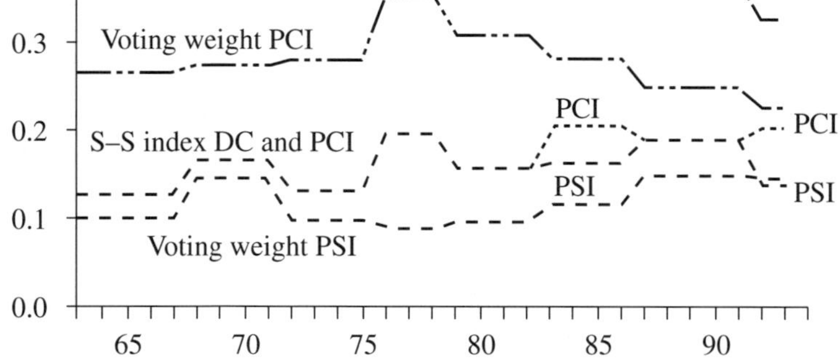

Figure 3.3 Chamber of Deputies: share of seats and S–S index for the three main parties (DC, PCI, PSI)

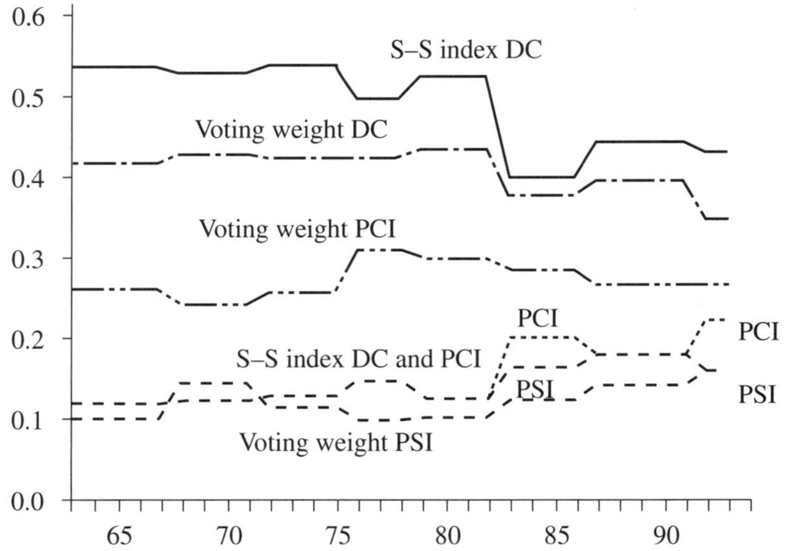

Figure 3.4 *Senate: share of seats and S–S index for the three main parties (DC, PCI, PSI)*

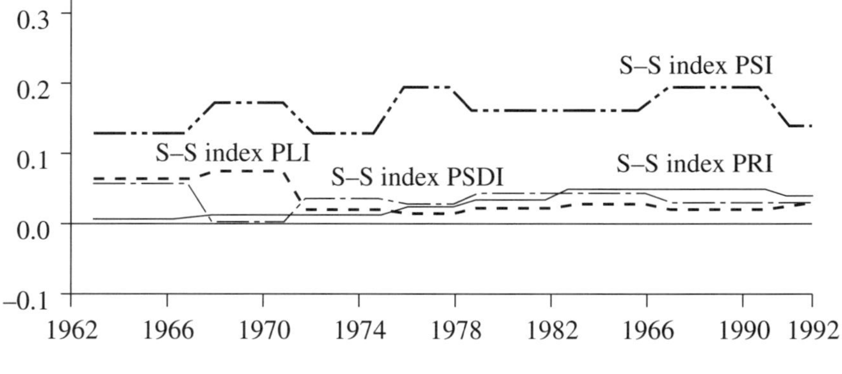

Figure 3.5 *Shapley–Shubik indices of the governing parties in the Chamber of Deputies*

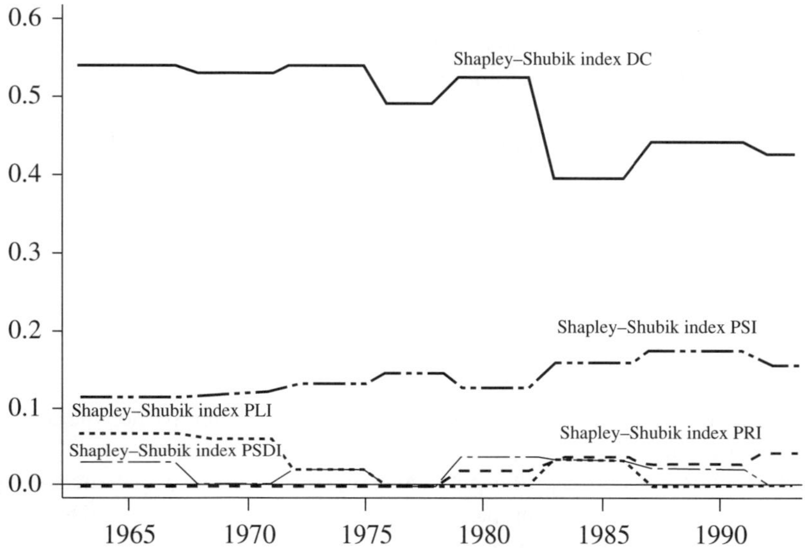

Figure 3.6 Shapley–Shubik indices of the governing parties in the Senate

the decision-making powers in the Chamber and in the Senate. Moreover, for the two governing parties the figures show how their voting weights are magnified in terms of voting powers. Notice that the difference between voting weights and voting powers helps to understand part of the reasons that might have led to the sequence of many governments similar to each other. This difference, jointly with the institutional practice of secret ballots, made the government, if in charge with a narrow margin of votes above the quota, run the risk of an unexpected loss of power because of the practice of 'snipers'.[14] Thus, with DC and PSI being the two main government coalition parties with an S–S index almost always above their voting weight, the requirement of some minor parties able to compensate both their electoral or unexpected loss of votes can be explained. Figures 3.5 and 3.6 show the compensative role played by the relevant minor parties in the governing coalitions.

6. THE IMPACT OF VOTING POWERS OF THE MAIN PARTIES ON DEBTS AND DEFICITS (1963–94) UNDER THE PROPORTIONAL REPRESENTATION REGIME IN A CHANGING INSTITUTIONAL SETTING

The correlations between the CGD/GDP and voting variables (in terms of shares of seats) that we have previously worked out are now verified with the

Table 3.3 Statistical correlation between CGD/GDP and the Shapley–Shubik index of the three main parliamentary groups (from IV to XI Legislatures)

Parliamentary groups	Statistical correlation between CGD/GDP and the Shapley–Shubik index	
	Chamber of Deputies	Senate
DC	–0.726250	–0.837727
PCI	0.742706	0.896206
PSI	0.418658	0.878143

Shapley–Shubik index of voting power. For the three main parties the results are reported in Table 3.3.

Now there emerges a relevant negative correlation between the voting power of the main governing party (DC) and the ratio of CGD to GDP and a positive correlation between the voting power of the two other parties and the same ratio.

As for the correlation between the S–S index of the DC party and the CGD/GDP the results in either Chamber of the Parliament are similar to those obtained with the simple correlation between the DC voting weight and the CGD/GDP. However, what clearly emerges now is that the higher the power of the PCI the higher the growth of CGD/GDP. As noted above, this is not surprising given the informal institutional change for which the PCI got the presidency of the Chamber and maintained it (see Table 3.4); also after the 1976–78 period of the so-called 'historical compromise' subsequently replaced by the so-called 'two oven' DC doctrine; that is, the strategy of potential alliance with the communists to counteract the power of the PSI that was blackmailing the existing majority led, in fact, by the DC. Notice, in this respect, the very high correlation between the CGD/GDP and the S–S index for the PSI in the Senate:[15] that is, the higher the power of the swing party the higher the increase of the gross government debt. The PSI would have been quite often in the position of forming a realistic government coalition with the PCI, that, however, has never occurred. This blackmailing power made the PSI quite relevant in determining the increasing trend of the CGD/GDP, while the 'historical compromise' and the 'two oven' doctrine gave a similar effect for the PCI. The higher the risk for the ruling party of losing the command chair, the higher the concessions it had to make, in the game for power, to its potential main ally – the PSI – and the higher the degree of collusion (institutionalised) with the main opposition party. Both practices led to higher expenditures and less tax discipline.

Notice that both the PCI and the PSI, being left-wing parties, as such, had

Table 3.4 The Presidents of the Chamber of Deputies from I Legislature to XII Legislature

		From	To
I Legislature (8 May 1948–24 June 1953)	Giovanni Gronchi (DC)	8 May 1948	24 June 1953
II Legislature (25 June 1953–11 June 1958)	Giovanni Gronchi (DC)	25 June 1953	29 April 1955
	Giovanni Leone (DC)	10 May 1955	11 June 1958
III Legislature (12 June 1958–15 May 1963)	Giovanni Leone (DC)	12 June 1958	15 May 1963
IV Legislature (16 May 1963–14 May 1968)	Giovanni Leone (DC)	16 May 1963	21 June 1963
	Brunetto Bucciarelli Ducci (DC)	26 June 1963	14 May 1968
V Legislature (5 June 1968–24 May 1972)	Sandro Pertini (PSI)	5 June 1968	24 May 1972
VI Legislature (25 May 1972–4 July 1976)	Sandro Pertini (PSI)	25 May 1972	4 July 1976
VII Legislature (5 July 1976–19 June 1979)	Pietro Ingrao (PCI)	5 July 1976	19 June 1979
VIII Legislature (20 June 1979–11 July 1983)	Leonilde Iotti (PCI)	20 June 1979	11 July 1983
IX Legislature (12 July 1983–1 July 1987)	Leonilde Iotti (PCI)	12 July 1983	1 July 1987
X Legislature (2 July 1987–22 April 1992)	Leonilde Iotti (PCI)	2 July 1987	22 April 1992
XI Legislature (23 April 1992–14 April 1994)	Oscar Luigi Scalfaro (DC)	24 April 1992	25 May 1992
	Giorgio Napolitano (PCI)	3 June 1992	14 April 1994
XII Legislature (15 April 1994–8 May 1996)	Irene Pivetti (LEGANORD)	16 April 1994	8 May 1996

Table 3.5 Statistical correlation between CGRD/GDP and the Shapley–Shubik index from IV to XI Legislature

Parliamentary groups	Statistical correlation between CGRD/GDP and the Shapley–Shubik index	
	Chamber of Deputies	Senate
DC	–0.553	–0.657
PCI	0.577	0.647
PSI	0.335	0.639

vast programmes of public spending in the areas of welfare, education and investments in public works and in public and private enterprises, and that while they normally did show a propensity to an increase of the tax burden, the DC party (as well as most of the minor parties) disliked it. As a result the combination of a steep increase in the ratio of public expenditure to GDP with reluctant choices in the same direction of the revenues could not but cause high deficits and increasing debts.

These features arising from the reduction of the voting power of the leading party, with the assignment of the Presidency of a Chamber of the Parliament to the minority, do not seem peculiar to a proportional electoral system. They may also occur under a uninominal electoral system. And they may occur even in the case that only two parties exist, provided that the 'mobility' of the members of parliament is institutionally allowed and/or snipers may operate under the protection of secret ballot.

Let us now check the validity of the above results with the CGRD/GDP ratio. The results of Table 3.5 broadly confirm the previous findings, although introducing a differentiation between the PSI correlation in the Senate much more significant than that in the Chamber of Deputies.

7. DEEPENING AND BROADENING THE ENQUIRY BY ENGLE AND GRANGER CAUSALITY METHODOLOGY

That voting weights and powers and related features in the institutions of parliamentary decision making are the sole determinant of the deficit and debt ratios to GDP seems to us a too simplistic conclusion. Indeed, we obtained an interesting correlation in both the Chambers for either debts or deficits with the voting power variables. But correlation does not necessarily imply causation. The statistical graveyard is full of sets of magnificent correlations, spurious or meaningless. Moreover, as noted above, the debt burden consequent to a given series of deficits is influenced by the level of the interest rate at which they are financed, thus, similar ratios of deficit to GDP may have (and in the case of Italy had) different consequences on the debt burden. And obviously the different cost of the debt service may cause differences in the new deficits. On the other hand, in order to determine the ratios of CGRD and of CGD to GDP, the GDP rate of growth is indeed relevant. Notice that, in real terms (not reported) the Italian GDP rate of growth was constantly higher than the European average for all the 1970s, then returned to European standards in the 1980s, showing that Italy during the 1970s was actually following an expansionary policy to promote growth and employment. In other words, the relation between the interest rate and GDP rate of growth plays an important role in the behaviour of these variables.

Figure 3.7 shows their peculiar behaviour (in nominal terms) during the period from 1962 to 1998. As one can see in the period 1962–80 the GDP nominal growth rate was higher than the long-run interest rate, whereas, with the exceptions of 1986 and 1988, during the 1980s the interest rate systematically exceeded the GDP rate of growth. The changing ratio between the interest rate and GDP rate of growth after 1981 was mainly caused by the monetary, institutional and fiscal policy changes (see Box 3.1) that we try to capture by including this ratio among the explanatory variables of the government finances.

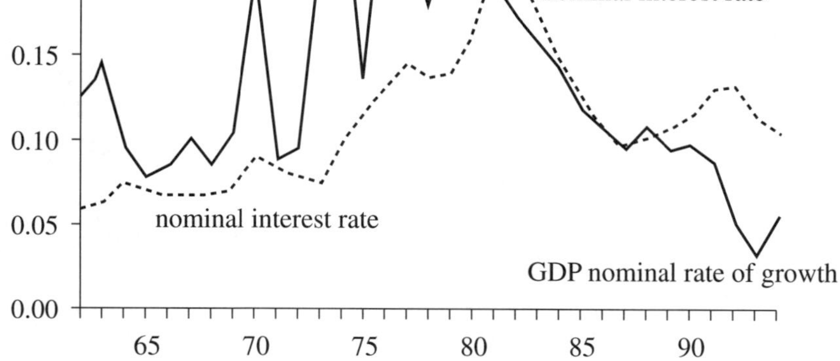

Figure 3.7 The interest rate and the GDP rate of growth

On the basis of these considerations, we tried a multivariate analysis by estimating by OLS (ordinary least squares), over the annual data set, the equations relating the CGRD/GDP – that we take as the parliamentary decision variable – to the ratio between the interest rate and the GDP rate of growth and to either voting weights or voting powers in both the Chamber of Deputies and the Senate. Unfortunately, none of the results obtained with the standard multivariate approach was acceptable. Given the peculiar behaviour of the individual political variables (see below), their mix with the economic ones gave strong problems of autocorrelation, with the consequence of meaningless, wrong signed estimates both when referring to voting weights and to voting powers. In order to find a 'solution' to the spurious correlation problem that emerged in the multivariate analysis, we used cointegration techniques,[15] with the view that the statistical notion of cointegration of time series is particularly apt to allow the consideration of long-run equilibrium relationships.

In practical application there might be some disadvantages to this procedure. One is related to the considerable degree of small sample bias which might occur in the parameter estimates (Banerjee et al., 1986). One other is related to the assumption made that the cointegrating vector is unique, which might not be the case. Finally, the procedure might not have a well-defined limiting distribution (see Johansen, 1988, 1989). Despite these difficulties a number of applications of the two-step procedure have provided a useful insight into the long-run relation amongst variables.

In the next section, the long-run equilibrium path of the CGRD/GDP is studied into the Engle and Granger framework. Then, by using the Engle and Granger (1987) results concerning cointegration and error correction models (ECM), the empirical analysis of the ECM containing the residuals lagged one period of the estimated cointegrating relation and the political variables is carried out to study the CGRD/GDP dynamic adjustment both for the Chamber of Deputies and the Senate.[16]

BOX 3.1 INSTITUTIONAL CHANGES EXTENDING (IN THE 1970s) AND REDUCING (IN THE 1980s) PUBLIC INTERVENTION IN REAL AND MONETARY ECONOMY AS AFFECTING THE MACROECONOMIC AND POLITICAL VARIABLES

Tables B.I and B.II in this box indicate the main institutional changes that had an effect in Italy in the two periods of the 1970s and the 1980s and seem to be relevant in explaining, together with the changing voting powers of the various parties (from which many of them derive), why and how CGRD/GDP and CGD/GDP behaved as they did.

The first decade with a weakened DC voting power and a strong PCI and PSI voting power (compare Figures 3.3 and 3.4) is characterised by the increased role of public intervention. Before the exogenous factor, such as the oil shock, a big social and political trend had been initiated in Italy to ask for deep institutional reforms, in particular, a new public pension scheme that became effective in 1969. From 11.3 per cent, the ratio of social expenditure to GDP continuously increased during the 1970s and was 14.8 per cent (about 40 per cent more) at the beginning of the subsequent decade.[18] Regions were created in 1970, mostly adding their new services to those of the state and also the 'general services' expenditure. It was 3.5 per cent of GDP in 1969–70 and rose during the 1970s, by one-third, reaching 50 per cent at the beginning of the subsequent decade. As a consequence of the extension of transfers to public economic institutions, the expenditures for 'economic services' rose from 5 per cent of GDP in 1969 to 6.4 per cent at the beginning of the 1980s. In the same period housing expenditures, mainly consisting of credit facilities and transfers doubled as a percentage of GDP, from 0.7 per cent to 1.4 per cent. From 1969 to 1981, net of the interest for the services of the debt, public spending rose from about 31 per cent of GDP to 40 per cent of GDP.[19] Only one percentage point of this increase occurred in capital expenditure. A substantial part of this increase was not due to the automatic effects of the original laws, but to successive amendments to them due to rent-seeking activities of pressure groups. On the revenue side, in 1971, a wide tax reform was approved introducing the global personal progressive income taxation in the place of the system of state real taxes complemented by a personal tax and a local family tax. The new value-added tax of the French type had to replace the previous state turnover tax and local consumption taxes. But the practical application of this reform was postponed until January 1974 because of its unpopularity. Furthermore, in the initial period it did not give the expected results. The expenditure on interest rates rose from 1.6 per cent of GDP to 6.2 per cent of GDP in 1981. Deflated from the loss of value of the debt stock, the rise was not so big: the nominal interest rate was kept at artificially low levels and the increase in the stock of debt in the 1970s was therefore only from about 35 per cent of GDP to 54 per cent: a level that even with the present Maastricht parameters, appears acceptable. The institutional features to keep the interest rate at a 'political price' level are described in Table B.I. Permissive monetary policy plus various state interventions sustained the GDP growth rate to an average 3 per cent, in spite of the new rigidities in the labour contracts. The result was a two-digit inflation. These institutional interferences were not bearable in the long run. One can see from Table B.II that in the 1980s most of them had to be repealed.

The recovery of voting power by the DC and the reduction of that of the PCI led, in the 1979–1983 Legislature, to (short-lived) governments' coalitions that realised important institutional changes in the monetary policy retreating from the manipulations of the 1970s. The main innovation was a consensual 'divorce' of the Bank of Italy from the Treasury, by which the first was no longer the residual purchaser of public debt. Mainly as a consequence of this divorce the interest rate rose substantially in real terms. And because most of the public debt in the 1970s had been short term, the burden of the debt increased not only because of the new deficits, but also as a consequence of a financing of the old one at market rates. On the other hand, the high rate of growth of GDP began to decline. Many factors, that are beyond the scope of this chapter, influenced this decline. However, one should not overlook the restrictive monetary policy related to the above-indicated institutional changes in the public debt policy and the distortions in the market economy indicated in Table B.I. The nominal interest rate rose above the GDP nominal growth rate, aggravating the debt burden. The new monetary policy was clearly related to the need to enter the European Monetary System in 1981: that was actually done with the safety net of a (provisional) broad band. In the 1983–1987 Legislature, the coalition DC–PSI dominated, with substantial continuity for the entire period. Other relevant institutional changes took place in connection with the exogenous factors of participation in the new phase of European integration: mainly the reduction of the escalator clause, the foreign exchanges liberalisation, the enactment of the European Directive vetoing the subsidies to public enterprises, with the corollary of the adhesion to the 'single European market' in 1996. The real rate of growth of GDP increased to 3 per cent but the nominal rate of interest remained at a level higher than the nominal GDP increase. The last part of the 1980s is characterised by pro-market institutional changes, undertaken in the perspective of the agreement on European monetary unification to be approved in 1992. In 1990 Italy thus entered the EMS narrow band. More and more these changes eroded the reason for collusion.

Table B.I Main institutional changes in the 1970s affecting CGD/GDP, CGRD/GDP, and the ratio between the interest rate and the GDP growth rate

30/11/1969	Institution of a general un-funded pensions' system.
28/01/1970	Institution of the 'Regions' with a statute allowing autonomous expenditure functions, via state transfers.
14/11/1970	Workers' statute of rights introducing rigidities in the labour contracts.
7/10/1971	Tax reform with radical changes and centralisation of revenues: local taxes replaced by transfers decided yearly by the Central Government and Parliament.
1974	Introduction of the ceiling to banking credit to the non-state sector.
25/01/1975	Generalised escalator clause on wages with a coverage of a uniform amount and subsequent extension to all the complements of the basic wage.
1976	Law n. 159 with severe controls and penalties on exports of capital.
5/07/1976	Assignment to the PCI of the presidency of the Chamber of Deputies and (only for the current legislature) of seven committees of the Chamber of Deputies.
5/08/1978	Institution of a financial law accompanying the budget, thus allowing the financing by deficit of the amount indicated in article 1 and related changes of expenditures and taxes.

Table B.II Main institutional changes in the 1980s affecting CGD/GDP, CGRD/GDP, and the ratio between the interest rate and the GDP growth rate

March 1981	Italy enters the EMS broad band.
July 1981	Divorce of the Bank of Italy from the Treasury whereby the former was no longer residual purchaser of public debt issues.
1982	Increase of ceilings of the bankers' credit to the non-state sector.
14/2/1984	The wages escalator clause is cut by the government.

Table B.II continued

17/2/1986	Approval of the Single European Act (SEA) setting the new rules of a free non-distorted single European market to be completed within 1992. Signing the SEA the member countries commit themselves to monetary integration.
1986	Italy applies the European Directive vetoing subsidies to public enterprises.
1987	Foreign exchange liberalisation.
11/3/1988	Institution of the document of fiscal planning before the budgetary session by which Parliament approves the fiscal guidelines by the Government for the next three years and the ceiling to the deficit for the incoming year.
13/8/1988	Abolition of the secret ballot.
29/7/1989	Final abolition of the wages' escalator clause.
12/5/1990	Reduction of the compulsory reserve of banks and related portfolio of public debt.
14/5/1990	Application of the EU Directive on complete currency liberalisation.
6/1/1990	Italy enters the narrow band of the EMS.
30/7/1990	Transformation in foundations of the public banks.
20/12/1990	Transformation in civil law corporations of remaining public credit institutions.
1991	Abolition of the current account of the Treasury with the Central Bank.
8/8/1992	Transformation of IRI, ENI, ENEL, INA in civil law private corporations and provisions for privatisation.
3/11/1992	Maastricht Treaty has effect in Italy.
Financial law for 1993	Reforms Health-care system and public pensions regime.

8. COINTEGRATION ANALYSIS OF THE LONG-RUN EQUILIBRIUM PATH OF CGRD/GDP

Before proceeding to test the mentioned set of variables for cointegration it is necessary to establish the properties of the individual series, given that much of the theory of cointegration has been developed for the case of first-order integration. We test for the order of integration of the two economic series, CGRD/GDP and Log(g/i) (or $[\text{Log}(g) - \text{Log}(i)]_t$) and of the S–S indices of the voting power of the DC, PCI, PSI, PLI and PSDI parties with the Augmented Dickey–Fuller tests (ADF) over the longest samples of data available to us,

Table 3.6 Unit roots tests for the economic variables

Variables	ADF (with neither intercept nor trend)	ADF (with intercept)	ADF (with both intercept and trend)
CGRD/GDP	–1.4296	–2.558	–2.362
Log (g/i)	–1.927	–1.751	–3.533
Δ (CGRD/GDP)	–6.216	–6.123	–6.245
Δ (Log (g/i))	–6.626	–6.808	–7.738
5% critical values	–1.950	–2.944	–3.538

that is, from 1962 to 1998 for the economic variables, whereas for the S–S index of voting power we tested over the whole proportional electoral period, that is, from the I Legislature until 1994.[20] Tables 3.6 and 3.7 report the ADF statistics for the economic and political series and for their first differences.

By looking at the level of the economic variables in the second and the third rows of Table 3.6, it is clear that none of them is a stationary process. Both the CGRD/GDP and Log(*g*/*i*) have negative highly insignificant test statistics. The fourth and fifth rows report the same tests for their first differences, that is Δ (CGRD/GDP) and Δ (Log (*g*/*i*)). In either case the ADF statistics are negative and significant at the 5 per cent level: if differencing once produces stationarity it is possible to conclude that these series are $I(1)$ and can form a cointegrating set. On the other side, the levels of the political variables in Table 3.7 seem not to indicate a stationary process. Nevertheless, although the tests for their first differences are negative and significant at the 5 per cent level, their peculiar behaviour – they are constant during each Legislature, indicating a first difference series made up of zero values with jumps in the years of the elections – suggests[21] that we exclude them from the cointegrating set and reconsider their level to explain the short-run adjustments in the ECM (see below).

On this basis, we tested for cointegration the OLS regression on the following equation:[22]

$$-\left(\frac{CGRD}{GDP}\right)_t = \text{constant} + [\text{Log}(g) - \text{Log}(i)]_t \qquad (3.1)$$

The results of the OLS estimates of model (3.1) are reported in Table 3.8. The above regression can be interpreted as depicting the long-run or

Table 3.7 Unit roots tests for the political variables in the two Chambers of Parliament

Variables	Chamber of Deputies ADF (with intercept)	Chamber of Deputies ADF (with both intercept and trend)	Chamber of Deputies ADF (with neither intercept nor trend)	Senate ADF (with intercept)	Senate ADF (with both intercept and trend)	Senate ADF (with neither intercept nor trend)
SS index DC	–3.011916	–2.998712	–2.094827	–0.970920	–3.316831	–1.392702
SS index PCI	–2.139888	–3.428571	0.380810	–0.345047	–3.361104	1.285565
SS index PSI	–2.581985	–2.641117	–0.132786	–1.126660	–3.206013	0.870117
SS index PLI	–1.909586	–2.081194	–0.828215	–1.863473	–1.880205	–1.537920
SS index PRI	–0.624200	–1.769843	–0.465627	–0.938452	–1.206009	–0.457091
SS index PSDI	–2.770803	–2.637699	–1.066499	–3.205259	–3.098600	–2.001573
Δ (SS index DC)	–4.744680	–5.078617	–4.527538	–4.726863	–4.666834	–4.519464
Δ (SS index PCI)	–4.757317	–4.836725	–4.519498	–4.590395	–4.616203	–4.293302
Δ (SS index PSI)	–4.460766	–4.756334	–4.390270	–4.595129	–4.533622	–4.397959
Δ (SS index PLI)	–4.474129	–4.585311	–4.513671	–4.474577	–4.456131	–4.527693
Δ (SS index PRI)	–4.548742	–4.448537	–4.247941	–4.221594	–4.974713	–4.268177
Δ (SS index PSDI)	–4.482390	–4.553160	–4.526925	–4.514707	–4.532467	–4.481229
5% critical values	–2.9286	–3.5136	–1.9483	–2.9286	–3.5136	–1.9483

Table 3.8 Dependent variable: (–CGRD/GDP) (adjusted for inflation with the consumer price index)

Variable	Coefficient	Std. Error	t-Statistic
Constant	0.0328	0.0039	8.520
Log(g/i)	–0.0192	0.0699	–2.762
R^2	0.179	ADF on Residuals = –3.233 (with neither intercept nor trend)	
CRDW=	0.907	ADF on Residuals = –3.292 (with intercept)	
		ADF on Residuals = –3.297 (with both intercept and trend)	

equilibrium path of CGRD/GDP, given that, in spite of the omission of any dynamic element inside the OLS estimates, it presents interesting properties if the variables are cointegrated: for example, Stock (1987) shows that if the variables constitute a valid cointegrating regression the OLS estimates are super-consistent since they converge to their probability limits at a higher speed than the standard OLS estimate). In Table 3.8, the test statistics reported are those used in Engle and Granger (1987), who also derive tables with the critical values for the two variables case. They are the standard squared R^2 associated with the regression, the ADF tests and CRDW (Cointegrating Regression Durbin–Watson).[23]

The CRDW shows that the regression residuals do not follow a stationary process, therefore we cannot reject the hypothesis of no cointegration at the 5 per cent level. However, the ADF statistics are at about their critical values. Given that the tests' power depends critically on the value of the autoregressive parameter ρ under the alternative hypothesis, it is likely to be very low for values of ρ less than, but close to, unity.[24] Thus, particular care has to be exercised in interpreting the results obtained from the unit root test and in rejecting the hypothesis of a non-existing cointegrating vector. For this reason, the Johansen (1988, 1989) procedure was also carried out as a counter-check that the variables of model (3.1) are indeed cointegrated.[25]

Despite the behaviour of the CGD/GDP showing a steep growth after the 1980s due to the change of the sign of Log(*g*/*i*) that becomes negative because of the divorce of the Central Bank from the Treasury, the parameter values of the estimated equation show how the CGRD/GDP follows the long-run equilibrium path from 1962 to 1998. That is, the important structural economic break affecting *g* and *i* seems not to have had irreversible effects on the behaviour of the

CGRD/GDP variable: the estimated coefficient of Log(g/i), although close to zero, is negative in the longest period we could consider.[26]

The standard errors are also reported in Table 3.8 even if they are highly misleading as it happens in the 'spurious' regression showing a low Durbin–Watson (CRDW) and an apparently high significance of the coefficients. Here, however, we were only looking for the values to be used in the second stage and for testing the equilibrium relationships.

9. THE IMPACT OF THE 'POLITICAL VARIABLES' ON THE DYNAMICS OF CGRD/GDP

Having specified the long-run estimates of the cointegrating relation with the Engle and Granger procedure, we now consider the one period lagged residuals of the estimated cointegrating equation, Z_{t-1}, as the 'error correcting' term of the short-run ('dynamic') models of deficit determination in the Chamber of Deputies and in the Senate. These provide two further tests of the existence of cointegration.[27] In other words, the estimated coefficient of the cointegrating equation are interpreted as the long-run parameters defining the long-run equilibrium between the CGRD/GDP and the log of the ratio between the GDP growth and the interest rates, whereas the residuals are considered as (statistically stationary) deviations from the equilibrium path.

Having the residuals Z_{t-1}, from the estimated model (3.1), we construct the short-run dynamic model for the CGRD/GDP *political* determination as follows

$$\Delta\left(-\frac{CGRD}{GDP}\right)_t = Constant + A(L)\Delta\left(-\frac{CGRD}{GDP}\right)_{t-1} + B(L)\Delta\left(\text{Log}\,\frac{g}{i}\right)_t$$
$$+ \text{dummies} + (POLITICAL\ VARIABLES)_t$$
$$+ Z_{(t-1)} + u_t \tag{3.2}$$

where $A(L)$ and $B(L)$ are finite order lag polynomials.

An important difference should be noted between our representation and the standard ECM including *only lagged values.* Here we allow for the *contemporaneous* effect both of $\Delta[\text{Log}\ (g/i)]_t$ – and also of what we have called $(POLITICAL\ VARIABLES)_t$, see below – something not allowed in a strictly endogenous model. This change is related to the fact that (3.2) represents a valid conditional model, that is, the explanatory variables are *weakly* exogenous (see Muscatelli, 1990 and Muscatelli and Hurn, 1992).[28]

We estimated the general model (3.2) over the period 1963–94 beginning with the inclusion, as for $\Delta[-(CGRD/GDP)]_{t-1}$ and $\Delta[\text{Log}(g/i)]_t$, of four lags both for the Chamber and for the Senate, and inserting as political variables the voting power indices of the main represented parties and a proxy of government instability (see next section). The voting power indices were introduced as follows: (1) we took the ratio of the Shapley–Shubik indices of the 'historical' governing parties over the 'historical' opposition party; (2) we took the ratios between the Shapley–Shubik indices of the 'historical' governing parties to depict the powers' relationship internal to the government coalition. A convincing empirical check of our thesis about the relevance of the power relations among the various parties to explain fiscal deficits was obtained, with a result not appearing peculiar to a proportional system, but to any situation in which the majority loses power with respect to the opposition.

At this point, one might object that perhaps working with less sophisticated measures of the importance of the various parties than their voting weights would give different results in line with Alesina–Perotti's mainstream. But the results we got on the basis of the voting weights appeared just worthless: something that should not be surprising, because mere voting weights do not capture the *game* features of the decision-making process of an assembly.

Thus referring to a general model as represented in (3.2), by successively eliminating insignificant regressors we found the results indicated in Table 3.9. Preliminarily, one may see that in Table 3.9, the economic variable and the lagged error term have the correct sign and are very significant, which implies that the long-run estimated economic equilibrium equation is statistically meaningful. Coming specifically to the impact of the political variables on the change of the variation of the CGRD/GDP, that is $\Delta\Delta[-(CGRD/GDP)]_t$ it seems that in the Chamber of Deputies it varied with the relative power of the main governing party (DC) with respect to the main opposition party (PCI), as represented by the ratio $(SS\ Index\ DC/SS\ Index\ PCI)_t$: when the value of this ratio diminishes the $\Delta\Delta[-(CGRD/GDP)]$ increases, that is when the DC loses power in comparison with its main opponent the PCI, the tendency to a deficit policy increases. But the variable 'Dummy PCI' is also very significant. This variable takes zero value over the period considered, but when the 'historical compromise' between the DC and the PCI occurred, with the PCI practically guaranteeing the DC government its support, the dummy took the value of 1 from 1976 to 1978. The dummy PCI was expected to capture the impact, on the fiscal variable, of the shock determined by the institutionalised collusion between the main governing party and the main opposition party, whereas in the former period of softer collusive democracy and in the

Table 3.9 Chamber of Deputies

Dependent Variable: $\Delta\Delta\left(-\frac{CGRD}{GDP}\right)_t$

Variable	Coefficient	Std. Error	t-Statistic
Constant	0.251368	0.106778	2.354117
$\Delta\left(\text{Log}\,\frac{g}{i}\right)_t$	–0.053168	0.018827	–2.823975
Z_{t-1}	–0.987837	0.304462	–3.244528
$\left(\frac{SS\ Index\ DC}{SS\ Index\ PCI}\right)_t$	–0.044774	0.019171	–2.335554
$\left(\frac{SS\ Index\ PRI}{SS\ Index\ PSI}\right)_t$	–0.466467	0.207054	–2.252879
$\left(\frac{SS\ Index\ PLI}{SS\ Index\ DC}\right)_t$	–0.563225	0.250350	–2.249752
DUMMY PCI	–0.087798	0.039401	–2.228347

R^2	0.646962			Mean dependent var	–0.000192
				S.D. dependent var	0.037062
Normality: Jarque-Bera (Probability)	3.2633434 (0.19559)			Akaike info criterion	–4.374799
LM (autocorrelation) F-statistic(4):	1.388 (0.27)	F-statistic(8):	1.186 (0.365)	Schwarz criterion	–4.050996
Breusch-Godfrey LM(4)	6.734 (0.15)	Breusch-Godfrey LM(8)	6.734 (0.17)		
Durbin–Watson	2.369			F-statistic	7.330211
RESET F[1, 31]	0.28			Prob(F-statistic)	0.000155

'two oven' period (subsequent to the 1979 elections) the role of the PCI was explained by the ratio (*SS Index DC/SS Index PCI*)$_t$. It is interesting to notice the estimated negative (although low) effect of the dummy on the real deficit. This might mean that when the two main parties formed a bloc, characterised by a short distance between their power (equal to unity) and the sum of their voting weights, the tendency to rent-seeking activities was reduced even in the presence of the secret ballots.

On the other hand, the estimated coefficients of the 'dummy PCI' and of the variable measuring the relative power of the DC with respect to the PCI, while significant, are quite low as compared with those representing the internal relations among the government coalition's fiscally 'severe' parties over those 'permissive' ones, as measured by (*SS Index PRI/SS Index PSI*)$_t$ and (*SS Index PLI/SS Index DC*)$_t$ where both the numerators have the power indices of the relevant anti-deficit[29] parties in the governing coalition.

As for the Senate, the dynamic of the variable [–(*CGRD/GDP*)]$_t$ *is* explained in Table 3.10.

Here again, the economic variable and the lagged error term are correctly signed and very significant. The impact of the political variables is somewhat different relative to the Chamber of Deputies given that, for example, those including the S–S index for the PSDI and the PLI in their relation with the other government parties have never been significant. Indeed, the small number of seats in the Senate very often made the elected representatives of the PSDI merge with those of the PSI; the PLI, in some Legislatures, did not even get seats, and when it did, its voting power was only significant when DC voting power was also very high, so that one may say that it was not really relevant for the DC strategy of remaining in power. Unexpectedly relevant in all the different specifications of the above dynamics was the S–S index of the PRI, which again plays its 'severe' role in relation with the PSI (the main left-wing party in the government coalition).

As in the Chamber of Deputies (*SS Index DC/SS Index PCI*)$_t$ is very significant in the Senate, although again the estimated coefficient is quite low with respect to (*SS Index PRI/SS Index PSI*)$_t$, representing the internal relations of the government's coalition. As before, it seems that as far as the two parties DC and PRI lose power relative to PCI and PSI, respectively, ΔΔ[–(*CGRD/GDP*)]$_t$ increases. Notice that in the Senate the variable 'Dummy PCI' has never been significant, possibly because the presidency of the Senate has never been given to the Communist party. Finally, notice that in either Chamber of the Parliament the variable used as a proxy of the government instability has never been significant. This aspect shall be reconsidered in the next section.

Table 3.10 Senate

Dependent Variable: $\Delta\Delta\left(-\frac{CGRD}{GDP}\right)_t$

Variable	Coefficient	Std. Error	t-Statistic
Constant	0.074647	0.03074	2.428203
$\Delta\left(\text{Log}\frac{g}{i}\right)_t$	–0.059144	0.01806	–3.274374
Z_{t-1}	–0.895936	0.28120	–3.186020
$\left(\frac{SS\ Index\ PRI}{SS\ Index\ PSI}\right)_t$	–0.169616	0.07269	–2.333281
$\left(\frac{SS\ Index\ DC}{SS\ Index\ PCI}\right)_t$	–0.017123	0.00711	–2.406279

R^2	0.646996			Mean dependent var	–0.000192
				S.D. dependent var	0.037062
Normality: Jarque-Bera	1.879886			Akaike info criterion	–4.512463
(Probability)	(0.390650)				
LM (autocorrelation)				Schwarz criterion	–4.281174
F-statistic(4):	1.1.0346	F-statistic(8):	0.803		
	(0.41)		(0.608)		
Breusch-Godfrey LM(4)	4.908	Breusch-Godfrey LM(8)	8.15		
	(0.297)		(0.419)		
RESET F[1, 31]	0.9951			F-statistic	12.07119
Durbin–Watson	2.234781			Prob(F-statistic)	0.000011

10. TESTING THE IMPACT OF THE 'FORMAL' GOVERNMENTS' INSTABILITY

As noted at the beginning, Grilli et al. (1991) argue, on the basis of average *countries*' statistical correlation, that short-lived governments cause the highest debt growth, no matter if they are an expression or not of the same political coalition and have the same premier or not. The inference is that the short duration of governments, *of any kind,* prevents long-run programmes.[30] We tried to test this hypothesis *for Italy from 1962 to 1994* using the Granger causality statistical methodology.

The Granger (1969) causality test is couched in terms of the relevance of all past information: the approach to the question of whether a variable *x* causes a variable *y* helps us to see how much of the current *y* can be explained by past values of *y* and then to see whether adding lagged values of *x* can improve the explanation. On this basis, say, *y* is Granger-caused by *x* if *x* helps in the prediction of *y*, or equivalently if the coefficients on the lagged *x*'s are statistically significant. Note that two-way causation is frequently the case: *x* Granger causes *y* and *y* Granger causes *x*.[31] We had a yearly economic data set. Therefore for the considered period we construct a variable that proxies the governments' instability. We called this variable 'changes of governments': it takes the value given by the number of governments during the year considered and it takes zero value when the government does not change (highest stability). The lag length chosen for the test was either the highest possible given the sample (that is 9 lags), or that corresponding to reasonable beliefs about the time over which one of the variables could help predict the other: in this latter case we run the test either for the legislature length, that is, 5 years or for the shortest length possible (2 lags). The bivariate regressions considered were of the form

$$y_t = \alpha_0 + \alpha_1 y_{t-1} + \ldots + \alpha_1 y_{t-1} + \beta_1 x_{t-1} + \ldots + \beta_1 x_{t-1}$$

$$x_t = \alpha_0 + \alpha_1 x_{t-1} + \ldots + \alpha_1 x_{t-1} + \beta_1 y_{t-1} + \ldots + \beta_1 y_{t-1}$$

for all possible pairs of (*x*,*y*) series in the group, where *x* is our annual proxy of the government length and *y* is alternatively the CGD/GDP and the CGRD/GDP. The reported F-statistics are the Wald statistics for the joint hypothesis

$$\beta_1 = \ldots = \beta_1 = 0$$

for each equation. The null hypothesis is therefore that x does not Granger-cause *y* in the first regression and that *y* does not Granger-cause *x* in the second regression. The results obtained are reported in Tables 3.11, 3.12 and 3.13.

Table 3.11 Pairwise Granger causality tests (9 lags)

Null Hypothesis:	Obs	F-Statistic	Probability
Deficit/GDP does not Granger cause 'Government changes'	22	2.31531	0.26471
'Government changes' does not Granger cause Deficit/GDP		1.34848	0.44639
CGD/GDP does not Granger cause 'Government changes	21	1.96078	0.38314
'Government changes' does not Granger cause CGD/GDP		0.88120	0.63651

Table 3.12 Pairwise Granger causality tests (5 lags)

Null Hypothesis:	Obs	F-Statistic	Probability
Deficit/GDP does not Granger cause 'Government changes'	26	4.18091	0.01403
'Government changes' does not Granger cause Deficit/GDP		1.20159	0.35510
CGD/GDP does not Granger cause 'Government changes	25	4.11984	0.01645
'Government changes' does not Granger cause CGD/GDP		2.04231	0.13445

Table 3.13 Pairwise Granger causality tests (2 lags)

Null Hypothesis:	Obs	F-Statistic	Probability
Deficit/GDP does not Granger cause 'Government changes'	29	0.45043	0.64263
'Government changes' does not Granger cause Deficit/GDP		0.61281	0.55009
CGD/GDP does not Granger cause 'Government changes	28	0.55611	0.58095
'Government changes' does not Granger cause CGD/GDP		0.48417	0.62235

In either case considered, we cannot reject the hypothesis that the variable 'Government changes' does not Granger cause either CGRD/GDP or CGD/GDP. Moreover, with 5 lags, we cannot reject its opposite or the hypothesis that either CGRD/GDP or CGD/GDP does not Granger cause 'Government changes'. *Therefore it appears that Granger causality runs, only for the 5-years length, one-way, and in a direction opposite to that expected.* Thus the proxy of government (in)stability, other than never being significant in the analysis done in the previous section, also did not affect the deficit and debt fiscal policy variables.

Alesina and Perotti (1994), with a particular consideration of the Italian case, maintain, in relation to the oil shock following the Yom Kippur war, that the short-lived governments of the 1970s may have not been willing and/or able to adopt and implement broad adjustment policies to cope with critical financial situations in *a structural way*. Thus the short governments' length implies the increase of both the total and primary government deficit, *in emergency* periods. No statistical evidence has been offered about this specific point. On the other hand, we found an explanation of deficits and debts, even for that period, in terms of the relative voting power of the main parties and of the informal institutional changes they implied. And the issue remains unexplored as to whether substantial governments' continuity with political homogeneity may have had positive effects on the structural variables of public policy. Fragmentation may coexist with enduring governments. But further research may be needed on these complex aspects.

11. SUMMARY AND CONCLUSIONS

Let us first summarise how we proceeded in our work. Unlike most of the empirical research in the area of the relations between political institutions and fiscal choices, we did not work on countries' cross-sections, but on Italian time-series. We mainly referred to the Shapley–Shubik *index of voting power* of the political groups, represented in the Italian Parliament, instead of their *voting weights*. We explained the behaviour of the CGD/GDP, that is a cumulative variable, with the analysis of the ratio between the total deficit and GDP, which was taken as a parliamentary decision variable once deflated to consider the big changes in the inflation rate. By adopting cointegration methodologies, we looked for a relation between the real deficit, the political variables and the trend of basic macroeconomic variables (the ratio of the interest rate to the GDP growth rate).

Our main results were the following:

1. From the 'political game' depicted in terms of the Shapley–Shubik index of voting power, *in the Italian case*, we did not get the (expected) picture of *fragmentation of decisional powers as a result of the proportional political system.* Indeed, rather than a fragmented Parliament unable to produce a clear leading government because of the multitude of small political groups, there emerged a clear division between the power of

three main parties (a leading, an opposition and a swing party) and those of all the other parties: that is, a situation similar to that under two-party plurality electoral systems with appeal to the median voter as potential swinger.

2. Moreover, as for the long run, by cointegration analysis, the only determinant of the public debt burden, via the real deficits, appeared to be the changing relation between the interest rate and the rate of growth of GDP. This ratio has been heavily influenced by institutions. In particular the interest rate, because of political constraints, for some time during the 1970s became negative in real terms, but returned to market levels afterwards. And to a certain extent it is also likely that the rate of GDP growth was influenced by institutional changes with lagged effects of the economic structure.
3. Given the electoral system (which in Italy remained unchanged from the first post-war election to 1994), the institutional variables have played an important role also in connection with the voting powers of the various parliamentary groups. But the political choices about *structural reforms* on taxation and on public expenditure operated on deficits within the constraints of the path traced by the macroeconomic variables. The short-run econometric analysis did show that the erosion of the voting power of the DC (with respect to the PCI and the PSI) was generally positively related to a pro-deficit policy. The dummy variable considering the increased political role of the PCI, as for the government decision-making process, was also very significant to explain the deficit adjustments, supporting the thesis that a bloc of the DC and the PCI, because of its high margin of 'safety', somewhat reduced the size of deficit caused by the need to stay in power. This result reinforces our general finding of an inverse relation between the voting power of the leading party and deficits. The positive relation between deficits and the power of a swing party, as with the PSI, could be explained by the costs of the policies of structural reforms and economic growth required by its programmes, plus the additional rents due to the precariousness of the coalition. These effects of a swing party, as such, cannot exist in a plurality system with two parties only (a feature not granted but only favoured by it). But a similar phenomenon may appear, under this electoral setting, in the tendency of both the majority and the opposition party to try to entice the electorate *that may swing*, by deficit spending, financing noble (but costly) ends and fiscal rents. On the other hand, there is an inverse relation between the real deficit and the voting power of a small, fiscally conservative, party such as the Liberals *vis-à-vis* the DC, as well as an inverse relation between the deficits and the increase of the ratio of voting power of the fiscally severe Republican party over that of the Socialists. Both the results seem to invalidate the view that under a proportional system, fragmentation makes the fiscal policy more permissive.

4. Proportional electoral systems are believed to be responsible for the growth of debts and deficits through the fact that they originate a tendency for short-lived governments. As noted for one theory this holds true only for *substantially* short governments. For another, it has empirical validity across countries for any kind of short-lived governments. We were not able to find any relation between the timespan of the different Italian governments *formally considered* and deficits and debts. It should be noted that there is no necessary connection between durability of governments and the proportional electoral system. Indeed countries like Germany, under a proportional system, have enduring governments because of the role of the leader. Italy had a tradition of short-lived governments under the uninominal electoral system that lasted from the creation of the national Kingdom in 1866 until 1919. In the Republic born after the Second World War, under the proportional electoral system, short-lived governments of different coalitions, always with DC as the leading party, were able, first, to get rid of the high deficits and inflation, then to have high GDP growth with low inflation and a small budgetary deficit until nearly the beginning of the 1970s. In the X Legislature, from 1977 to 1992, important institutional changes conditioning the path of the Italian economic and fiscal policy toward integration in the European single market economy and monetary unification with stabilisation of the debt burden, were undertaken, albeit with a questionable gradualism. This X Legistature *formally* had four governments: all of them with the same coalition, even if not always with a DC premier. Further research considering the relation between deficits and government duration, and also institutional variables other than the type of electoral system, may prove useful.

On balance, it seems to us that most of the factors found relevant to explain the long-run path and the short-run political behaviours in Italy were not peculiarly related to the type of the electoral system but to other variables. These appeared to be related to the changes in voting powers and in the institutions originating from them or from exogenous factors. Therefore, it seems to us that to focus on the type of electoral system to explain the deficits and debts path is unduly restrictive for a country that, under the same electoral rules, had such diverse deficit and debt trends. The fact that we argue that the electoral system is not, *as such*, a decisive variable to explain the greater or smaller tendency to public deficit and debts does not imply that we want to under-assess the value of the stability of governments to get (with appropriate institutions) an efficient governance. Stability of governments may be preferable to instability on grounds different from low bias to fiscal deficits and debts. Indeed it may well be that short-sighted, 'inefficient' governments do not make much deficit or debt because they are unable to engage in ambitious programmes of investments and structural spending. But one may argue that stable governments are more likely to make their expensive choices in longer-run perspectives. And this, in a proper institutional setting, might lead to GDP growth and employment. Still, the stability might be attainable under various institutional settings.[32]

NOTES

1. Accurately surveyed by Alesina and Perotti (1994).
2. After this chapter was written, Ireland, still under a proportional electoral system, resulted to be the best performing European country as regards the Maastricht parameters on debt and deficits.
3. See also McCubbins (1991), Von Hagan and Harden (1995) and Alesina and Rosenthal (1995).
4. Alesina and Perotti (1994) support their view on fragmentation on the basis of Drazen and Grilli (1993), Grilli et al. (1991).
5. See Appendix 3.1 for the sequence of the Italian governments.
6. Nevertheless, one should distinguish whether or not there is a leader of the coalition of the government.
7. And also without the German-type leadership system.
8. The correlation index we refer to is the following:

$$\rho_{x,y} = \frac{Cov(X, Y)}{\sigma_x \sigma_y} \text{ with } -1 \leq \rho_{x,y} \leq 1 \text{ and } Cov(X, Y) = \frac{1}{n} \sum_{j=1}^{n} (x_j - \mu_x)(y_j - \mu_y).$$

9. The share of seats in the Chamber of Deputies and in the Senate, that is the voting weights of the represented parties, are in Appendix 3.2.
10. The total domestic credit parameter and its shares for the government and for the market have been constantly utilised in Italian macroeconomic policy in the years we are referring to. In this chapter, we always refer to deficit of central government adjusted for inflation unless otherwise specified.
11. That is, only the winning coalitions have a 'non-zero', positive value and this value is assumed to be the same and equal to 1 for each winning coalition.
12. There are only two exceptions: the IX and the XI Legislatures. During the period of Craxi's leadership the PSI, unexpectedly, lost power in both the Chambers, despite the increase of its share of seats. During the XI Legislature the PSI lost both voting weight and voting power. The XI Legislature is, however, characterised by, at least, three political 'random shocks': the split of the Communist party into two parties, PDS (Left Democrats) and Rifondazione Comunista (Communists) – they, if pooled together as assumed in Figures 3.2 and 3.3 and in Table 3.A8 in Appendix 3.2, increase their power with respect to the previous positions; 'tangentopoli', which determined a relevant reduction of the PSI – as well as of other minor swing parties except the PRI – both in terms of voting power and voting weight; and the emergence of the Lega. See Table 3.A9 in Appendix 3.2 for the figures in terms of seats, voting weights and S–S index obtained by keeping separate PDS and Rifondazione Comunista (previously melted in the PCI).
13. The DC and PSI often formed, with all the government's coalition parties, called 'pentapartito'. Sometimes, without one of them, they formed a 'quadripartito'. And with only one of them, a 'tripartito'.
14. Although beyond the scope of the chapter, the analysis of the distance between voting

weight and voting power can be taken as a measure of the risk of losing power run by a (minimal) ruling coalition.

15. But notice the different results for the PSI obtained in the Chamber of Deputies presided over by the Communists and in the Senate where the presidency has never been assigned to them.
16. Engle and Granger (1987, p. 253) gave a definition of cointegration: a series x_t is integrated of order d and denoted as $x_t \sim I(d)$, if it has a stationary, invertible, non-deterministic ARMA representation after differencing d times. The components of the vector x_t are cointegrated of order d, b [$x_t \sim CI(d, b)$] if all the components of x_t are $I(d)$ and there exists a vector $\beta \neq 0$ so that $z_t = \beta' x_t \sim I(d - b)$, $b > 0$. The vector β is called the cointegrating vector.
17. The definition of cointegration given in the previous note for the ECM implies that if the level part of the ECM is made up of a cointegrated vector then this part of the error term will be non-stationary. Unless there is an exact offsetting nonstationarity coming from the difference term in the equation, the ECM error term will be non-stationary and the resulting estimates will be meaningless. Putting it in a different way, if the components of the vector x_t are all integrated of order 1, cointegration would mean that the equilibrium error would be $I(0)$ and the z_t will rarely drift far from zero if it has zero mean and z_t will often cross the zero line. It means that equilibrium will occasionally occur, at least to a close approximation, whereas in the absence of cointegration the z_t zero crossing would be very rare and the equilibrium concept would not have practical implications.

    With the Engle and Granger procedure the z_t error might be tested for stationarity and the cointegrating vector β can be imposed on the ECM estimated equation, therefore x_t is a properly cointegrating vector and the final equation is based on a consistent estimate of β.
18. For these and the following data on public expenditure increases we refer to Fedeli and Trotto (2001).
19. Out of these nine points in the increase of the ratio of expenditures net of interest to GDP, seven are explained by the items considered in the text.
20. Although not reported – see the next note – the same kind of analysis was also carried out with the voting weights of the Italian parties.
21. We tested for a cointegrating relation inclusive of the political variables in the context of the VAR model. We included the voting weights and the S–S indices of power (both levels and first differences). We were unable to find a valid cointegrating vector (unit roots are not reported here), which led us to the reported specification.
22. As in Figure 3.2 and in Tables 3.2 and 3.4, the original time series of the CGRD/GDP has been taken with negative sign only to simplify the exposition.
23. The CRDW is analysed to check whether the residuals are stationary. If they are not CRDW will tend to zero and therefore the null hypothesis of no-cointegration will be rejected for CRDW too high as suggested by Bhargava (1986). The ADF statistics here check the regression residuals with an auxiliary regression as depicted by Dickey and Fuller (1981) under the assumption that the first order model is correct. In two of the ADF tests, dynamic elements have been introduced.
24. Sargan and Bhargava (1983) note that the CRDW test is more powerful than the Dickey–Fuller type tests, but only when the alternative is a special case of a stationary first-order autoregressive process.
25. The procedure in this case provides a unified framework for estimation and testing of cointegrating relations in the context of the vector autoregressive (VAR) model. In the considered case the trace test (not reported) rejects the null hypothesis that there are zero cointegrating vectors, so we know that there is at least one. The likelihood ratio test that there are at most one or two cointegrating vectors is within the rejection criteria so there is clearly one cointegrating vector. The maximun eigenvalues statistics reject the hypothesis that $r = 0$ in favour of the alternative $r = 1$. A check of the OLS estimates obtained in Table 3.9 and the normalised estimated eigenvectors obtained with the Johansen procedure was also carried out as suggested by Hall (1986 and 1989). Not surprisingly, the signs of the estimated economic variables in the different inversions were always the same in either procedure. The results were, instead, slightly different in the values since the Johansen method is conditional upon the short-run dynamics of the VAR process.

    The first estimated normalized cointegrating eigenvector was the following:

$$\left(-\frac{CGRD}{GDP}\right)_t = 0.0359 - 0.0328\,[\mathrm{Log}(g) - \mathrm{Log}(i)]_t.$$

Nevertheless, the parameters so obtained seemed to offer less convincing interpretation, therefore we stick to the Engle and Granger procedure.

26. Given that the estimates over a longer period (that is, until 1998) are more prudential (or closest to zero) than those obtained in the (less prolonged) period until 1994, because of the highest relevance assumed by the reduction of the stock of public debt incorporated in the real deficit/GDP ratio, we referred to the sample 1962–98 as for the long-run equilibrium estimates.
27. Remember that the sign of Z_{t-1} and the t statistics in the dynamic equations provide two further tests of the existence of cointegration.
28. Notice that one could expect that the political variables affect the fiscal variables of the subsequent year. In this way, however, the often exploited possibility of corrective manoeuvres, which is explicitly allowed by the Italian system, would not be captured.
29. Unlike the PLI and the PRI, whose powers increase exactly when either the PSI or the DC lose their power. The PSDI, although belonging to a number of government coalitions, seems not to absorb the reduced power of the main governing party. Moreover, for some legislatures, the PSI and the PSDI merged in the same parliamentary group.
30. This situation is not peculiar to the proportional electoral systems. Indeed Germany has a proportional system and if the coalition government fails to gain support in parliament, new elections may be avoided only by an exceptional procedure of a 'no confidence constructive vote'. This institutional setting leads to enduring governments.

    The fact that short-lived governments may not be able to engage in medium-term long-run programmes may not imply that they cause more debts. These programmes may consist of ambitious investment plans and innovations in the role of the state that imply higher public spending as in Italy during the 1970s.
31. It is important to note that the statement '*x* Granger causes *y*' does not imply that *y* is the effect or the result of *x*. Granger causality measures precedence and information content but does not by itself indicate causality in the more common use of the term.
32. As noted, stability of governments may be assured, both under a plural system and under a proportional system such as that with the German institutions. It might also be achieved by the electorate's direct choice of the head of the government, as under the present Italian electoral rules for the Regions and for the local governments that are based, for the other representatives, on the proportionality principle.

REFERENCES

Alesina, A. and R. Perotti (1994), 'The Political Economy of Budget Deficits', IMF Working Paper, 85.

Alesina, A. and H. Rosenthal (1995), *Partisan Politics, Divided Government and the Economy*, Cambridge: Cambridge University Press.

Banerjee, A., J.J. Dolado, D.F. Hendry and G.W. Smith (1986), 'Exploring equilibrium relationships in econometrics through static models: some Monte Carlo evidence', *Oxford Bulletin of Economics and Statistics, Special Issue, Econometric Modelling with Cointegrated Variables*, D. Hendry (ed.), **48**.

Bhargava, A. (1986), 'On the theory of testing for unit root in observed time-series', *Review of Economic Studies*, **53**, 369–84.

Chiancone, A. (1993), 'Political theory and public debts', *Rivista di Diritto Finanziario e Scienza delle Finanze*.

Dickey, D.A. and W.A. Fuller (1979), 'Distribution of the estimators for autoregressive time series with a unit root', *Journal of the American Statistical Association*, **74**.

Dickey, D.A. and W.A. Fuller (1981), 'The likelihood ratio statistics for autoregressive time series with a unit root', *Econometrica*, **49**.

Drazen, A. and V. Grilli (1993), 'The benefits of crises for economic reform', *American Economic Review*.

Engle, R.F. and C.W. Granger (1987), 'Co-integration and error correction: representation, estimation, and testing', *Econometrica*, **55**.

Fedeli, S. and A. Trotto (2001), 'Il potere di voto nel sistema parlamentare italiano in regime proporzionale e la dinamica della spesa pubblica dal 1960 al 1990', Atti della XIII Conferenza SIEP, Pavia 2001.

Forte, F. (2001), 'Scelte pubbliche e debito pubblico: riflessioni sui contributi di Aldo Chiancone', *Rivista di Diritto Finanziario e Scienza Delle Finanze*, forthcoming.

Granger, C.W. (1969), 'Investigating causal relations by econometric models and cross-spectral methods', *Econometrica*, **37**.

Granger, C.W. (1986), 'Developments in the study of cointegrated economic variables', *Oxford Bulletin of Economics and Statistics Special Issue, Econometric Modelling with Cointegrated Variables*, D. Hendry (ed.), **48**.

Grilli, V., D. Masciandaro and G. Tabellini (1991), 'Political and monetary institutions and public finance policies in the industrial democracies', *Economic Policy*, **13**.

Hall, G.S. (1986) 'An application of the Granger and Engle two-step estimation procedure to United Kingdom aggregate wage data', *Oxford Bulletin of Economics and Statistics, Special Issue, Econometric Modelling with Cointegrated Variables*, D. Hendry (ed.), **48**.

Hall, G.S. (1989). 'Maximum likelihood estimation of cointegrating vectors: an example of the Johansen procedure', *Oxford Bulletin of Economics and Statistics*, **51**.

Johansen, S. (1988), 'Statistical analysis of cointegration vectors', *Journal of Economic Dynamic and Control*, **12**.

Johansen, S. (1989) 'Likelihood-based Inference on Cointegration: Theory and Applications', Mimeo, Institute of Mathematical Statistics, University of Copenhagen.

La Palombara, G.J. (1988), *Democracy Italian Style*, New Haven, CT: Yale University Press.

McCubbins, M., (1991), 'Party governance and US budget deficits: divided government and fiscal stalemate', in A. Alesina and G. Carliner (eds), *Politics and Economics in the Eighties*, Chicago: Chicago University Press.

Muscatelli, V.A. (1990), 'Exogeneity, cointegration and the demand for money in Italy', Discussion Paper, University of Glasgow.

Muscatelli, V.A. and S. Hurn (1992), 'Econometric Modelling Using Cointegrating Time Series', Discussion Paper, University of Glasgow.

Roubini and Sachs (1989a), 'Government spending and budget deficits in the industrial countries', *Economic Policy*, **8**.

Roubini and Sachs (1989b), 'Political and economic determination of budget deficits in the industrial democracies', *European Economic Review*, **33**.

Sargan, J.D. and A. Bhargava (1983), 'Testing residuals from least squares regression for being generated by the Gaussian random walk', *Econometrica*, **51**.

Shapley, L.S. and M. Shubik (1954), 'A method for evaluating the distribution of power in a committee system', *American Political Science Review*, **48**.

Stock, J. (1987), 'Asymptotic properties of least squares estimators cointegrating vectors', *Econometrica*, **55**, 1035–56.

Von Hagen, J. and I.J. Harden (1995), 'Budget processes and commitment to fiscal discipline', *European Economic Review*, **39**(3–4).

APPENDIX 3.1: THE ITALIAN GOVERNMENTS FROM IV TO XI LEGISLATURES

IV Legislature (16 May 1963–14 May 1968)

1° Leone (21-6-1963–5-11-1963); Government Political coalition: DC
1° Moro (14-12-1963–26-6-1964); Government Political coalition: DC-PSI-PSDI-PRI
2° Moro (26-7-1964–21-1-1966); Government Political coalition: DC-PSI-PSDI-PRI
3° Moro (23-2-1966–5-6-1968); Government Political coalition: DC-PSI-PSDI-PRI

V Legislature (5 June 1968–24 May 1972)

2° Leone (24-6-1968–19-11-1968); Government Political coalition: DC
1° Rumor (12-12-1968–5-7-1969); Government Political coalition: DC-PSI-PLI-PSDI
2° Rumor (5-8-1969–17-2-1970); Government Political coalition: DC
3° Rumor (27-3-1970–6-7-1970); Government Political coalition: DC-PSI-PSU
1° Colombo (6-8-1970–15-1-1972); Government Political coalition: DC-PSI-PSU-PSDI-PRI
1° Andreotti (17-2-1972–26-2-1972); Government Political coalition: DC

VI Legislature (25 May 1972–4 July 1976)

2° Andreotti (26-6-1972–12-6-1973); Government Political coalition: DC-PLI-PSDI
4° Rumor (7-7-1973–2-3-1974); Government Political coalition: DC-PSI-PSDI-PRI
5° Rumor (14-4-1974–13-10-1974); Government Political coalition: DC-PSI-PSDI
4° Moro (23-11-1974–7-1-1976); Government Political coalition: DC
5° Moro (12-2-1976–30-4-1976); Government Political coalition: DC

VII Legislature (5 July 1976–19 June 1979)

3° Andreotti (29-7-1976–16-1-1978); Government Political coalition: DC
4° Andreotti (11-3-1978–31-1-1979); Government Political coalition: DC
5° Andreotti (20-3-1979–31-3-1979); Government Political coalition: DC-PRI-PSDI

VIII Legislature (20 June 1979–11 July 1983)

1° **Cossiga** (4-8-1979–19-3-1980); Government Political coalition: DC-PLI-PSDI
2° **Cossiga** (4-4-1980–27-9-1980); Government Political coalition: DC-PSI-PRI
1° **Forlani** (18-10-1980–26-5-1981); Government Political coalition: DC-PSI-PSDI-PRI
1° **Spadolini** (28-6-1981–7-8-1982); Government Political coalition: DC-PSI-PSDI-PRI-PLI
2° **Spadolini** (23-8-1982–13-11-1982); Government Political coalition: DC-PSI-PSDI-PRI-PLI
5° **Fanfani** (1-12-1982–2-5-1983); Government Political coalition: DC-PSI-PSDI-PLI

IX Legislature (12 July 1983–1 July 1987)

1° **Craxi** (4-8-1983–27-6-1986); Government Political coalition: DC-PSI-PSDI-PRI-PLI
2° **Craxi** (1-8-1986–3-3-1987); Government Political coalition: DC-PSI-PSDI-PRI-PLI
6° **Fanfani** (17-4-1987–28-4-1987); Government Political coalition: DC-INDIPENDENTI

X Legislature (2 July 1987–22 April 1992)

1° **Goria** (28-7-1987–11-3-1988); Government Political coalition: DC-PSI-PSDI-PRI-PLI
1° **De Mita** (13-4-1988–19-5-1989); Government Political coalition: DC-PSI-PSDI-PRI-PLI
6° **Andreotti** (22-7-1989–29-3-1991): Government Political coalition: DC-PSI-PSDI-PRI-PLI
7° **Andreotti** (12-4-1991–24-4-1992); Government Political coalition: DC-PSI-PSDI-PLI

XI Legislature (23 April 1992–14 April 1994)

1° **Amato** (28-6-1992–22-4-1993); Government Political coalition: DC-PSI-PSDI-PLI
1° **Ciampi** (28-4-1993–16-4-1994); Government Political coalition: DC-PSI-PSDI-PLI

APPENDIX 3.2 THE SHAPLEY–SHUBIK INDICES OF VOTING POWER FOR THE ITALIAN PARTIES FROM 1963 TO 1994

Table 3.A1 IV Legislature (16 May 1963–14 May 1968)

	Chamber of Deputies			Senate		
Parliamentary Groups	Seats	Voting Weight	Shapley–Shubik Index	Seats	Voting Weight	Shapley–Shubik Index
Democratico Cristiano (DC)	260	0.41270	0.51984	134	0.41745	0.53571
Socialista Italiano (PSI)	62	0.09841	0.12460	32	0.09969	0.11667
Comunista (PCI)	166	0.26349	0.12460	83	0.25857	0.11667
Socialdemocratico (PSDI)	32	0.05079	0.05794	14	0.04361	0.03095
Repubblicano (PRI)	5	0.00794	0.00397			
Liberale (PLI)	38	0.06032	0.06111	19	0.05919	0.06905
Socialista It. Unita' Proletaria	25	0.03968	0.05000	12	0.03738	0.03095
Democratico Unita' Monarchica	8	0.01270	0.00397			
Movimento Sociale Italiano (MSI)	27	0.04286	0.05000	17	0.05296	0.06905
Misto	7	0.01111	0.00397	10	0.03115	0.03095
Total	630	1	1	321	1	1

Table 3.A2 V Legislature (5 June 1968–24 May 1972)

	Chamber of Deputies			Senate		
Parliamentary Groups	Seats	Voting Weight	Shapley–Shubik Index	Seats	Voting Weight	Shapley–Shubik Index
Comunista	171	0.27143	0.16508	77	0.23913	0.12024
Democratico Cristiano	265	0.42063	0.46389	137	0.42547	0.52976
PSI e PSDI Unificati	91	0.14444	0.16508	46	0.14286	0.12024
Liberale	31	0.04921	0.07579	16	0.04969	0.06310
Repubblicano	9	0.01429	0.00913			
Movimento Sociale Italiano	24	0.03810	0.05317	13	0.04037	0.05357
Dem. Unita' Monarchica	6	0.00952	0.00556			
Soc. It. Unita' Proletaria	23	0.03651	0.05317	13	0.04037	0.05357
Sinistra Indipendente				12	0.03727	0.05357
Misto	10	0.01587	0.00913	8	0.02484	0.00595
Total	630	1	1	322	1	1

Table 3.A3 VI Legislature (25 May 1972–4 July 1976)

Parliamentary Groups	Chamber of Deputies Seats	Chamber of Deputies Voting Weight	Chamber of Deputies Shapley–Shubik Index	Senate Seats	Senate Voting Weight	Senate Shapley–Shubik Index
Comunista	175	0.27778	0.12976	82	0.25466	0.12619
Democratico Cristiano	265	0.42063	0.53452	136	0.42236	0.53571
Socialista Italiano	61	0.09683	0.12976	36	0.11180	0.12619
Liberale	20	0.03175	0.02024	10	0.03106	0.02143
Socialdemocratico	30	0.04762	0.03452	12	0.03727	0.02143
Repubblicano	15	0.02381	0.01071			
Movimento Sociale Italiano	55	0.08730	0.12976	26	0.08075	0.12619
Sinistra Indipendente				11	0.03416	0.02143
Misto	9	0.01429	0.01071	9	0.02795	0.02143
Total	630	1	1	322	1	1

Table 3.A4 VII Legislature (5 July 1976–19 June 1979)

Parliamentary Groups	Chamber of Deputies Seats	Chamber of Deputies Voting Weight	Chamber of Deputies Shapley–Shubik Index	Senate Seats	Senate Voting Weight	Senate Shapley–Shubik Index
Comunista	222	0.35238	0.19524	99	0.30745	0.14524
Democratico Cristiano	262	0.41587	0.42619	136	0.42236	0.49524
Socialista Italiano	57	0.09048	0.19524	31	0.09627	0.14524
Socialdemocratico Italiano	15	0.02381	0.02659			
Repubblicano	14	0.02222	0.02262			
Liberale	5	0.00794	0.01151			
Socialdemocratico e Liberale				10	0.03106	0.02857
Partito Radicale	4	0.00635	0.00754			
Democrazia Proletaria	6	0.00952	0.01349			
Movimento Sociale Italiano	34	0.05397	0.08492	15	0.04658	0.06190
Sinistra Indipendente				18	0.05590	0.07857
Misto	11	0.01746	0.01667	13	0.04037	0.04524
Total	630	1	1	322	1	1

Table 3.A5 VIII Legislature (20 June 1979–11 July 1983)

	Chamber of Deputies			Senate		
Parliamentary Groups	Seats	Voting Weight	Shapley–Shubik Index	Seats	Voting Weight	Shapley–Shubik Index
Comunista	193	0.30635	0.15556	95	0.29503	0.12381
Democratico Cristiano	262	0.41587	0.46587	139	0.43168	0.52381
Socialista Italiano	61	0.09683	0.15556	32	0.09938	0.12381
Liberale	9	0.01429	0.01746			
Socialdemocratico Italiano	20	0.03175	0.03889	10	0.03106	0.03810
Repubblicano	16	0.02540	0.03095	7	0.02174	0.01905
Movimento Sociale Italiano DN	29	0.04603	0.06429	13	0.04037	0.05741
Partito Radicale	17	0.02698	0.03294			
Unita' Prol. Per il Comunismo (PDUP)	6	0.00952	0.00556			
Sinistra Indipendente				16	0.04969	0.07619
Misto	17	0.02698	0.03294	10	0.03106	0.03810
Total	630	1	1	322	1	1

Table 3.A6 IX Legislature (12 July 1983–1 July 1987)

	Chamber of Deputies			Senate		
Parliamentary Groups	Seats	Voting Weight	Shapley–Shubik Index	Seats	Voting Weight	Shapley–Shubik Index
Comunista	177	0.28095	0.20545	91	0.28173	0.19762
Democratico Cristiano	226	0.35873	0.38442	121	0.37461	0.39762
Socialista Italiano	73	0.11587	0.16140	39	0.12074	0.16190
Socialdemocratico Italiano	22	0.03492	0.03640	9	0.02786	0.03095
Repubblicano	29	0.04603	0.04672	12	0.03715	0.03095
Liberale	16	0.02540	0.02489	6	0.01858	0.03095
Movimento Sociale DN	42	0.06667	0.06894	18	0.05573	0.05952
Partito Radicale (PR)	11	0.01746	0.01656			
Democrazia Proletaria	7	0.01110	0.01020			
Sinistra Indipendente	20	0.03175	0.03481	18	0.05573	0.05952
Misto	7	0.01111	0.01021	9	0.02768	0.03095
Total	630	1	1	323	1	1

Table 3.A7 X Legislature (2 July 1987–22 April 1992)

Parliamentary Groups	Chamber of Deputies			Senate		
	Seats	Voting Weight	Shapley–Shubik Index	Seats	Voting Weight	Shapley–Shubik Index
Comunista	157	0.2491	0.18961	85	0.26235	0.17698
Democratico Cristiano	234	0.37143	0.42006	127	0.39198	0.44127
Socialista Italiano	94	0.14921	0.18961	45	0.13889	0.17698
Socialdemocratico Italiano	17	0.02698	0.02294	7	0.02160	0.02103
Repubblicano	21	0.03333	0.02908	9	0.02778	0.02460
Liberale	11	0.01746	0.01479			
Movimento Sociale DN	35	0.05556	0.05447	16	0.04938	0.04960
Federativo Europeo				6	0.01852	0.01389
Federalista Europeo (PR)	12	0.01905	0.01566			
Democrazia Proletaria	8	0.01270	0.01003			
Sinistra Indipendente	20	0.03175	0.02691	17	0.05247	0.05675
Verde	13	0.02063	0.01681			
Misto	8	0.01270	0.01003	12	0.03704	0.03889
Total	630	1	1	324	1	1

Table 3.A8 XI Legislature (23 April 1992–14 April 1994)[a]

Parliamentary Groups	Chamber of Deputies			Senate		
	Seats	Voting Weight	Shapley–Shubik Index	Seats	Voting Weight	Shapley–Shubik Index
Democratici Di Sinistra & Rifondazione Comunista	142	0.22540	0.20274	86	0.26380	0.21905
Democratico Cristiano	206	0.32698	0.38730	112	0.34356	0.38571
Socialista Italiano	92	0.14603	0.16082	51	0.15644	0.18571
Liberale	17	0.02698	0.02237			
Socialdemocratico Italiano	16	0.02540	0.02035			
Repubblicano	27	0.04286	0.03608	12	0.03681	0.05238
Movimento Sociale DN	34	0.05397	0.04199	16	0.04908	0.05238
Fed. Europeo (Lista Pannella)	6	0.00952	0.00902			
La Rete	12	0.01905	0.01573			
Lega Nord	55	0.08730	0.07424	25	0.07669	0.05238
Verde	16	0.02540	0.022035			
Misto	7	0.01111	0.00902	24	0.07362	0.05238
Total	630	1	1	326	1	1

Table 3.A9 XI Legislature (23 April 1992–14 April 1994)[a]

	Chamber of Deputies			Senate		
Parliamentary Groups	Seats	Voting Weight	Shapley–Shubik Index	Seats	Voting Weight	Shapley–Shubik Index
Democratici Di Sinistra (PDS)	107	0.16984	0.15459	66	0.20245	0.17976
Democratico Cristiano	206	0.32698	0.41465	112	0.34356	0.42738
Rifondazione Comunista	35	0.05556	0.04250	20	0.06135	0.04167
Partito Socialista Italiano	92	0.14603	0.13691	51	0.15644	0.15595
Liberale	17	0.02698	0.02259			
Socialdemocratico Italiano	16	0.02540	0.02089			
Repubblicano	27	0.04286	0.03500	12	0.03681	0.04167
Fed. Europeo (Lista Pannella)	6	0.00952	0.01043			
Movimento Sociale DN	34	0.05397	0.04200	16	0.04908	0.04167
La Rete	12	0.01905	0.01664			
Lega Nord	55	0.08730	0.07187	25	0.07669	0.05595
Verdi	16	0.02540	0.02089			
Misto	7	0.01111	0.01104	24	0.07362	0.05595
Total	630	1	1	326	1	1

[a] Tables 3.A8 and 3.A9 refer to the same Legislature. Table 3.A8's results are determined under the assumption that the two parties originating in the former PCI (that is the so-called Left Democrats and the Communists) are still joined in the same party. Table 3.A9 depicts the reality of the XI Legislature where the PCI is split into two separate parties.

4. Institutions matter for procedural utility: an econometric study of the impact of political participation possibilities

Alois Stutzer and Bruno S. Frey*

1. INTRODUCTION

Comparative institutional analysis judges institutions according to their contribution to human welfare. In economics, human welfare is normally evaluated by looking at individual income or measures such as the gross domestic product. Thus standard analysis only considers the outcome of different mechanisms of decision making. It neglects that people partly judge the *process* of decision making independent of the outcome. In addition to this alternative conceptual view referring to procedural utility, direct measures of subjective well-being offer new opportunities for empirical research of individual welfare.

Here *procedural utility* reaped from democratic decision making is theoretically discussed and empirically identified. Procedural utility goes beyond the utility gained from the favourable outcome that is generated by democratic institutions. A fundamental characteristic of democracy is the involvement of citizens in political decision making. Citizens have the possibility of participating in politics and thus the public or political sphere becomes responsive to them. This empowerment (see for example World Bank, 2000) is hypothesised to increase citizens' belief in political influence and, moreover, their subjective well-being.

In a cross-regional study for Switzerland, the effects of direct democratic

* Address: Institute for Empirical Research in Economics, University of Zurich, Blümlisalpstrasse 10, CH-8006 Zurich, Tel.: 0041–1–634 37 29, Fax: 0041–1–634 49 07, E-mail: astutzer@iew.unizh.ch, bsfrey@iew.unizh.ch. We thank Matthias Benz and Reto Jegen and the participants of the second Messina Conference for valuable comments. This study has been realised using the data collected by the Swiss Household-Panel, a project financed by the Swiss National Science Foundation Program, SPP, 'Switzerland Towards the Future' (Grant no. 5004–53205).

participation possibilities on reported satisfaction with life and the reported belief of political influence are analysed. To identify procedural utility, we consider people's nationality. As political participation in initiatives and referenda is restricted to Swiss nationals, only they can reap the respective procedural utility. We find supporting evidence that citizens gain more life satisfaction from direct democracy than foreigners. It is also shown that people think that they have more political influence in jurisdictions with more extended political participation possibilities. This effect is larger for citizens than for foreigners. However, the difference is small and not statistically significant. The two empirical findings go beyond previous results on the favourable effects of direct democratic decision making on political outcomes (for surveys see Eichenberger, 1999; Kirchgässner et al., 1999). Such findings are in line with previous research on procedural aspects of direct democracy. The discussion endogenously brought about by initiatives and referenda strengthens co-operation between 'winners' and 'losers' of a political decision, because both feel that their preferences have been seriously taken into account in a fair political process (Frey, 1994). This notion of procedural justice affects behaviour, for example with regard to tax compliance (Pommerehne and Weck-Hannemann, 1996; Frey, 1997).

The chapter proceeds as follows. Section 2 categorises the concept of procedural utility in economic research and puts forward subjective well-being measures for empirical work. In Section 3, the relationship between procedural utility and political participation possibilities is discussed. The section closes with two hypotheses. The empirical analysis is presented in Section 4. First, an index for political participation possibilities and measures for life satisfaction and the belief in political influence are discussed. Additionally, a descriptive analysis offers first evidence. Secondly, multiple regression analyses are conducted to control for correlated effects. Section 5 draws conclusions.

2. PROCEDURAL UTILITY

Democratic institutions structure the *process* of political decision making that is judged by the people independently of the generated political outcome. In this procedural view, people gain utility from the process itself. In the following sections, procedural utility is first discussed from a general perspective and is then applied to the possibilities of political participation.

The concept of procedural utility is a completely different approach to human well-being than the standard outcome oriented approach in social science research. On the one hand, research in the latter approach follows the tradition of Benthamite utility. It focuses on individual pleasures and pains. On the other hand, choices between possible outcomes are the basis for inferring utility or expected utility in the standard economic concept. Both approaches, Bentham's 'experienced utility' and 'decision utility', are purely outcome oriented (see Kahneman et al., 1997 for these terms). Therefore, Sen (1995) argues that procedural utility, for example in the case of gambling, is necessarily excluded from von Neumann–Morgenstern utilities.

Procedural utility refers to the pleasure and displeasure of a process as opposed to that of consequences. This utility has rarely been included in economic theory and empirical research. A recent exception is Le Menestrel (2001), who offers axioms for a model of rational behaviour combining processes and consequences. In other social sciences than economics, procedural utility has a long tradition and refers to the concept of Aristotelian eudaimonic well-being. In research done by social psychologists, for example, well-being consists of actualisation of human potentials (Ryff and Singer, 1998), of self-determination (Ryan and Deci, 2000) or of personal control (Grob, 2000; Peterson, 1999; Seligman, 1992).

Empirical research on individual welfare usually relies on measures, such as income, which are assumed to be close proxies to utility. Survey studies on subjective well-being, however, have shown that income is only weakly correlated with reported individual life satisfaction or happiness, and that in industrial countries the two measures of subjective well-being have been stable over time, despite marked growth of wealth per capita (see Frey and Stutzer, 2002 for a survey). Therefore, here we only rely on survey measures of subjective well-being. For outcome utility, people are usually asked to state their satisfaction with life or their happiness. For procedural utility, additional questions to do with human actualisation and self-determination are included in the surveys. It has been shown that the measures for both concepts are correlated (Compton et al., 1996). Thus, general questions on subjective well-being capture elements of outcome as well as procedural utility. It is difficult to disentangle them empirically. Therefore the conditions to identify procedural utility in the political process are discussed extensively in the next section.

3. PROCEDURAL UTILITY AND POLITICAL PARTICIPATION POSSIBILITIES

Political philosophers argue that procedural utility is derived from the democratic process. Special emphasis is put on individuals' possibilities to participate in the political process (Barber, 1984; Keim, 1975; Morell, 1999; Pateman, 1970). With regard to direct democracy, Cronin (1989) notes, for example, that 'giving the citizen more of a role in governmental processes might lessen alienation and apathy' (p. 11). Moreover, the political discussion induced by initiatives and referenda generates a common understanding for different political opinions and positions. This strengthens the social contract based on consensus and motivates people to act beyond narrow self-interest (Bohnet and Frey, 1994). Participation possibilities are thus considered an important source of perceived procedural fairness shaping individual behaviour. It has, for example, been shown that with more extensive democratic participation rights, people have higher tax morale and evade taxes less (Frey, 1997).

Research on 'procedural fairness' has previously been extensively undertaken by social psychologists (in particular Lind and Tyler, 1988; Tyler and Blader, 2000). They are able to show that people are at least as concerned with procedural justice as with the outcomes of these procedures. They evaluate procedures not only according to the results they yield but by the relational information that they convey, such as assessments of impartiality, trustworthiness of superiors and authorities, and the extent to which individuals perceive themselves to be treated with respect.

Here, procedural justice is evaluated with regard to utility. Political participation possibilities contribute to what Lane (1988) calls procedural goods of democracy. These contain, for example, dignity goods such as self-respect, feeling of personal control or understanding and public resonance. Democracy can further provide utility if it offers relief from procedural pain (e.g. fear, embarrassment or humiliation) or if it directly generates intrinsic pleasure, for example, by facing and meeting a challenge or by expressing oneself (Lane, 1988, pp. 179–85, see also Lane, 2000, chapter 13).[1]

In order to differentiate procedural utility from outcome utility, an identifying criterion has to be found. In this chapter, the status of citizenship is considered. In most countries, the status of being a national fundamentally differs from that of foreigners by having the possibility to vote. In many other ways, the law demands that they are treated equally. Thus, for example, they have the same human rights and, once admitted into the country, they have (with few exceptions) the same rights to participate in economic affairs. It cannot, of course, be denied that the national legislation and political decisions tend to be rigged in favour of nationals. However, it follows that, on average, the nationals derive more utility from political participation possibilities than foreigners do, provided nationals enjoy both outcome and process utility while the foreigners only enjoy outcome utility.

The distinction between nationals and foreigners is largely exogenous. Whether a person may become a citizen is determined by the law, in particular the requirement of having stayed in the host country for a sufficient number of years, having sufficient mastery of the local language and of the content of the constitution. Only after these stringent requirements have been met, does the individual have the choice of whether to become a citizen or not. Of course, whether those persons eligible for citizenship indeed accept it, depends *inter alia* also on their expected procedural utility, that is their wish to become a community member with full participation rights. Thus, some will decide not to change their citizenship. Becoming a citizen is more or less automatic for young persons and spouses once the head of the household has decided to do so. Resident citizens have no possibility of choosing their status of citizenship. They cannot give up their current citizenship without relocation. The distribution of residents in a country between the two categories, foreigners and citizens, thus strongly reflects formal exogenous criteria for citizenship and not revealed preferences for procedural goods. As a result of these considerations, one may assume that the distinction between nationals and foreigners influences the extent to which one benefits from outcome and process utility.

According to the previous discussion the following general hypothesis can be formulated:

Citizens value the possibility of engaging themselves directly in politically relevant issues, irrespective of the outcome.

Moreover, two empirically testable hypotheses can be put forward. Hypothesis I captures procedural utility in terms of subjective well-being.

Hypothesis I. The utility derived from the possibility of participating in the direct democratic process supports the subjective well-being of the citizens. Foreigners living in the same country, who are excluded from this process, experience lower happiness compared to the citizens.

A procedural 'good' that may mediate procedural utility from political participation possibilities is people's feeling of political effectiveness (see for example Bowler and Donovan, 2001). In Hypothesis II, this effectiveness is measured with survey data on people's reported belief that they exert some political influence.

Hypothesis II. The possibility of participating in political decision making increases people's belief that they exert some political influence. Foreigners, who do not have formal political participation rights, think that they have no political influence.

In both hypotheses, the strategy to identify procedural utility is based on the formal distinction between citizens and foreigners. The corresponding statistical approach is in analogy to the difference-in-differences estimator for time series. In a crude formulation, procedural utility is the additional positive effect of more extended political participation possibilities on citizens' well-being compared to that of foreigners (Hypothesis I). Or, an indicator for procedural utility is the difference between the increase in people's reported belief in their political influence due to more extended political participation possibilities for citizens and non-citizens, respectively (Hypothesis II).

4. EMPIRICAL ANALYSIS

4.1 Data and Descriptive Analysis

Political participation possibilities

It is hypothesised that citizens gain procedural utility from political participation possibilities. In Switzerland, there are several ways of engaging directly in the political process at three state levels over and above regular elections. The most important are the direct democratic instruments. They exist at the national level as well as at the level of the 26 cantons (states). Here the cantonal level is considered because the participation rights differ considerably between them. In cantons, the major direct democratic instruments are the popular initiative to change the canton's constitution or laws, a compulsory and optional referendum to prevent new laws, or the changing of existing laws, and an optional financial referendum to prevent new state expenditure. Due to the federal structure of Switzerland, major areas of competence reside within the cantons and, thus, there is a high potential influence of direct legislation on the outcome of the political process in Swiss cantons. However, citizens' access to the instruments mentioned above differs substantially from one canton to another. Thus, for example, the number of signatures required to launch an initiative or an optional referendum, or the time span within which the signatures have to be collected, varies. A referendum on public expenditures may be launched with different levels of additional outlays. We construct an index designed to reflect the extent of direct democratic participation possibilities in the 26 cantons (for details of the index construction, see the Appendix). This index is defined using a six-point scale, with 1 indicating the lowest, and 6 the highest degree of participation possibilities for the citizens.

The variation in citizens' possibilities in political participation is necessary to test our two hypotheses on the effects of these possibilities on subjective well-being and on the belief in one's political influence.

Subjective well-being

Hypothesis I is tested with data on people's reported subjective well-being or 'happiness'. In a number of studies, the validity of these survey measures has been documented. Happy people are, for example, more often smiling during social interactions (Fernández-Dols and Ruiz-Belda, 1995) and are rated as happy by friends and family members (Sandvik et al., 1993), as well as by spouses (Costa and McCrae, 1988). Furthermore, the measures of subjective well-being reflect life-changes (Ehrhardt et al., 1999), persons' recall of positive versus negative life-events (Seidlitz et al., 1997) and are, to a large extent, unbiased with regard to social desirability (Konow and Earley, 1999). But there is, of course, room for methodological concerns (for example Diener et al., 1999, pp. 277–8).

The survey at hand is the result of more than 6000 interviews with residents of Switzerland, collected by Leu et al. (1997)[2] The proxy measure for individual utility is based on the answers to the following question: 'How satisfied are you with your life as a whole these days?' Simultaneously, the respondents were shown a table with a 10-point scale of which only the two extreme values ('completely dissatisfied' and 'completely satisfied') were verbalised. The survey found a high general life satisfaction in Switzerland, with an average of 8.2 out of 10 points.

According to Hypothesis I, more extended participation possibilities are expected to increase reported satisfaction with life, due to a larger gain in procedural utility. In Table 4.1, the difference in life satisfaction between residents living in cantons with weak participation possibilities (index of participation possibilities is lower than 4) and with strong participation possibilities is listed. On average, residents with strong participation rights report a 0.22 point higher well-being. However, this calculated difference may also be due to a favourable outcome of the political process. There is ample evidence that, in more direct democratic jurisdictions, the outcome of the political process is closer to the wishes of the residents (see for example the surveys by Eichenberger, 1999 and Kirchgässner et al., 1999). To differentiate between

Table 4.1 Political participation possibilities and satisfaction with life, descriptive statistics

	Political participation possibilities		
	Weak	Strong	Difference
Whole sample	8.099	8.318	0.218
	(0.033)	(0.029)	(0.044)
Foreigners	7.625	7.602	–0.023
	(0.090)	(0.104)	(0.136)
Swiss citizens	8.176	8.402	0.226
	(0.036)	(0.029)	(0.046)
Difference	0.551	0.800	0.249
	(0.096)	(0.092)	(0.133)

Note: Standard errors in parentheses.

Data source: Leu et al. (1997).

outcome and procedural utility, the proposed identification criterion of people's nationality is considered. As foreigners are excluded from political participation rights, but not from the outcome of the political process, differences in levels of satisfaction between citizens and foreigners in cantons with weak and strong participation possibilities have to be compared. Where participation rights are weak, a difference in well-being between Swiss citizens and foreigners of 0.55 points is measured. The corresponding difference in cantons with extended direct democratic rights is 0.80 points. Both gaps in subjective well-being are due to differences in individual characteristics, incomplete assimilation and, above all, citizens' opportunity to reap procedural utility. The difference-in-differences between cantons with weak and strong participation possibilities then reflects the gain in procedural utility of citizens due to more extended participation possibilities (provided that individual characteristics and incomplete assimilation are distributed equally across cantons). The raw data show a large effect of procedural utility in terms of reported satisfaction with life, namely 0.25 points.[3] A multiple regression analysis has to test whether this result still holds if individual characteristics are controlled for. An ordered probit estimation and extended discussion of the result is provided in subsection 4.2.

Belief in political influence

Hypothesis II considers what people think about their political influence. This belief can be captured in surveys. We use answers to the following question: 'How much influence do you think someone like you can have on government policy?'. Respondents indicate their belief on a scale from 0 'no influence' to 10 'very strong influence'. The data are part of the first wave of the Swiss Household-Panel conducted in 1999/2000, in which 7521 people were interviewed and responded to the question about political influence. They believe, on average, that they have a political influence of 3.13 (with a standard deviation of 2.66) on the scale from 0 to 10.

Hypothesis II puts forward that people's belief in political influence is increased by more extended participation possibilities in political decision making. This hypothesis is not trivial, because it is sometimes argued that direct democratic participation possibilities 'disturb' the representative democratic process of elected politicians to follow the will of the voters. Critics of direct democracy often argue that political pressure from interest groups and random decisions in referenda by badly informed voters worsen the outcome of the political process and actually reduce the impact of citizens. An empirical test of Hypothesis II is thus also a test of this alternative argument.

The first row of Table 4.2 compares people's belief in their political influence in cantons with strong and weak participation possibilities. The

Table 4.2 Political participation possibilities and the belief of political influence, descriptive statistics

	Political participation possibilities Weak	Strong	Difference
Whole sample	2.836	3.408	0.572
	(0.044)	(0.043)	(0.061)
Foreigners	1.998	2.052	0.054
	(0.132)	(0.144)	(0.196)
Swiss citizens	2.950	3.544	0.593
	(0.046)	(0.044)	(0.064)
Difference	0.953	1.492	0.539
	(0.134)	(0.146)	(0.199)

Note: Standard errors in parentheses.

Data source: Swiss Household-Panel, 1999.

extent of participation possibilities is again measured with the index discussed above, whereby cantons with an index below (above) 4 are considered as the ones with weak (strong) possibilities. It shows that people in jurisdictions with developed participation possibilities report, on average, 0.57 index points higher belief in one's political influence than people with weak participation possibilities. However, perceived political influence may also be higher because the outcome of the political process corresponds better to people's preferences in these jurisdictions. In order to isolate the effect of the procedural differences from outcome considerations, the belief in political influence of citizens and foreigners is compared. As foreigners have no formal participation rights in political decision making, their perceived effectiveness in politics is assumed to be independent of the variation in the extent of participation rights across cantons. In the first column, capturing respondents living in cantons with weak participation possibilities, citizens think that they have, on average, a 0.95 points higher political influence than foreigners. In cantons with strong participation possibilities, this difference is 1.49 points. Thus the difference-in-differences estimate for the belief in political influence due to more extended participation rights is 0.54 points. This result is consistent with a gain in procedural utility by the citizens from political participation possibilities, as put forward in Hypothesis II.

In the next section, the robustness of this result is studied in a multiple regression analysis controlling for a large number of individual characteristics.

4.2 Multiple Regression Analysis

The descriptive analysis presented above offers preliminary evidence for positive procedural utility caused by more extended political participation possibilities for both measures: reported satisfaction with life and people's belief in their political influence. A multiple regression analysis has to show whether these results are robust. Once more a difference-in-differences estimation strategy is applied to identify procedural utility. Technically, an interaction term is included in the estimation equation that combines the variable that captures the proposed source of procedural utility with the identifying criterion. Here, the identifying characteristic is being a Swiss national or a foreigner. For the institutional variable political participation possibilities, the full variation on the index scale from 1 to 6 is considered.

Political participation possibilities and subjective well-being

Table 4.3 refers to Hypothesis I and presents the estimated coefficients and marginal effects of a microeconometric well-being function, taking into account political participation possibilities in addition to a large set of control variables. In order to exploit the ranking information contained in the originally scaled dependent variable, a weighted ordered probit model is applied. The weighting variable used allows representative results on the individual level for Switzerland.[4] Throughout the remainder of the chapter, we use a robust estimator of variance because random disturbances are potentially correlated within groups or clusters. Here, dependence refers to residents of the same canton.[5]

The estimation results show sizeable effects for both variables considered in Hypothesis I (see the top of Table 4.3). The overall effect of participation rights on reported satisfaction with life is positive. In an ordered probit estimation, a positive coefficient indicates that the probability of stating a well-being greater than or equal to any given level increases. This positive effect can be attributed to a gain in outcome or procedural utility in cantons with more extended participation rights. The interaction term in the second row reveals the difference in the positive effects for Swiss citizens and foreigners. The negative coefficient indicates that foreigners gain less from stronger participation rights than the people in the reference group, that is the citizens. This result is consistent with Hypothesis I that foreigners reap less procedural utility from direct democratic participation possibilities than Swiss nationals. If it is further assumed that foreigners do not reap any procedural utility at all, but cannot be excluded from the outcome of the political process, the relative size of procedural utility can be assessed. A comparison of the negative coefficient of the interaction variable, which under these assumptions captures procedural utility, and the coefficient for the variable participation possibilities, which captures combined

Table 4.3 Procedural utility: political participation possibilities and satisfaction with life

	Dependent variable: satisfaction with life Coefficient	T-value	Marginal effect (score 10)
Political participation possibilities	0.097	3.223	0.033
Political participation possibilities × foreigner	–0.067	–1.749	–0.023
Socio-demographic characteristics			
Age 30–39	–0.089	–0.998	–0.030
Age 40–49	–0.013	–0.169	–0.004
Age 50–59	–0.009	–0.149	–0.003
Age 60–69	0.302	4.244	0.108
Age 70–79	0.378	4.514	0.137
Age 80 and older	0.355	3.067	0.130
Female	0.033	1.019	0.011
Foreigner	–0.042	–0.287	–0.014
Bad health	–0.434	–7.631	–0.132
Middle education	0.077	2.217	0.026
High education	0.039	0.875	0.014
Separated, without partner	–0.590	–2.298	–0.163
Separated, with partner	–0.664	–1.823	–0.177
Widowed, without partner	–0.204	–4.015	–0.066
Widowed, with partner	0.078	0.511	0.027
Divorced, without partner	–0.348	–4.144	–0.107
Divorced, with partner	–0.094	–0.735	–0.031
Single, without partner	–0.175	–2.549	–0.058
Single, with partner	–0.085	–1.373	–0.028
Self-employed	0.056	1.061	0.019
Unemployed	–0.780	–4.564	–0.201
Student	–0.022	–0.238	–0.008
Housewife	0.119	2.086	0.042
Retired	–0.157	–2.584	–0.053
Other employment status	0.082	0.599	0.029
Equiv. income SFr. 2000–3000	0.065	1.861	0.022
Equiv. income SFr. 3000–4000	0.121	2.659	0.042
Equiv. income SFr. 4000–5000	0.259	4.665	0.093
Equiv. income SFr. 5000 and more	0.184	3.539	0.065
Member in associations	0.167	6.976	0.057
Urbanisation	–0.057	–1.340	–0.020
Language			
French-speaking canton	–0.075	–0.957	–0.025
Italian-speaking canton	0.297	4.302	0.108
Number of observations		6124	

Notes: Standard errors are adjusted for clustering on 26 cantons. In the reference group are 'people younger than 30', 'men', 'Swiss', 'healthy people', 'people with low education', 'married people', 'employed people', 'people with a lower equivalence income than SFr. 2000', 'people who are neither active nor passive members of associations', 'people living in non-urban areas' and 'people living in a German-speaking canton'.

Data source: Leu et al. (1997).

outcome and procedural utility, shows that two-thirds of the positive effect of more extended political participation possibilities are due to procedural utility and one-third stems from outcome utility.

A useful interpretation of the size of the effects is provided by the marginal effects. The marginal effect indicates the change in the proportion of persons belonging to a stated satisfaction level when the independent variable increases by one unit.[6] In the case of dummy variables, the marginal effect is evaluated with regard to the reference group. For simplicity, only the marginal effects for the top class of complete satisfaction with life (score 10) are shown in Table 4.3. An increase in the index of participation possibilities by one point raises the proportion of persons indicating very high satisfaction with life by 3.3 percentage points. For foreigners, however, this effect is smaller, as the interaction term has to be considered, so 2.3 percentage points of the increased probability to report maximum subjective well-being cannot be reaped by the foreigners. In our interpretation, this is because they are excluded from the political process and thus from procedural utility.

The effect of procedural utility as reflected in reported life satisfaction is in itself sizeable. This can be seen from a comparison with marginal effects for numerous control variables. The marginal effect capturing procedural utility is, for example, as large as the effect of living in the second-bottom (Sfr. 2000–3000) instead of the bottom income category (< Sfr. 2000). The effect is even larger when the total variation in participation possibilities is considered, that is when citizens in canton Basel Land (with the highest index for political participation possibilities, 5.69) are compared to citizens in canton Geneva (with the lowest index for political participation possibilities, 1.75). The former reap procedural utility that increases their probability to be completely satisfied by approximately 11.7 percentage points.

The results discussed so far hold *ceteris paribus*, that is a large number of determinants or correlates of happiness are controlled for. Most important are individual socio-demographic characteristics. In the estimation equation, the respondent's age, gender, health status, education level, civil status, employment status and household income are considered. The results for these variables are discussed in Frey and Stutzer (2000) and are in size and direction similar to those found in other microeconomic happiness functions (see, for example, Blanchflower and Oswald, 2000). In addition, four variables are included in the equation in Table 4.3 that control for three potential alternative explanations. First, a dummy variable for people's participation in clubs or associations is used to test whether in cantons with stronger participation possibilities citizens may have accumulated more Putnam (2000) style social capital and thus enjoy higher subjective well-being than citizens in cantons with less extended democratic participation possibilities. Second, a dummy variable for living in an urban area is included to investigate the argument that direct democratic participation possibilities could be weaker in urban areas where most of the foreigners live and thus the raw effect may reflect urbanisation. Third, dummies for the language that is spoken in the canton are included in order to test whether the patterns in the descriptive statistics may capture cultural differences within Switzerland instead of institutional variation. However, even controlling for these factors, political participation possibilities have a sizeable effect on individual procedural utility.

Political participation possibilities and people's belief in their political influence

The descriptive analysis in Section 4.1 showed that citizens are perceived to have more political influence than foreigners and that the difference is larger in cantons where citizens have more extended possibilities of participating in political decision making. This result is tested in a multiple regression approach in order to control for alternative explanations of the result. Similar control variables to the previous equation are included and the same econometric approach using ordered probit estimation is applied. The results of the micro-econometric estimation are presented in Table 4.4.

More extended political participation possibilities increase people's belief that they exert some political influence, *ceteris paribus*. The effect is smaller for foreigners, as indicated by the negative interaction effect between participation possibilities and being a foreigner. However, the interaction effect is not statistically significantly different from zero. Although a direct interpretation of the survey question would indicate higher procedural utility due to a higher perceived political influence in cantons with more extended political participation possibilities, the effect could also be due to outcome consideration. In cantons with stronger direct democratic participation possibilities, the outcome of the political process is closer to people's wishes and thus they perceive higher effectiveness. Our strategy to disentangle outcome and procedural effects using citizenship as an identifying criterion gives no clear answer. The coefficient of the interaction variable fails to be well determined. Its size is about one-third of the size of the coefficient for the general effect.

The general effect on citizens' perceived political influence is quite sizeable. If the marginal effect for the full variation of political participation possibilities is considered, the effect on what people think about their political influence (0.032) is almost half the size of having high education rather than low education (0.075). A marginal effect of 0.032 indicates that the proportion of people who believe they have political influence above 5 is increased by 3.2 percentage points, that is from a base probability of 18.5 per cent to 21.7 per cent.

For the interaction variable, the marginal effect for a one index point

Table 4.4 Procedural utility: political participation possibilities and the belief of political influence

	Dependent variable: belief of political influence		
	Coefficient	T-value	Marginal effect (scores 5 to 10)
Political participation possibilities	0.031	2.440	0.008
Political participation possibilities × foreigner	–0.011	–0.356	–0.003
Socio-demographic characteristics			
Age	–0.006	–4.363	–0.002
Female	–0.095	–2.513	–0.025
Middle education	0.157	3.458	0.042
High education	0.260	7.550	0.075
Foreigner	–0.449	–3.392	–0.101
Single	0.078	1.851	0.021
Separated	0.151	1.446	0.043
Divorced	0.008	0.131	0.002
Widowed	–0.173	–2.987	–0.043
Part-time paid work	0.026	0.602	0.007
School or apprenticeship	0.075	1.332	0.020
Work in the family company	0.030	0.285	0.008
Work in protected atelier	–0.546	–0.649	–0.110
Work at home	0.054	1.378	0.015
Retired	–0.023	–0.411	–0.006
Unemployed	–0.057	–0.440	–0.015
Other occupation status	–0.107	–0.921	–0.027
Member in associations			
Local or parents assoc. (active member, am)	0.172	3.393	0.049
ditto (passive member, pm)	0.015	0.283	0.004
Cultural assoc. (am)	0.069	2.209	0.019
ditto (pm)	0.133	3.562	0.037
Syndicate (am)	0.160	2.826	0.045
ditto (pm)	0.074	1.376	0.020
Political party (am)	0.409	8.994	0.126
ditto (pm)	0.265	4.849	0.078
Protection of the environment (am)	0.215	4.054	0.062
ditto (pm)	0.146	3.734	0.041
Charitable organisation (am)	0.156	2.865	0.044
ditto (pm)	0.014	0.365	0.004
Tenants rights assoc. (am)	0.180	2.484	0.052
ditto (pm)	0.007	0.183	0.002
Urbanisation	0.003	6.264	0.001
Language			
French speaking	–0.189	–3.424	–0.048
Italian speaking	–0.280	–5.414	–0.066
Number of observations	7079		

Notes: Standard errors are adjusted for clustering on 26 cantons. In the reference group are 'men', 'people with low education', 'Swiss', 'married people', 'employed people', 'people who are not members of a certain association' and 'German speaking people'.

Data source: Swiss Household-Panel, 1999.

increase in the political participation possibilities is –0.003. For the full variation in the interaction variable the effect is –0.017. Thus roughly half of the effect of more extended political participation possibilities on citizens' belief in their political influence is due to procedural considerations, as put forward in the general hypothesis.

There are several socio-demographic characteristics that also have a sizeable and statistically significant effect on one's belief in one's political influence. Younger people, men, people with more education and the Swiss perceive more political effectiveness than older people, women, people with low education and foreigners. Foreigners report a 10 percentage points lower probability than the Swiss in believing that they have political influence exceeding level 5.

Three sets of additional variables control for alternative explanations of the descriptive results.[7] Due to similar counterarguments to the previous section, we include several variables for Putnam-style social capital, a variable for urbanisation (measuring the share of urban population in a canton) and two variables for possible cultural differences within Switzerland.

Our data show that active members of all the associations explicitly listed in Table 4.4 have a higher perceived influence on the political process than non-members. The largest effect is estimated for active members of political parties. They report, with a 12.6 percentage points higher probability, a feeling of political effectiveness above 5. People in more urbanised cantons think that they have more political influence than people in less urbanised cantons. Compared to German speaking residents, French as well as Italian speaking people report a quantitatively sizeable lower feeling of political effectiveness.

Considering that these powerful alternative hypotheses are controlled for, the effect of more extended political participation possibilities on citizens' belief in their political influence is robust.

5. CONCLUSIONS

The concept of procedural utility represents a completely different approach to comparative institutional analysis than the standard outcome oriented approach in economics. Procedural utility refers to the utility that people gain from the decision-making process itself, irrespective of the outcome.

In this chapter, participatory decision making in politics is considered a possible source of procedural utility. Possibilities of participating directly in the democratic process give citizens a feeling that their preferences are seriously taken into account in a fair political process. Foreigners, who are excluded from political decision making, cannot reap such procedural utility. The results of our empirical analysis are consistent with this notion of procedural utility. Citizens, as well as foreigners, living in jurisdictions with more extended political participation possibilities enjoy higher levels of subjective well-being. The positive effect on reported satisfaction with life is, however, smaller for foreigners, reflecting their exclusion from procedural utility. It is thus empirically feasible to distinguish between outcome and process utility. Moreover, it is possible to get a notion of the relative size of outcome and process utility. The positive effect of participation rights is three times larger for citizens than it is for foreigners, that is a major part of the welfare gain from the favourable political process is due to procedural utility.

In the second test of the concept of procedural utility, we find that in cantons with more extended political participation possibilities, people think that they have substantially higher political influence. The maximum size of the institutional effect is almost half the size of having a high education rather than a low education. However, the institutional effect could also be due to outcome considerations as the difference in perceived political effectiveness between Swiss nationals and foreigners does not increase at the level of political participation possibilities in a statistically significant way.

Overall, the chapter can give a better understanding of what value individuals derive from specific institutions. We find that institutions matter for procedural utility and, in particular, that individuals derive substantial utility from political participation possibilities. Procedural utility is a source of welfare that has so far been neglected in comparative institutional analysis.

NOTES

1. Lane (1988) argues that '[d]emocratic theory makes inadequate provision for procedural goods other than distributive justice' (p. 186).
2. The survey data were collected between 1992 and 1994 in order to investigate the problem of poverty in Switzerland. The information contained in the data set is based on personal interviews and tax statistics.
3. An alternative differences-in-differences interpretation considers the rows in Table 4.1 instead of the columns. Given that foreigners cannot reap procedural utility from the democratic process because they are formally excluded, the difference in reported life satisfaction between people living in cantons with weak and with strong participation possibilities is due to a difference in outcome utility. For the raw data, differences in outcome utility are close to zero. In the case of Swiss citizens, the difference includes procedural as well as outcome utility. The raw effect of stronger participation rights is on average 0.2 points on the satisfaction scale. Considering foreigners and Swiss citizens, the differences-in-differences due to procedural utility is 0.2 points.
4. Due to clustering and stratification, in contrast to pure random sampling, weights are necessary to get approximately unbiased point estimates. Weights are proportional to the inverse of the probability of being sampled. In addition, the weights are adjusted to the demographic structure in 1992.
5. Ignoring the clustering in the estimation model is likely to produce downward biased standard errors, due to the effects of aggregate variables on individual data (Moulton, 1990). To get unbiased standard errors for the aggregate variable 'political participation possibilities', the 26 cantons are used as sampling units.

6. Alternatively, the marginal effect indicates the change of the probability belonging to a stated satisfaction level when the independent variable increases by one unit.
7. As two separate data sets are analysed, the additional control variables are not identical, but they are similar enough to capture the same correlated effects.

REFERENCES

Barber, Benjamin R. (1984), *Strong Democracy: Participatory Politics for a New Age*, Berkeley: University of California Press.

Blanchflower, Daniel G. and Andrew J. Oswald (2000), 'Well-Being Over Time in Britain and the USA', NBER Working Paper No. 7487. Cambridge, MA: National Bureau of Economic Research.

Bohnet, Iris and Bruno S. Frey (1994), 'Direct-democratic rules: the role of discussion', *Kyklos*, **47** (3), 341–54.

Bowler, Shaun and Todd Donovan (2001), 'Democracy, institutions and attitudes about citizen influence on government', *British Journal of Political Science*, **32** (2), 371–90.

Compton, William C., Maggie L. Smith, Kim A. Cornish and Donald L. Qualls (1996), 'Factor structure of mental health measures', *Journal of Personality and Social Psychology*, **71** (2), 406–13.

Costa, Paul T. and Robert R. McCrae (1988), 'Personality in adulthood: a six-year longitudinal study of self-reports and spouse ratings on the NEO personality inventory', *Journal of Personality and Social Psychology*, **54** (5), 853–63.

Cronin, Thomas E. (1989), *Direct Democracy. The Politics of Initiative, Referendum and Recall*, Cambridge, MA: Harvard University Press.

Diener, Ed, Eunkook M. Suh, Richard E. Lucas and Heidi L. Smith (1999), 'Subjective well-being: three decades of progress', *Psychological Bulletin*, **125** (2), 276–303.

Ehrhardt, J.J., W.E. Saris and Ruut Veenhoven (1999), 'Stability of Life-Satisfaction over Time', Mimeo, Erasmus University Rotterdam and University of Amsterdam.

Eichenberger, Reiner (1999), 'Mit direkter Demokratie zu besserer Wirtschafts- und Finanzpolitik: Theorie und Empirie', in Hans Herbert von Arnim (ed.), *Adaequate Institutionen: Voraussetzung für 'gute' und bürgernahe Politik?*, Schriftenreihe der Hochschule Speyer, Berlin: Duncker & Humblot.

Fernández-Dols, José-Miguel and Maria-Angeles Ruiz-Belda (1995), 'Are smiles a sign of happiness? Gold medal winners at the Olympic Games', *Journal of Personality and Social Psychology*, **69** (6), 1113–19.

Frey, Bruno S. (1994), 'Direct democracy: politico-economic lessons from Swiss experience', *American Economic Review*, **84** (2), 338–48.

Frey, Bruno S. (1997), 'A constitution for knaves crowds out civic virtues', *Economic Journal*, **107** (443), 1043–53.

Frey, Bruno S. and Alois Stutzer (2000), 'Happiness, economy and institutions', *Economic Journal*, **110** (466), 918–38.

Frey, Bruno S. and Alois Stutzer (2002), *Happiness and Economics: How the Economy and Institutions Affect Human Well-Being*, Princeton: Princeton University Press.

Grob, Alexander (2000), 'Perceived Control and Subjective Well-Being across Nations and across the Life Span', in Ed Diener and Eunkook M. Suh (eds), *Culture and Subjective Well-Being*, Cambridge, MA: MIT Press.

Kahneman, Daniel, Peter P. Wakker and Rakesh Sarin (1997), 'Back to Bentham?

Explorations of experienced utility', *Quarterly Journal of Economics*, **112** (2), 375–405.

Keim, D. (1975), 'Participation in Contemporary Democratic Theories', in J. Roland Pennock and John W. Chapman (eds), *Participation in Politics*, New York: Lieber-Atherton.

Kirchgässner, Gebhard, Lars Feld and Marcel R. Savioz (1999), *Die direkte Demokratie: Modern, erfolgreich, entwicklungs- und exportfähig*, Basel: Helbing and Lichtenhahn /Munich: Vahlen.

Konow, James and Joseph Earley (1999), 'The Hedonistic Paradox: Is Homo Economicus Happier?', Mimeo, Department of Economics, Loyola Marymount University, Los Angeles.

Lane, Robert E. (1988), 'Procedural goods in a democracy', *Social Justice Research*, **2** (3), 177–92.

Lane, Robert E. (2000), *The Loss of Happiness in Market Economies*, New Haven and London: Yale University Press.

Le Menestrel, Marc (2001), 'A process approach to the utility for gambling', *Theory and Decision*, **50** (3), 249–62.

Leu, Robert E., Stefan Burri and Tom Priester (1997), *Lebensqualität und Armut in der Schweiz*, Bern: Haupt.

Lind, E. Allan and Tom R. Tyler (1988), *The Social Psychology of Procedural Justice*, New York: Plenum Press.

Morell, Michael (1999), 'Citizens' evaluation of participatory democratic procedures: normative theory meets empirical science', *Political Research Quarterly*, **52** (2), 293–322.

Moulton, Brent R. (1990), 'An illustration of a pitfall in estimating the effects of aggregate variables on micro units', *Review of Economics and Statistics*, **72** (2), 334–8.

Pateman, Carol (1970), *Participation and Democratic Theory*, Cambridge: Cambridge University Press.

Peterson, Christopher (1999), 'Personal Control and Well-Being', in Daniel Kahneman, Ed Diener and Norbert Schwarz (eds), *Well-Being: The Foundation of Hedonic Psychology*, New York: Russell Sage Foundation, 288–301.

Pommerehne, Werner W. and Hannelore Weck-Hannemann (1996), 'Tax rates, tax administration and income tax evasion in Switzerland', *Public Choice*, **88** (1–2), 161–70.

Putnam, Robert D. (2000), *Bowling Alone: The Collapse and Revival of American Community*, New York, NY: Simon & Schuster.

Ryan, Richard M. and Edward L. Deci (2000), 'Self-determination theory and the facilitation of intrinsic motivation, social development, and well-being', *American Psychologist*, **55** (1), 68–78.

Ryff, Carol D. and Burton Singer (1998), 'The contours of positive human health', *Psychological Inquiry*, **9** (1), 1–28.

Sandvik, Ed, Ed Diener and Larry Seidlitz (1993), 'Subjective well-being: the convergence and stability of self-report and non-self-report measures', *Journal of Personality*, **61** (3), 317–42.

Seidlitz, Larry, Robert S. Wyer and Ed Diener (1997), 'Cognitive correlates of subjective well-being: the processing of valenced life events by happy and unhappy persons', *Journal of Research in Personality*, **31** (1), 240–56.

Seligman, Martin E.P. (1992), *Helplessness: On Depression, Development, and Death*, New York: Freeman.

Sen, Amartya K. (1995), 'Rationality and social choice', *American Economic Review*, **85**, 1–24.

Stutzer, Alois (1999), 'Demokratieindizes für die Kantone der Schweiz', Working Paper No. 23, Institute for Empirical Research in Economics, University of Zurich.

Trechsel, Alexander and Uwe Serdült (1999), *Kaleidoskop Volksrechte: Die Institutionen der direkten Demokratie in den schweizerischen Kantonen 1970–1996*, Basel, Genf, München: Helbling & Lichtenhahn.

Tyler, Tom R. and Steven L. Blader (2000), *Cooperation in Groups: Procedural Justice, Social Identity, and Behavioral Engagement*, Philadelphia, PA: Psychology Press.

World Bank (2000), *World Development Report 2000/2001*, Washington, DC: World Bank.

APPENDIX 4.A1

Index for Political Participation Possibilities in Swiss Cantons

Political participation possibilities are measured here in terms of direct democratic participation rights. In Switzerland, these rights exist at the national level and apply equally for all citizens. However, they are very heterogeneous on the cantonal level. An index is constructed to measure the different barriers to citizens entering the political process, apart from elections in the year 1992. The index is based mainly on data collected in Trechsel and Serdült (1999) (for details see Stutzer, 1999).

The four main legal instruments directly influencing the political process in Swiss cantons are (i) the popular initiative to change the canton's constitution, (ii) the popular initiative to change the canton's law, (iii) the compulsory and optional referendum to prevent new law or changing law and (iv) the compulsory and optional referendum to prevent new state expenditure. Barriers are in terms of (i) the necessary number of signatures needed to launch an instrument (absolute and relative to the number of citizens with the right to vote), (ii) the legally allowed time span to collect the signatures and (iii) the level of new expenditure per head allowing a financial referendum. Compulsory referenda are treated like referenda with the lowest possible barrier. Each of these restrictions is evaluated on a six point scale: 'one' indicates a high barrier, 'six' a low one. From the resulting ratings, a non-weighted average is calculated for the composite index, which represents the measure of participation rights in Swiss cantons. The results are presented in Figure 4.A1.

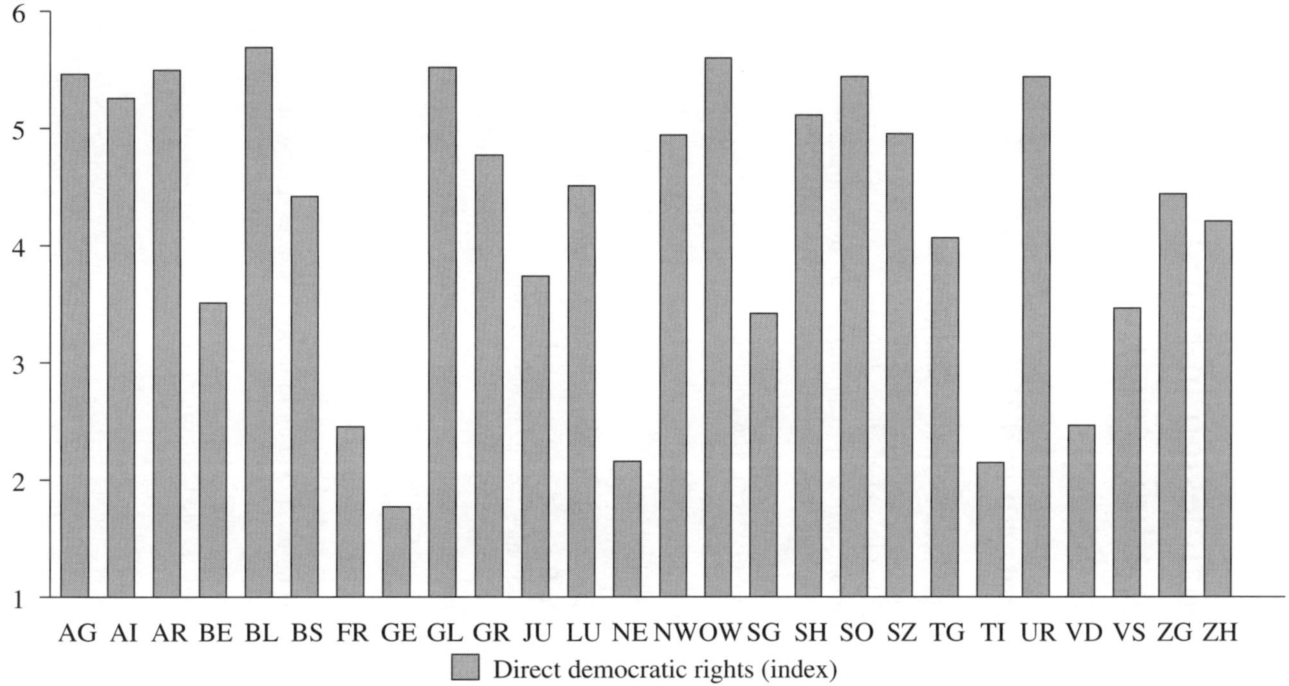

The figure shows the degree of direct democratic participation possibilities in the 26 Swiss cantons, namely Aargau (AG), Appenzell i. Rh. (AI), Appenzell a. Rh. (AR), Bern (BE), Basel Land (BL), Basel Stadt (BS), Fribourg (FR), Genève (GE), Glarus (GL), Graubünden (GR), Jura (JU), Luzern (LU), Neuchâtel (NE), Nidwalden (NW), Obwalden (OW), St. Gallen (SG), Schaffhausen (SH), Solothurn (SO), Schwyz (SZ), Thurgau (TG), Ticino (TI), Uri (UR), Vaud (VD), Valais (VS), Zug (ZG) and Zürich (ZH).

Figure 4.A1 Political participation possibilities in Swiss cantons

5. Institutional design in plural societies: mitigating ethnic conflict and fostering stable democracy*

Bernard Grofman and Robert Stockwell

A fundamental challenge faced by many countries is the accommodation of ethnic and religious diversity (Diamond and Plattner, 1994). Nations which are multiethnic in character but in which ethnic differences have been minimized in importance are commonly referred to as *pluralistic*. In contrast, *plural*, or 'deeply divided,' societies are those where politics is organized largely or entirely along ethnic lines, and two or more ethnic groups compete for power at the center of the political system. The potential for severe ethnic conflict is greatest in plural societies. In the worst case, in plural societies we may have civil wars between competing *ethnies*[1] that are fought with genocidal fury, as in Rwanda. But even in pluralist societies there are many domains where ethnic conflict remains possible, even if it is confined to individual acts of intolerance or small-scale protests or the occasional so-called 'race riot.'

In the post-World War II period, transnational migration, including an influx of people from former colonies (for example, Algerians into France, Indians and West Indians into the UK) and international refugees (whose recent impact, relative to total population, has been especially marked in Scandinavia), has led to significant changes in the ethnic composition of a number of industrialized nations. Moreover, ethnic issues that had previously been kept off the political agenda (for example, Quebec nationalism in Canada, Catalan nationalism in Spain, Scottish nationalism in the UK) have led to ongoing negotiations and/or major political reorganizations, including in many instances a large dollop of devolution/decentralization. In the US, changes associated with the Immigration Reform Act of 1965 and the Immigration Reform and Control Act of 1990 have led to a remarkable transformation of the ethnic landscape, with

* Prepared for delivery at the University of Messina Conference on 'The Political Economy of Institutional Development', August 14–17, 2000. Portions of this chapter draw heavily from the unpublished Ph.D. dissertation of the second author. We are indebted to Clover Behrend for bibliographic assistance and the first-named author is indebted to helpful conversations over the years with Arend Lijphart, but the views expressed in this chapter are solely those of the authors.

Hispanics soon to eclipse African–Americans as the nation's largest ethnically-defined minority, and substantial increases in immigration from various Asian nations as well. Moreover, in 'settler' nations such as Canada, New Zealand and the United States, long-buried issues about land claims and other rights of 'first peoples' reemerged.[2] In these and other pluralist nations, issues of national identity and of the meaning of citizenship have risen in political importance. Elsewhere in the world, the ending of colonial empires, including most recently the breakup of the Soviet Union, has created a multiplicity of states whose borders do not coincide neatly, or at all, with ethnic territorial boundaries, but where repressive former colonial regimes are no longer in place to suppress ethnic conflict.

In the study of the link between ethnic diversity and the prospects for democracy two key questions are debated: 'Is democracy possible in plural societies?'. And, if so, 'What are the mechanisms by which democracy might be achieved/strengthened?'. Students of ethnic conflict are deeply divided over the prospects for democracy in plural societies. One camp argues that, in plural societies, democracy is inherently unstable.[3] In such societies, it is argued, conflicts over division of resources will inevitably be fought primarily along ethnic lines, and thus will be inherently unresolvable, especially if the ultimate question is 'Who owns the state?'.

Indeed, it can even be argued that democracy, or at least attempts at democracy, can exacerbate conflicts in plural societies. As Brendan O'Leary, Chair of the Political Science Department at London School of Economics, and an expert on Northern Ireland, observed in a panel broadcast on BBC radio in April 2000: 'Democracy can cause conflict because it nationalizes territories, suggesting exclusive rights for one people, the Staatsvolk, the nation. . . . Unchecked democracy . . . can drive conflict.' On the other hand, Sisk (1996, p. ix) observes that 'democratic practices offer greater promise for long-term peaceful conflict management.'

In this chapter we will be interested in political arrangements in both pluralistic and plural nations, but almost all our attention will be on nations in the latter category. Our concerns in this chapter are also limited in a variety of other ways. Our focus will be on the impact of ethnic conflict on the prospects for democratization, and conversely. Even more importantly, our discussion will deal exclusively with *institutional arrangements* that might facilitate inter-ethnic accommodation and/or might mitigate the importance of ethnicity for political decision making so as to permit democracy to survive. Also, because the literature on ethnicity and ethnic conflict is vast, we will deal with many of the central issues in this literature (for example the debate about the extent to which extent identities are primordial in nature as opposed to manipulable at both the personal and the societal level,[4] and the debate about whether particular ethnic conflicts, such as that in the former Yugoslavia, could have been avoided) either not at all or only in passing. Similarly, we will only touch upon important questions such as when does ethnicity become politicized, or what are the conditions that lead from mere ethnic differences to actual ethnic conflicts (especially the likelihood of ethnic hostilities that lead to loss of life), or how can we best negotiate reduction in/reconciliation of ongoing ethnic conflicts.[5] Moreover, we make no claim to new major theoretical insights. Rather, we wish merely to provide a useful literature review based on a simple (2 × 2) typology of institutionalist approaches that is original with the present authors.[6]

Because we focus on institutions, a few words about how we view institutions are in order.

First, we share with Madison and Hamilton the *Federalist*'s assertion of the importance of political institutions and the notion that political institutions can be viewed as matters of explicit choices and tradeoffs.

Second, institutions may be thought of as either dependent or independent variables; sometimes used to explain and sometimes themselves in need of explanation (for example, as to origins and continued existence).[7]

Third, when thinking about institutions as objects of choice, by and large, we share the view expressed in John Ferejohn's pithy observation (personal communication, 1981): 'Preferences for outcomes condition preferences for institutions.' In that context, we would emphasize how the power of different actors affects the choice of institutional rules.[8] Frequently institutions are merely crystallizations of societal power relationships. Of course, this is not always true. Like the vermiform appendix, some institutions (for example, in the US, a bicameral legislature with two equally strong chambers) remain and have consequences long after the power relationships that brought them into being (for example, concerns about the relative power of large states and small states) have little or no current importance.

Finally, sometimes, especially where there are sufficient aspects of (long-term) choice behind a veil of ignorance and/or non-zero sum problems of coordinating collective action, institutions are better viewed primarily as problem-solving mechanisms. Thus, unless we understand the nature of the problem(s) to which particular institutional solutions are being directed, we are not likely to correctly understand the bases for the choices being made or the likely consequences of those choices.

This role of institutions as problem-solving devices is neglected if we look at institutions as a set of norms or as a synonym for a set of game-rules, or if we view institutions as primarily naturally evolving entities rather than objects of choice.[9] Unfortunately, in what is the closest to definitive review of different theoretical approaches to the study of institutions, Crawford and Ostrom (1995), the problem-solving aspect of what an institution is all about is not even mentioned explicitly, despite its centrality in Ostrom's own seminal work on institutions to solve collection action problems for common pool resources. Moreover, even those economists or political scientists who see institutions as problem solvers tend to focus on only one kind of problem, for example, how the organization of the firm provides a way to minimize transactions costs (Coase, 1937), or how choice of a particular *k/n* rule can solve the problem of balancing off costs and gains from collective action (Buchanan and Tullock, 1962), or how institutions can solve the problem of cycling among multidimensional alternatives (Shepsle, 1979 and Shepsle and Weingast, 1981). In contrast, earlier students of institutional design such as Madison and Hamilton, emphasized plural goals: in the *Federalist*, we see the notion that institutions can be the solutions to important problems: for example, harnessing self-interest, preventing factionalism, assuring that choices reflect long-term perspectives that resist the passions of the moment.

Elsewhere, one of the present authors (Grofman, 2000) has identified seven specific problems that constitutional arrangements might be directed to solving: to assure popular sovereignty, to prevent the rise of tyranny, to improve the competence of decision making, to prevent corruption, to foster participation, to protect liberty, and to strengthen the power of the polity to act collectively.[10] Here we are interested in institutions that can facilitate political stability within societies divided along ethnic or religious lines, within the context of democratic politics.[11]

INSTITUTIONAL DESIGN AND ETHNIC CONFLICT IN PLURAL SOCIETIES

In line with an insight of the noted sociologist Robin Williams (personal communication, February 2000), we believe it important to distinguish two bases for ethnic conflict: (1) fundamental conflicts over national identity, that is, over 'Who owns the state?', and (2) more focussed conflicts over particular resources or competition for jobs (for example, perceived unfair competition from immigrant Chinese *vis-à-vis* native Malays in the rubber business, or disputes about mineral or grazing or fishing rights).

For modernization theorists in political science, economic and political development is supposed to promote integration of ethnic groups based on national identities that override and displace 'parochial' attachments (Almond and Powell, 1966; Deutsch, 1953; Huntington, 1968). For Marxists, ethnicity has always represented a form of false consciousness that masks the class character of society; for them, to focus on ethnicity is to miss the 'real' driving force behind political conflicts (Brown, 1989). Similarly, economists who look at ethnic conflicts tend to view ethnicity as an epiphenomenon to 'real' interests in which an economic calculus of greed is masked in the guise of ethnic conflict. For example, Paul Collier, of Oxford University, an economist who is presently Director of Research at the World Bank in Washington DC, in the same April 2000 panel discussion broadcast on the BBC from which we have taken a previous quote stated: 'A lot of rebellions are either directly motivated by looting of natural resources or are financed and sustained by looting of natural resources. If we look at Africa, we find a number of rebellions, which are clearly related to diamonds. In the recent rebellion in one West African country, as soon as the rebel leader was offered the Ministry of Natural Resources, he stopped the combat. He was getting what he wanted without having to fight for it.'

However, it may not be possible to assuage ethnic conflict simply by bribing or otherwise coopting ethnic leaders, settling property rights disputes, or limiting economic competition between ethnies. Sometimes one group is seen by another as 'polluting' by their mere presence or by virtue of the 'heretical or blasphemous' nature of the ideas they espouse (Moore, 2000). As Brendan O'Leary observed on the same radio program, in rejoinder to Collier: 'Paul Collier's thesis that our conflicts are primarily about greed and resources rather than grievances or inequality should prompt the question "Where are the diamonds in places like Northern Ireland or the Balkans?" Surely there, if not everywhere, what's at stake are group identities and insecurities, self-determination, sovereignty and allegiance.'

A failure to reach an adequate political accommodation of how ethnic issues will be resolved may trigger the demise of democracy and/or the escalation of ethnic conflict. In societies that are ethnically divided, politics may be the continuation of war by other means. The dominant ethny (ethnies) may resort to undemocratic forms of governance to keep other ethnies in a subordinate position, and a government under the control of the dominant group may even institute (or at least do nothing to stop) an ethnically-based reign of terror directed against other ethnies.

Students in the camp who emphasize the strong impediments to stable democracy in plural society include not just the 'usual suspects,' that is, anthropologists, sociologists, and other theorists who take a 'cultural' perspective in which ethnicity is central to social identity, but Public Choice theorists who argue that ethnic resentments will be exploited by political entrepreneurs. Indeed, two noted Public Choice scholars, Alvin Rabushka and Kenneth Shepsle (1972) offer the clearest explication of why we ought to be pessimistic about the prospects for democracy in plural societies. In the Rabushka and Shepsle model (laid out in more detail in Appendix 5.1), in plural societies, ethnic salience and ethnic outbidding undermine multi-ethnic cooperation and inevitably lead to nondemocratic, ethnically-exclusive states. The key difference between the Public Choice perspective on ethnic conflict and that of 'cultural' theorists is that scholars with a more economic perspective tend to look closely at the structure of incentives (especially for elites), rather than regarding ethnic conflicts as completely foreordained. We shall be reexamining the bases for the Rabushka–Shepsle pessimism in the light of more recent work on incentive aspects of various specific features of constitutional design.

Pessimism about plural societies is empirically grounded in the large number of plural societies that have failed to sustain democracy, or suffered repeated lapses. An abbreviated list includes Burundi, Fiji, Guyana, Lebanon, Myanmar, Nigeria, Northern Ireland, Rwanda, Sri Lanka, Suriname, and Sudan, and now, of course, most of the parts of the former Yugoslavia.

Quantitative research that looks at the link between ethnic diversity and degree of democracy is generally consistent with the expectation of a negative relationship (Bollen and Jackman, 1985; Diamond, 1992; Hannon and Carroll, 1981; Muller and Seligson, 1994; Powell, 1982). On the other hand, a few researchers find no statistically significant linkage between the two variables once other factors are controlled for (Thomas et al., 1979); and others, while recognizing the difficulty of achieving ethnic accommodation in deeply divided societies, reject the claim that stable democracy is *impossible* in such societies. In defense of their more optimistic appraisal, they point to plural societies that have achieved democratic accommodation (Austria, Belgium, Canada, India, Mauritius, the Netherlands, South Africa, Switzerland, and Trinidad and Tobago). The case for at least partial optimism is bolstered by the fact that at least some of these plural societies lack the wealth (and substantial middle class) that are often held to be prerequisites of stable democracy.[12]

Those who hold out hope for democracy in plural societies are virtually unanimous in their belief that institutional design is the key to avoiding disaster, with constitutional engineering, particularly of electoral systems, treated as an important lever.[13] Prominent scholars of comparative politics (perhaps most notably Arend Lijphart) have asserted that *majoritarian political institutions*, especially *single member district elections* conducted under a first-past-the-post (plurality voting) rule and *presidential* (as opposed to *parliamentary*) systems, are *not* suited to plural societies and must be replaced. Because, in plural societies, ethnic issues are likely to be 'trump' cards in the quest for votes, and radical outbidding on divisive ethnic issues is pervasive (Rabushka and Shepsle, 1972; Sisk, 1996, p. 32), majority rule in such societies often ends up in permanent control over the political process by the largest (or most war-like) ethnic group, and permanent exclusion of minority ethnic groups. Similarly, the existence of a president, and the inevitable winner-take-all conflict for that office is also argued to be a factor that exacerbates ethnic tension, on the one hand, and provides a power base to the winner to use for ethnic subordination, as well (compare Lijphart, 1992; Linz and Valenzuela, 1994).

This anti-majoritarian point of view is well summarized in the remarks of Brendan O'Leary (BBC Radio, April 2000):

> Democracy is understood in two ways: consensually, the rule of as many as possible; or as majoritarian, the rule of the current largest number. Where majorities change frequently these rival understandings may not matter much, but where there are peoples with different ethnic allegiances, elections may become censuses, and majoritarian democracy an engine of domination and stored grievance – as it was in Northern Ireland for fifty years; and as it was in the Republic of Serbia when it included Kosovo.

The most prominent alternative to a majoritarian design is consociationalism (Lijphart, 1968, 1969, 1977, 1991, 1996). Lijphart argues that stable democracy in plural societies requires power-sharing arrangements, where by *power-sharing* is meant 'practices and institutions that result in broad-based governing coalitions generally inclusive of all major ethnic groups in society' (Sisk, 1996, p. vii). To achieve this end, the most clearly articulated form of power-sharing arrangements (Lijphart, 1977), *consociationalism*, has a particular constellation of institutional features as its hallmarks/defining characteristics: *grand coalitions* in parliament, *proportionality* rules for allocation of ministries and at all levels of government, *group autonomy* and *minority veto*. The consociational approach to democratic politics is one in which membership in discrete ethnic/religious/sociocultural groups is explicitly acknowledged, with a set of socially defined and governmentally recognized groups serving as the 'pillars' of civic inclusion. Also, consociational arrangements for power sharing are based on arrangements for accommodation and bargaining among political elites.[14]

However, there is a fundamental dispute between advocates of communalist perspectives (of which consociationalism is perhaps the best known variant) and those of a more integrativist bent. Thus, there is dispute between those who propose electoral systems that could be expected to strengthen party elites in ethny-based parties and foster allocation rules based on ethnic identification versus those that wish to create incentives for pan-ethnic parties and/or candidates who make cross-ethnic appeals and/or to minimize the importance of ethnicity, *per se*, as a basis for allocation/redistribution of societal resources. Also, there is a cross-cutting dimension: the degree of importance to be attached to designing mechanisms affecting the nature of the accommodations negotiated among political elites versus the need to affect the shape of broader social institutions and policies such as schools and language laws.

Even some who share Lijphart's lack of total pessimism regarding the prospects for democracy in plural societies question the wisdom of consociational arrangements. Among mainstream political scientists, the most forceful critic of consociationalism is Donald Horowitz (1985, 1991a, b, 1993).

Horowitz questions the consociational focus on accommodation at the elite level, and is concerned that consociational arrangements reinforce the importance of ethnic or religious cleavages. He argues for an integrative approach that seeks to deal with ethnic conflict potential through fostering political arrangements that will lead to bridging or transcending ethnic group differences. As laid out by Sisk (1996, p. 5), the goal of the integrative approach is to structure politics in such a way as to provide incentives for inter-ethnic cooperation and the creation of pre-election coalitions between ethnic parties or broad multi-ethnic parties based on interests (for example, region or common economic interests) that transcend ethnic identities.

Moreover, just as there is a dispute between advocates of communal and advocates of integrative approaches to mitigating ethnic conflicts, there are further divisions among those who advocate institutional solutions to mitigate ethnic conflict or reduce its political significance. In particular, even those who are sympathetic to the integrative approach do not have the same views about the specifics of choice among electoral rules. Horowitz (1985, 1991a, b, 1993) has been rather insistent that the *alternative vote* is the best electoral rule to foster voting patterns and that will cross ethnic lines and parties that will have a multi-ethnic base.[15] In contrast, Reynolds (Reynolds, 1999a; Reynolds and Grofman, 1994; Reynolds and Reilly, 1999) has argued for use of the *single transferable vote* (STV),[16] as have various authors familiar with its use in Northern Ireland (for example, O'Leary et al., 1993).

Our discussion of strategies to foster democratic modes of accommodation/dispute resolution in plural societies leads us to four-fold (2 × 2) categorization, whose horizontal axis represents communalist vs. integrative perspectives and whose vertical axis is the degree of emphasis on institutional mechanisms that foster elite accommodation as compared to institutional arrangements that affect the society as a whole (see Table 5.1).

The argument over the merits of mass-centered vs. elite-centered approaches can be thought of in political economy terms as, at least in part, a debate about the optimal tradeoffs between (a) making changes in those aspects of the incentive structures that are most easily changed and (b) making changes where changes are likely to have the greatest impact. Most students of ethnic politics would agree with Suzanne Lohmann's observation (personal communication, December 1999) that 'it is easier to change institutions than it is to change people.' Yet, if we succeed in changing people, that is, in leading citizens of a state to conceive of their self-interest in a different way or to see more commonalities between themselves and their fellow nationals regardless of ethnicity, this may have a far more profound effect on societal cohesion than negotiating elite deals that may, ultimately, come unglued (as in Lebanon, for example).

In contrast, the debate between integrative and communalist approaches to

Table 5.1 Categorizing institutional approaches to fostering stable democracy in plural societies

	Institutions that perpetuate the importance of ethnicity but seek to minimize its negative consequences (communal institutions)	Institutions that seek to minimize the importance of ethnicity and/or foster a multi-ethnic character to the state (integrative institutions)
Mass-oriented	Separate legal systems Specific provisions for group rights Separate school systems Ethnically-based allocative rules for jobs, etc. that draw on the norm of proportional representation	A legal system with a strong emphasis on individual rather than group rights Political distributions that are not tied to ethnicity Requiring a single common language or requiring multilingualism of all citizens Forbidding certain markers of group distinctiveness (e.g., the veil)
Elite-based	Ethnically rooted (territorial) federalism with considerable autonomy for subunits Mono-ethnic electoral constituencies (or, in the extreme, communal rolls) Elite power-sharing mechanisms (e.g., grand coalitions; minority veto, ethnically-based political parties, or, in the extreme, ethnically designated office-holding) Electoral rules that foster centralized elite control (e.g., list PR) Use of a parliamentary rather than presidential system	Forms of federalism that either do not coincide with ethnicity or that divide up ethnic blocs into multiple units so as to diminish prospects of ethnic solidarity STV in multi-ethnic con-constituencies (Reynolds and Reilly, 1999) The alternative vote in multi-ethnic constituencies (Horowitz, 1985)

institutional design might seem to involve irreconcilable differences in principle, with no possibility of a middle ground.[17] In Lijphart (1984, 1999) political institutions are viewed as naturally tending toward one of the two polar ends of the majoritarian (Westminster) vs. consensus continuum; this classification subsumes that in Lijphart (1977), with consociationalism now taken to be a particular form of consensual arrangements devised for societies with well-defined (and mutually exclusive and exhaustive) subgroup memberships.

A somewhat different perspective in institutional design for plural societies can be derived from the views on constitutional political economy in the *Calculus of Consent*.[18] Buchanan and Tullock (1962) consider deviations from the pure majoritarian or pure consensus model as being deliberate attempts to reach a particular tradeoff between two competing goals: the ability of governments to reach decisions and the avoidance of negative consequences of those decisions for some members of a society. In the context of plural societies, it is easy to think of those who enjoy/suffer particular (positive or negative) consequences as being members of particular subgroups of the society. As Sisk (1996, p. 4) puts it: 'A central challenge of managing ethnic conflict in the current era is to promote practices that successfully regulate competing group claims within a democratic framework.' Thus, from the Buchanan and Tullock perspective, it is natural to look for a *mix* of institutional mechanisms to deal with the problems confronted by plural societies, some of which will provide ways of strengthening the potential for collective action and others which will emphasize the protection of (group) rights/interests.

The 'optimal tradeoffs' perspective on constitutional political economy in the *Calculus of Consent* is directly relevant too in considering some of the more specific issues in designing electoral institutions for plural societies.[19] In terms of this perspective, Buchanan and Tullock identify four basic features of the rules under which representation takes place.[20] These four features can readily be thought of as ways to generate tradeoffs between consensus and majoritarian forms of conflict resolution.

Let N be the total number of voters; let n be the number of voters in a given constituency; let s (= N/n) be the size of the legislature.[21]

X_1, *the degree of agreement required to elect a representative*, generally ranging from plurality to n/n (unanimity).[22]

X_2, *the degree of randomness in the specification of the constituencies from which representatives are to be chosen*, ranging from maximally homogeneous constituencies (for example, a 'functional' form of representation such as election from within racial groupings or from occupational groupings, as the late Senator Paul Douglas once proposed in the 1920s) to a purely random assignment process.

X_3, *the degree of democracy*, ranging from $1/N$ (dictatorship) to N/N (direct democracy).
X_4, *the decision rule for internal legislative decision making*, ranging from $1/s$ to s/s (unanimity).[23]

For Buchanan and Tullock (1962), the anticipated consequence of a given mode of representation on the magnitude of the sum of 'external costs' plus 'decision-making costs' is what determines an individual's preferences among alternative forms of representation, where external costs are the costs imposed on the individual by having choices made that affect him negatively, and decision costs are the costs imposed (transaction costs, perhaps also side-payments) as part of the process of reaching agreement. Each of the four variables above can be thought of in terms of its consequences for these two types of costs. For example, if we look at X_2, as we move toward unanimity then we raise transaction costs and lower external costs. Similarly, if we have more than one parliamentary chamber, each with different modes of selection, then we increase the heterogeneity of the selection process and increase decision costs if the agreement of the two chambers is needed to pass legislation, while at the same lowering external costs by making changes from the status quo less likely.

For Buchanan and Tullock, the optimal set of rules is simply that in which the sum of 'external costs' plus 'decision-making costs' is minimized. Because choices that lower one of these two forms of cost tend to raise the other kind, Buchanan and Tullock emphasize tradeoffs between the two kinds of costs and complementarity across these variables, that is, we need to look at the costs consequences of each choice in the context of the full institutional specification, that is, we need to look at 'partial derivatives.' Hence, the costs and benefits of a particular institutional choice can only be properly weighed in the light of the total institutional package. In the context of plural societies, as noted earlier, we may readily translate from the purely individualist language of Buchanan and Tullock to one where here we may think of (some of) those whose interests need to be protected as members of a particular ethny.

A potentially important implication of the Buchanan and Tullock approach is that it suggests 'extreme solutions' (that is, those in which all institutions are 'of a piece' in terms of which type of costs they are most concerned with minimizing) are probably unlikely to be minimizing of total cost (and thus optimal from the Buchanan and Tullock perspective) in that the gains to be achieved by bringing down one type of cost are likely to be paid for by raising the other type of cost to a very high level. Thus, 'hybrid' sets of institutions may well prove more desirable than ones whose motivation is singularly in terms of minimizing one of the two types of institutional costs.

Before we turn to any further consideration of various of the specific mechanisms enumerated in Table 5.1 a few comments about the issues of secession/rectification of borders are in order.

The Secession/Partition Option

' "Self-determination" is the rallying cry of many aggrieved ethnic groups in every . . . region of the world. In 1992 a study [commissioned by] the Carnegie Endowment for International Peace identified more than sixty states with active subnational movements seeking self-determination' (Sisk, 1996, p. 1). Many of these groups were seeking their own state. Yet, as the political scientist, Samuel Huntington (1972, quoted in Sisk, 1996, p. 1) has noted, after the breakup of (colonial) empires into their component parts there has long been a strong opposition to further proliferation of nation-states on the part of the major world powers. Some advanced industrial nations had minority populations with separatist leanings; to help keep the lid on at home they may have sought to keep the lid on secessionist (and even regional autonomy) movements abroad. Perhaps even more importantly, during the Cold War, any changes in national boundaries were feared as destabilizing, and those on different sides in a civil war or war for independence often sought allies from opposite sides in the Cold War.

In the US, of course, secession still brings up memories of the War Between the States (a.k.a. the Civil War). Among Yankees, at least, the movement to secede is associated with a desire to oppress minorities. But the strong bias among US policy makers and academics against any further partition to create (more) ethnically homogeneous states has at least two other sources.

First, the US is committed to the nation-state as a form of voluntary social contract, joining those with a commitment to freedom and not merely those who share ties of blood or culture. Everyone can become an American. Ethnically defined states do not leave open the possibility of choice. Moreover, the exclusivity of the 'ethnic state' is thought likely to give rise to illiberal and even undemocratic policies – policies that do not recognize natural rights and that are likely to lead to various forms of ethnic segregation, ethnic cleansing or even genocide. Here memories of Nazi Germany still shape policy preferences.[24]

Second, the partition of existing nations into ethnically defined segments will, if carried out to its 'logical' conclusion, lead to the proliferation of mini- and micro-states. Such small-scale states are thought not to be economically viable.[25] And economic hardship is viewed as a near sure route to dictatorship, as well as a continuing push toward illegal immigration from these 'basket cases' to the wealthier nations of the world.

Furthermore, despite clear language about 'self-determination' in Article

1.2 of the UN Charter, there remains a strong 'bias against secession in international law and practice' (Sisk, 1996, p. 2). Still, recent events (including the end of the Cold War) have made secessionary movements at least somewhat more palatable (Sisk, 1996, p. 2). For example, the 'clean' separation of Czechoslovakia into Slovakia and the Czech Republic, the so-called 'velvet divorce,' was taken with equanimity in the West, largely because of the democratic way in which the sundering occurred and because the ethnic geography (and historic borders) allowed for partition without the gut-wrenching (and violence-ridden) movement of peoples that accompanied, say, the partition of British India into India and Pakistan.[26] Moreover, we are unaware of any argument contemporaneous with partition that Slovakia and the Czech Republic would, separately, be any less democratic than Czechoslovakia as a whole was expected to be.

Sometimes secession/partition might seem the only viable option.[27] Nonetheless, US (and UN) policy in the former Yugoslavia has exhibited remarkable naivete about the possibility of restoring a multi-ethnic character to various regions of that war-torn area and about the need to think about 'rectification' of borders.[28] Certainly the Hutu–Tutsi conflict might have been mitigated by some form of ethnic partition, with an externally monitored exchange of both territory and persons (albeit complicated by the problems of specifying who is Hutu and who is Tutsi). An attempt at international mediation in Rwanda in the early 1990s was a failure. But, as far as we are able to tell from secondary sources, neither boundary adjustment nor movement of persons was 'on the table' then (Kaufmann, 1997, pp. 297–8; Ganguly and Taras, 1998, pp. 241–4).

However, it is in large part a counsel of despair to think that moving borders or moving people are our only choices. There are simply too many different ethnic/linguistic groups for us to look to crafting of lines (or even movement of peoples) to be a viable solution to the 'problem' of plural societies. Moreover, as Sisk (1996, p. 2) reminds us, 'formerly internal conflicts may be transformed to international conflicts,' as with India and Pakistan and the continuing controversy over the fate of Kashmir. Thus we now wish to turn to a consideration of some of the more important of the specific mechanisms proposed in Table 5.1 as means for mitigating ethnic conflict within existing states. We may think of these as a menu of options, but recall that, following Buchanan and Tullock (1962), we are reluctant to view institutional design as 'either/or,' for example, designed exclusively with communalist aims in mind or designed to foster integration. Mechanisms of both types can coexist within the same political system, even if they fail to follow one or another 'grand logic.'

The discussion that follows in no way pretends to be exhaustive. We merely illustrate some of the cases where the mechanisms referenced in Table 5.1 have been put into use.

Territorial Federalism vs. a Unitary State

The American poet, Robert Frost, once proclaimed that 'Good fences make good neighbors' (Frost, 1919).[29] Territorial mechanisms of various sorts may be employed to minimize contacts/conflicts between ethnies. While it might be thought that differences in patterns of ethnic concentration across wide territorial areas may be used as the basis for 'natural' divisions into federal units, ethnic segregation is often 'unnatural,' that is, fostered by both state and private action,[30] an extreme case of which would be the creation of ethnic 'reservations.' In such cases, 'fencing off' is synonymous with oppression. In many settler states, 'first peoples' were driven off valuable land and confined to reservations in less desirable parts of the country (for example, the Cherokee and Seminole being transported from Georgia and Florida, respectively, to reservations in Oklahoma in the nineteenth century, or apartheid-driven white South Africa attempting to force its black population into Bantustans occupying only 13 per cent of the nation's land surface).[31]

Still 'fencing-off' of ethnies via territorial federalism in settings where geography and ethnicity are highly coincident may be a sensible mechanism to maintain national unity in the presence of strong ethnic and linguistic divisions. The model for a federal state is one in which the central government has responsibility for matters affecting the polity as a whole, for example, national defense and foreign policy, while the states (and subunits within them) deal with more 'local' matters.[32] Territorial federalism is commonly advocated as *the* constitutional design appropriate for plural societies – at least in contexts where ethnies are geographically concentrated. For example, Donald Horowitz, on the same April 2000 BBC radio show from which we have taken earlier quotes asserts:

> I think there's very good evidence that a great many countries could benefit from federalism and regional autonomy. Regional autonomy and federalism started out in the post-colonial world as dirty words because they were thought to be latter-day versions of techniques that the colonialists used to divide and rule, but slowly over the decades many states have come to realize that there's real utility in bringing government down to lower levels where members of ethnic groups will have more of a say over their own destiny. We're slowly learning that.[33]

On the other hand, because federal arrangements are seen as concessions to (separatist) minorities that challenge the dominant ethny's perception of the nature of the state they may be strongly resisted. In Estonia, for example, with its large proportion (over 30 per cent) of Russian 'colonizers,' native Estonians are unwilling to define the state in federal terms despite the geographic concentration of Russian speakers. Similarly, in Sri Lanka, history as 'remembered' by the Sinhalese majority defines the Tamils as interlopers – not entitled to a share in the state (Eller, 1999, chap. 3).[34]

At first blush there is little apparent relationship between the nation's degree of ethnic homogenity (or even ethnic dispersion) and its likelihood of adopting federal arrangements: some federal nations are effectively mono-ethnic (for example, Austria, Australia, Germany, Venezuela) or do not have ethnic divisions as the basis for territorial units (for example, the US), and some multi-ethnic nations are unitary in form (for example, Mauritius, Botswana, Indonesia). Nonetheless, at least if we confine ourselves to long-term democracies, a relationship between ethnicity and adoption of federal institutions does seem to emerge. As Lijphart (1999) summarizes the evidence, in long-term democracies, federal arrangements are most common in societies that are geographically large and/or ethnically and linguistically diverse, while the vast majority of monolingual and mono-ethnic states are unitary in form.[35] India is perhaps the most striking example of a multilingual and multiethnic federal nation.[36] While the original division of India into states did not match that well with the linguistic divisions in the country, additional states were created along linguistic lines and there was also some realigning of state boundaries in the 1950s and thereafter (Brass, 1990, pp. 146–56).[37] Belgium (after 1993) and Switzerland also leap to mind. In both countries, language and territory tend to coincide and federal arrangements obtain.

Mono-Ethnic Electoral Constituencies/Communal Rolls vs. Multi-Ethnic Electoral Constituencies

The greater the residential concentration of ethnic groups the harder it will be to create multi-ethnic constituencies. When there is virtually perfect residential segregation it may appear inevitable that we will end up with mono-ethnic constituencies. Still, in plural societies, if we are willing to allow for very large constituencies (in the limiting case the nation as a whole), or to engage in very creative gerrymandering, we can always create constituencies with substantial proportions of more than one ethny. However, we are unaware of any country that explicitly mandates the creation of multi-ethnic constituencies. But, there are many countries where the opposite is true.

For example, in the US, as a result of recent constitutional interpretation of the Equal Protection clause of the 14th Amendment (added to protect the rights of newly freed slaves after the Civil War) and of language in the Voting Rights of 1965 and the 1982 amendments to that Act, race-conscious districting (involving the drawing of 'majority–minority' districts) is mandated in situations where minority candidates of choice can be shown to regularly lose because of patterns of same-race voting and where there exists minority populations large enough and geographically concentrated enough to form the majority in a single member district (Grofman et al., 1992; Grofman and Davidson, 1992; Davidson and Grofman, 1994; Grofman, 1998).

The extreme case of a mono-ethic constituency is the *communal roll*, where only members of a given ethny may participate (Lijphart, 1986), as in the Maori seats in New Zealand. Involving only a handful of seats, the Maori seats are relatively noncontroversial (although there have been proposals to do away with them).[38] In contrast, in Fiji, communal seats (and communal quotas) are much more controversial because what is at stake is who will control the state (Stockwell, 2000).

Ethnically-Based vs. Non-Ethnically-Based Party Systems

When territory and ethnicity coincide, at least some parties are likely to be ethnically-based parties. There have been attempts to prevent the formation of ethnically-based parties, for example, Nigeria's constitution had an explicit prohibition against such parties (Sisk and Reynolds, 1998, pp. 37–54).[39] But such attempts are both anti-democratic and futile, since they may be circumvented by ethnically-based parties who officially organize around ostensibly non-ethnic issues. One of the more peculiar responses to the problem of ethnic-based conflict tied to the actions of ethnically-based party leaders came in Uganda. A June 29, 2000 referendum sponsored by President Yoweri Museveni was held on whether or not to make a multi-party system illegal, that is, to endorse a 'non-party' system. With 5l per cent turnout, the referendum carried, with 90.7 per cent of those voting expressing support! (Wasswa, 2000).

However, even if parties form on the basis of ethnicity, this need not be the whole story; there still may be mechanisms that allow for/foster cross-cutting cleavages. For example, in Belgium, while almost all parties are either Flemish parties or Walloon parties, by the 1980s most of the major parties can be viewed as language-based halves of a larger entity which is, at root, ideologically defined, for example, the Greens have been split (since 1981) into a Flemish and a Walloon half (Ishiyama and Breuning, 1998, p. 123).

Majoritarian vs. Proportional Electoral Rules

In post-1994 South Africa, even though the ANC could have virtually eliminated any competitors if it instituted a majoritarian electoral system, it deliberately chose PR (Reynolds and Grofman, 1994) partly to reassure whites and partly because it was ideologically committed to the principle of inclusive representation.

Use of a Parliamentary rather than Presidential System

Several leading students of comparative politics (perhaps most notably Juan Linz) have argued that presidential systems are particularly pernicious in their potential for conflict, especially when coupled with constitutional arrangements that create rival centers of power. For example, ill-defined borders between presidential powers and those of the legislature can be continual irritants leading to political unrest and may trigger crises that lead to the end of democracy. These scholars call attention to the instability in presidential systems, signaled by phenomena such as the high probability of military or other coups (for example, the self-coup by Fujimori in Peru). However, this point of view remains controversial, with some scholars (notably Shugart and Carey, 1992) arguing, *inter alia*, that we need to take into account regional controls (a high proportion of all presidential regimes are in Latin America, as are a high proportion of all coups). Lijphart (1992) offers a collection of many of the most important essays bearing on this debate.

The same arguments that are used against presidentialism, *per se,* have been used to argue that presidentialism exacerbates ethnic conflicts. In particular, presidentialism implies a single powerful office that tends to generate a strong likelihood of winner-take-all competition between rival ethnies.

Elite Power-Sharing Mechanisms

Grand coalitions

Sometimes the more comprehensive forms of power-sharing may be used only for transitional purposes. For example, in South Africa the transition from white rule took place under negotiated power-sharing arrangements that guaranteed every major (more than 5 per cent) party with a proportional share in the governing coalition. This arrangement for a 'grand coalition' was, however, only temporary (Sisk, 1995; Glickman, 1998; see also Johnston, 1994; Reynolds, 1994, 1999a, b).

Ethnically designated office-holding

Various countries have experimented with rules that specifically require that particular office-holders be of a given ethnicity or religion. In pre Civil-War Lebanon, there were power-sharing arrangements that made sure that not all major office-holders were from the same religious community. Similarly, conflicts between natives and 'Indians' in Fiji led to a 1999 constitution that contained communal arrangements intended to provide guarantees of Fijian majorities in the legislature regardless of changing demographic realities (Lal, 1999),[40] with 23 of the 71 seats reserved for native Fijians and only 19 for those of Indian descent.

In general, in our view, fixed quota rules are unlikely to prove stable. The problem with such rules is that they often attempt to preserve a particular status quo against changing demographic realities. Maintaining them almost invariably means refusing to permit new censuses to take place. The arrangements in Fiji, for example, have proven short-lived and the use of the alternative vote there did not have the desired consequences. In 1999, the Fijian Labor Party (FLP) not only won all 19 of the Indian communal seats but it also won 18 of the 25 geographically defined 'open' seats (each filled using the alternative vote), thus controlling a majority (37 of the 71 seats) in the Fijian legislature.[41] The FLP leader was Indo-Fijian, and assumed the position of prime minister – outraging some ethnic Fijians and leading to a successful coup (initiated in May 2000) by a group advocating a 'Fiji for Fijians' policy and arguing that existing constitutional arrangements failed to provide sufficient guarantees of native Fijian political control.

We are much more optimistic about a feature of the British–Irish Accord of 1998 (the 'Good Friday' agreement) that generated political inclusion without the need to treat religious identification as the sole touchstone of political identity in Northern Ireland and without attempting to freeze into place a particular (and otherwise temporary) balance of power. The 'trick' used was to require minimal representation for various parties, but to define those groupings entitled to special representation not by the religion of their supporters/representatives but by the policy positions they espouse (pro-Union, anti-Union, other).[42]

Another intriguing and unusual feature of the 'Good Friday' accord that we wish to call attention to because of the potential for its adoption in other settings is the mechanism the Accord specifies to determine the allocation of ministries across parties. After the prime minister (and associate prime minister) positions are allocated, the remaining ministries are determined by using the d'Hondt rule for proportional representation. However, the rule is used to do more than just determine what proportion of the ministries each party will be entitled to – a share proportional to its share of seats among the parties in the governing coalition. The *sequencing* aspects of d'Hondt are used to determine which party would get the first seat, which the second, and so on.[43] The party that is entitled to the first seat gets first pick of the ten ministries. The party that is entitled to the second seat gets second pick among the nine remaining ministries, and so on. The first use of this mechanism worked smoothly (O'Leary, 1999).[44]

To see how this sequencing works, we observe that any method for proportional representation that can be characterized as a divisor method (Balinski and Young, 1982) can be characterized by a unique vector of divisors (d_1, d_2, d_3, . . .). These divisors are (1, 2, 3, . . .) in the case of Jefferson/d'Hondt, and (1, 3, 5, . . .) in the case of Webster/Sainte Laguë. If there are *m* seats to be allocated,

Table 5.2a Illustration of d'Hondt divisor rule (elect 7)

D'Hondt divisor	Party 1	Party 2	Party 3
1	**0.47**	**0.32**	**0.21**
2	**0.235**	**0.16**	0.105
3	**0.157**	**0.107**	0.07

Table 5.2b Illustration of Ste Laguë divisor rule (elect 7)

D'Hondt divisor	Party 1	Party 2	Party 3
1	**0.47**	**0.32**	**0.21**
2	**0.157**	**0.107**	**0.07**
3	**0.094**	0.064	0.042

and the *i*th unit (or party) has a population (vote) share of p_i, the m highest quotients of the form p_i/d_j determine how many seats each geographic unit or party receives (Rae, 1971). For example, if three of the m highest quotients have p_1 in the numerator, then unit one/party one gets exactly three of the m seats.

Consider, for example, the allocation of seven seats among three parties, with vote shares of 47 per cent, 32 per cent and 21 per cent, respectively, as shown in Tables 5.2a and 5.2b. Here the d'Hondt and Ste Laguë rules give us different allocations.

The seven highest entries (highlighted in bold) in Table 5.2a give us three seats for party one, three seats for party two, and one seat for party three under d'Hondt; in contrast, for Sainte Laguë, while we again get three seats for party one, we now get two seats for party two and two seats for party three. If we arrange the ratios, p_i/d_j, from highest to lowest, the allocation of the m seats can be thought of as occurring in a particular sequence. If we are allocating seats to political parties, the party associated with the highest quotient from the set p_i/d_j can be thought of as being given the 'first' seat; the party with the second highest quotient can be thought of as getting the 'second' seat; and so on. From this insight, it is easy to think of generalizing this sequencing rule to the allocation of non-interchangeable units, for example, ministerial portfolios. Now, the party associated with the highest quotient from the set p_i/d_j can be thought of as being given the 'first pick' of ministerial portfolios; the party with the second highest quotient can be thought of as getting the 'second pick' among the set of (still open) ministerial portfolios; and so on.

For the data shown in Table 5.2a, under d'Hondt, party one gets the first, third, and sixth picks; party two gets the second, fifth, and seventh picks; and party three gets the fourth pick. For the Sainte Laguë allocation rule, as shown in Table 5.2b, in contrast, party one gets the first, third, and sixth picks, while party two gets the second and fifth picks, and party three gets the third and seventh picks. In this example, different aggregate allocations lead to different sequencing under d'Hondt and Sainte Laguë; however, O'Leary et al. (manuscript in progress) show that, even if the PR allocations are identical under two divisor rules, the sequencing need not be.

Minority veto

By requiring more than a simple majority or imposing especially complicated procedures, something very close to a minority veto may be implemented. For example, the transition phase of South Africa's transition to democracy imposed supramajoritarian requirements for certain kinds of decisions (Sisk and Reynolds, 1998).

Constitutional protection of rights

Many states have constitutions whose provisions regarding rights (or federal arrangements) either cannot be amended or require supermajorities or a popular referendum. In the 1999 Fijian Constitution, various quite specific safeguards pertaining to native Fijian rights and customs are written in. Moreover, amendment of these provisions required supermajorities in parliament (three-quarters approval) and the concurrence of the Council of Chiefs (Lal, 1999; Stockwell, 2000). Similarly, amendments to rights provisions of the new Spanish constitution require a two-thirds vote of both chambers, and automatically dissolve parliament if passed, with the proposed amendment submitted to the people for ratification by amendment (Stone Sweet, 2000, p. 59). Writing unamendable provisions into a constitution is also not unheard of. For example, it is a relatively little known fact about the US Constitution that the provision that each state must have at least one representative in the US House cannot be amended.[45]

Citizenship and Language Policies

Lijphart (1999, p. 196) observes that, although the Swiss Federation has four official languages, 22 of the 26 cantons (and half-cantons) are officially unilingual, only three (Bern, Fribourg, and Balais) are bilingual, and even the most linguistically polyglot (Graubünden) has only three official languages. In Belgium, the 'natural' division of the country is threefold, a Flemish-speaking area, a French-speaking area, and a bilingual area around Brussels. Nonetheless, in both countries, school policies encourage/require basic literacy in more than one language. In Spain, too, linguistic divisions are largely territorial in nature. A series of recent decisions there has given legitimacy to

Catalan, whose speakers are concentrated in Catalonia. In a number of economically developed countries (for example, Luxembourg, *par excellence*), virtually all citizens are, at minimum, bilingual, and many under the age of 40 are trilingual (with English as an additional language). In contrast, in Canada, while the central government has been committed since the 1960s to a policy of promoting bilingualism throughout Canada, this has been countered by Quebec insistence on French monolingualism in that province – the province in which the vast bulk of French speakers are located.

Many countries permit schooling in a 'native' language alongside schooling in the 'official' language of the country, and often such provisions are constitutionally embedded. In some countries the state takes responsibility for providing such instruction. In the US, for example, the Supreme Court held in the 1970s (in an important and still controversial decision) that students have a constitutionally protected right to be taught in a language that allows them to learn, such as their mother tongue.

When bilingual education is seen as compromising language learning in the 'official language,' it is often the subject of backlash. In the US, 'bilingualism' in the form of Spanish language instruction has been called for by some Hispanic activists, with the main pedagogical arguments being that instruction of particular topics in one's native language speeded learning and that grammatical skills developed in learning one's native language would carry over to acquisition of other languages. While there was little general resistance to 'transitional bilingualism,' when it appeared that some schools were requiring bilingual education for students for whom it had no compelling educational justification, and Spanish language instruction was being continued throughout the schooling process as a form of 'cultural preservation' rather than being viewed as temporary, with bilingual education serving a secondary role as a jobs program for Spanish speaking teachers and paraprofessionals (a portion of whom were effectively monolingual), given the poor performance of Hispanic students on standardized exams, the backlash was great. In California, in particular, there was a recent successful referendum to end (non-transitional forms of) bilingual education.

More generally, the growing presence of large numbers of people whose English language skills are minimal to nonexistent, symbolized in the public mind by the large influx of Spanish speakers to the US (a large number of whom are in the US illegally) has led to a number of campaigns for making English the official language of various states (most often states with large foreign-born populations), and for making English the official language of the US as a whole. (The US does not have an official language; and one state, New Mexico, is officially bilingual.)

Similar phenomena are found throughout the world. For example, in post-Soviet Bulgaria, where Article 36 of the 1991 Constitution guarantees that 'citizens whose mother tongue is not Bulgarian shall have the right to study and use their own language alongside the compulsory study of the Bulgarian language,' demands by the Turkish minority for 'the recognition of Turkish as an official language [in addition to Bulgarian] . . . have enraged xenophobic Bulgarian nationalists' (Ishiyama and Breuning, 1998, p. 25).

In many countries some level of demonstrated competence in the 'official' language is required for an immigrant seeking citizenship. Sometimes this language requirement is used as a barrier to limit naturalization; often it is used as a litmus test of a willingness to 'assimilate.' It plays both roles in parts of the former Soviet Union where there are 'leftover' Russian-speakers.

In Latvia, for example, knowledge of spoken Latvian is required as a prerequisite of naturalization. In 1994, Latvia also sought to set quotas on naturalization that would dramatically slow the rate at which Russians living in that country could gain citizenship. However, protest from within and outside the country led to an elimination of the quota, and in 1995 the language provisions of the citizenship law were further eased to allow those who had obtained language instruction in Latvian only schools or schools with Latvian language classes to automatically satisfy the language competence requirement (Ishiyama and Breuning, 1998, p. 95).[46]

DISCUSSION

Even if one believes that institutional solutions can mitigate ethnic conflict and foster stable democracy, the fact that such mechanisms exist does not mean that they will be adopted. Rabushka and Shepsle (1972) warn about the incentives for elites to engage in ethnic outbidding; even the much more optimistic Sisk (1996, p. xiii) warns about the likelihood that there will only be certain brief windows of opportunity.[47] On the other hand, integrative solutions may take decades before they shift political attitudes and reduce ethnic tensions, and there may be sparks that trigger ethnic conflicts long before these integrative solutions have had an opportunity to work. Gurr (1993) has identified 275 'politically significant' ethnic groups, in the 'Minorities at Risk' project that he headed. Fifty-seven of the 275 groups were in open rebellion, with 21 fighting medium-to large-scale guerrilla war, like the KLA in Kosovo (Gurr, 2000b).

Still, not all plural societies fail. Democracy has been multiply interrupted in Fiji and nonexistent in Guyana, but there have been clear democratic successes in Mauritius and Trinidad. Perhaps most importantly for optimism, India, despite a period of presidential rule under Indira Gandhi, clearly deserves to be labeled a democracy. Indeed, Lijphart (1999) treats it as one of his 36 major long-term democracies.

In the view of Stockwell (2000), democracy in plural societies depends upon the existence of cross-cutting class cleavages that mitigate ethnic divisions and the actions of ethnic elites who pursue inclusive, multi-ethnic coalitions and policies that promote relative equality in representation, appointments, and distribution. He emphasizes the choices made by ethnic elites in deciding whether or not to pursue a policy of multi-ethnic inclusiveness or ethnic exclusion. In addition to these social structural/class and elite-driven explanations of the democratic successes and failures of plural societies, here we would add the importance of good institutional design.[48]

But, alas, there does not seem to be a single royal road to success, nor does there even appear a royal road to failure *vis-à-vis* institutional design. Democratic success in Mauritius and Trinidad has been based on modified majoritarian institutions. Thus, power sharing is not a necessary condition for ethnic accommodation and relatively stable democracy in plural societies. Democracy has succeeded in Mauritius and Trinidad to the extent that it has[49] because cross-cutting class cleavages provided the foundation for moderate, nationalistic ethnic elites to pursue inclusive, multi-ethnic strategies, which mitigated the centrifugal force of ethnicity and contributed to the development of civic (national) identities that tempered ethnic attachments and deepened commitment to the democratic process among all ethnic groups.[50] Moreover, Fiji, which possessed semi-consociational arrangements and made use of the alternative vote, illustrates that even attempts to mix integrative and communal solutions may not overcome historical feelings of displacement generated by ethnic immigration.

Still, we do not wish to end on a negative note. Roughly 80 per cent of the ethnic groups identified in Gurr (1993) only pursued 'ordinary' politics, or at most engaged in non-violent protests such as mass demonstrations, to achieve their goals. For example, it was through ordinary politics that Inuits in Canada were given their own territory (Gurr, 2000b). Also, we would call attention to the incredibly complex yet very well-thought-out institutional design aspects of the British–Irish Agreement of 1998 for Northern Ireland (O'Leary, 1999). In the end, this agreement may not work, but at least it offers hope.[51]

NOTES

1. We use the term 'ethny' to designate groups that are viewed both by themselves and by non-group members as having a defined identity that allows members of the group to be clearly distinguishable from other citizens in terms of genotype, or phenotype, or language, or religion, or other cultural markers. This terminology is common in the sociological literature on ethnicity (personal communication, Robin Williams, February 2000).
2. In Canada, in 1999, 20 per cent of the country's land was used to create a new territory, Nunavut, for first peoples – with a considerable measure of self-governance and control over the area's rich natural resources for the 22,000 Inuits who reside there (Gurr, 2000a and b).

This land area is rich in natural resources, so the decision to turn its resources over to native control did not come easy.

3. To observers concerned with the expansion, consolidation, and deepening of democracy around the world, the second half of the twentieth century presents a mixed picture. On the positive side, more states than ever before have made transitions to democracy (Huntington, 1991). The recent wave of democratization has seen the end of dictatorships in Greece, Portugal, and Spain; democratic openings in Eastern Europe associated with the end of the Cold War; and births and rebirths of democracy in Africa, Asia and the Pacific, as well as North and South America. These developments support a cautious optimism about the prospects for the furtherance of human rights, increased economic development, and peace. But there remain a large number of states securely locked in authoritarian rule – half or more depending on how lenient a definition of democracy is used. Also, many democratizing states subsequently reverted back to authoritarianism. Moreover, most democratic transitions remain frail, unstable, and restricted; and many face severe economic and social problems that make democratic consolidation highly unlikely (Diamond, 1999; Huntington, 1996; Schmitter, 1994; Sørensen, 1998).
4. An immense amount of energy has been spent on the 'primordial' vs. 'constructed/instrumental' debate about the meaning of ethnicity. The use of the term 'primordial' to refer to ethnic and kinship attachments that are thought to be virtually impossible to change and providing fundamental social identity is commonly attributed to Shils (1957). Eller (1999, pp. 78–9) suggests that primordial theorists attribute three features to ethnicity: apriority, ineffability, and affectivity. *Apriority* means that ethnicity is 'just there, ascribed or founded upon characteristics that individuals are born into and cannot deny.' *Ineffability* means that 'primordial ethnic givens are inexpressible, inexplicable, overpowering and coercive in their social force.' *Affectivity* emphasizes 'the essentially emotional nature of ethnicity (with constant reference to ties, bonds, attachments, and sentiments).' For primordialists, the combination of these aspects of ethnicity makes ethnicity something whose effects can best be thought of as 'irrational or at least nonrational.' Some primordialists even offer a sociobiological basis for the intensity of ethnic attachments (van den Berghe, 1967).
5. Thus, in the terminology of the Carnegie Commission on Preventing Deadly Conflict, we are interested in aspects of 'structural prevention,' rather than in the 'immediate operational tasks to defuse a crisis' (Hamburg and Solomon, 1996, p. xviii). Important treatments of many of the general theoretical issues involving ethnic conflict include Smith (1981), Horowitz (1985), Montville (1991), McGarry and O'Leary (1993), Sisk (1996), Brown (1997), Eller (1999) and Gurr (2000a).
6. Our typology has a strong resemblance to that in Sisk (1996, pp. x–xi), but we have added a second dimension to better structure the discussion about alternative perspectives.
7. I take this point from discussions with Edwin Winckler (personal communication, 1996). See Grofman (1999) for further elaboration.
8. This perspective is closely related to that common in the political economy 'new institutionalist' literature, in which institutions are viewed as game-theoretic equilibria, but we would pay far more attention to considerations of political, military and economic power and considerably less to formal definitions of equilibrium than most game theorists do.
9. There are many variants of new institutionalism in addition to that familiar to economists. While the narrative historical approach, with its emphasis on institutions as organic growths whose understanding requires 'thick description,' tends to be insensitive to our view of institutions as problem solvers, there is a sociological literature on organizations that includes the 'garbage can model' of Cohen et al. (1972) in which problem solving is key, but this literature also tends to emphasize nonsystematic and unanticipated consequences of organizational choice and to emphasize the ways in which preferences are shaped by institutions more than the ways in which institutions are shaped by preferences (March and Olsen, 1989).
10. Grofman (2000) matches these problems (not intended to be an exhaustive list) with institutional solutions offered by three different schools of thought: the classic Athenian approach to direct democracy, the Madisonian approach to representative democracy, and contemporary Downsian and neo-Downsian approaches. Each of these traditions tends to address only some of the seven problems identified above.

11. One of the present authors is completing a dissertation that involves a comparative analysis of ethnic conflicts and democratization in Fiji, Guyana, Mauritius, and Trinidad (Stockwell, 2000).
12. In its classic articulation, Seymour Martin Lipset (1959, p. 75) writes, '[t]he more well-to do a nation, the greater the chances that it will sustain democracy.' High levels of wealth provide resources that mitigate the tensions produced by political conflicts. Economic development brings about higher rates of literacy and education, urbanization, and the development of mass media, factors conducive to democracy. A large number of empirical studies have generally supported Lipset's thesis (Diamond, 1992; Lipset, 1994). The strength of the association led Robert Dahl (1971, p. 65) to conclude that it is 'pretty much beyond dispute' that the higher the socioeconomic level of a country, the more likely that it would be a democracy. However, one of the present authors (Grofman) has work in progress casting doubt on this conclusion: arguing that the degree of inequality in the distribution of wealth (and related factors such as levels of citizen literacy) are more important in predicting sustainable democracy than mean GDP per capita *per se* (compare Bollen and Jackman, 1985).
13. However, even scholars who disagree with what my colleague, A Wuffle (personal communication, April 1, 1999), has referred to as the 'doom and gloom' view of the potential for democracy in plural societies would be likely to recognize the importance of other conditioning factors: perhaps, most notably, overall economic productivity and growth, degree of income inequality across ethnic groups, and the demography of ethnicity – with highly fractionalized plural societies generally regarded as having more hopeful prospects for democracy than those in which there is a single dominant ethny and one (or more) major contender(s). For example, work by one of the present authors, Stockwell (2000), argues that there are two critical factors that can operate in plural societies to prevent the consolidation of a unidimensional ethnic politics. The first is demographic/socioeconomic, and has to do with the existence of cross-cutting class cleavages that mitigate the effects of ethnicity, by providing the material basis for ethnic elites to forge and sustain multiclass and multi-ethnic coalitions and strategies. The second is the actions of ethnic elites themselves. Also, students of international relations (see for example, Ganguly and Taras, 1998) have looked at the role of external (uninvolved) players in either helping to resolve or helping to exacerbate ethnic conflict (consider, for example, the present role of the United States in Northern Ireland vs. past US involvement in ethnic conflicts in parts of Africa, such as Mozambique, that became proxies for Cold War conflicts between the US and the Soviet Union).
14. We take the key distinction between power sharing and majoritarian approaches to be the former's emphasis on consensus and full inclusion. We take the key elements of consociationalism to specify a particular form of power sharing (compare Sisk, 1996, pp. 5–6).
15. Under the *alternative vote*, best known for its use in Australia (Wright, 1986; see also various essays in Bowler and Grofman, 2000), voters must rank order their preferences for candidates. If no candidate receives a majority of first preference votes, the candidate with the fewest first preference votes is eliminated and, for those ballots where she was first choice, votes are reallocated to the next candidate on the voter's list. This process continues until some candidate receives a majority of first-place preferences.
16. The *single transferable vote*, also know as the *Hare* system (and, in Australia, as the *Hare–Clarke* system) requires that voters must rank order their preferences for candidates. If there are m seats to be filled and n voters, then winning candidates much receive a *Droop quota* of votes (the greatest integer bound of the quotient $n/(m + 1)$). If no candidate receives a Droop quota of first preference votes, the candidate with the fewest first preference votes is eliminated and, for those ballots where she was first choice, votes are reallocated to the next candidate on the voter's list. This process continues until exactly m candidates have received a Droop quota, or until the pool of eligibles is down to as many candidates as there are seats remaining to be filled.
17. Sisk (1996, p. ix) refers to this dimension as the 'integrative versus consociational' dimension. We prefer the term 'communal' – viewing consociationalism as a particular form of communal arrangement.
18. Parallels between the perspectives of mainstream political science specialists on democracy

such as Arend Lijphart and the approach in Buchanan and Tullock are discussed in Grofman (2000).

19. This book is rich in ideas about institutional design, but despite the fame of the book, a number of these ideas have largely been lost sight of in subsequent research. In our discussion we draw primarily on chapters 15–17 in *Calculus*, in our view the most neglected section of the book. Most of these chapters heavily reflect the ideas of Gordon Tullock.
20. Grofman (2000) suggests that four variables not directly considered by Buchanan and Tullock in *Calculus* are especially good candidates for addition to their select list of key representational variables: equality of treatment of voters, committee structure within the legislature, ease of constitutional amendment, and degree of legislator/legislative accountability. In addition, the domain of governmental action, a central concern of the early chapters in *Calculus* in our view, ought, we think, to be explicitly identified as one of the key variables in determining an optimal form of representation.
21. For convenience we may let N, n, and k be odd.
22. Buchanan and Tullock suggest this variable can take on values as low as $1/n$. These would be minoritarian processes of selection such as use of, say, the d'Hondt list PR method, with its *threshold of exclusion* for a national election of $1/(s + 1)$ (Grofman, 2001).
23. Contrasts in approach between Buchanan and Tullock and Lijphart can be overdrawn. For example, Lijphart (personal communication, 1995), is also concerned about interaction effects, for example, the interaction between the first and third of the variables in Buchanan and Tullock (1962), and takes the view (following the line of argument of John Stuart Mill, as elucidated by Duff Spafford (1985)) that PR is a more truly majoritarian institution than plurality (see discussion of this point in Grofman, 2000).
24. Even Israel remains suspect when Americans are reminded about the second-class status of its Arab citizens and its theocratic self-definition. Only the notion that Israel has been at war with its Arab neighbors (and the despotism of those neighbors) has served to (partially) shield Israel from the natural preference for 'universalism' among American intellectuals. (This preference for universalism is widely shared among the academics who write about ethnic conflict, regardless of their country of origin. For example, a book on the Baltic states by several Danish social scientists (Norgaard, 1996, pp. 188–220) takes Estonia and Latvia to task for failing to integrate the substantial number of Russophones living in those nations, without any recognition of the perspective of the 'natives' that the Russians came there only as 'occupiers,' who lived in Russian-speaking enclaves without ever being part of the 'nation.')
25. We would note, that in today's 'wired world,' with the widespread use of English as a lingua franca, and the remarkable economic success of states such as Taiwan and Singapore, claims about the economic non-viability of very small states seem much less plausible than they once did. But to pursue this topic would take us too far afield from our central concerns in this chapter.
26. On the other hand, secession may be chosen even if a compelling case for it cannot be made. In Czechoslovakia, for example, while potential ethnic conflicts were avoided by the famous 'velvet divorce,' many area specialists regard this as an outcome which was driven more by the relatively self-serving motivations of Czech and Slovak political elites than by strong voter preferences for an ethnically-based separation of the two parts of the country.
27. As Brendan O'Leary put it in one of his comments on the 1999 BBC radio program from which we have previously quoted: 'If borders cannot be adjusted, peoples may be adjusted instead – through genocide or expulsion.'
28. Paul Collier, on the 1999 BBC Radio program from which we have previously quoted, observes: 'Raising the question of borders with me is of course like a red rag to a bull in a sense because I argued in 1992 onwards in Yugoslavia that you would never get a resolution until you opened up the regional borders of the former Yugoslavia. Simply making their regions international borders and claiming that they were now independent countries could not resolve the basic fundamental problems that lay beneath it, and it was a great mistake not to do that. I argued publicly and even more strongly privately, well before the Kosovo war, that there was a deal available to exchange part of Bosnia-Herzegovina, that part round Pale which has simply not become integrated at all in Bosnia-Herzegovina in exchange for letting go the Kosovo Albanians.'

29. The most extreme form of such a fencing-off of ethnies is, of course, ethny-based partition. This was attempted by the British in dividing British India into (primarily Hindu) India and (almost entirely Muslim) Pakistan – with the latter nation having non-contiguous borders that eventually resulted in a successful secession movement that split west and east Pakistan into Pakistan and Bangladesh.
30. In many countries, ethnic territories are 'defended' by tactics ranging from legal enforcement of restrictive covenants to the cross-burnings, beatings and lynchings carried out by 'white-hooded' self-proclaimed protectors of ethnic purity or their latter-day equivalents, to (militarized) state-sanctioned ethnic cleansings.
31. As Muir (1975, p. 103) observed: 'The Bantustans are best interpreted in a political rather than an economic context, and the authorities hope that they will create an illusion of Bantu independence [and] reduce the dangerously high levels of Bantu in the four major South African cities.' According to Muir (1975, p. 103), it was anticipated that 'new industries will be established in white towns bordering the Bantustans, and that the Bantu, leaving their families behind, will live in segregated satellites where they will be deprived of political rights.'
32. However, as Morton Grodzins, one of the leading students of US federalism, once observed: responsibilities across units in federal systems more nearly resemble a 'marble cake' than a 'layer cake' (Grodzins, 1963) that is, domains of responsibility tend to overlap rather than be clearly assigned to either central or state units. Also, we must be careful about reading too much into designations of states as unitary or federal. For example, the Soviet Union purported to be a federal state, yet operated in a centralized manner; the United Kingdom, even before recent devolution of authority to parliaments below the Westminster level, although classified as a unitary state, had in place (albeit suspended) provisions for home rule for Northern Ireland and permitted a separate legal system in Scotland.
33. For more general discussion from a Public Choice perspective of the reasons for choosing federal arrangements see Mueller (1996, chapter 6).
34. For example, the Ceylon Citizenship Act No. 18 of 1948 deprived all Indian Tamils of citizenship in Ceylon, even if they had been born or had lived for a long time on the island (Eller, 1999, p. 124).
35. See Lijphart (1999, Table 10.1, p. 189).
36. But India also has majoritarian electoral rules and certain provisions that allow the central government to assume local power in 'emergencies.'
37. Of course, the plethora of linguistic groups and their geographic dispersion makes it impossible to create 'one language, one state' federalism in India.
38. Also, Maoris may choose whether or not to participate in the communal roll or be enrolled in a geographically-defined constituency.
39. For more general discussion of the Nigeria case see Diamond (1991), Nnoma (1995).
40. Many countries, including those not commonly thought to be communal in character, use proportional allocation rules that implement a kind of 'spoils system' – either formally (as in the Netherlands rule for TV time), or informally (as in the Italian practice of reserving government jobs for those nominated by party representatives of the various parties, in a fashion that was roughly proportional to party strength).
41. In addition, there were 3 communal seats reserved for groups other than native Fijians and Indians, and 1 seat for Rotuma.
42. For details see O'Leary (1999). For discussions of the background to the British–Irish accords see McGarry and O'Leary (1990), O'Leary and McGarry (1993 [1996]), O'Leary et al. (1993).
43. In the 1999 BBC Radio program from which we have previously taken material, Donald Horowitz observes that a constitutional framework should structure incentives and, at the same time, 'leave open an area of uncertainty about exactly how those are going to be pursued.' This sequencing rule for proportional allocations has that feature.
44. The London School of Economics political scientist, Brendan O'Leary, who has served as an adviser to the Labour Party on Northern Ireland was the first to suggest this mechanism (O'Leary et al., 1993) although he proposed using the Sainte Laguë method rather than that of d'Hondt. Subsequently, he (and one of the present authors) learned that this exact mechanism

was not original with O'Leary but had actually been used since the 1950s in allocating ministerial offices to parties in local governments in Denmark (O'Leary et al., manuscript in progress).

45. 'Rights provisions in the German constitution are considered to be possessed of "supraconstitutional" status, a natural law position' (Stone Sweet, 2000, p. 59).
46. Many western scholars have criticized the insistence on language competence in the 'official language' as a prerequisite for naturalization in countries like Latvia and Estonia as 'illiberal' and 'undemocratic.'
47. When 'ethnic conflict is at a nascent stage of tensions, parties may be unwilling to embrace power-sharing practices because they are not sufficiently desperate [for solutions]' (Sisk, 1996, p. xiii), or because they see their own side triumphing at relatively little cost to themselves. 'At a late stage of conflict, after significant violence, enmities may be too deep for parties to share power for mutual benefit' (Sisk, 1996, p. xiii).
48. For example, according to Stockwell (2000) democracy has failed to take clear hold in Fiji not only because insufficient cross-cutting class cleavages among Fijians militated against multiethnic strategies, but because ethnic Fijian elites sought to achieve exclusive Fijian control over the state. Similarly, he argues that democracy failed in Guyana despite the existence of cross-cutting class cleavages because ethnic elites, locked in a power struggle, pursued strategies of ethnic exclusion that provoked ethnic conflict.
49. There remain important discontents among darker-skinned citizens in both Mauritius and Trinidad. In Mauritius, skin color matters even among Afro-Mauritians, in that discontent is greatest among the Africans who are locally referred to as having 'no milk in their coffee,' that is, darker-skinned blacks. Discontent among this group was evidenced by rioting in 1999 following the death in police custody of Kaia, an Afro-Mauritian reggae singer. Afro-Creoles felt marginalized and excluded from three decades of economic growth. They remain the most economically disadvantaged group in Mauritius (News Report on Mauritius, 'The World' National Public Radio, February 25, 1999). Similarly in Trinidad, Afro-Trinidadians (especially those of darker skin) feel that they remain marginalized economically and socially. Demonstrations of discontent came with the Black Power movement of the 1970s as well as the Muslimeen insurrection of 1990 (Stockwell, 2000).
50. Democracy in Mauritius is aided by the fact there is no single majority bloc: the native population is in the minority and the Indian population is divided among Hindus and Muslims. (The country is 68.0 per cent Indo-Mauritian, 27.0 per cent Creole [African Creole, Colored Creole], 3.0 per cent Chinese and 2.0 per cent White [Franco-Mauritian]. Mauritians are largely tri-lingual, speaking French, English and a nativity language.) In Trinidad, there is also arguably no single majority bloc (The country is 40.3 per cent Indo-Trinidadian [East Indian or Indian], 39.6 per cent Afro-Trinidadian [African, Black], 18.4 per cent Mixed [Colored, Doogla, and so on], and 0.6 per cent White, 0.4 per cent Chinese, and 0.7 per cent Other.)
51. We may think of this agreement (in the spirit of the Oliver Wendell Holmes poem) as a 'wonderful one hoss shay.' It may last for a long time or it may fall apart early, but if it is implemented it is likely to be implemented 'all of a piece.' Remove one part and the whole may collapse.

REFERENCES

Almond, Gabriel and G. Bingham Powell (1966), *Comparative Politics: A Developmental Approach*, Boston, MA: Little Brown.

Balinski, M.L. and H.P. Young (1982), *Fair Representation: Meeting the Idea of One Man, One Vote*, New Haven: Yale University Press.

Bollen, K.A. and R. Jackman (1985), 'Political democracy and the size distribution of income', *American Sociological Review*, (50), 438–57.

Bowler, Shaun and Bernard Grofman (eds) (2000), *Elections in Australia, Ireland and*

Malta under the Single Transferable Vote, Ann Arbor: University of Michigan Press.

Brass, Paul (1990), *The Politics of India Since Independence*, Cambridge: Cambridge University Press.

Brown, David (1989), 'Ethnic revival: perspectives on state and society', *Third World Quarterly*, **11** (4), 1–16.

Brown, Michael E. (ed.) (1997), *Nationalism and Ethnic Conflict*, Cambridge, MA: MIT Press.

Buchanan, James M. and Gordon Tullock (1962), *The Calculus of Consent: Logical Foundations of Constitutional Democracy*, Ann Arbor, MI: University of Michigan Press.

Coase, Ronald H. (1937), 'The nature of the firm', *Economica*, **4**, 386–405.

Cohen, M.D., J.G. March and J.P. Olsen (1972) 'A garbage can model of organizational choice', *Administrative Science Quarterly*, **17**, 1–25.

Crawford, S. and E. Ostrom (1995), 'A grammar of institutions', *American Political Science Review*, **89** (3), 582–600.

Dahl, Robert (1971), *Polyarchy: Participation and Opposition*, New Haven: Yale University Press.

Davidson, Chandler and Bernard Grofman (eds) (1994), *Quiet Revolution in the South: The Impact of the Voting Rights Act, 1965–1990*, Princeton, NJ: Princeton University Press.

Deutsch, Karl W. (1953), *Nationalism and Social Communication*, Cambridge, MA: MIT Press.

Diamond, Larry, (1991), 'Nigeria's search for a new political order', *Journal of Democracy*, **2**, 54–69.

Diamond, Larry (1992), 'Economic development and democracy reconsidered', *American Behavioral Scientist*, **35**, 450–99.

Diamond, Larry (1999), *Developing Democracy Toward Consolidation*, Baltimore: Johns Hopkins University Press.

Diamond, Larry and Marc F. Plattner (eds) (1994), *Nationalism, Ethnic Conflict, and Democracy*, Baltimore: Johns Hopkins University Press.

Eller, Jack David (1999), *From Culture to Ethnicity to Conflict: An Anthropological Perspective on International Ethnic Conflict*, Ann Arbor, MI: University of Michigan Press.

Frost, Robert (1919), 'Mending Wall', in Louis Untermeyer (ed.), *Modern American Poetry: An Introduction*, New York: Harcourt, Brace & Howe.

Furnivall, J.S. (1948), *Colonial Policy and Practice: A Comparative Study of Burma and Netherlands India*, Cambridge, UK: Cambridge University Press.

Ganguly, Rajat and Ray Taras (1998), *Understanding Ethnic Conflict: The International Dimension*, New York: Longman.

Glickman, Harvey (1998), 'Ethnicity, Elections, and Constitutional Democracy in Africa', in Tim Sisk and Andrew Reynolds (eds), *Elections and Conflict Management in Africa*, Washington: United States Institute of Peace, pp. 37–54.

Grodzins, Morton (1963), *A Nation of States: Essays on the American Federal System*, Chicago: Rand McNally.

Grofman, Bernard (ed.) (1998), *Race and Redistricting in the 1990s*, New York: Agathon Press.

Grofman, Bernard (1999), 'Preface: Methodological Steps Toward the Study of Embedded Institutions', in Bernard Grofman, Sung-Chull Lee, Edwin Winekler and Brian Woodall (eds), *Elections in Japan, Korea and Taiwan under the Single*

Non-Transferable Vote: The Comparative Study of an Embedded Institution, Ann Arbor, MI: University of Michigan Press.

Grofman, Bernard (2000), 'Arend Lijphart and the New Institutionalism', in Markus M.L. Crepaz, Thomas Koelble and David Wilsford, *Democracy and Institutions: The Life Work of Arend Lijphart*, Ann Arbor: University of Michigan Press, pp. 43–74.

Grofman, Bernard (2001), 'Research note: a note of caution in interpreting the threshold of exclusion', *Electoral Studies*, **20**, 299–303.

Grofman, Bernard and Chandler Davidson (eds) (1992), *Controversies in Minority Voting: The Voting Rights Act in Perspective*, Washington, DC: The Brookings Institution.

Grofman, Bernard, Lisa Handley and Richard Niemi (1992), *Minority Representation and the Quest for Voting Equality*, New York: Cambridge University Press.

Gurr, Ted Robert (1993), *Minorities at Risk: A Global View of Ethnopolitical Conflict*, Washington, DC: United States Institute of Peace.

Gurr, Ted Robert (2000a), *Peoples vs. States: Minorities at Risk in the New Century*, Washington, DC: United States Institute of Peace.

Gurr, Ted Robert (2000b), 'Nonviolence in ethnopolities: strategies for the attainment of group rights and autonomy', *PS*, (June), 155–60.

Hamburg, David A. and Richard H. Solomon (1996), 'Forward', in Timothy Sisk, *Power Sharing and International Mediation in Ethnic Conflict*, Washington, DC: United States Institute of Peace.

Hannon, Michael T. and Glenn P. Carroll (1981), 'Dynamics of formal political structure: an event-history analysis', *American Sociological Review*, **46**, 19–35.

Horowitz, Donald L. (1985), *Ethnic Groups in Conflict*, Berkeley: University of California Press.

Horowitz, Donald L. (1991a), 'Ethnic Conflict Management for Policymakers', in Joseph Montville (ed.), *Conflict and Peacemaking in Multiethnic Societies*, Lexington, MA: Lexington Books, pp. 115–30.

Horowitz, Donald L. (1991b), 'Making Moderation Pay: The Comparative Politics of Ethnic Conflict Management', in Joseph Montville (ed.), *Conflict and Peacemaking in Multiethnic Societies*, Lexington, MA: Lexington Books, pp. 451–76.

Horowitz, Donald L. (1993), 'Democracy in Divided Societies', *Journal of Democracy*, **4** (4), 18–38.

Huntington, Samuel P. (1968), *Political Order in Changing Societies*, New Haven: Yale University Press.

Huntington, Samuel P. (1972), 'Foreword', in Eric Nordlinger, *Conflict Resolution in Divided Societies*, Occasional Papers in International Affairs No. 29, Harvard University.

Huntington, Samuel P. (1991), *The Third Wave: Democratization in the Late 20th Century*, Norman, OK: University of Oklahoma Press.

Huntington, Samuel P. (1996), 'Democracy for the Long Haul', *Journal of Democracy* **7** (2), 3–13.

Ishiyama, John and Marijke Breuning (1998), *Ethnopolitics in the New Europe*, Boulder, CO: Lynne Rienner.

Johnston, Alexander (1994), 'South Africa: the election and the emerging party system', *International Affairs*, **70** (4), 721–36.

Kaufmann, Chaim (1997), 'Possible and Impossible Solutions to Ethnic Civil Wars', in Michael E. Brown (ed.), *Nationalism and Ethnic Conflict*, Cambridge, MA: MIT Press.

Kuper, Leo and M.G. Smith (1969), *Pluralism in Africa*, Berkeley: University of California Press.
Lal, Brij (1999), 'Constitutional Engineering in Post-Coup Fiji', Paper presented at the Kellogg Institute Conference on 'Constitutional Design 2000', University of Notre Dame, December 9–11, 1999.
Lijphart, Arend (1968), *The Politics of Accommodation: Pluralism and Democracy in the Netherlands*, Berkeley: University of California Press.
Lijphart, Arend (1969), 'Consociational democracy', *World Politics*, **21** (2), 207–25.
Lijphart, Arend (1977), *Democracy in Plural Societies: A Comparative Exploration*, New Haven: Yale University Press.
Lijphart, Arend (1984), *Democracies: Patterns of Majoritarian and Consensus Government in Twenty-One Countries*, New Haven: Yale University Press.
Lijphart, Arend (1986), 'Proportionality by Non-PR Methods: Ethnic Representation in Belgium, Cyprus, Lebanon, New Zealand, West Germany and Zimbabwe', in Bernard Grofman and Arend Lijphart (eds), *Electoral Laws and their Political Consequences*, New York: Agathon Press, pp. 113–23.
Lijphart, Arend (1991), 'The Power Sharing Approach', in Joseph Montville (ed.), *Conflict and Peacemaking in Multiethnic Societies*, Lexington, MA: Lexington Press, pp. 490–510.
Lijphart, Arend (1992), *Parliamentary versus Presidential Government*, Oxford: Oxford University Press.
Lijphart, Arend (1996), 'The puzzle of Indian democracy: a consociational interpretation', *American Political Science Review*, **90** (2), 258–68.
Lijphart, Arend (1999), *Patterns of Democracy: Government Forms and Performance in Thirty-Six Countries*, New Haven: Yale University Press.
Linz, Juan and Arturo Valenzuela (eds) (1994), *The Failure of Presidential Democracy*, Baltimore: Johns Hopkins University Press.
Lipset, Seymour Martin (1959), 'Some social requisites of democracy: economic development and political legitimacy', *American Political Science Review*, **53**, 69–105.
Lipset, Seymour Martin (1994), 'The social requisites of democracy revisited', *American Sociological Review*, **59**, 1–22.
March, J.G. and Johan Olsen (1989), *Rediscovering Institutions: The Organizational Basics of Politics*, New York: The Free Press.
McGarry, John and Brendan O'Leary (eds) (1990), *The Future of Northern Ireland*, New York: Oxford University Press.
McGarry, John and Brendan O'Leary (eds) (1993), *The Politics of Ethnic Conflict Regulation: Case Studies of Protracted Ethnic Conflicts*, New York: Routledge.
Montville, Joseph (ed.) (1991), *Conflict and Peacemaking in Multiethnic Societies*, Lexington, MA: Lexington Books.
Moore, Barrington, Jr. (2000), *Moral Purity and Persecution in History*, Princeton, NJ Princeton University Press.
Mueller, Dennis C. (1996), *Constitutional Democracy*, New York and London: Oxford University Press.
Muller, Edward N. and Mitchell A. Seligson (1994), 'Civic culture and democracy: the question of causal relationships', *American Political Science Review*, **88** (3) (Sept), 635–52.
Muir, Richard (1975), *Modern Political Geography*, London: Macmillan Press.
Nnoma, Veronica (1995), 'Ethnic Conflict, Constitutional Engineering and Democracy in Nigeria', in Harvey Glickman (ed.), *Ethnic Conflict and Democratization in Africa*, Atlanta, GA: African Studies Association.

Norgaard, Ole (with Dan Hindsgaul, Lars Johannsen and Helle Willumsen) (1996), *The Baltic States after Independence*, Cheltenham, UK: Edward Elgar.

O'Leary, Brendan (1999), 'The British–Irish Agreement of 1998: Results and Prospects', Presented at the Kellogg Institute Conference on Constitutional Design 2000, University of Notre Dame, December 9–11, 1999.

O'Leary, Brendan, Tom Lyne, Jim Marshall and Bob Rowthorn (1993), *Northern Ireland: Sharing Authority*, London: Institute for Public Policy Research.

O'Leary, Brendan and John McGarry (eds) (1993 [1996]) (2nd edition), *The Politics of Antagonism: Understanding Northern Ireland*, Atlantic Highlands, NJ: Athlone Press.

O'Leary, Brendan, Bernard Grofman and Jörgen Elklit (manuscript in progress), 'Divisor methods to facilitate and sequence portfolio-allocation in a multi-party cabinet coalition: evidence from Northern Ireland', School of Social Sciences, University of California, Irvine.

Powell, G. Bingham, Jr. (1982), *Contemporary Democracies: Participation, Stability, and Violence*, Cambridge, MA: Harvard University Press.

Rabushka, Alvin and Kenneth A. Shepsle (1972), *Politics in Plural Societies: A Theory of Democratic Instability*, Columbus, OH: Merrill.

Rae, Douglas W. (1971), *The Political Consequences of Electoral Laws*, (1st edition, 1967), New Haven, CT: Yale University Press.

Reynolds, Andrew (ed.) (1994), *Election '94 South Africa: The Campaigns, Results and Future Prospects*, New York: St. Martin's Press.

Reynolds, Andrew (1999a), *Electoral Systems and Democratization in Southern Africa*, New York: Oxford University Press.

Reynolds, Andrew (ed.) (1999b), *Election '99 South Africa: From Mandela to Mbeki*, New York: St. Martin's Press.

Reynolds, Andrew and Bernard Grofman (1994), 'Choosing an Electoral System for the New South Africa: The Main Proposals', Presented at the Conference on Electoral Reform and Democratization, Columbia Institute for Western European Studies, Columbia University, April 18–19.

Reynolds, Andrew and Ben Reilly (1999), *Electoral Systems and Conflict Management in Divided Societies*, Washington, DC: National Research Council/National Academy Press.

Schmitter, Phillipe C. (1994), 'Dangers and dilemmas of democracy', *Journal of Democracy*, **4**, 57–74.

Shepsle, Kenneth A. (1979), 'Institutional arrangements and equilibrium in multidimensional voting models', *American Journal of Political Science*, **23**, 27–59.

Shepsle, Kenneth and Barry Weingast (1981), 'Structure-induced equilibrium and legislative choice', *Public Choice*, **37** (3), 503–19.

Shils, Edward (1957), 'Primordial, Personal, Sacred and Civil Ties', in Andrew Reynolds (ed.) (1994), *Election '94 South Africa: The Campaigns, Results, and Future Prospects*, New York: St. Martin's Press.

Shugart, Matthew Soberg and John M. Carey (1992), *Presidents and Assemblies: Constitutional Design and Electoral Dynamics*, New York: Cambridge University Press.

Sisk, Timothy (1995), *Democratization in South Africa: The Elusive Social Contract*, Princeton, NJ: Princeton University Press.

Sisk, Timothy (1996), *Power Sharing and International Mediation in Ethnic Conflict*, Washington, DC: United States Institute of Peace.

Sisk, Timothy and Andrew Reynolds (eds) (1998), *Elections and Conflict Management in Africa*, Washington, DC: United States Institute of Peace.

Smith, Anthony D. (1981), *The Ethnic Revival*, Cambridge: Cambridge University Press.
Sørensen, Georg (1998), *Democracy and Democratization: Processes and Prospects in a Changing World*, Boulder: Westview Press.
Spafford, Duff (1985), 'Mill's majority principle', *Canadian Journal of Political Science*, **18** (3) (September), 599–608.
Stockwell, Robert F. (2000), 'Democracy and Ethnic Conflict: A Comparative Analysis of Fiji, Guyana, Mauritius, and Trinidad', Unpublished Ph.D. diss., University of California, Irvine.
Stone Sweet, Alec (2000), *Governing with Judges: Constitutional Politics in Europe*, New York: Oxford University Press.
Thomas, G.M., F. Ramirez, J.W. Meyer and J.G. Gobalet (1979), 'Maintaining National Boundaries in the World System: The Rise of Centralist Regimes', in J. Meyer and Michael Hannan (eds), *National Development and the World System*, Chicago: University of Chicago Press, pp. 187–209.
Van den Berghe, Pierre L. (1967), *Race and Racism: A Comparative Perspective*, New York: Wiley.
Wasswa, Henry (2000), 'By a Huge Margin Ugandans Vote Against Multiparty Politics', *Austin American Statesman* (July 13).
Wright, Jack F.H. (1986), 'Australian Experience with Majority-Preferential and Quota-Preferential Systems', in Bernard Grofman and Arend Lijphart (eds), *Electoral Laws and their Political Consequences*, New York: Agathon Press, pp. 24–138.

APPENDIX 5.1: THE RABUSHKA AND SHEPSLE (1972) MODEL

The plural society perspective is grounded in the work of J.S. Furnivall (1948) and M.G. Smith (Kuper and Smith 1969), but its most systematic application to understanding the problem of achieving democracy in plural societies is Alvin Rabushka and Kenneth Shepsle's (1972) *Politics in Plural Societies: A Theory of Democratic Instability.* Writing in the early 1970s, and trying to explain why a large number of African and Asian plural states failed to maintain democracy following decolonization in the 1950s and 1960s, Rabushka and Shepsle make three simplifying assumptions regarding ethnic preferences. The first is intracommunal consensus: 'the members of an ethnic community perceive and express preferences about political alternatives identically. Thus all members may be represented by identical "ethnic preference functions" ' (p. 67). The second assumption is intracommunal conflict: 'ethnic communities are in disagreement on all issues that face the collectivity' (p. 67). The third assumption is perceptual consensus: 'alternatives are viewed according to a perceptual frame common to all actors . . . [A]mong the various communities, and especially among elites, there is agreement as to what constitutes the set of available alternatives. Moreover, how these alternatives benefit or harm each community is readily apparent' (p. 69).

Rabushka and Shepsle (1972) construct a five-stage paradigm to demonstrate why democracy is inherently unstable in ethnically-divided societies.

The first stage (pre-independence) is marked by elite-level inter-ethnic cooperation. Throughout this period, ethnic differences are submerged by colonial rule (a common enemy) and common aspirations for independence, which explains the early successes of African and Asian democratizing states (pp. 74–5). It is during stage two (post-independence) that strains begin to develop in the multiethnic coalition over the distribution of resources. Politicians respond by generating demand for national issues (for example, development) and remain intentionally ambiguous on communal issues (pp. 76–80). If they do this successfully, the multi-ethnic coalition remains in power.

Stage three (the early period of democratic rule) marks a critical turning point in the democratization process. The state's ability to manage the pressures created during this stage determines whether or not it spirals into a deeply divided society or evolves to become more pluralistic in orientation. During this period, national issues lose their salience, politicians 'fan the flames' of ethnic chauvinism, and ethnic appeals made by outbidders strain the unity of the multi-ethnic governing coalition (pp. 80–82).

According to Rabushka and Shepsle's theory, multi-ethnic coalitions cannot be sustained during stage three because of the actions of outbidders.

Outbidders are ethnic entrepreneurs who adopt extremist ethnic positions designed to advance the interests of a particular ethnic group. The success of outbidders depends on their ability to convince ethnic group members that ethnic extremism is necessary to protect the group from domination by other groups. If their appeals resonate, then outbidders can pressure moderate ethnic leaders to become more extremist by accusing them of 'selling out' their ethnic group. If the ethnic appeals of outbidders do not find a receptive audience, then outbidders will have little impact on the direction of politics in plural societies.

Rabushka and Shepsle suggest that, in most plural societies, outbidders are successful in pushing ethnic elites toward more extreme ethnic positions. The force that underlies their success is the ever-increasing salience of ethnicity. It is during stage four, when ethnicity becomes *the* defining political division, that the governing multi-ethnic coalition disintegrates. In plural societies that have become hyper-ethnicized (where ethnicity defines all political matters), multi-ethnic appeals no longer find an audience. Ethnic elites have difficulties cooperating with each other when forced by outbidders to mend fences in their ethnic communities. When ethnic elites can no longer appeal to multi-ethnic constituencies, they end up falling back on ethnically-based parties, which furthers the 'security dilemma' inherent in a situation of low social trust and intense ethnic division.

During stage four, ever-increasing ethnic salience, the divisive impact of ethnic outbidders, the consolidation of ethnically-exclusive parties, and the breakdown of trust and cooperation among ethnic groups inevitably leads to the creation of an ethnically-exclusive state, where public goods become the preserve of the advantaged ethnic group and ethnicity the criterion for their distribution. The state's inability to ensure the nonexcludability of public goods reinforces ethnic attachments and drives a spiral of deligitimation. Individuals seek out alternative sources of public goods and bases of statehood in their ethnic community. In a vicious cycle, ethnic communalism breeds attitudes of illegitimacy that reduce the states' effectiveness and thereby contributes to greater illegitimacy (pp. 82–6).

For Rabushka and Shepsle, the creation of an ethnically-exclusive state inevitably leads to the fifth and final stage, where democracy collapses and ethnic conflict ensues. Given ever-increasing ethnic salience and deepening ethnic divisions, the actions of outbidders, and the breakdown of multiethnic parties, ethnic movements emerge that demand total control over the state. Driven by concerns for communal self-preservation, ethnic elites exploit the state to secure and maintain ethnic group advantage. Democracy collapses because the temptation for majorities to enhance their power and minorities to seize power by nondemocratic means is overwhelming. The end of democracy is ushered in either shrewdly, through the exploitation of voting rules and methods of representation, franchise qualifications and vote counting, and gerrymander, or blatantly, through disenfranchisement, jailing opposition leaders, deregistration of political parties, forced emigration, militarist interference, and violent intimidation (pp. 86–8).

In addition to empirical support,[1] an obvious strength of the above approach is its delineation of process. By identifying key stages in the democratization process, it focusses our attention on critical junctures and forces that operate to bring about nondemocratic outcomes. Nevertheless, a critical weakness of plural society theory is the fact that it predicts only one outcome: instability and the end of democratic rule. Therefore, plural society theory cannot explain successful democracy outcomes. For example, it cannot explain how Mauritius and Trinidad (defined as plural societies by Rabushka and Shepsle) have managed to sustain stable democratic rule since independence.

NOTE

1. This model appears to be supported by the large number of plural societies that failed to maintain democracy and avoid ethnic conflict from the 1950s to the present. For example, it describes Guyana's democratization process quite well: ever-increasing ethnic salience created a unidimensional politics based on deep ethnic divisions; Guyanese elites played the ethnic card, contributed to increased ethnic salience, turned away from multiethnic accommodation, and constructed an authoritarian regime based on ethnic exclusion and repression (Stockwell, 2000).

6. Fiscal federalism and the Stability and Growth Pact: a difficult union

Fabrizio Balassone and Daniele Franco

1. INTRODUCTION[1]

During the 1990s, the process of integration between EU countries accelerated and monetary union was started. Over the same years, the degree of fiscal decentralisation in EU Member States increased. A process to enlarge the responsibilities of local governments in the management of public expenditure and taxation was set in motion in some countries not organised on a federal basis.[2]

While the European Monetary Union (EMU) renewed interest in institutional reform at the European level, less attention was paid to developments at the national level. The foundation of EMU and the process of national decentralisation had both political and economic motivations. Focusing on the latter, one can see that the two levels of institutional reform share a common denominator in that they aim at creating a more growth-oriented economic environment.

Decentralisation at the national level can foster an efficient allocation of resources. Monetary union can consolidate the progress made with the liberalisation of goods and capital markets. It can also create a wider area of monetary stability and lower uncertainty, thus acting as an incentive to investment.

Traditional theories of fiscal federalism, while pointing to the allocative advantages of local autonomy, stress the need to guarantee both control of national public finances and the possibility of carrying out countercyclical policies at the national level. To that end, the introduction of limits on transfers from the central government and on recourse to market financing by local governments is necessary. These constraints must be flexible in relation to cyclical events and to the need to spread the burden of public-sector investment over several generations. The indications of theoretical work have been confirmed by the legislation adopted in many countries. Variations of the so-called golden rule are often applied. Despite placing constraints on indebtedness, the possibility to compensate possible overshoots over several financial years is almost always permitted. On an annual basis the constraints apply *ex ante* but not *ex post*.

During the debate prior to the launch of EMU, the problem of fiscal regulation was given prominence.[3] Sound public finances were widely considered as a cornerstone in building the credibility of EMU economic policy framework. It has been argued that only a firm commitment to sound fiscal policy can allow a new institution like the ECB to gain credibility about its commitment to stable prices. It was also pointed out that, ultimately, the expected benefits of EMU would only materialise if Member States were able to master public finances. Their past record in this respect was not especially reassuring. At the same time, the loss of monetary sovereignty at the national level makes the availability of the fiscal instrument for stabilisation purposes all the more important. EMU fiscal rules have been designed to reconcile soundness and flexibility. The multi-country nature of the Union and the need to ensure a manageable monitoring procedure made the rules finally adopted less flexible than those adopted in several countries with federal structures;[4] they called for rules to apply to national states, with no reference to local governments.

The two processes of institutional reform, the national and European level, were not co-ordinated. The budgetary rules introduced in the framework of monetary union are based on the consolidated budgets of general governments and the different levels of government are not taken into account. Indeed, given the scale of changes involved, one can hardly imagine how co-ordination could have taken place. The consequences of this lack of co-ordination have not yet been adequately examined. This chapter proposes a first analysis of the compatibility between the degree of decentralisation decided at national level and the budget rules introduced at European level.

Although the operations of all levels of government are relevant to ensure compliance with the European regulations, in fact it is the central government that is responsible for compliance and for paying any penalty in the event of violation. Without suitable regulations, local governments that have the possibility to take on debt could free-ride on the back of central governments. More generally, a potential conflict exists between the constraints placed on national public finances and the flexibility allowed to decentralised public finances.

In those countries that are already organised on a federal basis and in those in which reforms are underway to increase the degree of decentralisation, the need to make national rules conform to the new European context is strong. The level of domestic flexibility must be made compatible with the lower level envisaged in the Stability and Growth Pact. The asymmetry between the responsibilities assigned to the central government and those assigned to regional and local governments must be corrected.

The analysis conducted in this chapter demonstrates the difficulty of reconciling the allocative benefits of fiscal decentralisation with full utilisation of the margins for countercyclical policies offered by compliance with the Pact. In considering possible solutions, particular attention is addressed to the solution proposed in Italy with the introduction of a domestic stability pact. It is pointed out that this solution will need to be substantially improved.

The second section of this chapter briefly examines the propositions which have gained wide consensus in the literature on fiscal federalism and compares the theoretical precepts with the practical solutions adopted in countries with federal structures. The third section summarises the European regulations on public sector budgets and examines their implications for the relationships among the different levels of government at the national level. The fourth section analyses the solution adopted by Italy in the context of increasing decentralisation of responsibility for expenditure and revenues.

2. FISCAL FEDERALISM AND BUDGET CONSTRAINTS

The current structure of national states is the result of a long process of aggregation and disaggregation of different jurisdictions, which over time have yielded some fiscal prerogatives while maintaining others. In recent decades a clear tendency to decentralise responsibility for expenditure and taxation has emerged in many countries (Ter-Minassian, 1997; Wildasin, 1997).

Economic theory also offers reasons favouring decentralised forms of government. Responsibility for the management of services should be entrusted to that level of government whose jurisdiction comes closer to the area in which the services are provided. In this way, supply could be adjusted to the needs and preferences of the citizens of each region, thus allowing closer monitoring of the conduct of elected representatives and competition among local governments to the benefit of citizens.[5] The expenditure functions assigned to each level of government affect the allocation of sources of tax receipts and financial relations between central and local governments.

This section examines the implications, in terms of instruments for controlling indebtedness in situations of decentralised finance, of two types of federation: the first type resembles a union of sovereign states (corresponding to the institutional structure of the European Union); the second is closer to the prescriptions of economic theories on fiscal federalism.[6] The solutions adopted by the leading federally-structured countries are also analysed.

2.1 Budget Constraints in a Situation of Radical Federalism

Let us consider a situation in which local governments enjoy absolute autonomy in matters of public expenditure, taxation and recourse to debt. In this context, the stability of monetary and financial conditions represents a public good to which all local governments contribute by maintaining sustainable budget positions. There is an incentive for each local government to exploit the benefits accruing from the discipline of others without itself complying with the rules (free-riding). This creates a double cost for the other entities: the free-rider's excessive indebtedness can put pressure on interest rates to rise; it can also result in bankruptcies requiring bail-outs.[7]

Before all else, we must ask if market regulations can avoid these kinds of situation. For regulations to be effective, certain conditions have to be met (Lane, 1993):

(a) no government body should have privileged access to the market;
(b) the market must have access to all the information necessary to evaluate the financial reliability of each body;
(c) the bailing-out of troubled bodies must not be allowed;
(d) mechanisms to ensure that entities react to market signals must exist.

These conditions are both very strict and unlikely to obtain simultaneously. In particular, the reaction times of decentralised fiscal authorities may be excessively long, for example when administrators work to short time horizons. It is also difficult to ensure absolute credibility of the ban on bail-outs. Finally, evaluation of the financial situation of a body could be hindered by 'creative accounting'.

Consequently, it may be useful to supplement market rules with the means to control the overall indebtedness of a federation's members. Excluding administrative controls, which require local governments to obtain prior approval of their financial strategies from central governments and which by their very nature are incompatible with a federal structure, two solutions may be considered:

(a) collective management of indebtedness;
(b) the introduction of rules (balanced budget, pre-fixed ceiling for the total deficit, golden rule) and sanctions for non-compliance.

With co-operative solutions, all levels of government must be involved in formulating the objectives of economic policy and be responsible for their attainment. However, these solutions do not eliminate the incentive for opportunistic behaviour. Moreover, co-operation may require protracted negotiations, especially when a large number of bodies is involved, to the detriment of the effectiveness of economic policy.

The introduction of rules also raises various problems, such as the credibility of their rigorous application, in particular for the management of bail-outs, and the possibility of efficient monitoring to avoid forms of creative accounting.

For these reasons an eclectic approach appears useful, one that combines rules with forms of co-operation based on peer pressure. Such an approach must in any case keep account of the need to allow margins of flexibility in order to offset cyclical effects on the budget without adopting pro-cyclical policies and to deal with exceptional circumstances that impact on the recourse to debt.[8]

Considerations of tax-smoothing and inter-generational equity may justify the funding of certain activities through limited recourse to debt. The problem is especially acute in the case of public-sector investment. The realisation of major projects requires a substantial temporary increase in total expenditure; without recourse to debt, this implies a peak in taxation, the intensity of which may lead to the projects being abandoned. In addition, since the benefits of the project may be spread over a long period of time, financing it through taxation would lead to an unfair division of the burden among generations.[9]

2.2 The Economic Theory of Fiscal Federalism

The literature on fiscal federalism is very extensive. A complete survey is beyond the scope of this chapter and we will therefore limit ourselves to summarising the key propositions on which there seems to be broad agreement.

The main advantage of a federal structure is increased efficiency resulting from the decentralisation of allocative functions. On the other hand, a central government can perform the functions of redistribution and macroeconomic stabilisation more efficiently.[10]

The crucial element in the production of public goods is the territorial range of the benefits: each public service should be produced and financed according to the preferences of the citizens residing in the area that enjoys the benefits. This area may coincide with national boundaries or it may be limited to a particular region. The fact that political processes are needed to disclose the citizens' preferences justifies the existence of several administrative jurisdictions.[11]

The redistribution function could also be interpreted as a local public good (Pauly, 1973), with each community being allowed to decide its own level. However, the analogy with the allocative function no longer holds if the effects on the citizens' choice of domicile are considered: where capital and labour are highly mobile, significant differences in redistribution levels may cause 'the rich to flee the poor and the poor to chase the rich' (Musgrave and Musgrave, 1984, p. 514).

A centralised authority for stabilisation is justified by the risk that the impact of built-in stabilisers and expansionary or restrictive measures decided at local level may be diminished or annulled if jurisdictions are closely integrated in economic terms.[12] The co-ordination of decentralised stabilisation policies may also be hindered by incentives for local authorities to behave as free-riders.

By virtue of the functions assigned to it, the central government should have access to the tax bases that are more mobile, more sensitive to cyclical factors and less uniformly distributed. A rigorous interpretation of this criterion would allocate the lion's share of tax bases to the central government. Income and capital transfers are adequate tax bases for redistribution policies. Moreover, income tax is particularly sensitive to the cycle, as is sales tax. Finally, corporate income tax should be allocated to the central government so as to avoid distortions in choosing where to locate productive activities.[13] Local governments would retain only property tax and public utility charges:[14] the former affect tax bases that are not very mobile; the latter permit full application of the benefit principle.

This implies that the revenue sources allocated to local governments may be insufficient to finance the expenditure relevant to the functions assigned to them. It may become necessary to make transfers to decentralised bodies or allow them a share of the central government's tax revenues. If qualitative and quantitative standards affecting the local production of public services are imposed at national level, the need for forms of financial support may increase.

Separating the responsibility for expenditure and its financing weakens the cost–benefit relationship associated with public services, reducing the allocative advantages of a decentralised system.[15] In addition, transfers not subject to predefined limits do not encourage efficient management;[16] central governments' financial support to local administrations has often been cited as one of the factors underlying the excessive growth in public expenditure.[17] In some circumstances, increases in local government spending can jeopardise macroeconomic stabilisation measures carried out by central governments.

Controls on the managerial efficiency of local authorities and limits on transfers and revenue-sharing are necessary. Just as controlling the indebtedness of local governments in conditions of 'radical federalism' cannot be rigid, nor can controls on transfers. There must be margins to offset the effects of cyclical swings or exceptional events on the budget and to permit tax-smoothing measures. One possibility is to allow recourse to debt, but this raises the problems already indicated in Section 2.1.

2.3 Fiscal Federalism in Practice

Reference to western nations provides a wide range of arrangements for the allocation of expenditure and revenue functions and for controls on local government indebtedness.

At the end of the 1980s, the share of central government outlays in total public-sector spending ranged from 41 per cent in Canada to 95 per cent in Paraguay (Ahmad et al., 1997). The allocation of expenditure functions among the different levels of government partly reflects theoretical indications: in several cases the territorial range of the benefits seems to be the criterion (most countries assign defence, foreign affairs and international trade to the central government but local transportation, firefighting and city police services to local governments). Central governments are generally responsible for redistribution. However, responsibility for particularly important expenditure functions, such as healthcare and education, is not predominantly assigned to any given level of government.

The contribution of local governments' own revenues to total public-sector revenue also varies greatly: in the early 1990s, in the industrialised countries, it ranged from 3 per cent in the Netherlands to 49 per cent in Canada (Norregaard, 1997). The solutions adopted are often based on theoretical indications: in general, property taxes are assigned to local governments, while corporate taxation is assigned to central governments (in relation to the different degree of mobility of the respective tax bases); income and sales taxes are assigned to the central government, on account of their sensitivity to the cycle and of the redistributive function of income tax.

There are three means of covering any imbalances between local governments' revenues and spending: sharing in central governments' tax revenues; transfers; and indebtedness. The importance of controlling local government spending is confirmed by widespread dissatisfaction with the utilisation of funds transferred from central governments (Ter-Minassian, 1997): varying kinds of organisational structures have been criticised, from 'conditional' transfers for healthcare and transportation utilised in Italy, to unconditional transfers for Medicaid and support of large families in the United States, to transfers based on full reimbursement of expenses for healthcare and higher education in Canada.

Recourse to debt is generally permitted. The industrialised countries rarely rely on market regulation alone; Canada is the only country that does not have provisions to limit the provinces' debt or other central government controls.[18] Brazil had relied on market regulation in the past, but in 1996 it introduced controls following the rapid accumulation of debt by the local governments. The market model was also not effective in Argentina. In Australia and the Scandinavian countries, central and local governments co-operate in defining the objectives for national public finance. Pre-determined regulations are in force in the United States, Spain and Switzerland. Germany utilises a combination of rules and co-operation. The rules generally limit the total deficit, permit indebtedness for certain objectives only or set a ceiling on expenditure for interest payable. The constraints on indebtedness generally apply *ex ante*: possible overshoots may be compensated for in subsequent financial years.[19]

Direct administrative controls are particularly widespread in non-federal states.

3. EUROPEAN TAX REGULATIONS AND THEIR IMPLICATIONS FOR NATIONAL LEGISLATION

3.1 European Balance Sheet Regulations

The model of European Union created by the Treaty of Maastricht is similar to the radical federalist system described in 2.1 above: member states have retained virtually total sovereignty in questions of expenditure and taxation.

A simple formalisation of the no-rules risk

The risk of free-riding posed by a Monetary Union without budgetary rules[20] can be represented in terms of simple games such as 'prisoner's dilemma' or 'hawks and doves'.

For the sake of simplicity, let us suppose there are only two member states (I and J) and that the game is perfectly symmetrical. The tax regime of each state produces a benefit (B) and carries a cost (C) – with B > C – and the benefits are divided equally between the two states, so that the outcome for each is B – C provided both are co-operative. If one country is not co-operative it will incur no costs but will continue to receive its part of the benefits produced by the other's co-operation (with the result B/2), while the other country will reap B/2 – C only. If both countries are not co-operative, each will obtain D (Figure 6.1).

If the order of possible outcomes is B/2 > B – C > D > B/2 – C the game is

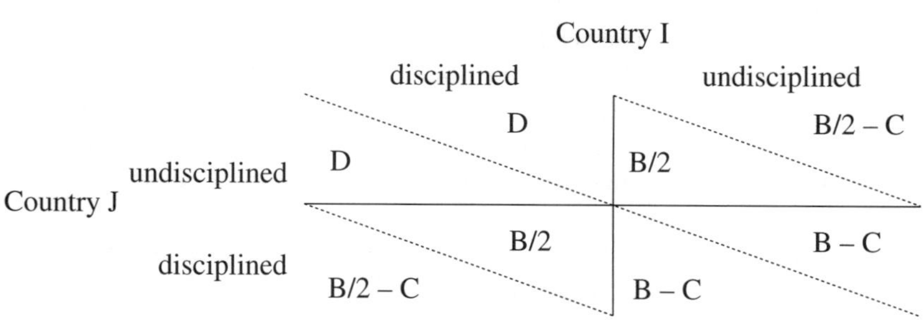

Note: [a]The outcome obtained by Country J is shown beneath the diagonal dotted lines; that obtained by Country I is shown above.

Figure 6.1 A general game at EU level[a]

		Country I: undisciplined	Country I: disciplined
Country J	undisciplined	D – S / D – S	B/2 – C / B/2 – C
	disciplined	B/2 – C / B/2 – C	B – C / B – C

Figure 6.2 A sanction is introduced

a prisoner's dilemma. If the order of possible outcomes is B/2 > B – C > B/2 – C > D the game is hawks and doves.

In the prisoner's dilemma the uncooperative strategy wins over the co-operative strategy (by guaranteeing a better outcome regardless of the other player's strategy) so that both countries have an incentive to adopt it. An equilibrium is thus the result of both countries adopting an uncooperative strategy. In hawks and doves there is no dominant strategy (non co-operation gives higher utility when the other player is co-operative but not when he is not); the game yields two equilibria in pure strategies; both imply the defection of one or the other players.

In this context sanctions (S) may change the result to make the co-operative strategy dominant (Figure 6.2). In the above example the sanction must comply with the stricter of the two restrictions: S > D – (B/2 – C) and S > – (B/2 – C).

The solution adopted

The problem of potential incentives for fiscal disobedience has been addressed at the European level and a series of rules, procedures and sanctions has been identified. Specifically, the Treaty of Maastricht sets quantitative ceilings for the government deficit and the public debt (of respectively 3 and 60 per cent of GDP) and envisages sanctions for wayward states; the Stability and Growth Pact approved in Amsterdam in June 1997 spelled out the objectives, control procedures and sanctions in greater detail.[21]

The Pact commits Member States to pursue the medium-term objective of 'a budget close to balance or in surplus'. The European Council later clarified that this objective should be achieved over the duration of the economic cycle.[22] The Pact may thus be considered as an attempt to reconcile counter-cyclical policies and sound public finances.[23]

Each state must define a budgetary target for the neutral phase of the cycle. In practical terms this means defining a cyclically-adjusted budget balance[24] around which the unadjusted balance fluctuates by virtue of built-in stabilisers and discretionary measures, if any. The further this balance lies below the 3 per cent ceiling, the greater is the margin available for countercyclical policies without incurring excessive deficits.[25]

The choice of a medium-term target for the neutral phase of the cycle is dictated mainly by three factors: (a) the depth of expected recessions; (b) the elasticity of the budget in relation to the cycle;[26] (c) the size of the discretionary measures that may be taken to enhance the impact of built-in stabilisers. Past experience suggests that in the majority of EU countries a cyclically adjusted deficit of between 0 and 1 per cent of GDP should make it possible for built-in stabilisers to become fully operative without incurring a risk of overshooting the 3 per cent ceiling (Buti et al., 1998).[27]

Any state with an excessive deficit is required to adopt corrective measures according to a fixed timetable. Failure to comply brings sanctions. Specifically, the country must pay a non-interest-bearing deposit equal to 0.2 per cent of GDP plus one-tenth of the difference between the 3 per cent ceiling and the actual deficit (up to a maximum of 0.5 per cent of GDP). For each successive year that the deficit is judged to be excessive only the variable component of the sanction must be paid.[28] Should the excessive deficit persist, the deposit is converted into a fine after two years.[29]

To the monetary costs of sanctions must be added their consequences in terms of loss of reputation, which could translate into the inclusion of a higher risk premium in yields on government securities. The approach taken is therefore actually less flexible than the solutions adopted in some federally structured countries:

(a) the rules are defined on the basis of established numerical parameters;
(b) *ex post* compliance with the parameters is required each year;
(c) margins of flexibility are envisaged only in connection with exceptional cyclical events (established *ex ante* as a decline in GDP) or in any case events beyond the governments' control;
(d) no margin of deficit is specifically reserved for investment expenditure;[30]
(e) monitoring procedures are envisaged, starting with an announcement of targets in special multi-year programmes (whose consistency with the rules is evaluated) and continuing with a mid-year examination of public finances and *ex post* verification of results;
(f) peer pressure is strengthened by the European Council's power to make formal representations to governments of the need to adopt corrective measures during the year;
(g) non-compliance triggers the application of pre-established monetary sanctions;

(h) overshoots must be rapidly dealt with; sanctions increase as situations of excessive deficit persist.

The public nature of the whole procedure can contribute to the efficacy of the control exerted by the market on governments' budgetary policies.

3.2 Implications of National Legislative Frameworks

The above rules apply to national governments. More specifically, compliance with budgetary rules is evaluated in respect of general government as defined in the European System of Accounts (ESA), that is, including central government, local governments and social security funds.[31] EU documents do not assign specific responsibilities to local governments.

While compliance with the rules involves the behaviour of all levels of government, it is effectively the central government that is held responsible and that bears the costs of non-compliance. It is, in fact, the European Council that ensures co-ordination of the general economic policies of the Member States and it is a representative of each Member State at ministerial level, authorised to commit the government of that Member State to sit in the Council.[32] Obviously, each Member State is free to define the necessary procedures and regulations to ensure co-ordination between different levels of government.

To understand the consequences of this asymmetry in a scenario in which decentralised levels of government enjoy some measure of independence in their budgetary policies, another example based on games may be helpful. Let us suppose that there is only one local government agency (LG) and that fiscal compliance by both local (LG) and central (CG) governments produces a benefit B at cost C, which is split equally between the two levels of government. Let us then suppose that the same benefit can be produced by CG's fiscal compliance alone, in which case, while the benefit is split equally between CG and LG, the cost C is borne wholly by CG. Lastly, let us suppose that LG's compliance does not produce any benefit by itself (the cost C of this fruitless effort is borne entirely by LG) and that the outcome when CG is non-compliant is D.

The table of outcomes for this game is shown in Figure 6.3. LG's dominant strategy is undisciplined (as $D > D - C$ and $B/2 > B/2 - C/2$). This situation can be interpreted as an extreme example of the incentive problem encountered in a federation in which the responsibilities for expenditure and taxation are separated. According to the arrangement of outcomes, CG may find it expedient either to comply or not to comply (the outcomes of the two equilibria resulting from CG's choice are indicated in bold type): the general government may turn out undisciplined, or CG may ensure compliance while LG plays the free-rider. If $D < [(B/2) - (C/2)]$, in other words if CG achieves a

		Local Government	
		undisciplined	disciplined
Central Gov.	undisciplined	**D** **D**	D – C D
	disciplined	**B/2** **B/2 – C**	B/2 – C/2 B/2 – C/2

Figure 6.3 The federal game at national level

better outcome when both governments are disciplined than it would by being uncooperative, the situation is one in which some form of control over local government deficits could usefully be introduced. The introduction of a sanction H (H > C) in the event of LG being undisciplined would alter the matrix, as shown in Figure 6.4, making LG's dominant strategy to co-operate (as D – H < D – C and B/2 – H < B/2 – C/2) and shifting the equilibrium to one of full co-operation (in bold type).

Monetary Union introduces two modifications with respect to the matrices in Figures 6.3 and 6.4:

(a) the cost of fiscal co-operation increases because the definition of co-operation is narrower than that used at the national level (in terms of both sanctions and the reference period for defining co-operation);
(b) the pay-off of strategies change, on account of the externality generated by the choices of other Member States.

Let us suppose that the new cost level is K (K > C) and that the externality is such as to determine an expected increase in the outcome achieved by CG in

		Local Government	
		undisciplined	disciplined
Central Gov.	undisciplined	D – H D	D – C D
	disciplined	B/2 – H B/2 – C	**B/2 – C/2** **B/2 – C/2**

Figure 6.4 The effects of control over local deficits

		Local Government	
		undisciplined	disciplined
Central Gov.	undisciplined	**D + E** / **D – H + E**	D + E / D – K + E
	disciplined	**B/2 – K** / **B/2 – H**	B/2 – K/2 / B/2 – K/2

Figure 6.5 The federal game at national level after EMU (without 'European' sanctions)

the event of non co-operation (from D to D + E) while leaving unchanged the outcome achieved by CG in the event of co-operation.[33] The new game table is shown in Figure 6.5.

In this environment the effect of national controls (the sanction H) may be cancelled by the higher cost of discipline (if K > 2H, LG's dominant strategy becomes 'undisciplined'). Moreover, the combined effect of the higher cost of co-operation and of the changed outcome determined by externalities may render undisciplined the dominant strategy for CG too (if D + E > B/2 – K/2). Again there are two possible equilibria (in bold type in Figure 6.5): general government may turn out to be undisciplined (a situation consistent with that described in Figure 6.1 in Section 3.1 above), or CG may ensure overall discipline while LG free-rides.

The sanctions envisaged in the Pact can be explained as a means of preventing some states (those where the equilibrium of the federal game at national level implies non co-operation) from free-riding at the expense of others. If sanctions are borne only by CG, the prevention of free-riding at EU level will not solve the problem at national level: a review of national controls is also needed (sanction H). This outcome is shown in Figure 6.6, in which the sanction introduced in the Pact (S, S > D + E + K – B/2) affects only the outcome that can be achieved by CG, which is obliged to allow LG to free-ride in order to ensure overall co-operation.

To conclude, the Pact increases the need for mechanisms to control decentralised governments. Two considerations, in particular, could render national rules inadequate:

(a) European regulations are generally speaking more restrictive than those adopted at national level; the resulting higher costs of co-operation could lead to national penalty systems becoming inadequate and to a conflict between the constraints on national public finances at the European level

		Local Government: undisciplined	Local Government: disciplined
Central Gov.	undisciplined	D + E − S; D − H + E	D + E − S; D − K + E
	disciplined	**B/2 − K**; **B/2 − H**	B/2 − K/2; B/2 − K/2

Figure 6.6 The federal game at national level after EMU (with 'European' sanctions)

and the flexibility allowed to decentralised institutions at the national level. For example, the level of local government investment prior to the Pact in countries applying the *golden rule* may determine excessive deficits;

(b) the allocation of responsibility for compliance with EMU fiscal rules among central and local governments and of the possible costs incurred because of non-compliance is asymmetrical; in the absence of adequate national rules, local governments that are able to contract debts could act as free-riders on the back of the central government.

3.3 Possible Solutions

In principle three strategies appear possible: the duplication of European rules at the national level; the amendment of existing legislative frameworks; the introduction of a market for 'deficit permits'.

Extending the Stability and Growth Pact to the national level

This solution poses several problems:

(a) if the bodies to be disciplined are too small in economic terms, it could be difficult to measure GDP and in any case the meaningfulness of available data (in regard to mobility of factors of production, for example) would be affected;

(b) the high number of bodies involved could make monitoring particularly costly. The evaluations needed for the cyclical adjustment of budgetary data could be especially problematic, as could those necessary for a case-by-case examination of 'exceptional' circumstances to justify excessive deficits;

(c) the financing of local investment expenditure through local taxation could pose particular problems, especially where unusually costly projects could lead to expenditure peaks.

The extension of European rules to the larger decentralised governments only (that is, in Italy, the Regions) could be a solution provided smaller decentralised governments have only limited autonomy; otherwise the cost of adjustment would merely be shifted from the central government to the larger local governments.

Adapting existing regulations at the national level

This approach cannot take the form of an introduction of administrative controls on the indebtedness of decentralised governments. As stated earlier, this solution would be in clear conflict with the spirit of a federal set-up.

Amendments would have to be aimed at allowing recourse to debt financing for both structural reasons (for example public-sector investment) and cyclical reasons (for example the absorption of cyclical effects on the budget).

Control systems in place in some states address these two aspects by setting flexible ceilings to the deficit: on the one hand the ceilings exclude capital expenditure (the golden rule); on the other hand they are applied only on an *ex ante* basis and if the deficit overshoots the ceiling the overshoot can be compensated in subsequent financial years: in some cases (for example some American states) the deficit overshoot must be financed through recourse to specially constituted 'rainy day funds', without recourse to the market.[34]

In the new scenario created by European regulations, these solutions appear most easily adaptable to structural aspects, in other words the financing of investment, while the cyclical aspect appears more complex. In both cases credible sanctions would have to be established to deal with non-compliance.

With regard to the structural aspect, adoption of the golden rule would have to be flanked by an overall ceiling on investment expenditure by local governments. When setting this limit, the need for the overall cyclically adjusted general government budget to be in balance or close to it would have to be taken into account: any deficits allowed to decentralised units would have to be compensated by a general government surplus with a generous enough margin to allow for the countercyclical measures.

Moreover, rules would have to be drawn up to define the criteria for allocating among decentralised bodies the overall deficit allowed for investment programmes. To this end, given the difficulties of defining an adequate reference parameter (population, amount of infrastructure, overall receipts, and so on) a co-operative approach could be contemplated. By involving decentralised governments in the process of defining overall budgetary targets, they would acquire greater responsibility for behaving consistently with the pursuit of the targets set and reaching agreement on the allocation of resources. The peer-pressure incentive for compliance generated in a co-operative framework could be strengthened by allocating any sanctions handed down by the EU among those agencies responsible for overshooting.

With regard to the absorption of cyclical effects on the budget, the application of ceilings that are valid only *ex ante* is clearly in contrast with European legislation, which as we have seen is based on *ex post* limits. On the other hand, the introduction of strict budgetary constraints that are valid *ex post* is problematic, since it would distort the allocation of resources (to the detriment of the more flexible expenses) and force decentralised units to adopt procyclical policies.

The establishment of rainy day funds could be a solution, though it would imply a review of the ESA accounting rules for calculating budgetary indicators. Under current rules transfers of resources to such funds are not included among the disbursements that comprise net indebtedness, nor is the use of such resources included among receipts; in neither case do movements of money through these funds alter the size of the deficit. The accumulation and use of these funds would have to be entered respectively under expenditure and receipts in the General government account; only in this way would their use avoid overshooting the 3 per cent threshold.[35]

A market in deficit permits

The thesis that the problems of externalities might be solved by creating appropriate ownership rights and allowing free trade in them was first put forward by Coase (1960). Casella (1999) suggested taking this approach to the question of fiscal discipline within the EMU. Comparing the negative externality produced by members running excessive deficits to that of pollution, this article suggested using the machinery developed in environmental economics.[36] With reference to the Italian domestic stability pact (Section 4), the Commissione Tecnica per la Spesa Pubblica (an experts' committee on public expenditure) raised the possibility of introducing a system of deficit permits for local and regional governments in its 1998 paper.

Once the overall ceiling[37] on permits and their initial allotment is set, market incentives would produce, through free trade, the most efficient allocation in relation to the financial needs of the various governments in any given year. The total volume of permits issued could be related to the national economic cycle, so as to allow both a 'structural' margin for investment and a variable margin to absorb the cyclical impact on the budget. Deficits above the amount fundable by the permits would result in a cut in the permits assigned the following year. The financial market could also be involved in the discipline by prohibiting borrowing or bond issues lacking debt permit coverage.

The system described is subject to three main difficulties. First, efficacy requires that the deficits of the various governments generate the same externality and are thus perfect substitutes. But the risk of triggering a financial crisis is not uniform across governments. If this risk were the function of a single variable, for example the level of debt, then one would merely have to make the value of the deficit permits of the governments inversely proportional to their stock of debt. However, the risk depends on a number of factors,[38] and determining the value of the permits held by each government is complicated.

Second, the efficiency of the market in permits depends on how competitive it is. This makes the mechanism ill-suited to situations in which the number of governments is small (within the EMU there would be just eleven players, and vastly different in size at that).[39]

Finally, there is no easy solution to the problem of determining the initial allotment of permits. The possible criteria (GDP, population, and so on) would produce greatly differing allocations. If the demand for permits exceeded the supply, then the countries with an allotment greater than their requirement would enjoy positional rents.

The first two objections appear more cogent for a permit market among Member States at EMU level than for one among local governments within each country. Presumably the risk connected with each entity's deficit is more uniform within than between countries: the size of the governments is smaller, and in many cases they have only recently acquired the power to issue their own debt. The number of market operators would be vastly greater. Of course, so extensive a market could entail higher administrative costs.

The third difficulty, which is strictly political, would be encountered at the national level as well. It would be compounded, at least initially, by local governments' problems in adapting to the new machinery for the allotment of resources.

Apart from these difficulties, the permit system seems better suited to financing investments than to buffering the budgetary effects of the business cycle. In the investment area, trading in permits could certainly contribute to greater efficiency in resource allocation. The financial needs connected with investment projects could be planned, and the realisation of works modulated, as a function of available resources. As to the cyclical effects, however, the initial allotment would necessarily be based on forecasts of national economic developments; the emergence of a discrepancy in the course of the year could result in overdemand for permits, which would penalise the governments of areas where cyclical performance was especially poor.

An overview

Each of the three solutions has drawbacks. Replicating the Stability Pact at national level is impeded by lack of the necessary data. Leaving room to buffer cyclical effects on local government budgets without compensating action by the central government (which would give local governments an incentive for opportunistic behaviour) requires solutions that are inconsistent with the ESA95 accounting rules. The formation of a deficit permit market faces the difficulty of finding an equitable criterion for the initial allotment of permits and that of the dubious ability of local governments to adapt to the new context.

In light of these problems, a combination of actions could usefully be evaluated.

(a) A domestic stability pact would appear to be feasible for the larger local government bodies (in Italy, the Regions), for which the problem of lack of data is solvable.
(b) The need to spread investment costs over a number of years could be addressed (albeit with the difficulties recalled above) by recourse to either market mechanisms or the application of rules.
(c) To buffer cyclical effects, the best solution appears to be the institution of reserve funds. As noted, however, this would require the revision of the European rules for national accounts.

4. ITALY: THE DOMESTIC STABILITY PACT

Some EU countries are faced with the necessity of adjusting relations between central and local government to the new European framework. Measures for budgetary co-ordination between the various levels of government are under study in Austria, Belgium and Germany.

Italy has taken a first step in this direction with the domestic stability pact introduced with the 1999 budget. This action was all the more necessary as a result of the decentralisation begun in the early 1990s. Decentralisation has brought a gradual transition from 'derived' regional finances, in which virtually the entire regional budget consisted of rigidly earmarked central government transfers, to fundamentally 'autonomous' financing, with revenues derived from regional taxes and percentage shares in certain central government taxes and their allocation increasingly left to regional decision.

4.1 Decentralisation

The main steps in regional decentralisation have been: the attribution to the Regions of health service contributions and automobile taxes in 1992; the abolition of state transfers (except for those for the health fund, for natural disasters and for purposes of major national interest), offset by the assignment to the Regions of a share of the excise tax on petrol and the institution of an equalisation fund (1995); the attribution to the regions of a new tax (the regional tax on productive activities, IRAP) and of a personal income tax surcharge (1997); the assignment of additional responsibilities under the 'Bassanini' Law (1997–98). Finally, Law 133/1999 envisages the abolition of health fund transfers, the assignment to the Regions of new shares and surcharges in central government taxes (petrol excises, VAT, personal income tax) and the redefinition of the financing and utilisation of the equalisation fund.[40]

Local government autonomy has also been enhanced. The main changes have been: the institution of the municipal real estate tax (1992); the reorganisation of minor local taxes (1993); the abolition of the municipal tax on professional activities and those on municipal concessions, offset by a share in IRAP (1997); the reorganisation of the system of central government transfers (enacted in 1996, with implementation however postponed to 2000); and the institution of a municipal surcharge on personal income tax (1998).

The transition to more pronounced forms of decentralisation has become a major political issue. The possibility of a federal reform of the Constitution has been broached by a number of observers.[41]

Within this general framework, before the domestic stability pact, the limits on local authorities' borrowing were set by a 'golden rule' (borrowing to finance current expenditure was prohibited) with an indirect ceiling (debt service could not exceed 25 per cent of own revenues). Frequently, however, there was unlimited year-end coverage of deficits (in the health and transport sectors, for instance) by the central government.

The emerging trend in institutional arrangements implied:

(a) a comparatively high degree of decentralisation;
(b) high sensitivity of local government revenues to the economic cycle;
(c) relatively lax constraints on indebtedness.

The analysis set forth earlier shows the risks that such arrangements entail for the observance of European budget rules.

4.2 The Domestic Stability Pact

The domestic stability pact is designed to involve the Regions and other local authorities in the effort to attain the objectives for general government budget under the European Stability and Growth Pact (see Ferro and Salvemini, 1999). The domestic pact requires local bodies to reduce deficits and their stock of debt.[42] The deficit referred to (DI) is the difference between total revenues (E) net of state transfers (T) and total expenditure (S) net of investment (K) and interest payments (I):[43]

$$DI = (E - T) - (S - K - I)$$

The definition differs widely from the European definition (DE), which is simply the difference between total revenue and total expenditure:

$$DE = E - S$$

The two definitions also differ in accounting rules. The domestic stability pact adopts a cash basis, while European rules, based on ESA95, refer to the accruals principle.

The target for the first three years of the domestic pact, beginning in 1999, is an annual reduction in the total deficit of local governments equal to at least 0.1 per cent of GDP. In the absence of data on local GDP, the contribution of each district is proportional to the level of primary current expenditure (S – K – I).[44]

The local governments' accounts will be monitored in the course of the year for consistency with the annual target. However, no sanctions for non-compliance are provided. The State–Region and State–Commune conferences will decide on any corrective measures. In 1999 the only consequence of detection of a potential overshoot was the proposal to increase the size of the reduction planned for 2000.

If Italy is sanctioned under the excessive deficit procedure, the fines will be levied on the entities that failed to meet their targets, in proportion to the part of the overshoot for which they are responsible.

An evaluation

The domestic stability pact is essentially a rule imposing deficit reduction on local authorities. It is based on an extended version of the 'golden rule' (interest payments too are excluded from the deficit[45]) with an indirect ceiling (the previous law limited the deficit to a level that would produce debt service payments not exceeding 25 per cent of own revenue[46]). In practice, carrying annual deficits forward appears possible. The eventual correction of yearly budget overshoots is entrusted to a co-operative mechanism (the conferences).

This set of rules is marked by a series of inconsistencies and lacunae:

(a) While the objective is deficit reduction, each government's contribution is correlated not with the deficit but with primary current expenditure. Thus if one region's budget is balanced or in surplus while another's is in deficit but the primary expenditure of the former is greater than the latter's, it would paradoxically have to make a larger contribution to the adjustment.

(b) Ultimately, the aim of the pact is to contain the relevant deficit for European purposes (DE). Taking a different budget variable (DI) as an intermediate objective makes it impossible to estimate the implications of local government targets for observance of the European rules. Specifically, it could be that the difference between the two balances (K + I – T) records an increase that more than offsets the reduction in the pact's reference balance (DI).

(c) Usually the golden rule excludes only investment spending from the reference deficit. Interest expenditure always forms part of the balance, the aim being to amortise the cost of public works over a number of years and thus share the burden among the generations that enjoy the benefits.

(d) Though the pact sets the objective of reducing local government debt, it introduces no machinery to assure its attainment. Reduction of the pact's reference deficit (which excludes major budget items, including interest expenditure) does not actually guarantee that net new borrowing will diminish. Furthermore, the debt ceiling imposed by the previous legislation based on the ratio between debt service and own revenue seems a weak instrument given increasing local taxation powers and relatively low interest rates.

(e) The pact divides a possible European sanction among the various government authorities in proportion to the share of the overshoot for which each is responsible. This formulation does strengthen the incentive for deficit reduction, but it also has certain undesirable characteristics. It would be better to impose sanctions for failure to achieve the deficit objective even if Italy is not fined at the European level. Apart from the fact that such conduct constitutes free-riding, failure to punish it could narrow the scope for national countercyclical measures within the 3 per cent ceiling. Moreover, if the overshoot is confined to a small number of governments, the size of the fine could be too large for credibility.

Certain features of the pact, moreover, appear ill-suited to strengthen Italian discipline consistently with the observance of European rules:

(1) even if recouped in the years following, any local government budget overshoots must be made good immediately by the central government;

(2) the problem of cyclical effects on local budgets is not dealt with (at a time when the devolution of tax base makes local government budgets more sensitive to macroeconomic conditions).

5. CONCLUSION

Our analysis underscores the problems inherent in the combination of increasing fiscal decentralisation within the EU Member States with rules set at

European level to guarantee sound public finances at national level and leave scope for countercyclical policy measures.

Specifically, we highlight the difficulty of reconciling full achievement of the allocative advantages of fiscal decentralisation with full exploitation of the scope for countercyclical policy action offered by compliance with the Stability and Growth Pact.

We have noted: (a) the reduced flexibility of the European approach compared with solutions adopted in federally structured states; (b) the asymmetry between the responsibilities laid on national and local governments by European rules (compliance with the rules depends on the conduct of all levels of government, but *de facto* it is the central government that is answerable to the EU and that must pay the price for non-compliance); (c) the consequent need for stricter controls over local governments to prevent free-riding; and (d) the difficulty of finding fully satisfactory solutions.

Devising appropriate solutions is hard for a number of reasons: (a) the mechanical extension of the Stability and Growth Pact is feasible only for the larger local bodies; (b) allowing local bodies to amortise investment expenditure over a number of years entails significant problems, whether market mechanisms or predetermined rules are used; (c) the best way (that is the use of a reserve fund) of buffering the effect of the economic cycle on local government budgets requires revision of the EU rules for national accounts.

The relevance of these difficulties is confirmed by the analysis of the Italian case. During the 1990s, institutional reforms increased the scope for decentralised decision making and the cyclical sensitivity of local government revenues was increased. But lax constraints on indebtedness were not removed. A domestic stability pact was introduced in 1998 so that these arrangements would not impede compliance with EMU budgetary rules. The domestic pact is essentially a rule requiring local governments to reduce their deficits. Our analysis has revealed a number of problems that require significant modifications of the pact's procedures and incentive structure.[47]

Both EMU and decentralisation at the national level represent cases of institutional overhaul. In this context, it is not surprising that full co-ordination between the two levels of reform has not been achieved. Prompt action is required to avoid a conflict between the two strands of reform which would endanger the economic benefits expected from both.

NOTES

1. A previous version of this chapter was published in *Journal of Public Finance and Public Choice*, No. 2–3, 1999, pp. 137–65.
2. In this chapter, the term federalism has been attributed a broad meaning. With regard to the significance of the term federalism and the classification of the various institutional structures

that can be defined federal, see for example Brosio (1996), Forte and Cerioni (1996) and Patrizii (1998).

3. For a review of this debate and, more generally, of the institutional and policy issues posed by EMU, see Brunila et al. (2001) and the papers there included.
4. The rules are defined in relation to numerical parameters that also have to be observed *ex post*; flexibility is envisaged only in connection with exceptional cyclical events or others beyond the control of governments; a monitoring procedure was introduced that provides for the formulation of multi-year financial programmes and the possibility formally to recommend corrective measures during the course of the year and to impose monetary sanctions in cases of default.
5. For a critical analysis of these indications, see Fausto (1996 and 1999).
6. The distinction made in this chapter is comparable to the more common one between confederations and federations.
7. Somewhat similar problems arise with regard to fiscal competition, that is, the introduction of preferential tax treatment in order to attract tax bases. On this subject, see for example Smith (1996).
8. The solution adopted by the European Union includes these features (see Section 3.1).
9. See Balassone and Franco (1998) and the references therein. For an analysis of the problems connected with public-sector investment within the framework of the Stability and Growth Pact, see Balassone and Franco (2000).
10. The principal bibliographical reference is Musgrave (1959). For an updated discussion of the problem of the allocation of expenditure functions, see Ter-Minassian (1997).
11. One difficulty arises from the fact that it is rare for public services to coincide with territorial divisions: theoretically, it could be necessary to provide as many jurisdictions as there are services to be produced. There are also problems in relation to free-riding and the difficulty of expressing preferences (see Olson, 1965, and Arrow, 1951). Solutions to these problems have been suggested (for example, Tiebout's 'voting with the feet', 1956). The classic reference on the optimal size of jurisdictions is Buchanan (1965); for an updated analysis, see Cornes and Sandler (1995).
12. The importance of these considerations for the allocation of stabilisation functions in the European Union tends to increase as the markets gradually become more closely integrated.
13. The assigning of mobile tax bases to decentralised governments also risks encouraging fiscal competition (see, for example, Smith, 1996).
14. The difficulty of evading taxes on natural resources makes them suitable to decentralised levels of government. However, the fact that the central government is responsible for their allocation among the different jurisdictions argues in favour of their attribution to the latter.
15. See, for example, Buchanan (1967) and Oates (1972).
16. The structuring of transfers so as to provide useful incentives is one of the most complex elements in the theory of fiscal federalism. Cullis and Jones (1992) offer a review of the budget constraints determined by different types of transfer. Garcia-Milà et al. (1999) stress the risks associated with heavy reliance on central government grants, especially when institutions make it difficult for the central government to avoid a regional government expectation of higher future grants in response to increased borrowing.
17. King (1984) examines explanations of the so-called 'fly-paper effect' (that is the fact that an increase in central government transfers causes an increase in local public-sector expenditure that is greater than that which would result from an equivalent increase in personal income); see also Oates (1979). For the implications of programmes in which the benefits are geographically concentrated and financing is met by general taxation, see Weingast et al. (1981).
18. The Canadian experience seems to suggest that there are large lags in the effects of market controls: despite a significant deterioration in its rating and a subsequent increase in risk premium, the debt of the Canadian provinces consistently increased for years before corrective budget policies were introduced (Ter-Minassian and Craig, 1997).
19. This, for example, is the case of the United States; for a detailed analysis, see McGranahan (1999).
20. For references to this risk, see among others: Canzoneri and Diba (1991), Allsopp and Vines (1996), Artis and Winkler (1999), Eichengreen and Wyplosz (1998).

21. For a review of the reasons adduced for introducing the Pact and an analysis of its potential macroeconomic implications, see European Commission (1997), Artis and Winkler (1997) and Eichengreen and Wyplosz (1998).
22. This interpretation is supported by the Resolution of the European Council of 16–17 June 1997, in Council Regulation no. 1466/97 of 7 July 1997 and in the Opinion of the Monetary Committee of 12 October 1998, later adopted by the Council.
23. Balassone and Monacelli (2000) emphasise the risk that the rules concerning the debt hinder the reconciliation proposed in the Pact. For an overview of the issue of fiscal sustainability in the context of EMU, see Banca d'Italia (2000).
24. We use the definitions given by the IMF, the OECD and the European Commission: budget corrections apply only to automatic reactions (that is, those determined by current legislation). For a methodological review of the methods for estimating structural balances, see Banca d'Italia (1999).
25. The Treaty establishes that the deficit may not exceed 3 per cent of GDP unless (a) exceptional circumstances obtain (these may include a recession leading to a reduction in real GDP of at least 2 per cent); (b) it is close to 3 per cent; (c) the overshoot is absorbed in the short term. These three conditions render the 3 per cent ceiling particularly strict (see Buti et al., 1997).
26. The term 'elasticity' is commonly used in preference to the term 'semi-elasticity' to indicate the ratio between the absolute change in the deficit/GDP ratio and the percentage change in GDP.
27. These figures are based on European Commission estimates for the period 1960–97 (a maximum output gap averaging 4 percentage points; average budget elasticity equal to 0.6). The choice of medium-term target should reflect the need to cover adverse circumstances other than those connected with the economic cycle (for example increases in interest rates), to reduce the public debt and to deflect pressures on spending generated by demographic trends. On this point, see the Opinion of the Monetary Committee of 12 October 1998, later adopted by the European Council.
28. The fixed component is intended to discourage excessive deficits, while the variable component is an incentive to limit their amount. The German Finance Minister, Theo Waigel, had initially proposed a deposit equal to 0.25 per cent of GDP for each point – or fraction thereof – between the actual deficit and the 3 per cent ceiling. This would have produced discontinuities in the application of sanctions and could, furthermore, have pushed the latter to politically unacceptable heights.
29. If no corrective measures are adopted, the sanctions can be applied in the same year in which the deficit is judged to be excessive.
30. No distinction is made in the Treaty between current and and capital expenditure for the purposes of determining the deficit. The volume of capital expenditure is included only among the relevant factors to be borne in mind when deciding whether there is excessive debt.
31. See Article 2 of the Protocol on procedures for excessive debt.
32. See Articles 145 and 146 of the Treaty establishing the European Community, as amended by the Treaty on European Union of 7 February 1992.
33. In other words it is assumed that an uncooperative state will benefit from other states' co-operation while not being penalised by their defection, whereas a co-operative state will not only benefit from other states' co-operation but also bear the cost of other states' defection.
34. See McGranahan (1999) for the US experience.
35. These operations would nevertheless have to be excluded when evaluating cyclically adjusted budgetary positions.
36. An early suggestion of a market in pollution permits is Dales (1968); later a vast literature has developed; for a discussion of the benefits and limitations of the approach see Baumol and Oates (1988).
37. The ceiling is needed to prevent the sort of problems cited in Sections 2.1 and 2.3 in relation to the possibility that financial markets can prevent excessive build-up of debt.
38. For instance, the risk may depend on the degree of exposure of the banking system, the degree of international openness, and so on. See among others Eichengreen and Portes (1986), Kharas (1984) and Hernandez-Trillo (1995).

39. The problem could be attenuated by a continuous double auction market (a system used in many financial markets); see Friedman and Rust (1993).
40. The resources should come from shares in central taxes and be distributed, after a transitional period in which allotments are to be based on past spending, according to fiscal capacity. The system of earmarking is to be phased out after a transitional period in which the Regions will be required to allocate to health an amount consistent with their per capita share in the financing of the health service established at national level.
41. See for example Buglione (1998), Fausto (1996), Forte and Cerioni (1996), Giarda (1996), Forum CEIS (1995).
42. Pica (1999) notes 'the anomalous use of the word "pact": the word assumes the existence of a forum in which local governments can agree (have the power to agree) on their conduct, bargaining with the central government. [Actually, however] . . . state law . . . constitutes [a] concrete means of coercion in the desired direction, not consent freely decided' (pp. 1–2; our translation).
43. Revenues are net of the proceeds of sales of financial assets and gross of the proceeds of sales of real estate assets. The same standard is used to calculate the deficit for European purposes.
44. The total correction, estimated at about 2.2 trillion lire, was divided among levels of government in proportion to total expenditure (S). The resulting targets for the individual categories of government were translated into specific objectives for each entity. For the Regions, the reduction was set at 1 per cent of primary current expenditure in 1998. For municipalities and provinces it was put at the larger between 1.1 per cent of primary current expenditure in 1998 and 3 per cent of the current-programmes' deficit for the year. The latter was calculated by each government body by augmenting the 1998 deficit by 80 per cent of the nominal GDP growth forecast for 1999.
45. However, the rule restricting market borrowing to cover only investment spending remains; consistency between the two rules would have to be ensured by state transfers.
46. Another limit is implied by the need to reduce the stock of debt. But no sanctions are provided if the debt increases. Moreover, the relevant definition of debt is not sufficiently well defined, increasing the scope for 'creative accounting'.
47. At the time of its introduction the EU Stability and Growth Pact gave rise to a wide debate. Many participants stressed that it provides no 'reward' for countries that are 'virtuous' during cyclical expansions, achieving budget balance or surplus. Bean (1998) observes that 'The problem with the pact as presently framed is that it is *all stick and no carrot*; rewarding good fiscal behaviour in booms rather than, or in addition to, punishing bad behaviour in slumps would surely make better sense' (p. 106). Paraphrasing this critique, one might say that Italy's domestic pact as it presently stands is 'neither stick nor carrot'.

REFERENCES

Ahmad, E., Hewitt, D. and E. Ruggiero (1997), 'Assigning Expenditure Responsibilities', in Ter-Minassian (ed.), pp. 25–48.

Allsopp, C. and D. Vines (1996), 'Fiscal policy in EMU', *National Institute Economic Review*, **4**, 91–107.

Arrow, K.J. (1951), *Social Choice and Individual Values*, New York: Wiley.

Artis, M.J. and B. Winkler (1997), 'The Stability Pact: safeguarding the credibility of the European Central Bank', CEPR Discussion Paper, 1688, August.

Artis, M.J. and B. Winkler (1999), 'The Stability Pact: Trading-off Flexibility for Credibility?', in A.H. Hallett, M. Hutchinson and S. Hougaard Jensen (eds), *Fiscal Aspects of European Monetary Integration*, Cambridge: Cambridge University Press, pp. 157–88.

Balassone, F. and D. Franco (1998), 'Investimenti pubblici e patto di stabilità e crescita: è opportuno introdurre la Golden Rule?', *Politica Economica*, **XIV** (3), 345–76.

Balassone, F. and D. Franco (2000), 'Public investment, the Stability Pact and the Golden Rule', *Fiscal Studies*, **21** (2), 207–29.
Balassone, F. and D. Monacelli (2000), 'EMU Fiscal Rules: Is there a Gap?', *Temi di discussione*, n. 375, July.
Banca d'Italia (1999), *Indicators of Structural Budget Balances*, Rome.
Banca d'Italia (2000), *Fiscal Sustainability*, Rome.
Baumol, W.J. and W.E. Oates (1988), *The Theory of Environmental Policy*, Cambridge: Cambridge University Press.
Bean, C. (1998), 'Discussion', *Economic Policy*, **26**, 104–7.
Brosio, G. (1996), 'Federalismo politico e federalismo fiscale', in E. Giardina, F. Osculati and M. Rey (eds), *Federalismo*, Milan: Franco Angeli, pp. 13–35.
Brunila, A., M. Buti and D. Franco (2001), *The Stability and Growth Pact*, London: Palgrave.
Buchanan, J. (1965), 'An economic theory of clubs', *Economica*, February, 1–14.
Buchanan, J. (1967), *Public Finance in Democratic Process*, Chapel Hill: University of Carolina Press.
Buglione E. (1998), 'Istituzioni e autonomia finanziaria in Italia', in E. Buglione and V. Patrizii (eds), *Governo e governi*, Milan: Giuffrè Editore, pp. 101–55.
Buti, M., D. Franco and H. Ongena (1997), 'Budgetary policies during recessions – retrospective application of the Stability and Growth Pact to the post-war period', *Recherches Economiques de Louvain*, **63** (4), 321–66.
Buti, M., D. Franco and H. Ongena (1998), 'Fiscal discipline and flexibility in EMU: the implementation of the Stability and Growth Pact', *Oxford Review of Economic Policy*, **14** (3), 81–97.
Canzoneri, M. and B. Diba (1991), 'Fiscal deficits, financial integration and a Central Bank for Europe', *Journal of Japanese and International Economies*, **5**, 381–403.
Casella, A. (1999), 'Tradable deficit permits: efficient implementation of the Stability Pact in the European Monetary Union', *Economic Policy*, **29**, 323–61.
Coase, R. (1960), 'The problem of social costs', *Journal of Law and Economics*, **3**, 1–44.
Commissione Tecnica per la Spesa Pubblica (1998), *Razionalizzazione e semplificazione dei documenti e delle procedure contabili*, Documento n. 3, ottobre.
Cornes, R. and T. Sandler (1995), *The Theory of Externalities, Public Goods, and Club Goods*, Cambridge: Cambridge University Press.
Cullis, J. and P. Jones (1992), *Public Finance and Public Choice Analytical Perspectives*, London: McGraw-Hill.
Dales, J. (1968), *Pollution, Property and Prices*, Toronto: Toronto University Press.
Eichengreen, B. and R. Portes (1986), 'Debt and default in the 1930s: causes and consequences', *European Economic Review*, **30** (3), 599–640.
Eichengreen, B. and C. Wyplosz (1998), 'Stability Pact: more than a minor nuisance?', *Economic Policy*, **26**, April, 67–104.
European Commission (1997), 'Economic policy in EMU', *Economic Papers*, nn. 124–5.
Fausto, D. (1996), 'Il federalismo fiscale: un falso rimedio nel caso italiano', *Economia delle Scelte Pubbliche*, n. 2–3, 175–96.
Fausto, D. (1999), *Note sulla teoria economica del federalismo fiscale*, mimeo.
Ferro, P. and G. Salvemini (2000), 'La riforma della pubblica amministrazione e la rilevazione di informazioni per il rispetto dei vincoli del patto di stabilità interno', *Queste Istituzioni*, forthcoming.
Forte, F. and E. Cerioni (1996), 'Proposte teoriche ed operative per il federalismo fiscale in Italia', in E. Giardina, F. Osculati and M. Rey (eds), *Federalismo*, Milan: Franco Angeli, pp. 265–79.

Forum CEIS (1995), *Federalismo, fisco e governo dell'economia*, Perugia.

Friedman, D. and J. Rust (eds) (1993), *The Double Auction Market: Institutions, Theories and Evidence*, New York: Addison-Wesley.

Garcia-Milà, T., T.J. Goodspeed and T.J. McGuire (1999), *Fiscal decentralization Policies and Sub-national Government Debt in Evolving Federations*, mimeo

Giarda, P. (1996), 'Alcune proprietà di un sistema di federalismo fiscale', in E. Giardina, F. Osculati and M. Rey (eds), *Federalismo*, Milan: Franco Angeli, pp. 36–61.

Hernandez-Trillo, F. (1995), 'A model-based estimation of the probability of default in sovereign credit markets', *Journal of Development Economics*, **46** (1), February, 163–79.

Kharas, H. (1984), 'The long-run creditworthiness of developing countries: theory and practice', *Quarterly Journal of Economics*, **3**, 415–39.

King, D. (1984), *Fiscal Tiers: The Economics of Multi-level Government*, London: Allen & Unwin.

Lane, T. (1993), 'Market Discipline', *IMF Staff Papers*, **40**, March, 53–88.

McGranahan, L. (1999), *State Budgets and the Business Cycle: Implications for the federal balanced budget amendment debate*, Federal Reserve Bank of Chicago, mimeo.

Musgrave, R.A. (1959), *The Theory of Public Finance: A Study in Public Economy*, New York: McGraw-Hill.

Musgrave, R.A. and P.B. Musgrave, (1984), *Public Finance in Theory and Practice*, New York: McGraw-Hill.

Norregaard, J. (1997), 'Tax Assignment', in Ter-Minassian (ed.).

Oates, W. (1972), *Fiscal Federalism*, New York: Harcourt Brace Jovanovich.

Oates, W. (1979), 'Lump-sum Intergovernmental Grants Have Price Effects', in P. Mieszkowski and W.H. Oakland (eds), *Fiscal Federalism and Grants in Aid*, Coupe Papers in Public Economics, Washington, DC: Urban Institute.

Olson, M. (1965), *The Logic of Collective Action*, Cambridge MA: Harvard University Press.

Patrizii, V. (1998), 'Rappresentanza ed efficienza in un sistema di governo a più livelli', in E. Buglione and V. Patrizii (eds), *Governo e governi*, Milan: Giuffrè Editore, pp. 17–99.

Pauly, M. (1973), 'Income redistribution as a local public good', *Journal of Public Economics*, **1**, February, 35–58.

Pica, F. (1999), *Fatti ed opinioni in materia di 'federalismo fiscale' italiano*, mimeo.

Smith, S. (1996), 'European Integration and Local Government Finance', in G. Pola, G. France and R. Levaggi (eds), *Developments in Local Government Finance*, Cheltenham, UK, Northampton, MA: Edward Elgar, pp. 273–91.

Ter-Minassian, T. (ed.) (1997), *Fiscal Federalism in Theory and Practice*, Washington, DC: IMF.

Ter-Minassian, T. and J. Craig (1997), 'Control of Sub-national Government Borrowing', in Ter-Minassian, pp. 156–74.

Tiebout C.M. (1956), 'A pure theory of local government expenditures', *Journal of Political Economy*, October, 416–24.

Weingast, B.R., K.A. Shepsle and C. Johnsen (1981), 'The political economy of benefits and costs: a neo-classical approach to distribution politics', *Journal of Political Economy*, **89** (4), 642–64.

Wildasin, D.E. (ed.) (1997), *Fiscal Aspects of Evolving Federations*, Cambridge: Cambridge University Press.

PART II

Institutions and Business Activity

7. The changing institutional form of innovation: from exploiting market power to developing corporate technological capability

John Cantwell

1. INTRODUCTION

In this chapter the Schumpeterian theory of profits and growth through innovation is revisited and recast, with explicit reference to the changing institutional form of innovation during the twentieth century. It is shown how many clues for the restatement and modernisation of Schumpeter's approach can be found in Edith Penrose's theory of the growth of the firm, her 1959 book having benefited from her reading of what for our purposes are the crucial aspects of Schumpeter (1943). The chapter has three sections following this introduction. Section 2 sets out an evolutionary and institutional account of how profits are created through innovation, which is contrasted with the standard interpretation of Schumpeter's theory found in the literature. It is argued that the standard interpretation does not do justice to Schumpeter's theory, but that the original theory requires adaptation in any case to better reflect the means by which capitalist institutions have promoted innovation during and beyond the twentieth century. The third section reviews Penrose's work on the growth of the modern firm, demonstrating how she incorporated Schumpeter's insights into her thinking, and explaining how her approach provides a link between Schumpeter's theory and the modern institutional form of innovation in the large firm. The remainder of the chapter in Section 4 illustrates and elaborates upon the argument through some evidence on the changing form of innovation in large firms in the major industrialised countries during a first phase roughly from 1900 to 1970, and a more recent phase from around 1970 onwards.

It is contended that innovation has relied on the creation of technological or social capability, through problem-solving or learning activities principally within (and between) large firms. The development of new products and processes is the outcome of a path-dependent building upon established capabilities and achievements, by the critical revision of emergent new products or methods and the search for relevant novelty. This insight into the form of innovation is an amalgam of the conclusions of the work of Usher (1954) and Rosenberg (1976, 1982, 1994) on the history of technology, Nelson and Winter (1982) on the evolutionary theory of economic change, as well as Penrose's (1959) theory of the growth of the firm. Thus, innovation depends upon the generation of feasible new capabilities, the operation of which adds new value to the existing circular stream of income, and thereby creates new profits and higher income.

By contrast, the standard interpretation of Schumpeter's theory of profits through innovation focuses upon the quasi-monopoly positions developed in markets by entrepreneurial firms that enjoy first mover advantages. This common approach to Schumpeter's theory renders it understandable within the conventional framework of market-based analysis, in which institutions are discussed only with regard to their role in the process of economic exchange, primarily through markets (or with reference to a hypothetical alternative market in the case of transactions within firms). Since the leading innovators establish a temporary monopoly within some output (product) or input (process) markets they obtain 'super' profits from innovation, typically associated with higher output prices and lower input prices or costs. But this brings us back to issues of the distribution of the circular flow of income, a flow that is sustained through markets, rather than the question of how that flow can be increased over time as new value-generating activities are added into the stream. In other words the standard treatment reduces the means by which profits can be earned through innovation to a matter of the capacity for static appropriability through the exercise of market power, and hence analytically no different to any other kind of 'normal' profits. The relevant markets may be new, but their newness is significant only for its relationship to the scope for temporary monopolies. The distinctiveness of Schumpeter's notion of adding to the existing circular flow of income is lost.

Schumpeter's (1934) original theory of innovative profits emphasised the role of entrepreneurship (his term was entrepreneurial profits) and the seeking out of opportunities for novel value-generating activities which would expand (and transform) the circular flow of income, but it did so with reference to a distinction between invention or discovery on the one hand and innovation, commercialisation and entrepreneurship on the other. This separation of invention and innovation marked out the typical nineteenth century institutional model of innovation, in which independent inventors typically fed discoveries as potential inputs to entrepreneurial firms. After his early work on entrepreneurship, Schumpeter became only too aware of the rise of in-house corporate research and development (R&D) in large firms in the twentieth century, to the extent that the literature now distinguishes his 'Mark I' model of innovation from his 'Mark II' model in which innovation was envisaged as a more routinised process within large firms (Phillips, 1971). The Mark I model is associated with Schumpeter (1934) originally published in 1911, and the Mark II model with Schumpeter (1943). Indeed, this shift in Schumpeter's thinking towards the role of large oligopolistic firms as the key agents for innovation might be thought to reinforce the conventional interpretation of his earlier theory of innovative profits, since these large firms certainly exercise market power, and in what has become known as the 'Schumpeterian hypothesis' Schumpeter himself is now widely believed to have thought in terms of a link running from market power to the extent to which resources are devoted to innovation. However, I argue here that the so-called 'Schumpeterian hypothesis' which links profits based on market power with innovation is a misunderstanding of Schumpeter (1943) which is due to an attempt to recast his insights from within what he labelled traditional theory; and that Schumpeter himself did not revise his earlier theory of profits when advancing his Mark II model, but in fact reiterated his view of the distinctiveness of profits from innovation as opposed to market power, although without working through the implications of endogenous innovation in large firms for his theory.[1] In any case, recent empirical research has cast doubt upon the alleged association between market power, firm size and innovation, and suggests that smaller firms may be highly innovative as well, especially through their interactions with large firms in the same industry (Pavitt et al., 1987; Audretsch, 1995). In other words, the critical contribution of large firms to modern innovation may lie instead in their creation of novel technological capability run by skilled teams and developed through their continual problem-solving activity, which becomes a resource for other firms with which they cooperate as well as for themselves (Loasby, 1998). This alternative perspective returns us to Schumpeter's original emphasis on creating new value-generating activities as a means of searching for higher profits from innovation, as opposed to statically maximising profits by appropriating higher rents from an existing income stream.

In Section 3 of the chapter it is argued that Penrose (1959) relied on an approach to profits and innovation in the firm that implicitly embodies the most important elements of Schumpeter's original theory (that is, the elements which are most important for our purposes), and she explicitly incorporated the role of in-house research and development and endogenous innovation in large firms. As such, she helps us to link together these two aspects and from that vantage point to expand upon Schumpeter's theory of innovation, profits and growth for a modern institutional setting. What is more, as is perhaps better known, she anticipated the recent approach to technological change and the firm with her resource-based perspective on corporate growth. Hence, we can trace to Penrose the foundations of the approach taken here, which aims to connect Schumpeter's theory of innovation, profits and growth to the changing institutional reality of innovation since the start of the twentieth century.

In the final Section 4 we relate our discussion to some evidence of recent studies on the changing institutional form of innovation over the last hundred years. By understanding how profits are created from innovation in an alternative evolutionary way through corporate learning and search processes, it can be appreciated how innovative profits are of steadily rising significance relative to the more traditional kind of profits derived from market power, given the way in which capitalist institutions have evolved during the twentieth century through to today. In the first phase or paradigm in about the first three-quarters of the twentieth century, science-based innovation in large-scale production facilities (as documented by Chandler, 1990) depended upon the capabilities that were associated with the rise of in-house corporate R&D in large industrial firms. Large firms became the key actors in combining the processes of invention and innovation, each individual firm being technologically specialised in a way that reflected the specific profile of corporate technological competence that it accumulated through cumulative path-dependent learning processes. An inter-company variety of capabilities gradually extended the reservoir of social capability for innovation, and hence broadened the foundations for the creation of profits through innovation.

In the most recent phase or paradigm from the latter part of the twentieth century onwards, science-based innovation has been combined with information and communication technologies in computerised and flexible production facilities. Large firms have remained the key actors in the accumulation of technological capabilities, but in an institutional context that now emphasises the economies of scope to be obtained from the fusion of interrelated capabilities, and a new role for the internationalisation of economic activity. Between firms this has taken the form of a growing number of inter-company alliances for the purposes of promoting innovation. Within large firms in-house R&D is increasingly directed to the emergent benefits of corporate technological diversification through novel and more complex combinations, and to the development of technological competence through internal international company networks. These latter international corporate networks for innovation mark a change in the institutional character of multinational firms in terms of how they innovate and organise their R&D. While in the past the internationalisation of firms was mainly a matter of the internationalisation of their markets and hence supporting through adaptation the wider exploitation of their established technological competences, it is now also becoming a matter of the internationalisation of their ability to create technological competences through the combination of geographically distinct lines of innovation. Of course, the greater scope for establishing such international research-based networks has depended upon organisational innovation and new types of managerial capabilities, as stressed by scholars of business strategy. The emergence of institutions that can accommodate successful international integration of corporate innovation implies a shift away from obtaining profits through the exploitation of established capabilities through new positions of market power abroad, towards the creation of innovative profits by building new capabilities through knowledge exchanges and cooperative learning, and thereby utilising cross-border networks for the establishment of new value-generating activities. These recent changes have further reinforced the growing relative importance of innovative profits of the original Schumpeterian or Penrosian kind, when the conceptualisation of innovative profits is suitably reinterpreted to fit the current institutional conditions for innovation.

2. SCHUMPETER'S THEORY OF PROFITS THROUGH INNOVATION REVISITED

Schumpeter (1934) relied on a distinction between two realms of economic analysis, and corresponding to these realms are two different means for creating profits. The first realm is grounded on the circular flow of income, and this is the realm of traditional economic theory focused upon the determination of prices and quantities in the markets that link together the flows of inputs and products. In this realm the economy is most easily analysed as either stationary or as growing at a steady state in the form of a simple reproduction of at least some existing elements of the economy on an expanded scale. Profits derive from positions of market power (some might say from market imperfections), since in perfectly competitive conditions profits would be driven to zero. However, Schumpeter (1943) argued that perfectly competitive markets had never existed and would never exist, so comparisons with this hypothetical state are unhelpful. So let us suppose that there is some irreducible degree of market power inherent in every market in practice, which is then associated with positive 'normal' profits (in equilibrium, leaving aside issues of recession or declining demand and the like). In this traditional context of price and quantity setting in the realm of circulation or markets, an increase in profits to values above the normal must be attributed to a rise in the degree of market power. Now when profits are achieved through the market-based adjustment of prices and quantities by firms that possess the market power to do so, then it is appropriate to use the conventional apparatus for the analysis of profit maximisation and optimisation by rational economic agents. This is the sphere of most mainstream or orthodox economic analysis.[2]

The second realm is that of novelty-creating economic activity which generates new sources of value-adding productive endeavour, and which disturbs the circular flow of income. In this realm growth must be understood as an inherently disruptive rather than as a smooth process, which the later Schumpeter (1943) termed 'creative destruction' (although this term is also often misunderstood, as the disruption referred to relates to the circular flow and established market structures, but the creative process itself is likely to be cumulative and incremental, as argued below and by Cantwell and Fai, 1999). Profits derive from creating new fields of productive activity, given that there is an inertia in the wages of the firms responsible, such that their wage costs only rise with a lag. A traditional theorist might reply here that such profits are still conditioned on the fact that markets do not adjust instantaneously (wages being bid up immediately in the labour market to match higher productivity), but the source of the profits is the creative process that added new value to the income stream – and this type of departure from a hypothetical absence of any kind of market power is highly socially beneficial, since everyone enjoys higher income in the long run as a result. Following successful innovation workers do earn higher wages on average, but only high enough to leave room also for a return to the creation of a collective social capability, which is jointly exercised especially in large firms, and does not initially accrue to the individuals that make up an innovating firm's team. The value created by the collective operation is greater than the sum of the parts, and the individuals concerned could not appropriate a higher return on their own particular knowledge or contribution were they to set up independently, so in this sense there is no market failure or departure from rational behaviour. Increase in profits over and above the normal is not due to an increase in the degree of market power at a given point in time, but rather is due to a continual process of creating new value-adding activities. It is a process of incessant change and improvement despite a tendency within markets for such profits to be subsequently whittled away (were there no further change) through technological competition. The elements of market power in the position of an innovating firm are not the source of the new value, but are rather a coincidental by-product (when viewed from the perspective of the realm of circulation) of the uneven character of the creative process (which stems principally from the realm of production). Given the uncertain and the experimental nature of the process of innovation which follows a course of trial and error including an inevitability of some mistakes (Nelson and Winter, 1982), this second category of profits is best characterised analytically in a framework of a search for higher profits, and not within the standard framework of profit maximisation strictly interpreted (even if stylised as 'long-run' profit maximisation, since this is not achievable as a behavioural strategy in the context of experimentation).

These two different realms of profits, which correspond to two different realms of economic analysis with alternative focuses of attention and corresponding methodologies, can also be linked with two different functions of the firm, as discussed by Penrose (1959) in the early sections of her book. The firm is in part a price and output decision-taker, in which guise it can earn higher profits through increasing its degree of market power, but the firm is also a device for innovation, problem-solving and cumulative learning in production, the incentive for which is to generate higher profits through creating new areas of social or productive capability. While Schumpeter suggested that the first realm of the market-based allocation of resources and coordination could be left to the closed system of Walras and his own contribution was focused instead mainly on the second realm of innovation, for her part similarly Penrose suggested that the first realm could be left to the conventional theory of the firm which was thus set apart from her separate theory of the *growth* of the firm ('so long as it cultivates its own garden and we cultivate ours', Penrose, 1959, p.10) (see Loasby, 2000).

It turns out that both the common misunderstandings of Schumpeter's two primary arguments to which we have referred earlier can be reduced to attempts to recreate his contentions about the source of innovative profits and their relationship to market power within the framework and constraints of the first realm of analysis, when they can only be properly and fully comprehended when placed in their original and more appropriate context of the second realm. His theory of innovative profits depends upon creating new fields of productive endeavour to add to and restructure the established circular flow of income and cannot be understood by means of a simple reference to the building of temporary positions of market power within that circular flow. Likewise, Schumpeter's view that when areas of market power are the occasional effects of a continuous stream of innovation from within large firms, such monopolistic positions in the market are an incidental by-product and not the source of innovative profits, became inverted in the so-called 'Schumpeterian hypothesis' which held that market power is the cause of innovation by providing resources and safeguarding against the potential downside of risk-taking activity. The attribution of the latter idea to Schumpeter (1943) seems to come from a misreading of his Chapter 8 on Monopolistic Practices, in which his criticisms of the notion of perfect competition and its inconsistency with a regime of innovation and creative destruction were taken as an advocacy of the benefits of market power and imperfect markets for innovation, when viewed through the lens of conventional market-based analysis. Instead, Schumpeter's real point was that the very intellectual framework which gave rise to the hypothetical concept of perfect competition as an extreme point on a spectrum of market structures was misplaced when it comes to the analysis of innovation, but this point could hardly be absorbed by those whose objective it was to try and introduce reference to the scope for innovation within the confines of the traditional analysis of market structure and resource allocation. His idea was simply too revolutionary to be taken on board, and so it could only be accommodated partially and hence in the process in a misleading fashion.

So in order to better understand and appreciate the significance of Schumpeter's own view let us allow him to speak for himself. First of all, it is important to understand the context which was set for his chapter on Monopolistic Practices by the preceding Chapter 7 on The Process of Creative Destruction. In a quotation that is now well known amongst evolutionary economists, as part of an effort to show the need for the analysis of a process in its own right and not through the device of comparative statics, Schumpeter (1943, p. 82) says: 'The essential point to grasp is that in dealing with capitalism we are dealing with an evolutionary process. It may seem strange that anyone can fail to see so obvious a fact which moreover was long ago emphasised by Karl Marx.'[3]

The profits that derive from evolutionary processes over time can be best characterised as the outcome of profit-seeking activities, in contrast to the strict notion of profit maximisation which better describes the profits that result from coordinating activities at a given point of time and with given technology; and over the longer term innovative profits are probably more important:

> A system – any system, economic or other – that at *every* given point in time fully utilises its possibilities to the best advantage may yet in the long run be inferior to a system that does so at *no* given point in time, because the latter's failure to do so may be a condition for the level or speed of long-run performance. (Schumpeter, 1943, p. 83)

Crucially, in order to understand how to interpret Schumpeter's subsequent discussion of monopolistic practices (which follows immediately in his book), he goes on to argue that when monopolistic positions are created through innovation they are not intentionally profit-maximising despite any appearance of being so since they are merely one aspect of a wider process of transformation, and so innovation requires competition to be analysed in a fundamentally different framework:

> In other words the problem that is usually being visualised is how capitalism administers existing structures, whereas the relevant problem is how it creates and destroys them . . . However, it is still competition within a rigid pattern of invariant conditions, methods of production and forms of industrial organisation in particular, that practically monopolises attention. But in capitalist reality as distinguished from the textbook picture, it is not that kind of competition which counts but the competition from the new commodity, the new technology, the new source of supply, the new type of organisation . . . (Schumpeter, 1943, p. 84)

Schumpeter claims that with innovation output expands despite restrictive practices, unlike in the conventional account of the effect of monopoly, but this is not because these restrictive practices are themselves the source of the incentive to innovate. In this context the motive for restrictive practices is to facilitate further learning and inter-company knowledge transfer in an environment of rapid change, within which such practices provide some temporary stability so as to be able to introduce new products or processes more gradually (in an evolutionary and path-dependent fashion, learning in the process) and hence more effectively, so as to raise the longer-term growth of output. Thus, any monopolistic price and output decisions in a changing market are a coincidental (and transitory) source of profits, and should be distinguished from the profits due to innovation as such:

> Thus it is true that there is or may be an element of genuine monopoly gain in those entrepreneurial profits which are the prizes offered by capitalist society to the successful innovator. But the quantitative importance of that element, its volatile nature and its function in the process in which it emerges put it in a class by itself. The main value to a concern of a single seller position that is secured by patent or monopolistic strategy does not consist so much in the opportunity to behave temporarily according to the monopolistic schema, as in the protection it affords against temporary disorganisation of the market and the space it secures for long-range planning. (Schumpeter, 1943, pp. 102–3)

This is a quotation which we can be sure does not appear in orthodox references to the Schumpeterian hypothesis, since it disputes the so-called Schumpeterian hypothesis and challenges the very notion of analysing innovation as the outcome of the degree of market power associated with one particular kind of market structure as opposed to another. Schumpeter then goes on to show how the hypothetical regime of perfect competition would be even less desirable with respect to technological dynamism, but he does so in the context of a thorough critique of the conventional market structure framework as a whole, rather than (and indeed explicitly not) to associate innovative profits with market power. From here, in what would become a link with Penrose, Schumpeter argued that the large firm was more an innovator and an organisational device for learning beyond being a price and quantity decision taker, and within innovation (much more clearly than in his first book) he stresses the centrality of technological change in production:

> What we have got to accept is that it [the large-scale establishment or unit of control] has come to be the most powerful engine of that [economic] progress and in particular of the long-run expansion of total output not only in spite of, but to a considerable extent through, this strategy which looks so restrictive when viewed in the individual case and from the individual point of time. . . . Was not the observed performance due to that stream of inventions that revolutionised the technique of production rather than the businessman's hunt for profits? The answer is in the negative. The carrying into effect of those technological novelties was of the essence of that hunt. (Schumpeter, 1943, pp. 106 and 110)

So we have seen that far from abandoning his earlier theory of innovative profits in his analysis of the later phase of trustified capitalism, Schumpeter reasserted that theory and continued to draw a clear conceptual distinction between the profits which are due to the market power of monopolistic or oligopolistic firms and the profits they earn from their capacity to innovate, and indeed to insist on the priority of the latter over the former. However, in this event the original theory was in need of extension in order to accommodate the significance of inter-company technological cooperation as well as competition, and the blurring of the distinction between innovation and imitation to which Schumpeter continued to adhere, but which is by now more obviously unsustainable (since with greater technological complexity imitation requires the related absorptive capacity that comes from innovation, and innovation always incorporates some elements of imitation). In this respect the problem with the original formulation of the theory is that it stresses the need to identify the original sources of innovation as opposed to subsequent imitation in order to determine the distribution of innovative profits, with the initial leaders (innovators) earning the higher share. It is true that a useful recent literature has continued in this tradition to distinguish between 'Schumpeter Mark I' and 'Schumpeter Mark II' technological regimes, according to whether innovations are introduced mainly by new entrants or by established firms (Malerba and Orsenigo, 1995; Breschi et al., 2000). Yet moving beyond this to link innovation with the distribution of profits and growth across firms, a drawback of Schumpeter's approach is that the first mover in a successful innovation does not always perform best.

Empirical evidence indicates that among large firms technological leaders tend to retain leadership positions from one phase of development to another (they are the companies specialised in the fields of technological opportunity), but at the level of the industry innovative profits and technology-based growth are highest the faster that other firms catch up (Cantwell and Andersen, 1996). This suggests that innovative profits are created by 'followers' and not just by 'leaders'. What is more, the technological leaders are not in general the firms that earn the highest profits within the industry or experience the most rapid growth (Teece, 1992; Andersen and Cantwell, 1999). Now none of this need be a problem once we accept that although social capability is created through internal learning processes within firms, such learning is interactive and involves continuous exchanges of knowledge, whether through deliberate cooperation in learning or independent exchanges through licensing, imitation or the like (Cantwell and Barrera, 1998). Defining innovation to be what is new to a firm with its own differentiated area of expertise or what is new to a particular local context rather than as something new to the world as a whole (Nelson, 1993), the most effective corporate innovators are not necessarily the technological leaders whose expertise is focused on the leading edge fields as such. They may be other firms that have found the most productive industrial applications of the leading edge technologies, which applications themselves require further innovation and other supporting capabilities – linked in part to the process of critical revision of new technologies which enhances their workability and effectiveness, as emphasised by Usher (1954) and Rosenberg (1982).

This line of argument is now entirely intelligible in terms of the most recent literature on the evolutionary approach to technological change which has stemmed from the work of Nelson and Winter (1982) and Rosenberg (1982), and in the process rediscovered the contribution of Penrose (1959). In the evolutionary theory of technological change innovation is always context-specific and localised, and so requires the cost of further innovation to be transferred into some other context, but the cost or difficulty of subsequent innovation depends upon the initial degree of technological relatedness or complementarity between the activities (Cantwell and Barrera, 1998), and upon the degree of absorptive capacity in the recipient or imitating firm (Cohen and Levinthal, 1989). When firms have a higher degree of technological complementarity between their profiles of specialisation they will each have a greater absorptive capacity with respect to taking advantage of the knowledge being created by the other, and so they will be better able to mutually make use of technology-based alliances and the external capabilities that can be accessed through inter-firm cooperation (Cantwell and Colombo, 2000). In the network of inter-company interaction in innovation the greatest profits are likely to accrue to the firm with the best fit between initial capabilities and the new field of opportunity, as opposed to the firm that first initiates a new line of innovation. The greatest benefits go not to the 'first to discover' or the 'first to commercialise' a core technology with important implications, but rather to firms whose social capabilities are best adapted to absorb and to further develop and entrepreneurially to apply the new lines of innovation that emerge from the areas of greatest technological opportunity to novel contexts and in new combinations with other branches of (and perhaps more traditional) technology.

According to this view Schumpeter's theory of innovative profits should be retained, but his underlying theory of innovation needs to be strengthened in the modern institutional context. It is not necessarily technological leaders that become the best innovators, let alone the only innovators, but rather the firms that succeed in making the most effective combinations between new and old technologies and uncovering the most conducive new fields of application. Actually, abolishing the hard distinction between innovation and imitation only goes to reinforce Schumpeter's point about the distinctiveness of innovative profits which has been stressed above. Innovative profits should not be understood as the returns to the temporary positions of monopolistic market power enjoyed by first movers, but rather represent a return to the creation of the social capability that enables firms to experiment with new technological combinations and solve the problems that arise in doing so, and hence to learn and to innovate in production successfully.

3. PENROSE ON PROFITS, GROWTH AND PATH-DEPENDENT LEARNING IN LARGE FIRMS

Penrose identified herself clearly with those such as Schumpeter who were mainly interested in the second realm above of innovation, productive experimentation and novel creativity, rather than in the first realm of coordination, exchange and market power. She focused on innovation as the source of profits, which would be achieved through learning to develop new applications of the current resource base of the firm, as opposed to profits due to the market positioning of the firm or the rents achieved through market power. So like Schumpeter before her and Nelson and Winter subsequently, Penrose stylised the firm as a profit-seeker rather than as a profit-maximiser. She argued that in the most successful and longest-standing firms (on which her attention was concentrated) profits were typically desired for the sake of the firm itself, to facilitate a stream of continued longer-term profit creation through the expansion of the firm, by developing and taking advantage of the opportunities provided by the firm's capabilities or resources. Thus, she claimed that the goals of profit-seeking and raising through appropriate investment the long-run rate of growth of the firm became equivalent, since each was derived from the innovative adaptation and extension of the firm's resource base. Echoing Schumpeter's view that innovation is the only reliable basis for longer-term corporate growth as distinct from the shorter-term gains that might be made from monopolistic practices or market power she states: 'Examples of growth over long periods which can be attributed *exclusively* to such protection [market power] are rare, although elements of such protection are to be found in the position of nearly every large firm' (Penrose, 1959, p. 113).

While acknowledging that the firm could create new opportunities through marketing and advertising by better exploiting its established competence as well as through the development of new technological competence, Penrose suggested that such a strategy is only feasible within its existing market areas. To diversify into new areas of specialisation requires the appropriate technological base to do so. In other words she asserted the ultimate primacy of the realm of productive and technological competence over that of exchange and selling relationships, since purely market exploiting activity works only within the confines of an established market area, and so must sooner or later run up against limits. Like Schumpeter she contrasted the attainment of a monopolistic market position and technological progressiveness as conceptually alternative (although in practice quite possibly correlated) routes to profitability and corporate survival. She argued that the seeking of the innovative profits needed for longer-term survival led to a wider range of diversification based on the underlying technological complementarity or relatedness of activities:

> Firms . . . 'specialize' . . . in a much wider sense than the logic of industrial efficiency [cost minimisation and price competition] would suggest, for the kind of 'specialization' they seek is the development of a particular ability and strength in widely defined areas which will give them a special position *vis-à-vis* existing and potential competitors. In the long run the profitability, survival and growth of the firm does not depend so much on the efficiency with which it is able to organize the production of even a widely diversified range of products as it does on the ability of the firm to establish one or more wide and relatively 'impregnable' bases from which it can adapt and extend its operations in an uncertain, changing and competitive world. (Penrose, 1959, p. 137)

Hence, Penrose had little use for her purposes for the standard model of the firm as a price and output decision-taker (the coordination-based theory of the firm), which was not designed for the analysis of a firm that is free to internally vary the kind of products it produces as it grows and to innovate by creating from within new products and processes (as in the capabilities-based approach to the firm, which she effectively initiated). She remarked: 'we will be dealing with the firm as a growing organization, not as a "price-and-output decision maker" for given products' (Penrose, 1959, p. 14).

She goes on to explain how the very nature of the social capabilities of the firm as embodied in its organisational structure is transformed as the technological base of the firm is expanded and increased in complexity. She was especially interested in large successful firms not because she believed them to be representative of the population of firms as a whole (indeed she was careful to distinguish between the two), but rather because it is these large firms that encapsulate a repository of competence for the economy of which they are part, which today we might refer to as social capability but which she termed administrative organisation. Penrose spent some time discussing the relationship between the productive competence of firms and market demand, acknowledging of course that external changes in the structure of demand may be responsible for growth opportunities. However, as noted above she argued that a firm which lacked an adequate technological base would lack the capability to diversify, while conversely a firm with a strong degree of technological competence would find its opportunities for expansion likely to be so prevalent that it would have to choose carefully between many different possibilities of action. Indeed, in a view that anticipates quite well the later Cohen and Levinthal (1989) argument about the role of absorptive capacity, she emphasised that the very ability to perceive opportunities in the firm's external environment (including new market opportunities) depended upon the initial capabilities and resources of the firm:

> I have placed the emphasis on the significance of the resources with which a firm works and on the development of the experience and knowledge of a firm's personnel because these are the factors that will to a large extent determine the response of the firm to changes in the external world and also determine what it 'sees' in the external world. (Penrose, 1959, pp. 79–80)

In this context Penrose referred as well to Schumpeter's contention that new products may be forced on consumers by the initiative of entrepreneurs where the latest fashion or model comes to be desired in its own right, but this is not necessary to understand why she wished to focus on the firm as a repository of capabilities or resources as opposed to the coordination functions of the firm. Rather she believed that innovation-based profitability and growth is essential to the firm's longer-term survival, that it is 'built into' or inherent in the characteristics of every successful firm, and hence that the firm can be most usefully depicted as a device for learning and the posing and solving of new problems in its field of expertise and production. New products and processes are in her view created through learning from the established resources and technological base of the firm, by extending and adapting it for novel purposes:

> Consequently if we can assume that businessmen believe there is more to know about the resources they are working with than they do know at any given point in time, and that more knowledge would be likely to improve the efficiency and profitability of their firm, then unknown and unused productive services [from existing resources] immediately become of considerable importance, not only because the belief that they exist acts as an incentive to acquire new knowledge, but also because they shape the scope and direction of the search for knowledge . . . both an automatic increase in knowledge and an incentive to search for new knowledge are, as it were, 'built into' the very nature of firms possessing entrepreneurial resources of even average initiative. Physically describable resources are purchased in the market for their known services; but as soon as they become part of a firm the range of services they are capable of yielding starts to change. The services that resources will yield depend on the capacities of the men using them, but the development of the capacities of men is partly shaped by the resources men deal with. The two together create the special productive opportunity of a particular firm. (Penrose, 1959, pp. 77–9)

Indeed, Penrose began her book by remarking that there are forces inherent in the nature of firms that induce expansion even if all external conditions remain unchanged, and that the internal interaction between inherited resources and managerial perception is a dynamic process which encourages continuous corporate growth, but which constrains the achievable rate and direction of growth. From all this the centrality to her perspective of capabilities, corporate learning and innovation is quite clear, and as with Schumpeter conceptually separate from issues of market power or other aspects of the exchange and coordination of established products or activities. What is interesting here is not just her linking of Schumpeter's second realm of innovative profits to the resource-based theory of growth of the firm, but also the way in which as a result she depicted the direction of corporate learning and growth as a path-dependent resource-constrained process. In this respect she anticipated current ideas on the evolutionary approach to technological change, and in particular the notions of corporate technological trajectories (Dosi, 1982), corporate technological diversification (Pavitt et al., 1989; Granstrand and Sjölander, 1990; Granstrand et al., 1997) and corporate coherence in diversification (Teece et al., 1994). Anticipating as well the argument of Cantwell and Fai (1999) that since innovation is rooted principally in internal learning within the firm, technological competence evolves gradually and changes much less dramatically than the composition of downstream products or markets, Penrose claimed that each successful firm had a continuity which was provided by its capabilities or resources:

> In practice the name of a firm may change, its managing personnel and its owners may change, the products it produces may change, its geographical location may change, its legal form may change . . . [yet] the identity of the firm can be maintained through many kinds of changes, but it cannot survive the dispersal of its assets and personnel nor complete absorption in an entirely different administrative framework. . . . The general direction of innovation in the firm (including innovation in production) is not haphazard but is closely related to the nature of existing resources . . . and to the type and range of productive services they can render. . . . The Schumpeterian process of 'creative destruction' [of established products] has not destroyed the large firm; on the contrary, it has forced it to become more and more 'creative' [in the adaptation and application of its capabilities]. . . . when it [a firm] develops a specialized knowledge of a technology which is not in itself very specific to any particular kind of product . . . it [research] enables at least the large firms to turn aside the process of 'creative destruction' and to thrive on the novelty which might otherwise have destroyed them. (Penrose, 1959, pp. 22–3, 84, 106 and 115)

As was argued at the start of this chapter (and that has now actually occurred), from here Penrose was led to forecast that there would be an increasing impetus to innovation as the basis for profits (innovative profits, as opposed to profits due to market power) as the role of technological competition rises. However, at the same time she noted that greater technological competition would compel firms to specialise in a narrower range of basic areas of production, since resources would be increasingly tied up in continual innovation which would restrict the rate at which they can diversify their fundamental activities (Penrose, 1959, pp. 106–7). This was a remarkable anticipation of the modern trend towards corporate technological diversification or more properly a restructuring of diverse technological capabilities around the clusters of greatest interrelatedness (Cantwell and Santangelo, 2000), accompanied by greater product concentration (less diversification across products or lines of business activity). However, as was more appropriate to the historical period in which she herself was writing, and to the earlier stages of large firm growth, Penrose tended to stress how technological diversification would in general facilitate and support greater product diversification:

> There is no reason to assume that the new knowledge and services [from corporate exploration and research] will be useful only in the production of a firm's existing products; on the contrary, they may well be useless for that purpose but still provide a foundation which will give the firm an advantage in some entirely new area. (Penrose, 1959, pp. 114–15)

As has now been described in a detailed historical survey by Chandler (1990), and as Penrose had observed from her own collection of case study evidence, for most of the twentieth century large firms grew through a combination of technological diversification from their initial resource base linked to related product diversification, or what Chandler later depicted as the interlinkage between the economies of scale and scope. Penrose indicated as well that the greater market spread that accompanied technological diversification through innovation from within the resource base of the large firm may entail either product diversification or geographical diversification. Hence, industrial diversification or internationalisation could be considered substitutes for a particular firm at a given point in time given the resource constraint upon its overall rate of growth (see Cantwell and Piscitello (2000) for a discussion of how this relationship later shifted from one of substitutability to one of complementarity). However, it should be underlined that for Penrose the substitutability between different types of new market entry was not a result of her trying to focus on the realm of market exploitation rather than competence creation (selecting between alternative ways of exploiting a given competence), but was on the contrary the outcome of her focus upon the nature of competence creation in the specific historical context in which she was writing, at which time any diversification of the basic market area(s) of the firm tended to require a supporting diversification of the firm's technological base. This emphasis upon capability formation from the resource base of the firm rather than market exploitation should already be clear from what has been said of Penrose's central focus upon the firm as a device for innovation and knowledge creation rather than as a means of coordinating established activities. However, she believed that the scope of feasible technological diversification would not only regulate the degree of market spread, but a move into markets that require a complementary technological base may result in positive feedbacks to further innovation. If there were no such feedbacks the long-term rationale for common ownership in the firm would be weak and the character of the investment association between the parts of the enterprise would be qualitatively different than in a coherent corporate group:

> expansion by acquisition does not necessarily, or perhaps even usually, mean that a firm is entering a field for which it would otherwise have no qualifications. Acquisition is often a profitable process precisely *because* the firm has peculiar qualifications in the new field. . . . In some cases [of exceptions in which foreign subsidiaries operate independently of their parents] . . . the acquisition of foreign subsidiaries should be treated . . . simply as an investment akin to investments in financial assets [as a portfolio rather than as a direct investment]. (Penrose, 1959, pp. 129 and 193)

Thus, Penrose asserted the need for coherence in the technological and productive activities of the firm from the perspective of the capacity to continue to innovate and grow as a combined organisation, although not necessarily from the perspective of the pure realm of coordination, which may be instead essentially a financial perspective. In terms of feedback to subsequent growth perhaps Penrose also to some extent anticipated the notion of intra-firm networks of competence creation, but at an international level for cross-border innovative feedback to become fully effective it had to wait for the new historical phase of integrated multinational firms from around 1980 onwards (Cantwell, 1989; Cantwell and Piscitello, 2000).

4. THE CHANGING INSTITUTIONAL FORM OF INNOVATION

Something has already been said of the way in which the institutional conditions for innovation in large firms have shifted since Schumpeter's day, and to some extent since Penrose's early contribution as well, although she said much which anticipated these changes. The importance of this shift in institutional regime has been to reinforce the significance of innovative profits as against the profit and growth strategies associated with market power. Hence, the arguments of Penrose and Schumpeter are still more relevant today than at the time they were writing, once their essential themes are related to the modern context. The two major reasons why innovative profits are now even more relatively important are: first, that innovation has been increased in what modern Schumpeterians such as Freeman (1987) have termed a new techno-economic paradigm, and with a greater intensity of international competition, positions of protected market power are increasingly under threat; and second, the firm must now rely on more complex combinations of related technologies to serve even more narrowly-defined product markets, so relative to some given level of cost of the innovative development of resources the opportunities for establishing downstream monopolistic positions are reduced in this way as well. A by-product of these changes is that inter-company cooperation between large firms is increasingly motivated by the need for mutual technology-based exchanges and coordinated learning relative to the more traditional collusion to secure jointly exercised positions of market power.

Taking a step back for a moment, in the first phase of the growth of large firms that ran up until about 1970, as described by Chandler (1990) there was an interleaving between the economies of scale and scope. Large firms grew by diversifying their technological base, and in the process diversified their product markets in similar proportion, and together this combined diversification supported a rise in the scale of output. An essential plank behind this process was the rapid growth of in-house corporate R&D in the largest firms, as stressed by Schumpeter, which improved their innovative search activities, and their capacity for problem-solving and learning in an age in which science and technology began to become more interdependent with one another. Using the patents that large firms are granted from these problem-solving activities, we can trace their individual profiles of technological specialisation (Cantwell, 1993; Cantwell and Fai, 1999; Cantwell, 2000). What emerges from these studies is that these patterns of corporate technological specialisation are differentiated and firm-specific, that groups from common countries of origin have certain country-specific features in the form of their expertise, and that the profiles of specialisation persist over time, reflecting a path-dependent technological accumulation or corporate technological trajectories.

One other aspect of this empirical evidence on the history of corporate innovation patterns is worth emphasising in particular. This is the relationship between the degree of diversity of technological activity in the firm and the overall scale of technological effort, the latter serving as a proxy as well for the scale of output of the firm since the various measures of size tend to be correlated across firms. It is well established that the degree of diversification rises with size, and we can plot a size–diversification relationship across large firms (size is measured by the total number of patents granted, and diversification by the reciprocal of the coefficient of variation across sectors in the index of corporate technological specialisation – see for example Cantwell and Santangelo, 2000). Now the interesting point is that whether we are working with firms (Cantwell and Fai, 1999) or at the level of countries (Cantwell and Vertova, 1999) for most of the twentieth century the size–diversification frontier did not shift very much. That is, most growth took the form of the joint achievement of increased scale and greater scope through a movement along the frontier as diversification and growth went hand in hand, a statistical confirmation of the case study conclusions of Penrose and Chandler. However, in more recent times the size–diversification frontier has shifted quite markedly (Cantwell and Santangelo, 2000), which shows how the relationship between technological diversification and growth has become less simple than in the past. For firms the size–diversification frontier has tended to shift upwards (so the average extent of technological diversification controlling for size has risen), but it has also shifted rotationally so that the very largest firms have tended to reduce the diversity of their technological profiles. There is now an impetus for firms to achieve a minimum threshold degree of technological diversification to take advantage of greater interrelatedness, but the combinations constructed by the firm must also be coherent enough to focus upon potential linkages in which interrelatedness or technological complementarity is at its highest. At the level of countries instead the size–diversification frontier has shifted downwards, which shows that on average countries have increased the extent of their technological specialisation for any given size (Cantwell and Vertova, 1999). This is likely to be due to the effects of internationalisation of activity, leading locations to become more focused in their efforts while the largest firms span more technological fields and more geographical areas.

The increasing significance for firms of technological interrelatedness and fusion is one aspect of the historical shift mentioned earlier as having been termed a new techno-economic paradigm (Freeman and Perez, 1988). In this context a techno-economic paradigm is a system of scientific and productive activity based on a widespread cluster of innovations that represent a response to a related set of technological problems, relying on a common set of scientific principles and on similar organisational methods. The old paradigm until around 1970 was based on energy and oil-related technologies, and on mass production with its economies of scale and specialised corporate R&D. In recent years this has gradually been displaced by a new paradigm grounded on the economies of scope as distinct from scale, and derived from the interaction between flexible but linked production facilities, and a greater diversity of search in R&D. Individual plant flexibility and intra-company network linkages both depend upon the new information and communication technologies (ICTs).

Part of the reason for the increased extent of technological interactions within and between firms lies in the more sophisticated modern system of production as well in the more intensive linkages between science and technology in the current techno-economic paradigm, which relies on flexibility through computerisation and diversity through new combinations drawing upon a wider range of disciplines. Firms increase the returns on their own R&D through suitably adapting their underlying tacit capability so that they can absorb and apply the complementary knowledge acquired from other locations or from other firms more intensively in their own internal learning process. Technological diversification and internationalisation have become positively related in more internationally integrated multinational corporations (MNCs) since around 1980 (Cantwell and Piscitello, 2000). Apart from the rise in technological interrelatedness, the potential opportunities for cross-border learning within MNCs have been enhanced by an increased take-up of ICTs (Santangelo, 1999). ICT specialisation seems to amplify the firm's technological flexibility by enabling it to fuse together a wider range of formerly separate technologies. In this sense, in the current ICT-based paradigm government intervention is better geared towards the promotion of cross-firm and cross-border knowledge flows (presuming that firms follow the model of a continually interactive search for better methods and improved products, and hence a search for higher profits through experimental innovation in the fashion of Schumpeter and Penrose); rather than to provisions to protect the monopolistic and separate exploitation of knowledge by those that have independently invested in its creation (which could be more easily represented through an underlying model of static profit maximisation by firms through the exercise of market power) (Cantwell, 1999). Yet as stressed above, the theory of innovative profits needs revising in this era of greater technological interrelatedness in which firms must not only sustain an adequate spread of coherent in-house diversification but must be able to access other related capabilities through partnerships. It is not leadership in ICT as such that is likely to count for most, but rather the capacity to blend ICT with other technologies as a means of fusing them together and creating new combinations.

However, the creation of technology may be locationally concentrated or dispersed according to the degree of complexity embedded in it. Some kinds of technologies are geographically easily dispersed, whilst the uncodified character of others makes cross-broader learning within and across organisations much more difficult. Thus, although multinationals have shown a greater internationalisation of their R&D facilities recently, it depends upon the type of technological activity involved. The development of science-based fields of activity (for example ICT, biotechnology and new materials) and an industry's core technologies appear to require a greater intensity of face-to-face interaction (Cantwell and Santangelo, 2000). Nonetheless, it may sometimes still be the case that science-based and firm- and industry-specific core technologies are dispersed internationally. The main factors driving the occasional geographical dispersion of the creation of these kinds of otherwise highly localised technologies are either locally embedded specialisation which cannot be accessed elsewhere, or company-specific global strategies that utilise the development of an organisationally complex international network for technological learning (Cantwell and Santangelo, 1999).

The more typical pattern of international specialisation in innovative activity within the MNC is for the development of technologies that are core to the firm's industry to be concentrated at home, while other fields of technological activity may be located abroad, and in this sense the internationalisation of research tends to be complementary to the home base. Thus, when science-based technology creation is internationally dispersed it is most often attributable to foreign technology acquisition by the firms of 'other' industries – for example, chemical industry MNCs developing electrical technologies abroad, or electrical equipment MNCs developing specialised chemical processes outside their home countries (Cantwell and Santangelo, 1999, 2000; Cantwell and Kosmopoulou, 2002).

Evidence has now emerged that the choice of foreign location for technological development in support of what is done in the home base of the MNC depends upon whether host regions within countries are either major centres for innovation or not (termed 'higher order' or 'lower order' regions by Cantwell and Iammarino, 1998, 2000). Whereas most regions are not major centres and tend to be highly specialised in their profile of technological development, and hence attract foreign-owned activity in the same narrow range of fields; in the major centres much of the locally-sited innovation of foreign-owned MNCs does not match very well the specific fields of local specialisation, but is rather geared towards the development of technologies that are core to the current techno-economic paradigm (notably ICT) or earlier paradigms (notably mechanical technologies) (Cantwell et al., 2000). The need to develop these latter technologies is shared by the firms of all industries, and the knowledge spillovers between MNCs and local firms in this case may be inter-industry in character. Thus, ICT development in centres of excellence is not the prerequisite of firms of the ICT industries, but instead involves the efforts of the MNCs of other industries in these common locations.

It may also be the case that the development of the capability to manage a geographically complex international network lies in a firm's specialisation in ICT. The opportunities created for the fusion of formerly unrelated types of technology through ICT has made feasible new combinations of activities, the best centres of expertise for which may be geographically distant from one another. The enhanced expertise in ICT seems to provide a company with greater flexibility in the management of its geographically dispersed network, and an enhanced ability to combine distant learning processes in formerly separate activities. If this is the case for manufacturing companies in general, it is all the more true for electrical equipment and ICT specialist companies. Affiliate networks are increasingly used to source new technology. Accordingly, global learning has become an important mechanism for corporate technological renewal within MNCs.

The key importance of ICT to the now more complex management of innovation in MNCs is that it enables firms to better exploit their corporate technological diversification across national boundaries (Cantwell and Piscitello,

2000), owing to the role of ICT as a means of combining fields of knowledge creation that were previously kept largely apart (or what Kodama, 1992, terms technology fusion). However, while this use of ICT has led many smaller firms to extend the breadth of their technological diversification to create new combinations, in some of the very largest MNCs the extent of technological diversification has been reduced, so as to better focus on the most promising possible combinations from amongst the broader initial dispersion of innovative activity that such companies have inherited from the past (Cantwell and Santangelo, 2000). Thus, we find some convergence in the average degree of technological diversification across large firms, including amongst others in the pharmaceutical industry (Cantwell and Bachmann, 1998).

Freeman and Perez (1988) had argued that in the latest techno-economic paradigm ICT has become a 'carrier branch' or a 'transmission belt' for the transferral of innovation across sectors, analogous to the role played by the capital goods sector in the mechanisation paradigm in the nineteenth century (Rosenberg, 1976). Company evidence now suggests more than this that ICT has also become a core connector of potential fields of technological development within firms (or between firms in technology-based alliances) that facilitates the technological fusion of a formerly disparate spread of innovative activity. Thus, while in the past the machine-building industry simply passed knowledge of methods from one field of mechanical application to another, ICT potentially combines the variety of technological fields themselves and so increases the scope for wider innovation. Hence, innovation has become a still more central part of corporate development in the ICT age. Internationalisation through the MNC to connect together in a network related streams of locationally specialised innovation, in-house technological diversification and inter-company technology-based alliances, and the corporate development and application of ICT have become intertwined in a new era of innovative capitalism. The perspective of Penrose and Schumpeter on innovation, profits and growth in the large firm has not only stood the test of time, but provides a crucial theoretical backdrop to the analysis of this modern form of innovative and international capitalism.

NOTES

1. My attention was called to this by Richard Nelson's presentation in the plenary session 'Joseph Schumpeter 50 years on' at the International J.A. Schumpeter Society conference held in Manchester in June 2000, in which he argued that there was no evidence of what has subsequently become known as the 'Schumpeterian hypothesis' to be found in Schumpeter's own writings.
2. It should be noted in passing that it is also the sphere of a lot of non-orthodox economic analysis, such as that of Marxists who emphasise the market power of multinational firms, or neo-Ricardians who emphasise the bargaining strengths of capitalists as against workers.

3. In turn, in order to understand the context for this remark it should be recalled that the first four chapters of Schumpeter's book were devoted to an appraisal of Marx, from which there are three points worth noting for our purposes. First, Schumpeter draws a contrast between the evolutionary Marx as an economist and the revolutionary Marx as a sociologist, and believed that it was possible to isolate the evolutionary economic aspects of his work: 'To say that Marx, stripped of phrases, admits of interpretation in a conservative sense is only saying that he can be taken seriously' (Schumpeter, 1943, p. 58). Although Schumpeter's view runs against the whole tenor of twentieth century Marxism, perhaps it might be more readily accepted today. Second, Schumpeter criticises Marx's supposed solution to the question of the origins of profit (surplus value) through the concept of a market for labour power in place of the conventional labour market. But in doing so Schumpeter focuses his attack on Marx's use of this device to explain the creation of absolute surplus value through lengthening the working day or increasing the intensity of work; while arguably the more significant application was how Marx explained the creation of relative surplus value through productivity-raising innovation, and hence introduced the distinction between the two types of profit emphasised by Schumpeter himself. Third, indeed, just as Marx learned much through an intense criticism of Ricardo (as noted by Schumpeter), so Schumpeter appears to have learned much from his detailed critique of Marx, and this is reflected in his own theory of innovation which incorporates many of Marx's insights (on which see Rosenberg, 1976, 1982, 1994). Just as Marx took the parts of Ricardo that he needed and critically demolished the redundant parts that did not fit with his argument, so Schumpeter did the same with Marx.

REFERENCES

Andersen, H.B. and J.A. Cantwell (1999), 'How firms differ in their types of technological competence, and why it matters', *University of Manchester ESRC Centre for Research on Innovation and Competition Discussion Papers*, no. 25.

Audretsch, D.B. (1995), *Innovation and Industry Evolution*, Cambridge, MA: MIT Press.

Breschi, S., F. Malerba and L. Orsenigo (2000), 'Technological regimes and Schumpeterian patterns of innovation', *Economic Journal*, **110**, 388–410.

Cantwell, J.A. (1989), *Technological Innovation and Multinational Corporations*, Oxford: Basil Blackwell.

Cantwell, J.A. (1993), 'Corporate Technological Specialization in International Industries', in M.C. Casson and J. Creedy (eds), *Industrial Concentration and Economic Inequality: Essays in Honour of Peter Hart*, Aldershot: Edward Elgar.

Cantwell, J.A. (1999), 'Innovation as the Principal Source of Growth in the Global Economy', in D. Archibugi, J. Howells and J. Michie (eds), *Innovation Policy in a Global Economy*, Cambridge: Cambridge University Press.

Cantwell, J.A. (2000), 'Technological lock-in of large firms since the interwar period', *European Review of Economic History*, **4**, 147–74.

Cantwell, J.A. and H.B. Andersen (1996), 'A statistical analysis of corporate technological leadership historically', *Economics of Innovation and New Technology*, **4**, 211–34.

Cantwell, J.A. and A. Bachmann (1998), 'Changing patterns in technological leadership – evidence from the pharmaceutical industry', *International Journal of Technology Management*, **21**, 45–77.

Cantwell, J.A. and M.P. Barrera (1998), 'The localisation of corporate technological trajectories in the interwar cartels: cooperative learning versus an exchange of knowledge', *Economics of Innovation and New Technology*, **6**, 257–90.

Cantwell, J.A. and M.G. Colombo (2000), 'Technological and output complementarities, and inter-firm cooperation in information technology ventures', *Journal of Management and Governance*, **4**, 117–47.
Cantwell, J.A. and F.M. Fai (1999), 'Firms as the source of innovation and growth: the evolution of technological competence', *Journal of Evolutionary Economics*, **9**, 331–66.
Cantwell, J.A. and S. Iammarino (1998), 'MNCs, technological innovation and regional systems in the EU: some evidence in the Italian case', *International Journal of the Economics of Business*, **5**, 383–408.
Cantwell, J.A. and S. Iammarino (2000), 'Multinational corporations and the location of technological innovation in the UK regions', *Regional Studies*, **34**, 317–32.
Cantwell, J.A., S. Iammarino and C.A. Noonan (2000), 'Sticky Places in Slippery Space – the Location of Innovation by MNCs in the European Regions', in N. Pain (ed.), *Inward Investment, Technological Change and Growth*, London: Macmillan.
Cantwell, J.A. and E. Kosmopoulou (2002), 'What Determines the Internationalisation of Corporate Technology?', in V. Havila, M. Forsgren and H. Håkanson (eds), *Critical Perspectives on Internationalisation*, Oxford: Penguin.
Cantwell, J.A. and L. Piscitello (2000), 'Accumulating technological competence – its changing impact on corporate diversification and internationalisation', *Industrial and Corporate Change*, **9**, 21–51.
Cantwell, J.A. and G.D. Santangelo (1999), 'The frontier of international technology networks: sourcing abroad the most highly tacit capabilities', *Information Economics and Policy*, **11**, 101–23.
Cantwell, J.A. and G.D. Santangelo (2000), 'Capitalism, profits and innovation in the new techno-economic paradigm', *Journal of Evolutionary Economics*, **10**, 131–57.
Cantwell, J.A. and G. Vertova (1999), 'Historical Evolution of Technological Diversification', paper presented at the Annual Conference of the European International Business Academy, Manchester, December.
Chandler, A.D. (1990), *Scale and Scope: The Dynamics of Industrial Capitalism*, Cambridge, MA: Harvard University Press.
Cohen, W.M. and D.A. Levinthal (1989), 'Innovation and learning: the two faces of R&D', *Economic Journal*, **99**, 569–96.
Dosi, G. (1982), 'Technological paradigms and technological trajectories: a suggested interpretation of the determinants and directions of technical change', *Research Policy*, **11**, 147–62.
Freeman, C. (1987), *Technology Policy and Economic Performance: Lessons from Japan*, London: Frances Pinter.
Freeman, C. and C. Perez (1988), 'Structural crises of adjustment, business cycles and investment behaviour', in G. Dosi, C. Freeman, R.R. Nelson, G. Silverberg and L.L.G. Soete (eds), *Technical Change and Economic Theory*, London: Frances Pinter.
Granstrand, O. and S. Sjölander (1990), 'Managing innovation in multi-technology corporations', *Research Policy*, **19**, 35–60.
Granstrand, O., P. Patel and K.L.R. Pavitt (1997), 'Multi-technology corporations: why they have "distributed" rather than "distinctive core" competencies', *California Management Review*, **39**, 8–25.
Kodama, F. (1992), 'Technology fusion and the new R&D', *Harvard Business Review*, July–August, 70–78.
Loasby, B.J. (1998), 'The organisation of capabilities', *Journal of Economic Behavior and Organization*, **35**, 139–60.

Loasby, B.J. (2000), 'Connecting Principles, New Combinations and Routines: Reflections Inspired by Schumpeter and Smith', paper presented at the Biannual Conference of the International J.A. Schumpeter Society, Manchester, June–July.

Malerba, F. and L. Orsenigo (1995), 'Schumpeterian patterns of innovation', *Cambridge Journal of Economics*, **19**, 47–65.

Nelson, R.R. (ed.) (1993), *National Innovation Systems: A Comparative Analysis*, Oxford and New York: Oxford University Press.

Nelson, R.R. and S.G. Winter (1982), *An Evolutionary Theory of Economic Change*, Cambridge, MA: Harvard University Press.

Pavitt, K.L.R., M. Robson and J. Townsend (1987), 'The size distribution of innovating firms in the UK: 1945–1983', *Journal of Industrial Economics*, **35**, 291–316.

Pavitt, K.L.R., M. Robson and J. Townsend (1989), 'Technological accumulation, diversification and organisation in UK companies, 1945–1983', *Management Science*, **35**, 81–99.

Penrose, E.T. (1959), *The Theory of the Growth of the Firm*, Oxford: Basil Blackwell (reprinted in 1968).

Phillips, A. (1971), *Technology and Market Structure*, Lexington, MA: Lexington Books.

Rosenberg, N. (1976), *Perspectives on Technology*, Cambridge and New York: Cambridge University Press.

Rosenberg, N. (1982), *Inside the Black Box: Technology and Economics*, Cambridge and New York: Cambridge University Press.

Rosenberg, N. (1994), *Exploring the Black Box: Technology, Economics and History*, Cambridge and New York: Cambridge University Press.

Santangelo, G.D. (1999), 'Multi-Technology, Multinational Corporations in a New Socio-Economic Paradigm based on Information and Communications Technology (ICT): The European ICT Industry', Ph.D. thesis, University of Reading.

Schumpeter, J.A. (1934), *The Theory of Economic Development*, Cambridge, MA: Harvard University Press (originally published in German in 1911; reprinted by Transaction Publishers, New Brunswick, New Jersey in 1997).

Schumpeter, J.A. (1943), *Capitalism, Socialism and Democracy*, London: Allen & Unwin (originally published in the USA in 1942; reprinted by Routledge, London in 1994).

Teece, D.J. (1992), 'Strategies for Capturing the Financial Benefits from Technological Innovation', in N. Rosenberg, R. Landau and D.C. Mowery (eds.), *Technology and the Wealth of Nations*, Stanford: Stanford University Press.

Teece, D.J., G. Dosi, R. Rumelt and S.G. Winter (1994), 'Understanding corporate coherence: theory and evidence', *Journal of Economic Behavior and Organization*, **23**, 1–30.

Usher, A.P. (1954), *A History of Mechanical Inventions*, Cambridge, MA: Harvard University Press, 2nd edition.

8. Institutions, entrepreneurship, and growth: biomedicine and polymers in Sweden and Ohio

Bo Carlsson

INTRODUCTION

What are the linkages between institutions, entrepreneurship, and growth? The purpose of the present chapter is to examine the role of institutions in explaining the differences in performance with respect to entrepreneurship and growth in two industry clusters in two countries.

In a series of papers, my colleagues and I have studied the biomedical and polymer clusters in Ohio and Sweden.[1] The main reason for selecting biomedicine and polymers is that these clusters include the fastest-growing industries in both regions over the past two decades. They are also very different in terms of supporting institutions and other infrastructure.

Given the focus in this chapter on institutions, entrepreneurship, and growth, it is desirable to compare regions that can be expected to differ in these dimensions while not being too dissimilar in other dimensions. The differences in economic growth between Europe and the United States over the last two decades makes it interesting to compare regions on both sides of the Atlantic. The diversity within Europe and the US and the difficulty of obtaining data makes it impractical to compare Europe and the United States as a whole. The main reasons for the choice of regions are that Sweden and Ohio are similar in size (population 8.8 and 11.2 million, respectively in 1996), income level ($27 794 GDP per capita in Sweden and $27 240 in Ohio in 1996 at official exchange rates), and industrial history (especially, heavy reliance on engineering and metalworking industries); and that both suffered economic setbacks in the 1980s and 1990s.[2] The fact that Sweden is a country and Ohio a US state raises some problems that will be addressed in the analysis that follows.[3] The location and affiliation of the researchers involved in the project made it possible to collect the detailed information required for the analysis.

In the present chapter, the aim is to examine the institutional differences that have contributed to the differences in economic performance. Even though the industrial history and the composition of industrial output in general are quite similar in the two regions, and even though the Ohio economy is only about 25 per cent larger than that of Sweden, both of these clusters are about twice as large in Ohio as in Sweden. Why have these particular clusters grown faster and become larger in Ohio?

The chapter is organized as follows. We begin with a discussion of the rationale for looking at clusters and why certain economic activities tend to cluster. This is followed by an overview of the biomedical/biotechnology and polymer clusters in Ohio and Sweden and their development in the 1990s. Next, we examine the institutional factors that we have identified in our previous work as important in understanding the differences in industry structure and performance. The concluding section formulates the policy issues to which the analysis gives rise.

CLUSTERING OF ECONOMIC ACTIVITY

In recent years there have been numerous studies of clustering of economic activity, particularly in 'high technology' sectors such as biotechnology and electronics. Clusters may refer to concentrations of activity either geographically or in related sectors and industries, and sometimes both.[4] One of the main advantages of studying clusters of economic activity is that it emphasizes the context, both institutional and otherwise, in which the activity takes place.

Biotechnology is a field in which economic activity tends to be heavily concentrated geographically. Most of the activity in this rapidly evolving field is located in two main areas in the United States – California and the northeastern seaboard from Massachusetts to North Carolina; in two areas in Britain – Oxford and Cambridge; and a scatter of smaller clusters elsewhere in Europe (UK Department of Trade and Industry, 1999). The main reason for this geographic concentration is the strong dependence of economic activity in this domain on academic research which happens to be located in these particular regions (Prevezer, 1997; Zucker and Darby, 1996). Studies have shown that the spillover effects of academic research tend to be highly local in nature (for example, Jaffe et al., 1993); this is certainly true in biotechnology (Audretsch and Stephan, 1996).

If the field of study is broadened to include not only biotechnology (narrowly defined as genetic engineering) but also medical technology more broadly – pharmaceuticals, medical devices, medical instruments and equipment, and so on, referred to here as biomedicine and defined more in detail below – the geographic concentration is no longer as strong. The science base is not as concentrated and clearly defined, and the links to other industries (particularly engineering) exert a stronger influence than in biotechnology (Zucker et al., 1994). Thus, the previously existing industrial activities play more of a role (path dependence). But due to the fact that this broader field is not well defined and cuts across several conventional statistical categories, not much is known about the magnitude, growth, and location of economic activity.

Thus, the biomedical cluster consists of a wide variety of activities in various industries. The defining feature of the cluster is that the goods and services produced all have the same end use: they are inputs in the provision of health care, either directly by patients or indirectly via hospitals, clinics, physicians, and so on.

Similarly to biomedicine, the polymer cluster consists of activities in many different industries. The major applications of polymers are in building materials, fibers and textiles, packaging materials and coatings, transparent and optical materials, biological and medical materials. All of these materials are classified in different manufacturing industries. The common feature which makes it useful to look at these products as belonging to the same cluster is that the same material (polymers) is used.

Thus, neither the biomedical nor the polymer cluster corresponds well to any particular Standard Industrial Classification codes. They represent goods and services as well as technologies and competencies which are produced in many different types of businesses. The supporting infrastructures go beyond the 'industry' in that they encompass entities outside the market process, in addition to firms within the industry and those in upstream and downstream activities.

The fact that both of the clusters are made up of firms in a variety of industries – manufacturing and services – and that these firms represent only a fraction of the total activity in those industries means that it is difficult to identify the population and therefore also to measure the size of each cluster. We ended up using the membership directories of the Edison BioTechnology Center (EBTC) and the Edison Polymer Innovation Corporation (EPIC) in Ohio, while surveys of the Scandinavian plastics industry, the Nordic biomedical industry and the Nordic biotechnology industry were used to gather the data for the Swedish clusters.[5] These data were supplemented with information from the Harris Directory and the Central Register of Firms (Centrala Företagsregistret), respectively. See Carlsson and Braunerhjelm (1999 and 2002) for details.

The measurement problems are even more difficult if we want to examine how the clusters have developed over time. It is easy to measure growth in sales, the number of firms, and the number of employees in the industries which fall entirely within the cluster. But it is not easy to determine how much of the growth in industries whose coverage falls only partially within the cluster should be attributed to firms belonging to the cluster, unless one assumes that the coverage remains the same over time. What we did instead was to examine how much of the total activity (measured in terms of sales, employment, and number of firms) in each cluster in 1996 was attributable to firms established in 1990 or later.

Having identified the population of firms in each cluster in both countries, we then supplemented our data through interviews with a sample of firms. Through previous studies (especially Carlsson and Braunerhjelm, 1999) we had also identified the other actors in supporting activities and interviewed a sample of them as well. In total, 43 interviews were conducted in Ohio (21 in biomedicine, 10 in polymers, 5 with venture capitalists, 4 with academic institutions and 3 with other organizations) and 32 in Sweden (8 in biomedicine, 10 in polymers, 3 with venture capitalists, 10 with academic units, and 1 with a 'bridging institution').

OVERVIEW OF THE BIOMEDICAL/BIOTECHNOLOGY AND POLYMER CLUSTERS IN OHIO AND SWEDEN

As summarized in Table 8.1, both the biomedical/biotechnology and the polymer clusters are roughly twice as large in Ohio as in Sweden in terms of number of firms. The differences are even larger in terms of employment and revenues. The biomedical/biotech cluster has 422 firms and more than 52 000 employees in Ohio, compared with 230 firms and nearly 26 000 employees in Sweden. The polymer cluster consists of more than 2800 firms and 273 000 employees in Ohio vs. about 1400 firms and 76 000 employees in Sweden. The total revenues are more than twice as large in Ohio as in Sweden in biomedicine ($15 billion vs. $6 billion) and more than three times as large in polymers ($59 billion vs. $18 billion). The Ohio firms are larger than their Swedish counterparts in both clusters, due in part to the fact that they tend to be older: the average Ohio biomedical firm was established in 1972 vs. 1981 in Sweden. The average polymer firm was established in 1962 in Ohio and in 1969 in Sweden.

Table 8.1 also provides summary data about new firm formation. Of the Ohio biomedical firms surviving in 1996, 108 were established during the period 1990–96 vs. 73 in Sweden. This means that a larger fraction of surviving firms in Sweden were established during the 1990s than in Ohio. The same is true for the polymer cluster: 242 (17.4 per cent) of the surviving firms in Sweden were established during 1990–96 vs. only 94 (3.3 per cent) in Ohio. Thus, this comparison points to a potential problem in Ohio with the rate of new firm formation, less so in Sweden.

However, the picture changes dramatically if we look at the growth of the

Table 8.1 Biomedical/biotech and polymer firms in Ohio and Sweden, 1996

	Number of Firms		No. of Employees		Revenues, $ billion		Employees/firm		Revenues/firm, $ million	
	Ohio	Sweden	Ohio	Sweden	Ohio	Sweden	Ohio	Sweden	Ohio	Sweden
All firms										
Biomedicine/Biotech	422	230	52 175	25 768	15.0	6.1	123.6	112.0	35.5	26.6
Polymers	2 832	1 387	273 413	76 271	58.7	18.1	96.5	55.0	20.7	13.1
Firms established 1990–96										
Biomedicine/Biotech	108	73	1 791	982	1.7	0.1	16.6	13.5	15.4	1.8
Percentage of total	25.6	31.7	3.4	3.8	11.1	2.2	13.4	12.0	43.3	6.8
Polymers	94	242	6 166	6 268	1.6	1.1	65.6	25.9	16.5	4.7
Percentage of total	3.3	17.4	2.3	8.2	2.6	6.3	67.9	47.1	79.5	36.0

newly established firms. The 108 new biomedical firms in Ohio created nearly 1800 new jobs, compared with less than 1000 jobs in the 73 new Swedish firms. In terms of revenues, the Ohio firms were more than 8 times as large. In polymers, the story is similar: the 94 new Ohio firms created almost as many new jobs as the 242 Swedish firms, and the average revenues per firm were nearly four times larger than in the Swedish firms.

This suggests that there are factors at work which encourage new firm creation (entrepreneurship), particularly in Sweden, and also factors which inhibit growth in Sweden relative to Ohio. The findings also suggest that there are important differences not only between the countries but also between the clusters.

Before proceeding to the analysis of these differences and the role various institutions play, it is necessary to outline the product composition (specialization) of output, size distribution of firms, and geographic concentration of each cluster.

The Biomedical Cluster in Ohio

In terms of sales, the cluster in Ohio may be divided into four roughly equal groups: pharmaceuticals, medical equipment, diagnostics, and 'other' (consisting of services, medical supplies, and software). The distribution of employment and number of firms across these groups are quite different, however, with medical equipment and medical supplies together representing more than half of the totals. This reflects large differences in employment and sales per firm. The largest firms in terms of both sales and employment are pharmaceutical and service firms.

About half of the sales in the biomedical cluster in Ohio are made up of medical and diagnostic equipment. Three of the largest companies, each with annual sales exceeding $700 million, are Picker International (manufacturer of CAT scanners and other imaging equipment), Invacare (the world's largest manufacturer of wheelchairs), and Steris (manufacturer of sterilization equipment). Picker International was established in 1915 and Invacare in 1971; the manufacturing activities of both these companies are closely related to the industrial machinery cluster which has long dominated the industrial landscape in Ohio. Steris was founded much more recently (1987), with both capital input and other support from Invacare. The manufacturing know-how in these companies is part of the old manufacturing base in Ohio, while the marketing is oriented to the medical sector rather than other manufacturing industries. The older companies (particularly Picker International and Invacare) have continued to grow rapidly as a result of acquisitions of other companies (often overseas) in related products.

The biomedical cluster includes a number of young and small companies in entirely new areas. Some of these are biotech companies which are much more research-intensive than their older counterparts. In fact, many of them have no products at all to sell; all their revenues consist of research funding in the form of research grants as well as seed or venture capital. Several of these companies are university spin-offs or have other important ties to academic research, particularly at Case Western Reserve University (CWRU). Once the companies are established, their local ties become less important as they network with and recruit from universities everywhere. Other companies are software companies, consulting firms, and specialized manufacturing, engineering, and other service companies.

Geographically, the biomedical/biotechnology firms are heavily concentrated in the major metropolitan areas where the major universities are also located. About three-quarters of the firms and employment and almost 90 per cent of the sales are associated with firms in Cleveland, Cincinnati, and Columbus, the three largest metropolitan areas. Each of these cities is home to at least one major research university: Case Western Reserve University, the University of Cincinnati, and the Ohio State University, respectively. These three regions also have a disproportionate share of the newest firms. The chemically-based drug industry is heavily concentrated in Cincinnati (strongly associated with Procter & Gamble), while the biotechnology-based sector is tied primarily to Cleveland.

The Biomedical Cluster in Sweden

The Swedish biomedical cluster is more strongly dominated by pharmaceutical companies than is that in Ohio. The Swedish drug companies represent nearly two-thirds of total sales in the biomedical cluster, with medical equipment firms making up another 30 per cent. Thus, the drug companies make up a much higher share than in Ohio.

The pharmaceutical industry has a long history in Sweden and has enjoyed extraordinary sales growth in the 1980s and 1990s while at the same time undergoing rapid consolidation. The number of major drug companies was reduced from seven in the late 1970s to only two today (Stankiewicz, 1997, p. 95): Astra, the largest company, merged in early 1999 with Zeneca, a British company. Its rapid sales growth has been generated by extremely successful innovation in the form of new drugs, including the first beta blocker to be approved by the Food and Drug Administration in the United States, and Losec, the peptic ulcer drug which is currently (1999) the world's best-selling drug. The second largest company is Pharmacia–Upjohn, the result of a 1995 merger of Pharmacia with the US-based Upjohn company.

The medical equipment industry in Sweden is dominated by Gambro (founded in 1964) and Siemens, a German firm which had already established production in Sweden in 1927. Similarly to the Ohio medical equipment companies, these firms may be seen as closely related to the industrial machinery industry, with sales oriented to the medical sector rather than other manufacturing industries.

There is also a large number of small medical supply firms Sweden. This is the only field in the biomedical area in which there are more firms in Sweden than in Ohio. But these are generally quite small firms; they are similar in size to those in the software and diagnostics sectors. These latter companies are much more heavily represented and are also much larger in Ohio than in Sweden.

Similarly to Ohio, the geographic location of economic activity in this field is strongly tied to universities with high research capability. The Stockholm–Uppsala region dominates, with other clusters based in Göteborg and Lund and also in Linköping and Umeå. There is a certain amount of specialization among the regions. The Linköping region is relatively large in biomedical software; Göteborg is specialized in medical instruments and supplies, while Uppsala is biggest in diagnostics. However, the Stockholm region is largest in most fields.

The Polymer Cluster in Ohio

The polymer cluster in Ohio consists of more than 2800 firms with a total employment of nearly 275 000 and sales of about $59 billion in 1996. Nearly two-thirds (about 1800) of these are small firms engaged in fairly simple processing of plastic products. Another major segment (nearly 400 firms, generally much larger than in the previous group) is made up of materials manufacturers. The remaining firms are machinery manufacturers, mold manufacturers, tool and die manufacturers, and providers of various services (for example distribution). Thus, the polymer cluster is made up of a combination of very large, multinational firms and numerous small firms.

It is noteworthy that the large (mostly tire and rubber) companies have elected to keep their headquarters and major research units in Ohio, even though they have shifted a large part of their manufacturing activities elsewhere. As will be shown below, this is due in large measure to the presence of high quality universities and infrastructure – or, more generally, an environment highly conducive to close interaction and strong linkages among people with the right skills, high-performance mold-making companies, suppliers, metal-cutting industry, and compounders, as well as firms providing highly developed financial and legal services. In addition, proximity to major markets has been advantageous. The area between Akron and Cleveland is often referred to as 'Polymer Valley' because of its high concentration of polymer firms. Ohio's polymer firms are heavily concentrated in the large cities. This distribution is identical to the location of heavy industrial activity in general.

The Polymer Cluster in Sweden

As mentioned before, in the Swedish polymer cluster there are only about half as many firms and one-third the employment and sales as compared to the corresponding cluster in Ohio. Swedish polymer firms are broadly scattered throughout the country, although a few distinct clusters can be identified close to the three largest cities. Noteworthy is a large polymer cluster around Gislaved, a small southwestern town without a university. This, along with the relatively even distribution of polymer firms, suggests that a substantial part of the technology used in polymer production is well-known and relatively easy to apply and that dependence on know-how from the universities is modest.

A characteristic feature of the Swedish polymer production is the dominance of companies which to a large extent are foreign-owned (for example, BASF Svenska AB, Bayer Sverige AB, Borealis Industrier AB, Norsk Hydro Sverige AB, and Akzo Nobel AB). Hence, Sweden does not have the same tradition of production in domestically owned chemical firms as does Ohio.

THE ROLE OF INSTITUTIONS

The question that arises, then, is: what are the differences between Ohio and Sweden which have led to the observed differences in patterns and rates of growth in biomedicine/ biotechnology and polymers?

One set of explanatory factors surely reflects differences in the economic environment. Between 1990 and 1996, the Swedish GDP grew hardly at all (only 3 per cent over the period as a whole) as Sweden went through its worst slump in the entire postwar period. Similarly, most other countries in Europe also experienced slow growth. Meanwhile, the Ohio economy expanded by about 16 per cent, and the US economy by 13 per cent. The fact that Ohio firms have easier access to the large and rapidly growing US market than do Swedish firms to the more slowly growing European market probably also plays a role. But it is difficult to determine how much of the differences in growth should be attributed to such economic factors and how much to other factors. In the following, we will focus on some institutional factors which have emerged in the studies referred to earlier.

In a previous study, 'institutions' were defined as

> the normative structures which promote stable patterns of social interactions/transactions necessary for the performance of vital societal functions . . . By the institutional infrastructure . . . [is meant] a set of institutional arrangements (both regimes and organizations) which, directly or indirectly, support, stimulate and regulate the process of innovation and diffusion of technology. The range of institutions involved

> is very wide. The political system, educational system (including universities), patent legislation, and institutions regulating labor relations are among many arrangements which can influence the generation, development, transfer, and utilization of technologies. (Carlsson and Stankiewicz 1995, p. 45)

In the present study, however, only a subset of these institutions are considered. Left out, for example, are the broader aspects of the political and educational systems and the regulations pertaining to the labor market. Remaining for consideration here are several institutional factors which we have found in our work on biomedicine and polymers as important in understanding both the differences between the two clusters and the differences between the regions. These may be summarized in the following four groups:

1. the science base and mechanisms of technology transfer;
2. the density of networks and the role of business support services and companies in related industries;
3. the entrepreneurial climate, especially the availability of finance;
4. the policy environment and other infrastructure.

THE SCIENCE BASE AND MECHANISMS OF TECHNOLOGY TRANSFER

There are important differences between the two types of clusters with respect to the role of science, reflecting differences in the nature of knowledge and in the appropriate mechanisms of knowledge sharing or technology transfer. We begin, therefore, with a discussion of the nature of knowledge in each field.

Nature of Knowledge in Biomedicine

Even though we are treating biomedicine and biotechnology here as parts of a single cluster in each country, there are distinct differences between the two fields as far as the knowledge base is concerned. Biotechnology relies heavily on basic science, primarily biology and biochemistry, and is therefore closely tied to academic research. Even large pharmaceutical companies (especially those based on chemical traditions) tend to outsource basic research to academia or to small, specialized biotechnology companies. The biotechnology companies, in turn, are often spin-offs from universities. They tend to focus on research rather than production. There is a clear division of labor: universities or scientific institutions are the main creators of knowledge; small start-up firms are the intermediaries which carry the research out from the universities and make the technology ready for use by large firms;

and large firms manufacture, market, and distribute the products. This specialization seems to be most pronounced within the United States, partly propelled by the higher propensity of large US firms to engage in outsourcing of R&D. However, there is evidence that a similar structure is slowly evolving in Sweden as well.

The market for new biotechnology products is highly uncertain; approval from the appropriate authority is necessary (the Food and Drug Administration in the US) and requires a long process of patenting, phase I and phase II trials, clinical testing, and so on. Therefore, it takes many years before the first output is sold, and the risk of failure is high. Finance comes from pharmaceutical companies and/or venture capital firms. Generally, the patented product is sold to large companies, or patenting is done together with a large company as a joint venture. As a result, biotech companies rarely become large.

In biomedicine, by contrast, the basic technology comes from biomedical engineering, with secondary inputs from mechanical and electrical engineering and computer science, as well as from macromolecular science and materials science. Thus, in addition to the life sciences, engineering and computer sciences are indispensable disciplines for the development of technology in the biomedical cluster. The relations between business and academia are not as tight as in the biotechnology case, however. Biomedical firms are oriented more to applied research and production. These firms either spin off from existing businesses or from academia. Their main focus is on the application of an innovation in production. The FDA approval process or its equivalent is relatively short. Markets are more certain, and the risk is lower than in biotechnology. Production and sales start immediately, and return on investment starts in a relatively short period. Firms may grow rapidly and become large.

Nature of Knowledge in Polymers

This contrasts sharply with the nature of knowledge in polymers. There are four classes of polymers: (1) thermoplastics (when heated they flow: plastics); (2) thermosets (solids, for example rubber); (3) fibers; (4) films and coatings. The main research is currently in the area of thermoplastics and is concentrated primarily on catalysts which are used to manipulate the polymer structure. But polymer research does not have a strong disciplinary base in the academic structure. Even though chemistry departments in the universities might seem to be the natural place for polymer studies, this is not where polymer research is typically done. Chemistry departments are traditionally conservative. Polymer research does not fit well with their well-defined, well-structured approach to research. It is much more experimental. But at the same time, chemical engineering, although an applied discipline and very different in character, culture, and approach from chemistry, does not offer a natural habitat for polymer research either. Chemical engineering continues to be concerned chiefly with the design of heat flows, cooling towers, and reactions. It is only the demands of industry that have forced universities to put the experimental, non-traditional polymer researchers together in their own departments. But this has happened only in a few universities and only fairly recently.

The technological changes take place in molecular structure as well as in the interaction between material and machine. As a result, chemistry, polymer science, and chemical engineering are all becoming connected to mechanical engineering. Besides macromolecular science, mechanical engineering, material science, and computer science are indispensable disciplines for the development of technology in the polymer cluster. This broadening of the required competence base is increasingly problematic for many of the smaller firms in both countries. It also means that the bulk of the research, even basic research, takes place in large companies. The research is highly application-oriented and does not lend itself to the discipline-based academic structures. The main function of universities is to educate and train highly skilled researchers; the research results are of secondary importance.

As a result of these differences in the nature of knowledge as well as the locus of knowledge creation, the mechanisms of commercialization of new scientific breakthroughs are quite different in the two clusters.

Technology Transfer and Commercialization

Biomedicine

The transfer of technology from the research lab to production units and the commercialization of innovations are critical ingredients in the dynamics in the biomedical cluster. The technology transfer problem arises because of the fact that, as stated already, a large share of the research takes place in universities. Technology transfer from academia and research institutions often takes the form of formation of new firms, that is, the technology is carried directly by the researcher into a new firm. Another possibility is licensing of a patent to an existing firm. Successful transfer requires well-functioning institutions either for new firm formation or for commercialization via licensing, or, both. Many universities have established an 'Office of Technology Transfer' (OTT) to facilitate commercialization.[6] The system features which promote start-ups will be discussed further in a subsequent section.

The commercialization activities cover a wide range of activities: managing the legal and contractual framework within which research partnerships operate, along with the intellectual property that may emerge; providing mechanisms for distribution of income resulting from invention and discovery between the university, the researcher, and outside entities; helping start-up firms or researchers file government grant applications such as for Small Business Innovation Research; providing business incubator services to entrepreneurs; providing private industry opportunities to locate close to the campus; training researchers for commercialization activities; promoting the use of inventions and discoveries for public good; and developing effective communications with industry.[7]

The attitude towards commercialization of research results in the Swedish academic community was for a long time fairly negative. This has gradually changed, however. Today commercialization of research is promoted, and universities and institutes of technology have adopted plans for the commercialization of research results. In fact, Swedish universities have been assigned three specific tasks by the government. In addition to education and research, the third task of the universities is to strengthen the collaboration and interaction with the commercial sector, particularly manufacturing. The commercialization of research and development conducted at universities and institutes of technology is therefore seen as one way to improve the competitiveness of Swedish firms. It is also recognized that this may be important for start-ups and growth of new firms.

Neither Ohio nor Sweden is a leader in the area of technology transfer. In this regard, Ohio's universities lag behind many successful universities elsewhere in the United States, such as Stanford and MIT. Even though there are no OTTs in Sweden, recent new legislation has allowed the universities to start firms for the purpose of promoting the commercialization of research results. The Swedish intellectual property rights state that the research results are owned by the researcher, not the university. However, the researchers usually have no knowledge, and little experience, of the commercialization process. Thus, the Swedish university-owned firms have a similar task as the OTTs. They help the researchers with the expensive and time-consuming patenting process, provide contacts with venture capital firms and other firms (for example, industrial firms) that might be interested in the new technology and assist them in contract negotiations. The university-owned firms charge the researchers for their services, for example by getting part of the license revenues.

Firms are very active in searching and analyzing the available technologies through technical publications, conferences, and patents. Because of the complex legal and technical issues involved, they all rely on outside firms to carry out their patenting. This service is outsourced to a larger extent in the United States than in Sweden.

Polymers

In the polymer field, technology transfer from academia to industry takes place through large firms, not small and medium-sized firms. There are three reasons for this. First, large firms are the only ones capable of financing academic research and of absorbing the results. If large firms fund the research and are willing to buy the results, the researchers' incentive to go out to industry and set up firms to commercialize their own technologies is sharply reduced. Secondly, the funding affects the direction of research and orients it more towards the needs of large firms, which usually means product and process development, sometimes quite firm-specific in nature. However, an important portion of the research budget is also spent on basic science. But this type of research does not lead to new start-ups and is not sold to small firms. Again, large firms with well-structured research departments (with large R&D budgets and highly trained employees) are in a much better position to understand basic science and appropriate it for their own use. Thus, the market structure seems to be one explanation for the low diffusion of technology in the polymer cluster.

Thirdly, the competencies of firms are based mostly on production technology involving, for example, polymerization, low-cost manufacturing, and use of computers. Firms maintain, renew and develop their competence through in-house research and university contacts. Large firms are not risk-takers in terms of pursuing new lines of research. The firms which conduct R&D are mostly large and well established, and they fund their research internally.

The leading universities in the polymer field have a wide spectrum of research capabilities. But while many academics think that specialized firms could work with high engineering polymers and thousands of new polymers in their labs, industry does not generally find many interesting prospects among these for the near future. Unlike firms in the biotechnology field, polymer firms commercialize their own technologies without the use of specialized intermediaries.

The nature and organization of research has changed over the last few decades. Twenty or thirty years ago, most large firms had central R&D labs at headquarters and conducted a fair amount of basic research. Occasionally they would also ask polymer departments in universities to do basic research. Today, their R&D function having been decentralized and much more closely oriented to individual divisions or product lines, industry's requests for academic research projects are much more targetted and operations-oriented. The scope for networking with academic researchers is much more limited now than it used to be. But a common method of technology transfer is still for companies to hire the PhD students whose research they funded. This type of transfer involves large companies almost exclusively; only rarely does it involve the start-up of a new company. Our data show that the Ohio firms are not only larger but also somewhat older (34 years old vs. 27) than their Swedish counterparts. Thus, even though the Swedish firms spend more on

R&D in relation to sales (approximately 2 per cent versus about 1 per cent in Ohio), the research base in absolute terms is considerably larger in Ohio, particularly on the industrial side, and Ohio firms are in a better position to exploit the results commercially.

Given the infrastructure, the nature of knowledge, and the technological change, and so on, examined in this section, it is not surprising that most of the growth in this system in Ohio has come through expansion within large firms rather than through establishment and growth of new firms. In Sweden, where the polymer technology base is weaker, especially in large firms, and where the system is less mature, more of the growth has come from new start-ups.

Biomedical R&D

Ohio

The biomedical R&D infrastructure in Ohio consists of universities and hospitals, medical clinics, policy organizations and other institutions. In biomedical engineering research, the largest units in Ohio are the Cleveland Clinic Foundation (one of the largest and most highly ranked hospitals in the United States) and Case Western Reserve University (CWRU) whose Department of Biomedical Engineering is one of the leading institutions in its field in the United States. Other engineering departments as well as the School of Medicine at CWRU, other hospitals in the Cleveland area, and the University of Akron are other important research units. Together these institutions in northeast Ohio spend about $17 million on biomedical engineering research annually.[8] To this amount should be added the research which is conducted in other parts of Ohio. Based on our interviews and other materials available to us, we estimate that the total amount spent annually on academic biomedical engineering research in Ohio is about $25–30 million. Most of this research is funded by the National Institutes of Health, the National Science Foundation, and other federal sources.

Sweden

In Sweden, the Cancer Foundation, the Swedish National Board for Industrial and Technical Development (NUTEK), the Technology Research Council (TFR), the Medical Research Council (MFR), and the Science Research Council (NFR) are among the leading units that organize and financially support biomedical research. In the field of medicine as a whole, the Swedish academic research expenditures in 1995/96 amounted to around $500 million. Among the private companies Astra is the most important actor with a total research budget of about $1 billion, half of which is spent in Sweden. We estimate that there are about 100 research units in Sweden in the medical field, including universities, research institutes, and private companies. The expenditures on biomedical research appear to have increased during the 1990s.

The Swedish universities are also important actors in the biomedical technological system. Several of them conduct world-leading research. For example, one of the youngest universities, Umeå University in the northern part of Sweden, has a good international reputation in biotechnology. The largest academic unit is Karolinska Institutet in Stockholm with more than 1500 teachers and researchers (including 200 professors), and approximately 7000 students (of which 1700 are graduate students). About 200 PhDs graduate at Karolinska Institutet each year. The research hospitals are a third group of important actors in the biomedical technological system. They carry out their own research and have extensive contacts with the universities. The science parks and NUTEK are the main bridging organizations that try to facilitate the commercialization of research results.

Polymer R&D

Ohio

The concentration of the United States rubber industry to northeast Ohio is the main reason why two of the top three academic polymer research institutions in the United States are located in the area: the College of Polymer Science at the University of Akron and the Department of Macromolecular Science at Case Western Reserve University (CWRU) in Cleveland.[9] If we also include the University of Cincinnati, the Ohio State University, and other universities, the total academic polymer research in Ohio is estimated at about $20 million annually.[10]

The academic research is important (especially as a producer of PhDs, less so as a producer of research results), even though it is literally dwarfed by the R&D carried out by major corporations. Goodyear alone spends about $300 million a year on R&D, but only a small portion of that is fundamental research. Other major companies with polymer-related R&D are BF Goodrich, BP Chemicals, Bridgestone/Firestone, Ferro, GenCorp, and Loral. According to industry sources, a good guess is that somewhere around 2–3 per cent of sales of materials manufacturers is spent on R&D. This would mean that corporate polymer-related R&D in Ohio is in the neighborhood of $400–$600 million a year, and perhaps as much as twice that amount if machinery, mold, and tool and die manufacturers are also included.

Sweden

About a decade ago, it was estimated that a total of about 60 million SEK (about $9 million) was spent annually on polymer-related research in Sweden at that time, with almost half being funded by the Swedish National Board for

Industrial and Technical Development (then STU, subsequently NUTEK). Only 2 million SEK was spent annually on fundamental work in polymer chemistry and physics and was divided among numerous research units (STU, 1989). There seems to be an inadequate amount of polymer science in the training of college graduates. This means that, similarly to Ohio, there is limited access to research for the large majority of small and medium-sized firms, and very limited absorptive capacity. The large international companies in Sweden can get their research needs met both in Sweden and abroad, and they are well connected to both Swedish universities and research units elsewhere.

More recent figures estimate polymer-oriented research in Swedish universities to be about $12 million annually (compared to $20 million in Ohio). The magnitude of industrial R&D is not known. But since much of the research is concentrated in the parent companies, and since many of the Swedish companies are subsidiaries of multinational companies headquartered outside Sweden, this reduces the R&D intensity in Sweden. Assuming that the average R&D intensity in the polymer firms is about 2 per cent of sales, which is below the average in the Swedish manufacturing sector, total research expenditures – including universities, government support and the industry – are estimated at approximately $375 million.

Altogether, the academic and research infrastructure for polymers in Sweden seems to be somewhat inadequate. The need for bridging institutions in Sweden similar to EPIC in Ohio (whose role is explained below) in the polymer sector is also evident.

Density of Networks and the Role of Business Support Services and Companies in Related Industries

Biomedicine

In biomedicine, new companies are often based on original ideas and new products. The founders need good networks of relationships and knowledge of the market in order to be able to raise the venture capital needed for growth. Older firms have a large network of relationships with other companies and universities globally. In the initial stage, start-up firms are highly dependent on local actors, even though they also have relationships with more distant entities. The importance of local links drops radically when firms proceed to the later stages of their technology.

Both biotechnology and biomedical firms, and the institutions supporting them, show a strong tendency towards cooperation in research, usually of a long-term nature. Institutional contacts involve hospitals, universities, government organizations (such as NIH), intermediary organizations (such as EBTC and EPIC – see further below), and industrial associations. Firms have relationships not only with local universities but also with national universities as well as with foreign ones. These firms are highly specialized, and in case the local university is not satisfactory, they go and search for expertise wherever it may be found.

The type and degree of connectivity (linkages among various entities) in Sweden are similar to those in Ohio. The main differences can be attributed to the role of hospitals supporting the biomedical cluster. Biotechnology products are subject to strict clinical tests that cannot be performed without the existence of a strong hospital infrastructure. Due to the weaker bridging institutions similar to EBTC in Sweden, the hospitals, especially via their central purchasing agency in each county, play an even more important role in Sweden than in Ohio. Besides academia, the interviewed biotechnology firms also work closely with the pharmaceutical firms that buy their products.

Polymers

Polymer firms network with their customers, joint-venture firms, sister firms, parent firms, and other local firms. But the degree of collaboration among firms is not high. However, firms are quick in picking up new developments by hiring good engineers away from each other. The R&D staff in most large polymer firms have informal relationships with their counterparts in other firms. They read the same journals, attend the same meetings, and live in the same neighborhoods, at least in Ohio where the geographic clustering is stronger than in Sweden. The majority of the case study firms in Ohio have established relationships either with local universities or with local community colleges. Multinational firms also have contacts in foreign countries.

Given the competitive pressure on production costs, polymer firms try to rationalize their investments in research and concentrate more on product and process development. To the extent that they engage in basic research at all, they employ outside experts such as university professors to perform the research for them.

There seem to be significant differences in connectivity between the Swedish and the Ohio polymer clusters. Generally the interviewed polymer firms in Sweden had little or no contact with universities and other research institutes. Employees and managers also had little formal education; university degrees are uncommon. The technology used is low-tech and developed in-house. The firms usually do not apply or search for new technology. Instead, they continuously improve the existing technology in a process of trial and error. Cost minimizing is extremely important and the major source of competitiveness for several of the interviewed firms.

The main sources of knowledge among Swedish polymer firms emanate from close linkages with customers and suppliers, who give impulses to improvements. Customers and suppliers are more or less regarded as strategic partners, and the polymer firms use them when developing new products and improving existing ones.

ENTREPRENEURIAL CLIMATE AND THE ROLE OF FINANCE

Neither Ohio nor Sweden is particularly known for a favorable entrepreneurial climate. Both economies have traditionally been dominated by heavy manufacturing industry, and both have struggled in the last two decades to restructure and find new areas of growth. Due to resource limitations, our inquiries thus far have focussed primarily on only one particular aspect of the entrepreneurial climate, namely the availability of finance.

In 1998 there were 17 venture capital firms in Ohio with a total capital of \$9.6 billion, about \$2 billion of which is estimated to be committed to biomedicine. All but four of these firms were founded after 1980. In addition to these local companies there are also venture capitalists whose main activities are outside Ohio. There are also 'business angels' who are willing to provide 'seed' and 'start-up' capital.

It appears that although there are venture capital firms active in this field in Sweden, they are much fewer in number than in Ohio. We have been able to identify only a handful of firms active in 1996–98, some of them foreign. But this does not mean that there is a shortage of capital. In recent years new actors have also become increasingly interested in the biomedical sector. For instance, Investor, the 'holding company' of the dominant Swedish industrial group (the Wallenberg group), has recognized the biotechnology/biomedical industry as a potential high growth (profit) industry and acquired a company (Novare Kapital AB) for the purpose of investing in this area. However, as compared to the US, our interviews indicate that Sweden hosts few 'business angels' and 'competent' venture capital firms, connecting new ventures to management and marketing competence, that is, the primary inputs provided by venture capitalists. The Swedish venture capital market is also less specialized and offers fewer alternatives than the more mature and differentiated venture capital market in the US.

Finance is usually the problem considered most important by the biomedical firms. It is related not only to the cost of research but also to the cost of clinical tests, patenting, and FDA approval. It is only during the later stages of technological development that venture capital (VC) firms become interested. If the founders do not have a good network of relationships and knowledge of the market, raising venture capital is difficult. This is where business incubators can play a crucial role (see further below).

We found that five of six Ohio biotech start-ups but only one in three

Swedish firms were university spin-offs. Among the non-biotech biomedical firms in Ohio, university spin-offs also dominated. In Sweden, company spin-offs turned out to be more common. This reflects both the general industrial structure in Sweden in which large firms tend to dominate and the prominent role of pharmaceutical firms in the whole biomedical cluster in Sweden.

We also found that few firms in our Swedish sample received support in the form of finance, laboratory equipment, networks, and people from their host (either the university or the company from which they were spun off). By contrast, the Ohio firms were found to have access to both finance and equipment. Even more importantly, they also benefit from network and managerial support during their initial years. This is because of the active involvement of venture capital firms, intermediary organizations, and parent companies.

The VC firms supply not only finance but also provide other services which are at least as important to their clients: finding a chief executive officer; assigning one or more of its employees as a member of the board of directors of the client; helping to establish the client's network with other producers and customers; supplying management know-how; improving the client's marketing capability; evaluating and improving business ideas; advising and, if necessary, intervening in strategic decisions of the client, such as mergers and investments; preparing the client's initial public offering; communicating with suppliers; and forming a network with other venture firms that work in the same business. Hence, VC firms are important not only for the finance they provide but also because they are a major part of the mechanism that provides linkages to other actors in the cluster.

In Sweden, the venture capitalists have played a more limited role, largely limited to finance, than in Ohio where they also provide management competence and networking capability. This appears to be changing now in Sweden as venture capitalists there become more numerous and competent.

In biomedicine, most of the case study firms in Ohio have encountered financial problems also in the later (post start-up) stages of their technology development (clinical testing/phase III). These funding problems are often solved through licensing and joint ventures. The cost factor is in fact one of the main reasons behind the industrial structure in the biomedical cluster, since financial constraints mitigate against small firm growth.

In Sweden the bottlenecks to growth are different from those in Ohio. According to the interviewed firms, growth is hindered primarily by lack of managers with entrepreneurial experience. While Sweden has a large number of well-managed and successful multinational firms, the skills required to manage such firms are quite different from those required to manage new start-ups. There is a good supply of researchers, some of them world leading, with good technical skills and inventions with the potential to become profitable investments. However, commercialization is hampered by a shortage of people competent to manage new start-ups. In particular, the lack of business angels, or other agents fulfilling the same tasks, was pointed out as an important obstacle to growth. Since the Swedish tax system makes it difficult to accumulate private wealth through productive activities, there are very few business angels active in Sweden.

Our data indicate, somewhat surprisingly, that firms in the Ohio biomedical cluster receive more government finance than do those in Sweden. One possible explanation is the existence of a variety of resources by both state and federal government agencies in the US, particularly via SBIR (Small Business Innovation Research) grants.[11]

In the polymer cluster, venture capital plays a much less prominent role than in biomedicine in both Ohio and Sweden. On the one hand, polymer-based firms have had difficulty attracting venture capital in both locations; venture capitalists are looking for higher returns and faster pay-off in other types of ventures. On the other hand, many start-ups tend to be spin-offs from larger companies and thus obtain finance through the parent companies. The higher degree of geographic concentration in Ohio and the much higher density of firms have undoubtedly given Ohio firms an advantage over the Swedish ones.

POLICY ENVIRONMENT AND OTHER INFRASTRUCTURE

The substantially higher density of both venture capitalists and other service firms in Ohio than in Sweden explains a great deal of the observed differences in the growth of new firms once they are established. Another potentially contributing factor is public policy. Contrary to what might be expected, Ohio has taken a much more pro-active policy stance than Sweden in both the biomedical/biotechnology field and the polymer field. The Ohio Edison program is the main vehicle for technology policy in Ohio. It consists of funding for seven 'centers of excellence' in various technology fields, two of which happen to be biomedicine/biotechnology and polymers.

In the biomedical field, the Edison BioTechnology Center (EBTC) plays an important dual role as a 'bridging institution' between academic research (particularly at CWRU) and industry and between new start-ups and potential financiers. EBTC, founded in 1987, is an independent nonprofit organization affiliated with the Ohio Edison Program. It works closely with the leading universities and medical institutions, businesses, foundations, and civic and state organizations in Ohio. EBTC also collaborates with Enterprise Development, Inc. (EDI), a joint venture between the Weatherhead School of Management at CWRU and the Edison Program. EBTC's primary task is to encourage and support the creation of new firms based on biomedical engineering and biotechnology.[12] This is done in collaboration with EDI through technical and business assistance and advice (especially in writing business plans), training courses and seminars, and especially through two business incubators in which newly started companies have free access to office space, laboratory facilities and equipment, office services, and advice in exchange for a modest rent during a maximum of five years.[13] During the incubator phase, there is often no marketable product at all, just some ideas that need to be developed, along with a business plan. The funding is primarily in the form of research grants, often from government sources. Other sources of seed capital are personal savings and business angels. An important function of EDI is to arrange conferences a few times each year to bring together venture capitalists with people interested in presenting their business plans.

To a limited extent NUTEK, a governmental organization, serves the same purpose in Sweden. In addition, science parks and industrial parks represent another type of bridging institution. When the first parks were established in Sweden (in the 1980s), they had already been around for at least 30 years in the US.[14] The primary objective of science parks is to foster a closer cooperation between academia and industry. They also assist in raising venture capital and management support. Today 24 such parks exist in Sweden. The largest is located just north of Stockholm and hosts about 350 companies with 23 000 employees. The parks usually specialize in one or a few major spearhead technologies, usually information technology or biomedicine. Studies indicate that Swedish science parks have not performed well in an international comparison in terms of creating employment opportunities (Lindholm-Dahlstrand, 1997, 1998). The best record can be found in those Swedish science parks that have the closest ties to universities or multinational firms.

In addition to the services offered by venture capitalists, incubators, and science parks, many firms, particularly in biotechnology/biomedicine, may require a whole range of other services. Computer software (genomics, bioinformatics), legal services, regulation-related services, and intellectual property rights services are the main groups of services. Geographic proximity and density of networks play an important role here in enhancing the degree of specialization. This is an area in which Ohio firms have an advantage over Swedish ones.

In the polymer field, the Edison Polymer Innovation Corporation (EPIC) plays a similar role. Its function is to support polymer research and technology at Ohio universities in collaboration with local industry, and to provide technical services. The primary task is to support existing industry and to be a 'change agent for cultural change' within the industry rather than to create new businesses.[15] Since EPIC's establishment in 1986, the research has been divided between generic research whose results are available to all members and research on specific topics specified by each sponsoring firm, the results of which are proprietary.

Several difficulties have been encountered in pursuing this strategy. One has to do with the dual structure of the industry. The large firms have extremely high technical competence, often on a par with the universities from whom they hire their PhD scientists. For these firms it is not always the case that the small amounts (compared to the total R&D budget) spent on EPIC projects (whether generic or specific) could not be better spent on internal projects. By contrast, the problem for the large bulk of small processor firms is that their absorptive capacity is too limited. In addition, many of these smaller firms are currently undergoing a generational shift. The older generation is often fiercely independent, reluctant to join any organization, and resistant to change. As the management and ownership shift to a new generation, numerous changes may occur, particularly involving consolidation of firms and upgrading of competence in all areas. Meanwhile, EPIC's strategy has recently shifted towards increased emphasis on research consortia through which member companies undertake joint research in specific areas on a much larger scale than previously.

There are many other factors which form the institutional infrastructure for business activity but which we have not been able to cover in this study. For example, in a recent paper, Henrekson and Johansson (1999) hypothesize that the failure of Swedish firms to grow to medium or large size is caused by a number of institutional impediments: the level of taxation and design of the tax system, credit market regulation, the Swedish wage negotiation system, the negative effects of the pension system on private savings, the labor security legislation with particularly detrimental effects on small firms, and the dominance of the public sector in services which could be produced in small firms.[16]

CONCLUSIONS

What are the policy issues arising from the preceding analysis? Let us address each of the four sets of institutional factors.

It was demonstrated that the science base appears strong in both regions in biomedicine/biotechnology and strong in Ohio also in polymers. Further, it was shown that the science base is much more important in biotechnology than in polymers and that the ability to absorb research results in polymers resides primarily in large firms. Thus, even though the science base in polymers in Sweden is weak, increased expenditures on research and development in polymers are not likely to yield positive results unless they are coupled with efforts to raise the absorptive capacity (receiver competence) in the industry (in both large and small firms). The lack of major domestic polymer companies in Sweden is a problem in this regard. In biomedicine (particularly biotechnology), the main constraint with respect to the science base appears to be in converting scientific research into commercially exploitable technology (that is, technology transfer). The transfer mechanisms currently existing in Ohio started to be developed a decade or so earlier than in Sweden, but clearly they need to be developed much more in both regions. Sweden's heavy reliance on (strongly science-based) pharmaceuticals makes it especially important to improve technology transfer to new start-ups, while in Ohio the lack of major pharmaceutical firms is a major barrier to effective technology transfer.

The density of the networks depends significantly on geographic proximity. For this reason, the larger population and smaller land area give Ohio an advantage. The existence of bridging institutions such as EBTC and EPIC also contributes to better networking opportunities. The creation of similar institutions in Sweden is an obvious public policy issue, as is the strengthening of their functions in Ohio.

The entrepreneurial climate appears to be the area where the preceding analysis indicates the most significant differences between Ohio and Sweden. Our research has identified the greater availability of finance (especially venture capital but also seed funding and business angels) as one of the main factors explaining the higher growth rates of new start-ups in Ohio than in Sweden. The easier access to both financial markets and product markets outside Ohio (that is, in the United States as a whole) undoubtedly plays an important role. Improving the conditions for a thriving venture capital market should be a high priority for public policy in both Ohio and Sweden (reinforcing the developments in this direction in Sweden in the last few years). Other aspects of the entrepreneurial climate not dealt with in this chapter (taxes, regulations, the functioning of the labor market, and so on) are also likely to be important, but much more systematic comparative research is needed before specific policy recommendations can be made.

NOTES

1. Braunerhjelm et al. (1998); Braunerhjelm et al. (2000); Carlsson and Braunerhjelm (1999), (2002); Cetindamar and Laage-Hellman (2002); and Braunerhjelm et al. (2002). The present chapter draws upon material from these studies.
2. For further information see Carlsson and Braunerhjelm (2002).
3. Sweden became a member of the European Union in 1996. The fact that the United States exhibited higher growth than the European Union in the 1990s probably contributed significantly to the better economic performance in Ohio than in Sweden during the same period. But as will become clear in the analysis to follow, most of the institutions that are relevant for our comparison, particularly in the policy arena, are local or state-wide in Ohio (rather

than US-wide) and are therefore comparable in scope to the local and national institutions in Sweden. In the entrepreneurship and growth dimensions, the differences among states in the US are as great as among countries in Europe.

4. The theoretical literature suggests two main explanations for agglomeration of economic activities: (1) supply and demand (input–output) linkages and (2) technological spillovers which tend to be highly localized. For a review of the literature and a methodology for identification of clusters, see Braunerhjelm and Carlsson (1999).
5. The following sources were used for the Swedish data: Grönberg (1996, 1997), Ekonomisk Litteratur AB (1996), and the database Svenska Aktiebolag.
6. The Bayh–Dole Act (1980) fundamentally transformed the legal environment for technology transfer in the United States by transferring the property rights to research results obtained in projects funded by federal agencies from the funding agencies to the universities.
7. The most developed clusters, such as Silicon Valley, are characterized by access to highly specialized and differentiated services.
8. Data obtained from Cindy Brogan, unpublished scientific paper, EBTC.
9. The third and perhaps leading institution in the United States is the University of Massachusetts at Amherst.
10. There appears to be no similar concentration of academic polymer research anywhere else in the world, the leading rivals being in Germany (Max Planck Institute and the University of Mainz) and Japan (the universities of Tokyo and Kyoto).
11. The SBIR program receives funds from various federal agencies such as the National Science Foundation and the Department of Commerce and invests these funds in small high-tech businesses as well as in academic research. In 1996, SBIR investments amounted to $916 million. Another such award program, Small Business Technology Transfer (established in 1994), invested $64.5 million in high-tech firms in 1996 (SBA, 1999).
12. This is in contrast to EPIC's role which is primarily to support R&D in Ohio universities in collaboration with existing firms in the industry.
13. It is important to note that these incubators are specialized in biotechnology/biomedicine. There are eight other Edison incubators in Ohio, plus a number of incubators not associated with the Edison program.
14. The science park phenomenon stems from the US (for a more detailed description and review of the literature, see Hauschildt and Steinküler (1994) and Keeble and Oakey (1997). Originally they were set up to enable entrepreneurial academics to link their findings to the market. The Stanford Research Park, later the base of Silicon Valley, is the classic example of a successful research park.
15. To this end, EPIC has a research budget of about $1–1.5 million a year to support such efforts; none of the research is done in-house but is carried out at CWRU, the University of Akron, and more recently at the Ohio State University.
16. For further analysis of these and similar issues, see Andersson et al. (1993), Jakobsson et al., (1998).

REFERENCES

Andersson, T., P. Braunerhjelm, B. Carlsson, G. Eliasson, S. Fölster, L. Jagrén, E. Kazamaki Ottersten and K.R. Sjöholm (1993), *Den långa vägen – den ekonomiska politikens begränsningar och möjligheter att föra Sverige ur 1990-talets kris* (The Long Road – The Limitations and Possibilities of Economic Policy to Bring Sweden out of the Crisis of the 1990s), Stockholm: IUI.

Audretsch, D. and P. Stephan (1996), 'Company–scientist locational links: the case of biotechnology', *American Economic Review*, **86** (3), 641–52.

Braunerhjelm, P. and B. Carlsson (1999), 'Industry clusters in Ohio and Sweden, 1975–1995', *Small Business Economics*, **12** (4), 279–93.

Braunerhjelm, P., B. Carlsson and D. Johansson (1998), 'Industriella kluster, tillväxt och ekonomisk politik', *Ekonomisk Debatt*, **26** (6), 419–30.

Braunerhjelm, P., B. Carlsson, D. Johansson, and D. Cetindamar (2000), 'The old and the new: the evolution of polymer and biomedical clusters in Ohio and Sweden', *Journal of Evolutionary Economics*, **10** (5), 471–88.

Braunerhjelm, P., D. Johansson and D. Cetindamar (2002), 'The Support Structure of the Biomedical System: Research, Intermediary, and Financial Organizations', in B. Carlsson (ed.), *Technological Systems in the Bio Industries*, Boston, London and Dordrecht: Kluwer Academic Publishers, pp. 123–44.

Carlsson, B. (ed.) (1995), *Technological Systems and Economic Performance: The Case of Factory Automation*, Boston, London and Dordrecht: Kluwer Academic Publishers.

Carlsson, B. and P. Braunerhjelm (1999), 'Industry Clusters: Biotechnology/ Biomedicine and Polymers in Ohio and Sweden', in D. Audretsch and R. Thurik (eds), *Innovation, Industry Evolution and Employment*, Cambridge: Cambridge University Press, pp. 182–215.

Carlsson, B. and P. Braunerhjelm (2002), 'The Biomedical Clusters in Ohio and Sweden: An Overview', in B. Carlsson (ed.), *Technological Systems in the Bio Industries*, Boston, London and Dordrecht: Kluwer Academic Publishers, pp. 53–79.

Carlsson, B. and R. Stankiewicz (1995), 'On the Nature, Function, and Composition of Technological Systems', in B. Carlsson (ed.), op. cit., pp. 21–56.

Cetindamar, D. and J. Laage-Hellman (2002), 'Micro-Level Analysis of Firms in the Biomedical/Biotechnology System in Ohio and Sweden', in B. Carlsson (ed.), *Technological Systems in the Bio Industries*, Boston, London and Dordrecht: Kluwer Academic Publishers, pp. 81–122.

Ekonomisk Litteratur AB (1996), *Skandinavisk plastindustri 97*, Ekonomisk Litteratur AB, Stockholm.

Grönberg, Ann-Marie (1996), *Nordiska företag i medicinsk teknik* (Nordic Firms in Medical Technology), Huddinge: Bioprint Publishing and Consulting AB.

Grönberg, Ann-Marie (1997), *Nordiska företag i bioteknik* (Nordic Firms in Biotechnology), Huddinge: Bioprint Publishing and Consulting AB.

Hauschildt, J. and R. Steinküler (1994), 'The Role of Science and Technology Parks in NTBF Development', in R. Oakey, (ed.), *New Technology-Based Firms in the 1990s*, London: Paul Chapman Publishing.

Henrekson, Magnus and Dan Johansson (1999), 'Institutional effects on the evolution of the size distribution of firms', *Small Business Economics*, **12** (1), 11–23.

Jaffe, A.B., M. Trajtenberg and R. Henderson (1993), 'Geographic location of knowledge spillovers as evidenced by patent citations', *Quarterly Journal of Economics*, **63** (3), 577–98.

Jakobsson, U., L. Bergman, P. Braunerhjelm, S. Fölster and M. Henrekson (1998), *Entrepreneurship in the Welfare State. Summary and Conclusions. SNS Economic Policy Group Report 1998*, Stockholm: SNS.

Keeble, D. and R. Oakey (1997), 'Spatial Variations in Innovation in High-Technology Small and Medium-Sized Enterprises', in A. Cosh and A. Hughes (eds), *Innovation: National Policies, Legal Perspective and the Role of Smaller Firms*, Cheltenham: Edward Elgar.

Lindholm-Dahlstrand, Å. (1997), 'Spin-Off and Acquisition of Small Technology-Based Firms', in D. Jones-Evans and M. Klofsten (eds), *Technology, Innovation and Enterprise*, London: Macmillan Press.

Lindholm-Dahlstrand, Å. (1998), 'Incubators for Small Technology Based Firms', mimeo, Chalmers University of Technology, Gothenburg.

NUTEK (Swedish National Board for Industrial and Technical Development) (1998), *Den biomedicinska industrin i Sverige* (The Biomedical Industry in Sweden), NUTEK Report B 1998:8, Stockholm: NUTEK.

Prevezer, Martha (1997), 'The dynamics of industrial clustering in biotechnology', *Small Business Economics*, **9** (3), 255–71.

SBA (US Small Business Administration), 1999.

Stankiewicz, R. (1997), 'The Development of Beta Blockers at Astra-Hässle and the Technological System of the Swedish Pharmaceutical Industry', in B. Carlsson (ed.), pp. 93–138.

STU (Swedish National Board for Technical Development) (1989), *Report of the International Evaluation Committee on Swedish Polymer Research and Technology*, STU-info no. 723–1989, Stockholm: STU.

UK Department of Trade and Industry (1999), 'Biotechnology Clusters. Report of a Team Led by Lord Sainsbury, Minister for Science', http://www.dti.gov.uk/biotech-clusters.

Zucker, L.G. and M.R. Darby (1996), 'Star scientists and institutional transformation: patterns of invention and innovation in the formation of the biotechnology industry', *Proceedings of the National Academy of Science*, **93** (23), 12709–16.

Zucker, L.M., M. Darby and M. Brewer (1994), 'Intellectual Capital and the Birth of U.S. Biotechnology Enterprises', National Bureau of Economic Research Working Paper No. 4653.

9. Corporate governance and capital markets in the two capitalisms

Martin Ricketts

1. BASIC FEATURES OF THE TWO CAPITALISMS

Political events in the 1980s seem, at least for the foreseeable future, to have resolved arguments about the relative merits of centrally planned compared with market systems. The fall of the Berlin Wall and the retreat of the Soviet Empire were outward physical and political signs of a parallel intellectual collapse in support for state planning. Debate about the role of markets in economic life did not diminish in the 1990s, however, but changed its focus. In place of a crude bifurcation between 'plan' and 'market' there is now a more subtle division of the economic world into 'communitarian' and 'Anglo-American' capitalism. Albert (1993) provided a celebrated exposition of this division between types of capitalism contrasting the German or 'Rhineland' model with Anglo-Saxon norms. Similarly Williams (1994) investigated Japanese economic and political development. He argued that Japanese institutions have decisive advantages over the Anglo-American competition. The intervening years since the mid-1990s have seen Japan struggling to escape recession and Germany facing the continuing problems of reunification. Meanwhile, a long period of Anglo-American growth up to 2001 has made the work of Albert and Williams less fashionable. Nevertheless, discussion of 'the third way' has been a feature of British politics since the Labour administration came to power in 1997 and controversy is likely to revolve around the efficiency of differing 'varieties of capitalism' for the foreseeable future. This chapter aims to unravel and examine the main arguments in the debate.

All markets exist to facilitate exchange but the arrangements used by contractors vary widely. At one end of a spectrum of contractual relations can be found the arm's-length spot market contract. Such a contract might be found on commodities markets or financial markets where conditions are impersonal. The terms of the contract are clear and uncomplicated – the delivery of a certain grade of a commodity at a particular time at a specified price. There is no expectation that a particular buyer will again trade with the same seller. Confidence is high that the terms of the contract will be scrupulously observed. At the other end of the contractual spectrum are 'obligational relationships'. If the goods and services being bought and sold are very complicated, heterogeneous or subject to continual changes in specification, detailed written contracts could not possibly cover all the possible contingencies that might arise. In practice, sellers gradually learn over time about the requirements of buyers, and buyers similarly accumulate knowledge about the problems faced by sellers. Contracts do not specify what is required of the parties under all eventualities but set the framework for an evolving association. The terms are 'implicit' and rely on the gradual development of trust between the contractors. These 'relational' contracts are therefore durable and are supported by institutional features such as procedures for settling disputes short of recourse to the formal legal system.

The debate between advocates of the two capitalisms is about the nature of the contractual arrangements that link participants in the market. In particular, critics of the Anglo-American system claim the following:

(i) In the United States and the United Kingdom the prevailing contractual norms veer towards the impersonal arm's-length end of the spectrum relative to the norms prevailing in other capitalist countries such as Japan and Germany.
(ii) These contractual preferences have adverse consequences for economic efficiency.

Exchange is not costless. It requires people to generate information about the opportunities available from trade, it requires them to negotiate terms, and it requires a sufficient degree of trust that agreements will be honoured and that property rights in the resources exchanged will be respected. In a world of perfect information, uncontested property rights and costless enforcement of contracts, all exchange could be transacted on spot markets. There would be no institutional structures in existence other than the market itself with the 'state' as a costless enforcer of contracts. Bowles and Gintis (1993, p. 98) criticise economists for implicitly claiming that the state is capable of supporting such arrangements. They write that 'Capitalism's neoclassical defenders have themselves presumed an omnipotent state at least in one area: its powers and information allow the state to enforce contracts at no cost to the exchanging parties'.

As Coase (1937) recognised, it is imperfect information and the resulting transactions costs which give rise to the institutions of capitalism. The structure of the firm is a response to the problem of producing and disseminating information as well as policing and enforcing agreements. Critics of Anglo-American norms are arguing that the institutions of the United Kingdom and the United States, seen in this light, are less effectively organised than those of other countries. Potential gains from exchange are sacrificed because transactors are less well coordinated, information is not disseminated and used productively, and agreements are less effectively policed. In short, some varieties of capitalism cope with the hazards of transacting more efficiently than others.

2. GOVERNANCE SYSTEMS IN THE TWO CAPITALISMS

Differences in contractual norms permeate through an economic system. Buyer–supplier relationships, labour contracts, training incentives, marketing methods and the organisation of research and development can all be seen as part of the wide issue of how property rights in different types of economic asset (especially information and human skills) are established and defined, how contractual relations concerning these property rights are governed, and hence how institutional design affects economic performance. In no other area has controversy been greater and the contrast between systems more starkly presented, however, than in that of corporate governance. The following subsections briefly describe what Kaldor might have called the 'stylised facts' of the two capitalisms in the area of corporate governance. It should not be assumed that these 'facts' are undisputed or that their implications for economic efficiency are obvious. These points will be explored later.

The Anglo-American System or 'Market' System

Finance is supplied to the corporation in the Anglo-American system through impersonal arm's-length mechanisms. In particular a number of investigators have drawn attention to the following broad characteristics:

1. Shareholdings are widely dispersed and risk is highly diversified.
2. As a consequence of characteristic 1 there is little incentive for any individual shareholder to monitor management activity closely.
3. Outside auditors have a duty to prepare informative accounts but are not liable for any losses incurred by shareholders from trading on misleading information.
4. There is a single (Unitary) Board of the Company which includes non-executive directors. The appointment of these directors is likely to be controlled by the management group rather than by shareholders.
5. Financial institutions such as pension funds, investment trusts and insurance companies are the major holders of US and UK company shares. The trustees of these institutions have a fiduciary duty to protect the

interests of future pensioners, policy holders and contributors to the funds under their control.

6. Substantial investment by financial institutions in information gathering and monitoring of performance would risk falling foul of legislation against 'insider dealing'. If they wish to maintain their freedom to trade, shareholders must not have access to inside information. They must remain 'outsiders'.
7. Dissatisfaction with management performance results in shareholders (mainly financial institutions) selling the firm's shares. This results in a falling price of the shares on the market.
8. Management discipline is imposed by the market in corporate control. Under-performing companies will find themselves vulnerable to hostile takeover raiders.
9. Fear of takeover leads managers to pay close attention to the price of the company's shares on the market.
10. Unwillingness to permit the share price to fall results in a tendency for managers to distribute a higher percentage of earnings as dividends than is normal in other countries.
11. In the absence of direct shareholder influence, incentive packages are designed to give managers protection from the takeover threat and the prospect of fairly rapid short-term gains. These incentive packages link management bonuses to the stock price and give managers an incentive to engineer high stock prices in order to benefit from generous stock options.
12. In spite of dispersed shareholdings and the status of shareholders as 'outsiders', the takeover threat and the structure of management remuneration ensure that investment decisions are heavily influenced by the likely impact on the price of the firm's shares.

The Bank-Orientated System

Corporations in Germany and Japan have quite a different governance structure from those in the US and the UK.

1. Shareholdings are less dispersed across investors in bank-orientated systems than is the case in market systems. For a sample of companies in the UK, Mayer and Alexander (1991) found that there were, on average, fewer than two holdings in excess of 5 per cent of the outstanding equity. In Germany, on the other hand, holdings of more than one-quarter of the shares are common.
2. Given a more concentrated structure of share holding, the incentive to monitor management activity is higher than in the market system. This

monitoring is said to be undertaken by banks – especially the 'main bank' in Japan or the 'Hausbank' in Germany – who hold equity stakes in companies and (in Germany) exercise the voting rights of those shares which people deposit with them.

3. The transmission of information to 'outsiders' via auditors is less important when the major shareholders are 'insiders'. Because the banks and other principal shareholders maintain their interest in a company over very long periods, they become very well informed about its operations.
4. The German system of corporate governance has a two-tier board structure in contrast to the unitary structure of the US and the UK. The supervisory board is made up equally of representatives from the employees and the shareholders.[1] Members of the management board are appointed by the supervisory board, which must be informed about the policies and performance of the company.
5. Institutional holdings of shares are important in Germany and Japan as they are in the US and the UK. In Japan, for example, the structure of holdings – one-quarter individual and three-quarters institutional – is similar to that in the UK. The nature of the institutions is different however. Instead of independent insurance companies and pension funds, the institutional holders are banks, companies with close links as buyers or suppliers, or other companies within a keiretsu group. In Germany, company pensions are not financed by the specific payment of funds to an independent trust. As much as 60 per cent of the pension funds are implicitly invested within the firm and the pension obligations are unfunded long-term liabilities of the company (see Schneider-Lenne, 1994, p. 295).
6. Maintaining an ability to trade their shares at all times is not a high priority of Japanese or German institutional shareholders. Corbett (1994, p. 319) estimates, for example, that two-thirds of Japanese equity is held by stable shareholders. She notes that 'the most actively traded shares are those held by the household sector'– the opposite of the situation in the UK.
7. Adverse business conditions or management misjudgements do not necessarily result in the heavy selling of a company's shares. In Germany, for example, the banks use the power of their proxy votes and their seats on supervisory boards to monitor management performance. It is argued by some observers that the banks in Germany are prepared to lend on more favourable terms over longer periods and to be more supportive in times of crisis than is the case of banks in the UK or the US.
8. It follows from 7 that the market in corporate control is far less active in bank- than in market-orientated systems of corporate governance. In

spite of increasing numbers of mergers and acquisitions in Germany in recent years, Schneider-Lenne (1994, p. 300) still reports that 'so far the hostile takeover has been the absolute exception in Germany rather than the rule'. In Japan also, the US-style takeover is virtually unknown.[2]

9. The existence of long-term shareholders willing to give sustained support to a firm implies that the share price is a less important factor in management decision making.
10. The percentage of earnings distributed as dividends is lower in bank than in market systems. The dividend payout ratio has been estimated to be twice as high in the UK compared with Germany (Schneider-Lenne, 1994, p. 293). For non-financial corporations the ratio of dividends to gross income was about four times higher in the UK than in Japan in the late 1980s.[3]
11. Greater direct monitoring by shareholders reduces the use of management remuneration packages linked to share prices and share options. Kaplan (1994) reports that the percentage of ownership accounted for by Japanese top executives is typically one-half of that associated with equivalent US executives and one-quarter when stock options are included in the calculations (Kaplan, 1994, Table 4, p. 535).
12. It is sometimes claimed that bank-orientated systems encourage the direct monitoring of managers and lead to a more effective pursuit of long-term firm value. More usually, however, the system is seen as giving a voice to a wide group of 'stakeholders' – including employees, managers, bondholders, and other buyers or suppliers. As has been seen, the German supervisory board consists of employee representatives as well as representatives of shareholders. In Japan, top managers are promoted from within the company and see themselves as mediators between the interests of the various constituencies within the firm (see Aoki, 1989).

3. SHORT-TERMISM AND THE CRITIQUE OF THE ANGLO-AMERICAN MODEL

At the heart of the criticism of the Anglo-American system of corporate governance is the assertion that it leads to an obsession on the part of managers with short-term financial returns. The system, it is argued, inhibits investment – especially investment in 'intangible' human capital and research activity. In the United States many recent reports have emphasised this basic point as an explanation of the so-called 'productivity slowdown'. Dertouzos et al. (1989, p. 53), for example, write that 'there is evidence, difficult to quantify but ultimately convincing to us, that other forces [than higher interest rates] drive

American business to excessive preoccupation with immediate profit, even to the sacrifice of longer-term opportunities'. Jacobs (1991, pp. 9–10) is quite explicit about the cause. 'I believe the primary cause of business myopia is the distant relationship between the providers of capital (shareholders and lenders) and the users of capital (corporate Managers)'. Porter (1992, p. 75) asserts that 'in general, the U.S. system is geared to optimise short-term private returns; the Japanese and German systems optimise long-term private and social returns'.

In the United Kingdom, identical concerns have been expressed in very similar phraseology. A *Guardian* survey in 1993 lamented that 'short-termism intrudes into every nook and cranny of British business life. It is this that holds back the process of British wealth generation'.[4] Hutton (1995, p. 157) is one of the foremost exponents of the view that the City of London induces managerial myopia and undermines investment. 'British companies not only suffer one of the highest costs of capital in the world, but the febrile stock market compels them to earn a very big mark-up over even that cost of capital to fend off the threat of takeover and keep their shareholder base stable'. He quotes with approval Mayer's (1993) identification of the 'fundamental deficiency of the UK economy; a systematic failure to commit'.

The precise connections between particular features of the Anglo-US system of corporate governance and the alleged existence of short-termism are complex. There are at least three main lines of argument which have been used to justify the assertion that markets in the United States and the United Kingdom are short-termist.

Generation of Information

Arm's-length contracting, it is argued, implies that people expect to maintain an association for only very limited periods of time. Resources recontract on the market at frequent intervals and this encourages activities likely to enhance market value – for example the accumulation of skills which can be easily assessed and which can be used in many different industrial and commercial settings. This restless recontracting and mobility of resources inhibits the accumulation of certain types of information however. Knowledge of the particular capabilities of suppliers, of the special requirements of customers and of the productive potential of a team requires time and a continuing association to develop. People contracting at arm's length will not have the incentive to invest in the acquisition of such information.

In Japan the system of 'lifetime employment' is supposed to provide more appropriate incentives. Employees gain wide experience within the firm and are not confined to a particular 'function'. They are rewarded for flexible and cooperative behaviour over a long period of time. Aoki (1986) sees the typical

'J' firm as a 'horizontal hierarchy', that is a system that encourages rich horizontal communication between departments. In contrast, the 'A' firm is a 'vertical hierarchy' which limits people within a particular function and is mainly concerned with discipline and control. Several writers have seen this contrast as critical to an understanding of the problems of American capitalism. Porter (1992, p. 72) argues that 'American managerial innovations have resulted in less face-to-face consultation, information flow, and direct management involvement in investment choices' whereas 'Japanese innovations . . . such as just-in-time manufacturing, total quality management, and greater cross-functional coordination, have resulted in more vertical and horizontal information flow and involvement by management in decisions'. Porter concludes (p. 72) that 'the extensive flow of information is perhaps the most potent strength of the Japanese and German systems'.

Information Asymmetry

All exchange relationships must face the problem that each party is unlikely to be equally informed. The provider of finance to a joint stock company will find it difficult to assess the effort and effectiveness of the managers. As has already been observed, individual shareholders are unlikely to find it worthwhile to invest in better information about a company if they hold only small quantities of a company's shares. The scope for 'managerial behaviour' (that is the use of the firm's resources in pursuit of goals which do not benefit the shareholders) is therefore substantial. Two 'market-orientated' responses to this moral hazard problem may both be seen as leading to short-termism.

(a) The first response is to design contracts which give managers an interest in pursuing shareholder value even when they are not being closely monitored. Such contracts might involve bonus payments linked to profits, managerial shareholdings and share options. Critics argue, however, that unless these contracts are extremely carefully devised, managers will either receive large 'windfalls' unrelated to effort or will devote their time to attempted manipulation of the share price rather than to improving the long-run health of the company. In a bull market, for example, even rather poor management might benefit substantially from share options. Alternatively, share options that were related to the performance of a firm relative to other firms in the same sector would be better designed but more complex and costly to administer.

(b) An alternative mechanism for inducing managerial effort uses the power of reputation. Managers will be safe from takeover only if they can induce people to hold shares at a sufficiently high price. They have to find a means of reassuring shareholders that their interests will not be

> ignored. This they do by establishing a reputation, period after period, for paying regular dividends. Dividend payments become a way of committing the managers to a minimum level of performance [see Easterbrook, 1984]. The payment of a high proportion of earnings as dividends would not matter if shareholders and managers were equally informed about future prospects. Critics argue, however, that the payment of dividends transfers resources from those who have information about long run investment opportunities to those who do not. Thus, investment is inhibited by the necessity of paying regular and substantial dividends.[5]

This assumption that 'outsiders' are relatively poorly informed about the true prospects of companies leads to a further problem.[6] Managers wishing to avoid takeover will, if the market is undervaluing their firm, try to correct this false valuation. They cannot do so merely by publicly reporting good news since the reliability of this information would always be questionable. Instead they may 'signal' that the future looks good by raising dividends. A 'signal' in economics is an observable action that would not be rational unless undertaken by firms or individuals with certain (unobservable) qualities. In this case, raising the dividend (an observable action) would not be in the interests of the management if the firm's prospects (assumed unobservable by outsiders) were actually poor. Thus a rise in the dividend can act as a convincing signal that good times are just around the corner.[7] The problem as perceived by critics of the market-orientated system is once more that the payment of dividends might divert resources away from investment. Paradoxically, the effort to communicate the opportunities available to a firm involves the dispersal of the very means required to exploit them. Managers might, according to this view, be induced to act in a myopic or 'short-termist' way as a by-product of their efforts to convey information to the market.

Fear of 'Hold-Up'

The investment process will often involve the accumulation of assets which are highly specific to a particular operation. A classic example is investment in a pipeline to collect natural gas from a particular field. Once built, the pipeline cannot be transferred at low cost to alternative uses. The pipeline owner will feel vulnerable to attempts on the part of gas producers to renegotiate the price of carrying gas. Technically, the return to the pipeline after it has been built is a *quasi rent*. Even if the carriage rates are insufficient fully to service the capital costs of the pipeline, it will still be sensible to use the pipeline rather than close it down. Bargaining over the quasi rents which accrue to specific assets can therefore be very disruptive, and suppliers will try to avoid placing themselves in a position of dependency on particular buyers.

Investment in assets which result in dependency will therefore only occur if long-run contracts can be made sufficiently 'cast iron' and proof against opportunism or if the market is suppressed and replaced by internal organisation. Clearly, if pipeline owner and gas producer are the same firm (that is the industry becomes vertically integrated) the problem of 'hold-up' will not occur. It no longer matters whether the quasi rents accrue to the distribution or the gas production part of the business. The lack of trust between suppliers and buyers when specific assets are at stake has been used to explain the greater degree of vertical integration in British and American industry compared with Japanese or German norms. In the United States, for example, automotive companies purchase a lower proportion of parts from outside than do companies in Japan yet they typically deal with a much larger number of suppliers (see, for example, Kester, 1991).

Vertical integration cannot resolve every problem associated with specific assets, however. It can work only where the property rights in specific assets can be brought together under the ownership of a single party. In the case of specific human skills, the title to which cannot be transferred between contracting parties, the hold-up problem can be addressed only through the development of trust. As an employee, I will be prepared to invest in highly firm-specific knowledge and expertise only if I confidently expect the firm to pay a return on this investment.

It is here that issues of corporate governance become central to the analysis. Suppose, for example, that a firm has a workforce which operates as a highly effective team. Individual workers are more productive than they would be in alternative employment. Their higher productivity is reflected in higher wages than are available outside the firm. A portion of their wage, in other words, is a return to the accumulation of specific skills. Opponents of the market-orientated system of corporate governance argue that the return to these human assets is vulnerable to opportunism. Through the takeover mechanism, another firm might gain control and renegotiate the contracts of the workforce. The new owners might upset the existing distribution of rents on the firm's resources and divert a greater portion towards themselves. Takeover would then involve a breach of trust, and the threat of takeover would make people wary of committing themselves to a particular enterprise (Shleifer and Summers, 1988).

Collaborative ventures between firms are also vulnerable to sudden changes in ownership. A celebrated recent case was the sale of Rover to BMW by British Aerospace that effectively destroyed the long-term collaboration between Rover and Honda on complex matters such as design and engineering. A number of business commentators saw this sale as further confirmation that the British financial system was incorrigibly short-termist. Anatole Kaletsky (1994) wrote in *The Times* that 'the sheer stupidity and immorality of this betrayal is too scandalous to be ignored' and that 'the Rover fiasco looks like becoming another milestone in the long march of British public opinion back from the free market dogmas of the 1980s'.

4. THE COUNTER-CRITIQUE

Whereas charges of short-termism and 'casino-capitalism' have been levelled against British and American institutional arrangements, the more 'communitarian' models outlined in Section 2 have also been subjected to reappraisal. As Japan has struggled to overcome the legacy of the 'bursting of the bubble' in the late 1980s and to cope with the decade of relatively low growth and asset price deflation which followed, the governance arrangements which accompanied these events have come under much greater critical scrutiny. The idea, for example, that Japanese corporations are able to pursue long-term strategies in research and development, marketing, production techniques and so forth is dismissed as a myth by Mochizuki (1994). An alternative interpretation is that much of the investment so admired by American and British observers reflects 'a lack of accountability due to insufficient corporate governance, rather than far-sighted management'. Insiders with close associations with banks and with no takeover threat to consider are able to squander shareholders' funds. Most controversially Mochizuki argues that 'stable employment and corporate loyalty praised by many western commentators could generate stagnation and xenophobia'.

Japanese industrialisation and economic growth have undoubtedly been facilitated in the past by the discipline, conformity, reliability, loyalty and consensus associated with organisational arrangements. However, the problems associated with 'catching-up' with other industrialised economies and the problems of achieving further advance in the new (post catch-up) era are rather different. As Mikuni (1992) argued, the old system reflected the remnants of a kind of 'anachronistic wartime footing' in which economic objectives were relatively simple. In the new system, more entrepreneurial judgement is necessary and adjustments in the direction of market norms might be required to encourage mobility of resources between sectors and to finance innovation.

Gradual changes in Japanese economic organisation have been taking place in response to the pressures of technical change and economic recession. Some companies have responded to the information boom and the increasing technical links between hitherto separate industries by a policy of diversification. Ubukata (1991) noted that the increased movement of workers between companies was leading to 'the breakdown of the lifetime employment system' and the undermining of the seniority system (p. 22). Similarly, *The Economist* (10 August 1991) noted that 'Nissan . . . poaches experienced employees from other firms for many of the new businesses, such as mobile telecommunications, into which it is diversifying'. Mochizuki (1994) argued that 'lifetime employment is a phenomenon only temporary for the period after 1945 and limited to larger corporations' and that it will never again be the same 'as at the time of the continuous economic growth'. In the academic literature Clark and Ogawa (1992) showed that by the mid-1980s in Japan the value of a year of job tenure in a particular firm had fallen below the value of a year's general experience. The incentive to remain with a single firm was therefore falling and the remaining years of the 1990s can only have reinforced this trend.

In the financial sector too, changed conditions began to influence Japanese corporate governance. A regulated system designed to produce low-cost finance for large-scale industry is being liberalised and some studies have concluded that the cost of capital is no longer lower in Japan compared with the United States. The reform of the Japanese financial system which began in 1996 has been dubbed the 'Big Bang' after the London 'Big Bang' of 1986. It involves changes to the operation of the stock market such as the liberalisation of the commission on stock trading; reforms of financial institutions enabling banks to extend their range of activities; the establishment of a regulatory system to police the markets and the introduction of standardised international accounting conventions. These reforms might be expected to move Japanese corporate governance in the Anglo-American direction. Restrictions on insider dealing, the provision of information to the market and protection for 'outside' stockholders, for example, are likely gradually to undermine the dominance of 'insiders'.

Further, substantial capital losses on shareholdings in recent years have put many banks and other financial institutions under pressure. As that pressure has mounted the 'patience' of these 'long-term' investors has been sorely tried and its limits tested. The willingness to extend long-term finance in the expectation of eventual profitability has been reduced. Stefan Wagstyl (1992) for example, records the falling capital spending in Japanese companies even in areas such as R&D. With Japanese firms unable to escape the emerging constraints on growth he argues that 'the chase after sales seems certain to give way to a pursuit of profits'.

Germany has also undergone some reappraisal of its system of corporate governance in recent years. Ziegler (2000) describes proposals to reform the supervisory boards and extend shareholder rights, thus moving towards a more Anglo-American system. A celebrated attempt by Krupp to launch a hostile takeover of Thyssen in 1997 led to such negative political reactions, however, that it was transformed into a friendly merger. This sequence of events 'marked a clear setback for the proponents of a more open market for corporate control in Germany'. Nevertheless, as Chapman (1996) reports, the rescue packages provided by the banks to a raft of companies such as

Metallgesellschaft, Daimler-Benz, Bremer Vulkan and Klockner-Humboldt-Deutz (KHD) in the mid-1990s attracted considerable criticism and revealed 'how lenient the German system of corporate governance is'. A few years later (in 2000) Vodafone's successful acquisition of Mannesmann became the first example of a successful hostile bid in German corporate history.

Disenchantment with bank-orientated systems of corporate governance derives therefore from the very features which make it attractive to critics of the market-orientated system. For the latter, long-term stable relationships give rise to well-informed owners willing to sacrifice immediate returns for the future development of the firm. The alternative view is that long-term stable relationships between financial institutions and firms ultimately lead to a system which is too forgiving, permits empire building on the part of managers and makes radical innovation very difficult.

To supplement this sceptical appraisal of the consequences of bank-orientated systems of corporate governance, the counter-critique of the Anglo-American model defends that system against charges of short-termism. The defence is mounted at two levels – methodological and empirical.

Methodology

The building of sophisticated models along the lines reported in Section 3 embodying particular assumptions about information asymmetry and the existence of specific human capital does not, in itself, prove anything about the relative performance of actual systems. If we are to avoid the 'nirvana' fallacy[8] it is necessary to compare the behaviour of feasible alternative sets of institutional arrangements. Further, it is not valid merely to assert that one system is characterised by a particular 'information structure' or that another system embodies a high level of trust among the participants. Given the subjective nature of these judgements it will usually only be possible to *infer* such matters from indirect empirical evidence.

Empirical Evidence

Defenders of the Anglo-US system argue that a great deal of evidence exists which contradicts the short-termist critique. The finding, for example, that announcements of R&D expenditure and long-term capital expenditure more generally are associated with stock price increases seems inconsistent with the idea that investment in research and development is discouraged by the stock market.[9] Similarly, Hall (1988) could not detect any effect of mergers on R&D performance. This casts doubt on the idea that firms undertaking investment in research attracted takeover raiders who tried to steal the returns to these 'undervalued' assets.

Studies of takeovers during the 1980s showed that share prices of target companies rose sharply at the announcement of a bid.[10] Critics believe that this premium represented the present value of a redistribution of income towards shareholders of target companies rather than gains in productive efficiency. Jensen (1988) argues, however, that social gains amounting to about 8 per cent of the combined value of the companies involved were achieved by the average takeover in the United States. The takeover mechanism, in Jensen's view, was particularly effective in the 1980s in prising resources away from cash-rich companies in the oil and other industries. These resources would otherwise have been wasted by managers on low return projects within the target firms rather than used for higher yielding projects elsewhere.

This theory has become known as the 'free cash flow' theory of takeovers. The use of surpluses in the petroleum industry for further exploration, for example, made it cheaper at one stage to acquire reserves by buying companies than by actual search. In the process of takeover, cash was disgorged to the shareholders of target companies who were then free to consider alternative uses for their funds. The 'free cash flow' theory of takeover activity is controversial. Goldstein (2000) investigates a sample of hostile takeovers in the US from the years 1978–89 and concludes that the free cash flow hypothesis is not supported. Other studies confirm the effectiveness of the takeover as a constraint on managerial moral hazard. In the United States, some individual states restrict takeover activity in the banking sector while others do not. Schranz (1993) finds that banking firms are more profitable in those states that have an active takeover market.

For defenders of the market-orientated system of corporate governance, therefore, it is as reasonable to accuse the bank-orientated system of overlongtermism as it is to accuse the market system of short-termism. The Anglo-American system offers the advantages of great flexibility, an effective weapon against managerial waste, and a means of preventing overinvestment whether this be in oil reserves, physical equipment or the currently fashionable areas of training and research.

5. INSTITUTION BUILDING IN THE SINGLE CAPITALISM

Underlying the debate about the relative merits of different varieties of capitalism or systems of corporate governance there lurks a seductive idea of dubious validity that by some collective decision it might be possible to adopt whichever system has the best properties. The idea is of dubious validity for two reasons.

(i) There may not be a single 'best' system of governance. A whole range of possible governance structures may instead be feasible and suitably adapted to differing conditions. The whole 'two capitalisms' debate can be seen as overlooking the main underlying issue. If some governance arrangements are likely to be more efficient than others, what are the impediments which prevent them from being adopted – not by government but by those individuals with the most at stake in the circumstances of each case? The choice of a governance structure for a firm is rather like the choice of a 'constitution'. The dynamic processes of competition might be expected to produce effective governance arrangements – selecting out poor performers and replacing them with firms better structured to survive in the particular environment in which they find themselves.

(ii) If governance arrangements do tend to gravitate towards differing 'norms' this may reflect a long process of historical evolution. The effectiveness of a particular structure may, in other words, depend upon the existence of other supporting institutions which influence the behaviour of the entire system. Whether, for example, a company decides to appoint its top managers from inside the organisation or uses the external managerial labour market will to some extent depend upon how well developed the latter institution has become. Are there specialised agencies able to assist in executive recruitment and selection? Are there information channels good enough to mitigate the adverse selection problems that will exist? Is there a sufficiently deep pool of managers with enough accumulated reputational capital for this to act as a disciplining force? Again, the extent to which a substantial venture capital market has developed will determine whether innovative ideas can be undertaken by new 'entrepreneurial' firms or are confined to older and larger 'managerial' ones.

These interdependencies mean that 'governance systems', as distinct from the arrangements adopted by particular individual firms, are not really there for the choosing – even through collective mechanisms. If the United States suppressed the managerial labour market or restricted takeovers in the interests of encouraging 'long-term commitment' it would not thereby create an environment similar to that in Japan. If Japan wished to emulate the success of venture capital markets in the United States and the United Kingdom it would be likely to find that its evolved conventions and institutions made precise imitation impossible. Recognising that bits of one system cannot easily be grafted onto another, reformers emphasise the importance of 'systemic' action. Porter (1992, p. 76) for example, argues that 'the only real solution to the failure of the U.S. capital allocation system is to address the system as a "system" '. A number of inter-related reforms should be undertaken in his view 'ideally all at once' (p. 77).

6. THE NEW INSTITUTIONAL ECONOMICS AND THE FIRM

At the root of discussions about corporate governance in the two capitalisms, therefore, is the question of how institutional structures evolve and whether this evolution can be expected to produce social gains. Contracting at arm's length is unlikely always to provide the best method of coordinating economic activities. It is bemusing to many supporters of market processes to find themselves accused of denying this proposition. For many years, economic theorists such as Ronald Coase (1937), Armen Alchian (1977), Harold Demsetz (1983) and Oliver Williamson (1985) have investigated the institutions of capitalism. These institutions, they argue, are structured so as to economise on transactions costs and to cope with the inevitable hazards of contracting. Contracts may range from exchanges on arm's-length spot markets to the most intimate and durable of relationships enforced by accrued trust and social convention. Capitalism is not, therefore, to be confused with trading on spot markets; it is about choice of contracting arrangements.

Transactions-cost analysis leads us to expect a huge variety of institutional forms in an efficiently functioning capitalist system. Labour-managed firms, partnerships, cooperatives, profit-sharing firms, non-profit enterprises, charities, closely-owned companies, and joint-stock companies are all possible. As Hansmann (1996) argues, each type of firm may be seen as an appropriate response to particular sets of transactional hazards depending upon factors such as the costs of monitoring; the scale of the enterprise; the risk aversion of financiers, managers and employees; the vulnerability of the various stakeholders to opportunism and so forth. Within the joint-stock sector it is possible to structure managerial incentives to encourage care of shareholder value; to make takeovers more or less difficult by adjustments to corporate charters or the introduction of 'poison pills'; to institute profit-sharing arrangements or other schemes[11] which protect assets vulnerable to hold-up; and to introduce employee representation on company boards if that were considered advantageous. Given the scope for innovation and experiment in governance structures why do the critics fear that institutional failure is widespread in the United States and the United Kingdom? Such failure might be expected to be associated with high returns to successful institutional innovation and a correspondingly high incentive to try new ideas.

Interdependence between Institutions

One 'sophisticated' answer to this question is that the benefits of certain institutional changes may not all accrue to those implementing them – there are external benefits that leak away to others. Suppose, for example, that a firm is set up with a few well-informed shareholders who monitor managers carefully. The shareholders face greater risks and monitoring costs but the benefits of greater managerial effort and better decisions more than compensate. The existence of such a firm will have 'external' effects if managers elsewhere in the same industry respond to the 'tighter' and more competitive environment by raising their own effort levels. 'Managerial' firms with widely dispersed shareholders work more effectively if they face competition from firms with more concentrated ownership. In these circumstances competition between governance arrangements might be expected to result in 'too few' classically structured firms since these provide indirect monitoring services to managerial firms for which they receive no reward.[12]

Similar arguments have been devised to justify the assertion that profit-sharing arrangements will be under-provided. Certain highly skilled individuals might greatly raise the productive potential of a team of profit sharers. If another company entices these skilled people away by paying them more, the loss to the sharing team as a whole may be more than the gain to the deserters. In this case the existence of classically structured firms reduces the productivity of profit-sharing firms. These arguments, however, tell us more about the ability of economists to 'dream up' circumstances in which anyone's pet governance arrangements deserve support than about the actual processes of institutional competition and innovation.

Government Regulation and Institutional Structure

It is probably not these theoretical possibilities that underlie the suspicion that Anglo-US governance arrangements are flawed. A more persuasive line of argument is that a bias in favour of arm's-length contracting and market-orientated governance is the 'unintended consequence' of government regulation and not the result of experiment and evolution in a free market. Governments may deplore 'short-termism' but their regulation of contracting has tended to support the arm's-length model. Consider the following examples of government regulation.

(a) Insider-dealing regulations try to ensure that all shareholders trade on the basis of publicly available information. No shareholder should be in a privileged position relative to other shareholders. Insider status is discouraged because it implies restrictions on the ability of the insider to trade on the information acquired.
(b) Takeover rules restrict the ability of bidders to build up substantial positions in a company secretly. Once more this is designed to protect the small shareholder who will be less likely to sell unwittingly to a raider at a price below the post-takeover value. By discouraging takeovers and

protecting small shareholders these rules buttress the system of widely dispersed shareholdings.

(c) In the United States, anti-takeover laws passed by various states in response to the takeover wave of the 1980s make leveraged buyouts (and hence the concentration of ownership) more difficult to achieve.

(d) The recently repealed Glass-Steagall Act (1933) in the United States forbade commercial banks from underwriting, holding or dealing in corporate securities. In 1940 the Investment Company Act had a similarly discouraging effect on the corporate governance activities of mutual funds. In the light of this regulatory background it seems hardly surprising that a bank-orientated system of governance failed to evolve. It is interesting that one justification for restricting banks in this way was that underwriting new securities and lending to firms created a conflict of interest. Banks who knew firms were in trouble might avoid losses by underwriting new share issues, the proceeds of which could be used to pay off the bank's loans. Recent work has shown, however, that prior to the Glass-Steagall Act commercial banks underwrote *higher* quality issues than independent investment banks and that public awareness of conflicts of interest was sufficient to constrain the banks in their operations (see Krozner and Rajan, 1994). Arguments that markets 'fail' because of asymmetric information and 'adverse selection' may be plausible and popular with economic model builders, but evidence that markets are unable to cope is often entirely lacking. Nevertheless, the interpretation of Glass-Steagall is likely to be debated for many years to come. Time will tell whether this Act 'put salutary limits on the economy's ability to speculate with other people's money' – thus providing a necessary damper for the Anglo-American financial system as suggested by Kuttner (1999); or whether it unnecessarily prevented the evolution of closer and more long-term relations between business and the banks.

(e) In the field of pensions, government policy has encouraged 'portability' and flexibility. It is widely felt that people should not suffer a reduction in their pension entitlement when they leave an organisation. It has for long been a principle of British pension provision that the funds should not be concentrated in one firm but that risks should be spread widely. The capital market enables people to break the link between the size of their pension and the performance of the firm in which they happen to work. This freedom from dependency on a particular organisation is considered very desirable by most people. Yet lifetime employment systems require dependency. In Japan, for example, the large 'separation payments' that are paid at retirement represent 70 per cent of the value of retirement benefits provided by companies (see

Aoki, 1989, p. 58). An employee who leaves the firm for 'private reasons' before retirement would expect to lose a substantial portion of these separation payments.

(f) Monopolies, mergers and restrictive practices legislation presents another area of paradox to the proponents of close long-term relationships. In the interests of fostering competition, a great deal of this legislation is devoted to keeping firms apart. There is a long tradition in economics reflected in competition law that where people in the same trade gather together, training and research and development will not constitute the most prominent topics of conversation. Changed perceptions about the consequences of restrictive practices legislation have led in recent years to exemptions for certain classes of agreement, particularly those involving joint projects or vertical associations which are now seen as protecting quality and reputation. Few economists have been prepared to go as far as Shenfield (1983), however, and argue that antitrust policy since the Sherman Act has been a complete waste of time and resources.

These various examples indicate that the forms of corporate governance that have become established in the US and the UK may be as much the result of government policy interventions as of competitive adaptation. A recent book by Mark Roe (1994) argues strongly that the political distrust of concentrated financial power has acted systematically to prevent the type of corporate ownership patterns seen in Germany and Japan. Many of the policy proposals suggested by Porter (1992) are concerned with relaxing existing regulatory restrictions in the US. He suggests, *inter alia*, removing restrictions on the ability of investors to hold significant corporate stakes; permitting financial institutions to hold both debt and equity; permitting the disclosure of 'insider' information to significant long-term owners; and loosening restrictions on institutional board membership (see Porter, 1992, pp. 77–9).

More generally, societies which are suspicious of all concentrations of power and are intolerant of dependency (even when this can plausibly be ascribed to agreements which are voluntarily entered into) are very likely, through the political process, to gravitate towards an arm's-length system of contracting. It is perhaps not too fanciful to see changes in the tax treatment of families and to divorce laws as part of the same general phenomenon. The strong desire to protect personal autonomy within marriage and to minimise dependency by lowering the cost of 'exit' have combined to produce an institution of marriage which looks short-termist and in which the incentive to make specific investments in child rearing and other matters is undermined (see Brinig and Crafton, 1994).

7. CONCLUSION

The superiority of arm's-length over other forms of contracting is not, *pace* Kaletsky, a free market dogma. It may be that the dominance of the 'perfectly competitive', anonymous, 'level playing field' conception of capitalism in certain academic circles has led to the neglect of institutions in economic analysis. Theorists from Coase onwards who have made economic institutions the centre of their studies, however, have never subscribed to this idea.

Competitive capitalism is as much about the development of institutional forms as it is about the development of new products and processes. The corporate governance systems that have developed in the US, UK, Germany and Japan have very different characteristics (Section 2). The Anglo-US system has been subject to much recent criticism for encouraging short-termism (Section 3). Practitioners and academic writers have also pointed out possible failings in other systems that are equally serious (Section 4). Underlying the 'two capitalisms' debate, therefore, is the question of whether institutions can be relied on to adapt over time and take on the structures most suitable to their circumstances (Section 5). It is probable that systems do have a coherence of their own and that the governance arrangements adopted by one firm will not be entirely independent of the choices made by other firms. Nevertheless, a major determinant of governance arrangements in the corporate sector and of contractual arrangements more generally is state regulatory intervention (Section 6). This is so in Japan as well as in the US and the UK. A climate of financial and business regulation which is more neutral in its effects on corporate governance is therefore likely to be a prerequisite of institutional change.

NOTES

1. This is true for AGs (stock corporations) with more than 2000 employees. Those with fewer than 2000 employees must have supervisory boards with one-third of the members representing employees.
2. Outsiders are especially unlikely to succeed in acquiring Japanese business assets by takeover. T. Boone Picken's attempt at taking over Koito was entirely unsuccessful. See 'What T. Boone's Slim Pickin's Say About Japan', *The Wall Street Journal*, Monday May 6 1991.
3. The UK figure was about 40 per cent compared with around 10 per cent in Japan. See Prevezer and Ricketts (1994, table 12.1, p. 250).
4. 'Rebuilding Britain: The Agenda for Economic Recovery', *The Guardian*, 16 March 1993, p. 14.
5. It is worth pointing out that this is directly counter to the 'old' standard position that dividends were likely to be good for overall investment because managers only knew of possibilities within their own firms while outside investors would transfer resources to the fastest growing and most productive sectors. As will be seen in a later section, a great deal hangs on our beliefs about how well informed participants in the outside capital market really are.

Critics of the market-orientated system tend to assume that managers are capable of using investable funds in a host of productive projects while outside investors are prey to speculative fads and short time horizons. Defenders are apt to assume that managers are capable of squandering any amount of resources in empire building or wishful thinking while outside investors can make a detached and prudent assessment of possibilities. The 'nihilists' amongst us are prone to accept the second assumption of the critics and the first assumption of the defenders.

6. In general the problem with information which is hidden from one of the parties to a contract is that it leads to 'adverse selection'. Adverse selection refers to the tendency of high-quality suppliers to leave the market if buyers are, *ex ante*, unable to distinguish low- from high-quality goods and services. Adverse selection can be countered by the development of reputation, through repeat dealing, and by market 'signalling' (see text).
7. For a formal model see Stein (1988).
8. See Demsetz (1969). The fallacy consists in implicitly comparing an actual situation with some idealised alternative in which the problems of existence have altogether faded away.
9. Office of the Chief Economist of the United States' Securities and Exchange Commission (1985). Also McConnell and Muscarella (1985).
10. Bid premia averaged about 30 per cent in the mid-1980s.
11. Golden parachutes, for example, give certain employees rights to severance pay that can be seen as providing reassurance that the value of firm-specific skills cannot simply be stolen.
12. Hart (1983) presents a model of this type.

REFERENCES

Albert, M. (1993), *Capitalism against Capitalism*, London: Whurr Publishers.

Alchian, A.A. (1977), *Economic Forces at Work*, Indianapolis: Liberty Press.

Aoki, M. (1986), 'Horizontal versus vertical information structure of the firm', *American Economic Review*, **76** (5), 971–83.

Aoki, M. (1989), *Information, Incentives and Bargaining in the Japanese Economy*, Cambridge: Cambridge University Press.

Bowles, S. and H. Gintis (1993), 'The revenge of homo-economicus: contested exchange and the revival of political economy', *Journal of Economic Perspectives*, **7** (1), 83–102.

Brinig, M.F. and S.M. Crafton (1994), 'Marriage and opportunism', *Journal of Legal Studies*, **23** (2), 869–94.

Chapman, C. (1996), 'German corporate governance under fire', *Internal Auditor*, **53** (5), 11.

Clark, R.L. and N. Ogawa (1992), 'Employment tenure and earnings profiles in Japan and the United States: Comment', *American Economic Review*, **82** (1), 336–45.

Coase, R.H. (1937), 'The nature of the firm', *Economica*, **4** 386.

Corbett, J. (1994), 'An Overview of the Japanese Financial System', in N. Dimsdale and M. Prevezer (eds) (1994), *Capital Markets and Corporate Governance*, Oxford: Clarendon Press, pp. 306–24.

Demsetz, H. (1969), 'Information and efficiency: another viewpoint', *Journal of Law and Economics*, **12**.

Demsetz, H. (1983), 'The Structure of ownership and the theory of the firm', *Journal of Law and Economics*, **26** 375.

Dertouzos, M.L., R.K. Lester and R.M. Solow (1989), *Made in America: Regaining the Productivity Edge*, Cambridge, MA: MIT Press.

Easterbrook, F.H. (1984) 'Two agency cost explanations of dividends', *American Economic Review*, **74** (4), 650–59.

Economist, The (1991), 'Japan encourages its young', 10 August, Management Focus, p. 57.
Goldstein, D. (2000), 'Hostile takeovers as corporate governance? Evidence from the 1980s', *Review of Political Economy*, **12** (4), 381.
Hall, B.H. (1988), 'Effects of Takeover Activity on Corporate Research and Development', in A.J. Auerbach (ed.), *Corporate Takeovers: Causes and Consequences*, Chicago: NBER, University of Chicago Press, pp. 69–96.
Hansmann, H. (1996), *The Ownership of Enterprise*, Cambridge MA: Harvard University Press.
Hart, O.D. (1983), 'The market mechanism as an incentive scheme', *Bell Journal of Economics*, **14** 366.
Hutton, W. (1995), *The State We're In*, London: Jonathan Cape.
Jacobs, M.T. (1991), *Short-Term America: The Causes and Cures of Our Business Myopia*, Boston, MA: Harvard Business School Press.
Jensen, M.C. (1988), 'Takeovers: their causes and consequences', *Journal of Economic Perspectives*, **2** (1), 21–48.
Kaletsky, Anatole (1994), 'Rover was really sold to the City', *The Times*, 22 February.
Kaplan, S.N. (1994), 'Top executive rewards and firm performance: a comparison of Japan and the United States', *Journal of Political Economy*, **102** (3), 510–46, esp. Table 4, 535.
Kester, W. Carl (1991), 'Governance, Contracting, and Investment Time Horizons', Working Paper 92–003, Harvard Business School.
Krozner, S.R. and R.G. Rajan (1994), 'Is the Glass-Steagall act justified? A study of the U.S. experience with universal banking before 1933', *American Economic Review*, **84** (4), 810–32.
Kuttner, R. (1999), 'A Requiem for Glass-Steagall', *Business Week*, Issue 3655, p. 28.
Mayer, C. (1993), 'Promiscuity and the UK financial system', University of Warwick.
Mayer, C. and I. Alexander (1991), 'Stock markets and corporate performance: A comparison of quoted and unquoted companies', Centre for Economic Policy Research, Discussion Paper.
McConnell, J.J and C.J. Muscarella (1985), 'Corporate capital expenditure decisions and the market value of the firm', *Journal of Financial Economics*, **14**, 399–422.
Mikuni, A. (1992), 'The Nikkei: A Casualty of Japan's Outmoded Economy', *Wall Street Journal Europe*, 28–29 August, p. 6.
Mochizuki, K. (1994), 'Tomorrow's capitalism in a Japanese perspective', *RSA Journal*, (October), 37–45.
Porter, M.E. (1992), 'Capital disadvantage: America's failing capital investment system', *Harvard Business Review*, September–October.
Prevezer, M. and M. Ricketts (1994), 'Corporate Governance: The UK Compared with Germany and Japan', in N. Dimsdale and M. Prevezer (eds), *Capital Markets and Corporate Governance*, Oxford: Clarendon Press, pp. 237–56.
Roe, M. (1994), *Strong Managers, Weak Owners: The Political Roots of American Corporate Finance*, Princeton: Princeton University Press.
Schneider-Lenne, Ellen. R. (1994), 'The Role of the German Capital Markets and the Universal Banks, Supervisory Boards, and Interlocking Directorships', in N. Dimsdale and M. Prevezer (eds), op. cit, p. 295.
Schranz, Mary S. (1993), 'Takeovers improve firm performance: evidence from the banking industry', *Journal of Political Economy*, **101** (2), 299–326.

Shenfield, A. (1983), *Myth and Reality in Anti-Trust*, Wincott Memorial Lecture, Occasional Paper 66, London: Institute of Economic Affairs.
Shleifer, A. and L.H. Summers (1988), 'Breach of Trust in Hostile Takeovers', in A.J. Auerbach (ed.), *Corporate Takeovers: Causes and Consequences*, Chicago: NBER, University of Chicago Press, pp. 33–56.
Stein, J.C. (1988), 'Takeover threats and managerial myopia', *Journal of Political Economy*, **96** (1), 61–80.
Ubukata, Yukio (1991), 'Stepping out of the pyramid', *Intersect*, **7** (3), 18–24.
Wagstyl, Stefan (1992), 'The big squeeze in Japan', *Financial Times*, Monday 27 April.
Williams, D. (1994), *Japan: Beyond the End of History*, London and New York: Routledge.
Williamson, O.E. (1985), *The Economic Institutions of Capitalism: Firms, Markets, Relational Contracting*, London: Collier Macmillan.
Ziegler, J.N. (2000), 'Corporate governance and the politics of property rights in Germany', *Politics and Society*, **28** (2), 195.

10. Political orientation and multinational investment flows into Italy

Ram Mudambi, Pietro Navarra and Giuseppe Sobbrio

1. INTRODUCTION

In the post-Soviet era, governments of all hues tend to view multinational enterprises (MNEs) as sources of scarce investment funds and desirable high value added jobs (UNCTAD, 1997). The ideal MNE investment from the point of view of the local government consists of a single facility with regional and preferably global R&D, production and marketing responsibility. Such a facility is a large employer, with a highly skilled, productive, and high-wage workforce, and a high level of local purchases to generate macro multiplier effects (Young et al., 1994). Whether or not the government takes an activist role in attracting MNE investment, ensuring that the investment is close to the ideal requires an understanding of the forces that underlie the multinational mode of operation (Mudambi, 1998).

In their seminal work, Buckley and Casson (1976) analyze the multinational enterprise (MNE) using the tools of transaction cost economics developed by Coase (1937). Here, the MNE is seen as a form of hierarchical international organization that is put in place when the transaction costs involved with using market operations, typically through exports, become too high. Dunning's (1980, 1988) eclectic or O-L-I paradigm, under which MNE investment decisions are based on ownership, location and/or internalization advantages, can be seen as a means of fleshing out the transaction costs involved in international activity. In the literature, the role of the government is typically subsumed within the location dimension (Davidson, 1980; Mudambi, 1995; Loree and Guisinger, 1995). Thus, the government may increase a location's attractiveness to MNE investors either directly, by providing investment supports, or indirectly by improving the location's fundamental advantages, that is, its infrastructure and labor force.

Direct incentives to invest may well be viewed with suspicion by MNEs that may fear less favorable treatment once investments are in place and their bargaining position is considerably weakened. This question also affects the evaluation of the raw measures of location-specific advantage. Brewer (1992) finds that MNE–government relations tend to be characterized by a mixture of cooperation (in relation to issues such as investment supports) and conflict (in relation to issues such as regulation). He is mainly concerned with tangible issues that have tangible effects.

Previous studies of the role of political factors on MNE investment decisions have focussed on this issue of risk. For example, it has been pointed out that an unstable political climate does not necessarily equate with an unprofitable investment potential and that political risk must be treated like another component of business risk (Kobrin, 1979; Simon, 1984). Brewer (1983) examines the relationship between political instability and changes in government policy relating to MNE funds transfers. He differentiates between industrial and developing countries and finds that the relationships are actually stronger for industrial countries. Miller (1993) develops an instrument for measuring managers' perceptions of country risk, which includes political factors.

Thus, the literature on political risk has mainly been concerned with identifying factors underlying observable government policies towards MNEs. However, such analysis ignores the subtler aspects of the location's business culture (Casson, 1991) and its overall attitude towards MNE investors. These attitudes may be summarized by the political culture in the location, reflected in the political orientation of the government. These can have tangible effects on an MNE even if no policy pronouncements are made explicitly. This leads to the following question: does the political orientation of a government have any impact on the foreign direct investment (FDI) decisions of MNEs?

The question is difficult to address empirically, as locations differ in many dimensions (Amin and Malmberg, 1992). The effect of the political orientation of the government, which may not be overriding in any event, may not be easy to isolate. We therefore address this question by examining MNE investment location decisions with regard to different regions within a single country. The country we examine is Italy, which exhibits one of the highest levels of variation with regard to the political orientation of its regional governments.

Our study complements the work of Mariotti and Piscitello (1995), who study FDI into the Italian regions from the perspective of information costs. They find that the pattern of intra-country FDI is influenced by the asymmetry of information between domestic firms and foreign investors. Thus, they find that certain types of economic intangibles are important in influencing FDI. In contrast, we are interested in studying the influence of political intangibles.

We assume that firms take the political environment as given and exogenous. In this approach, the role of MNEs in manipulating the political environment (Boddewyn, 1988; Boddewyn and Brewer, 1994) is not considered. The returns to overt political behavior on the part of MNEs are likely to be higher in developing countries where the domestic corporate opposition is much weaker. Thus, a passive political strategy is likely to be optimal for investments in industrialized countries like Italy (Poynter, 1985; Doz, 1986). For example, it is reported that US, UK and German MNEs follow a 'whiter than white' policy in adhering to transfer pricing laws (Coates et al., 1992).

We find that political orientation does seem to influence MNE investment decisions. However, this effect is found to be secondary, while the primary factors underlying investment location decisions appear to be the economic location advantages. Thus, the subtler aspects of political culture do seem to matter. When considering the secondary importance of the estimated effects of these factors, it should be borne in mind that the primary factors are likely to be roughly equal in most locations that are short-listed by MNE investors. When this occurs, the secondary factors will be critical in determining the outcome of the investment location decision.

The chapter is organized as follows. In the second section we set up our formal research hypotheses and discuss our methodology. In the third section we describe our data, explain our estimation procedure and results. Finally, some summary comments are offered in the last section.

2. RESEARCH HYPOTHESES AND METHODOLOGY

Our objective in this chapter is to focus on the link between the political orientation of governments and the location of activities by MNEs. In studying the linkage between these two topics, we are interested in two questions. First, whether any statistically significant link exists; second, if there is a link, is the government's political orientation a primary factor influencing location or is it a secondary factor, exerting only a residual effect. These two questions give rise to the following two nested hypotheses.

- H1: The political orientation of the government has a direct or primary effect on the MNE investment location decision, along with location-specific variables.
- H2: The government's political orientation has an incremental or 'second-stage' effect on MNE investment, *after* accounting for firm- and location-specific factors.

H1 and H2 are based on different assumptions regarding the decision processes within MNEs. Under H1, MNEs view the government's political orientation as a key variable in the investment location decisions, along with location-specific variables. Thus, the decision process involves a general appraisal of all variables simultaneously. However, under H2, MNEs view government political orientation as a marginal variable. Under this scenario, the MNE decision process is a two-stage one, in which location factors are the major decision variables, with government political orientation exerting an incremental influence on residual investment. A rejection of H1 implies that government political orientation is not a primary variable in MNE investment location decisions. However, a rejection of H2 implies that government political orientation is totally irrelevant in the context of MNE investment location. This hypothesis-testing procedure has the advantage of being able to assess the impact of government political orientation in a *three*-way categorization, that is, whether it is a major factor, an incremental factor or of no importance whatsoever.

Assuming that government political orientation has a direct effect on MNE investment, we may set up a general equation determining investment expenditure at a particular location as:

$$Y_i = f[\text{LOC, POL}] + u_i, \qquad (10.1)$$

where

Y_i = level of investment by firm 'i' in a given period
LOC = vector of location-specific variables
POL = vector of measures of government political orientation

The estimation of (10.1) may be used to test H1.

On the other hand, if as postulated in H2, government investment incentives have an incremental effect on the location of R&D, we may model the process as follows:

$$Y_i = f_1[\text{LOC}] + v_i, \qquad (10.2)$$

$$v_i = f_2[\text{POL}] + w_i \qquad (10.3)$$

The estimates obtained from (10.2) and (10.3) differ systematically from those obtained in (10.1). In (10.1), the LOC and POL regressors are used jointly and their covariance appears in the estimation of the parameters. To the extent that we expect these factors to be correlated, this 'muddies the waters'. In (10.2) and (10.3), the covariance does not appear, so the estimates of the parameters of the LOC factors are free of the effects of the POL factors. This methodology for estimating marginal effects using residuals is used by Cantwell and Mudambi (2000), who formally derive the properties of the two estimators (see Appendix 10.2).

Thus, the specification in (10.1) implies that political factors are co-determinants of MNE investment location, along with locational and infrastructural factors. The specification in (10.2) and (10.3) implies that the major influence on the location of investment emanates from locational and infrastructural factors, while political orientation is influential at the margin, affecting the residuals. This is not to say that political orientation is unimportant. Under H2, political orientation will play a key role in a decision between two possible sites where the major locational parameters are very similar. Such situations are likely to be the rule rather than the exception in MNE investment location.

3. DATA, ESTIMATION AND RESULTS

Political orientation, particularly in terms of party identity, is a very country-specific characteristic and comparing party orientations across countries is very difficult. Thus, party A in country 1 may be considerably more hostile to foreign investment than party B in country 2. However, this tells us little about the relative political orientation of the two parties if country 1 is a very closed economy while country 2 is extremely open. With this in mind, we restrict our focus to a single country, Italy, so that the political orientation is generally comparable along party lines.

3.1 Data

The FDI data used in this study was taken from Cominotti and Mariotti (1994, 1997). The data on regional macroeconomic indicators was obtained from Prometeia, a Milan-based agency. Finally, the data on regional infrastructures was obtained from an unpublished manuscript compiled by the Istituto Guglielmo Tagliacarne (1998). Using these sources, it was possible to generate a data set consisting of two region-wise cross-sections. These were stacked for the purpose of estimation.

The variables assembled for use in the study correspond to the requirements of estimating equations (10.1), (10.2) and (10.3). FDI, infrastructure and political data were available on a regional basis. The dependent variable was the level of FDI in a region.

The level of FDI for each of 20 regions was obtained for the years 1992, 1994 and 1996, generating three 20-element panels for a total of 60 observations. We use four separate measures of FDI into Italy. The first measure is the (region-wise) total number of factories in which non-Italian MNEs have an ownership interest (FACALL). The second measure is the (region-wise) number of factories in which non-Italian MNEs have a *majority* ownership interest (FACMAJ). This second measure is obviously a sub-set of the first and perhaps a finer measure of FDI. The third measure is the (region-wise) level of employment in *all* MNE enterprises (EMALL). The fourth measure is similar to the second and is the (region-wise) level of employment in those enterprises where non-Italian MNEs have a *majority* ownership interest (EMAJ).

Two groups of regressors were used. The first group, (the LOC group), consisted of traditional economic location variables, that is regional levels of infrastructure and factor endowments. This group includes measures of the regional infrastructure, income (representing regional development) and labor force. To capture the inherent time period involved between decision making and implementation of FDI, these variables were lagged two years. This lag is fairly typical in the international business literature (see for example, Czinkota et al., 1998). However, the results are fairly robust to the choice of lag.

The second group of regressors (the POL group), consisted of measures of regional government political orientation, political institutions and political concentration. Since we are interested in the intangible effects of political orientation, which develop over long periods of time, we consider these variables over the period 1968–91. Regional government political orientation was measured using the political orientation of the region in terms of the level and trend in the electoral power of the Center-right (Christian Democrats), the Center-left (Socialists) and Far-left (Communists) political formations. During the period in question, these formations constituted the only national political groups and they accounted for at least 70 per cent of the total votes cast in every region.

Political institutions were measured using an index based on Putnam et al. (1993), which uses data for the period 1978–85. Political concentration was measured by constructing the Cubbin–Leech (1983) power index for the upper house in each region. This variable was constructed using data for the period 1968–87.

The details of all variables extracted and used in the study are provided in Appendix 10.1. Summary statistics relating to all variables used in the analysis are presented in Table 10.1.

3.2 Estimation and Results

Baseline estimates were obtained using ordinary least squares (OLS). These involved estimating equation (10.1) and are presented in Table 10.2. The overall fit of the equation is extremely good, for all four measures of FDI, with an adjusted R^2 value in the region of 90 per cent. Since the regions differ considerably in terms of the levels of FDI, heteroskedasticity is a concern. The Breusch–Pagan test is failed in all cases, indicating that this concern is justified (see Tables 10.2, 10.3 and 10.4). Therefore, in all our estimations, we use White's heteroskedasticity-consistent variance–covariance matrix and are able to successfully deal with this problem.

Table 10.1 Summary statistics

Variable	Mean	S.D.
FACALL	111.23	187.1558
FACMAJ	92.96	161.0337
EMALL	25846.20	57412.1583
EMAJ	20769.80	48052.1533
LTRANS	180.62	51.9296
FTRANS	146.35	66.3363
SERV	82.38	39.6217
UTIL	287.91	47.1838
GDP	66490.08	62021.6772
URATE	11.7261	6.6438
EMIND	252.42	300.3575
CDAVE	0.3665	0.0880
CDTR	–0.0138	0.0133
PCIAVE	0.2793	0.1143
PCITR	0.0008	0.0076
PSIAVE	0.1092	0.0334
PSITR	–0.0017	0.0062
INSTM	4.00	1.8866
ALFA	0.8454	0.0143

The data for estimating equations (10.1) and (10.2) is a panel data set with three 20-element panels. Therefore, we also obtained panel estimators. We used the random-effects approach, since some of the regressors are not time-varying. However, in testing the panel model against the OLS model, the OLS model cannot be rejected (see Tables 10.2 and 10.3 for the test results). This implies that the panel effects are insignificant, so that the panel specification is poorer than the OLS specification. In interests of brevity, we do not report the panel estimates. All the reported results are based on the OLS specification.

The influence of the variables appears to be in line with the predictions of the theoretical literature. Thus, increases in a region's foreign transportation links in terms of its airport and seaport facilities seem to be positively associated with MNE FDI inflows. Further, the quality of the utility facilities (electricity, gas and water) is a significant positive factor. However, the quality of the local transportation network (road and rail) does not appear to be significant. The same is true for the quality and availability of services. Regional GDP appears positive and significant for FACALL and the regional unemployment rate for FACALL and FACMAJ. The size of the region's industrial workforce appears significantly positive for EMALL and EMAJ.

Table 10.2 Estimation of MNE inward investment activity (single equation estimates using location and political orientation variables)

	Regressand			
Regressor	FACALL	FACMAJ	EMALL	EMAJ
Constant	–232.72 (0.68)	–98.29 (0.31)	–108800 (0.76)	–58173 (0.46)
LTRANS	0.302 (1.39)	0.218 (1.09)	–162.05 (1.69)	–165.55 (1.83)
FTRANS	1.604 (4.32)**	1.322 (3.87)**	365.44 (2.67)*	253.73 (2.16)*
SERV	–0.623 (1.11)	–0.475 (0.91)	295.02 (1.53)	290.32 (1.60)
UTIL	2.138 (3.29)**	1.820 (3.08)**	633.97 (2.84)**	501.04 (2.46)*
GDP	0.0024 (2.18)*	0.0018 (1.82)	–0.190 (0.44)	–0.245 (0.64)
URATE	10.695 (2.92)**	8.759 (2.66)*	1371.3 (1.09)	1030.5 (0.93)
EMIND	0.155 (0.86)	0.177 (1.07)	206.77 (2.72)**	187.07 (2.72)**
CDAVE	300.89 (1.15)	213.66 (0.93)	–87301 (0.87)	–87475 (0.98)
CDTR	–1361.9 (0.59)	–521.09 (0.25)	1729900 (1.71)	1881900 (2.06)*
PCIAVE	296.15 (1.40)	175.28 (0.90)	–68446 (0.79)	–108050 (1.45)
PCITR	2227.2 (1.15)	2333.4 (1.31)	1528600 (1.81)	–1697600 (2.16)*
PSIAVE	446.09 (1.65)	476.55 (1.92)	332810 (1.55)	289000 (2.79)**
PSITR	–9638 (4.74)**	–7788 (4.08)**	–1723700 (0.05)	–1049500 (1.35)
INSTM	2.490 (0.27)	2.368 (0.28)	6844.9 (1.80)	4542.2 (1.32)
ALFA	–773.11 (1.39)	–732.67 (1.47)	–45019 (0.21)	–36241 (0.19)

Table 10.2 continued

	Diagnostics			
Regressor	FACALL	FACMAJ	EMALL	EMAJ
Adj. R^2	0.9326	0.9218	0.8927	0.8765
F(15, 44)	55.44	47.34	33.74	28.92
Log-Likelihood	–308.8257	–304.2859	–666.3364	–659.8808
S.E. (residuals)	48.5811	45.0409	18802.5120	16884.5279
AIC	10.828	10.676	22.745	22.529
Breusch–Pagan Test	34.520	34.3721	37.2208	40.2006
$\chi^2(15)$, ('p' value)	(0.0029)	(0.0030)	(0.0012)	(0.0004)
LM Test of Panel				
Model vs. OLS	0.19	0.07	0.24	0.21
$\chi^2(1)$, ('p' value)	(0.6625)	(0.7948)	(0.6229)	(0.6470)

Notes
White's heteroskedasticity-consistent 't' statistics in parentheses.
* Estimate statistically significant at the 5% level.
** Estimate statistically significant at the 1% level.

Table 10.3 Estimation of MNE inward investment activity (estimates using only location variables)

	Regressand			
Regressor	FACALL	FACMAJ	EMALL	EMAJ
Constant	–287.09	–265.33	–135910	–120930
	(3.74)**	(3.81)**	(4.32)**	(4.31)**
LTRANS	–0.189	–0.156	137.25	113.83
	(0.94)	(0.90)	(2.26)**	(2.16)*
FTRANS	0.612	0.545	236.1	192.34
	(3.34)**	(3.38)**	(3.65)**	(3.61)**
SERV	0.036	–0.0078	256.3	213.38
	(0.09)	(0.02)	(1.99)	(1.78)
UTIL	1.024	0.940	435.07	381.65
	(3.09)**	(3.24)**	(3.92)**	(3.92)**
GDP	0.00031	0.00026	–0.111	–0.068
	(0.49)	(0.45)	(0.49)	(0.31)
URATE	5.36	4.929	2795.1	23.99
	(3.04)**	(2.98)**	(3.55)**	(3.36)**
EMIND	0.558	0.481	195.51	155.83
	(5.53)**	(5.07)**	(4.77)**	(3.86)**
		Diagnostics		
Adj. R^2	0.8993	0.8909	0.8576	0.8404
F(7, 52)	76.25	69.85	51.76	45.40
Log-Likelihood	–325.8980	–319.2663	–679.8497	–672.5838
S.E. (residuals)	59.3971	53.1818	21664.6978	19193.7806
AIC	11.130	10.909	22.928	22.686
Breusch–Pagan Test	35.5848	34.5466	37.5379	36.3269
$\chi^2(7)$, ('p' value)	(0.000)	(0.000)	(0.000)	(0.000)
LM Test of Panel				
Model vs. OLS	0.61	0.31	0.00	0.00
$\chi^2(1)$, ('p' value)	(0.4340)	(0.5770)	(0.9209)	(0.9136)

Notes
White's heteroskedasticity-consistent 't' statistics in parentheses.
* Estimate statistically significant at the 5% level.
** Estimate statistically significant at the 1% level.

Generally, few of the measures of political orientation emerge as significant. The level of support for support for the Center-left is significant and positive for EMAJ, while the trend of Center-left support is significant and negative for FACALL and FACMAJ. The trend of support for the Center-right is significant and positive and the trend of support for the Far-left is significant and negative, each for EMAJ. Given the excellent quality of the fit of the equations as measured by the adjusted R^2 and the F statistic, the level of statistical significance observed in the regressors is low. This suggests that multicollinearity is a problem. The problem is confirmed by examining the correlation matrix associated with the regressors.

The implication of this result is that since political orientation and FDI location factors are strongly correlated, it is not possible to disentangle their independent effects on MNE investment decisions using a single-equation estimation methodology. We deal with this problem by estimating equation (10.2), that is, by dropping the political orientation variables from the original specification. This results in a more parsimonious model. The estimates of this model are presented in Table 10.3. The overall fit of the equation as measured by the adjusted R^2 value of almost 90 per cent is nearly as good. Further, the pattern of variable significance now corresponds to the excellent fit of the equation, suggesting that the problem of multicollinearity has been resolved.

While the quality of foreign transportation links and utilities remain significantly positive, both the size of the industrial workforce and the unemployment rate are consistently and significantly positive. Indeed, the size of the industrial workforce is the single most important regressor. Thus, it appears that labor force considerations are particularly important for MNEs investing in Italy, appearing both in terms of the general availability of labor and in terms of the availability of skilled labor.

Finally, we examine the estimates of equation (10.3), which are presented in Table 10.4. The salient feature of these estimates is that once the confounding effect of the location variables is removed, the pattern of statistical significance of the regressors changes dramatically. We now find that the trend of support of the Center-right (Christian Democrats) is significant and directly related to residual FDI. This implies that regions with an increasing trend in Center-right support have enjoyed increasing FDI, *after normalizing for location factors*. However, the level of Center-right support does not appear to be significant.

However, in the case of the Far-left (Communists), both the level and trend of support are significant and inversely related to residual FDI. This implies that regions with high levels of Far-left support, *ceteris paribus*, have lower levels of FDI. Further, an increasing trend in Far-left support is associated with lower FDI. By implication, a region with a falling level of Far-left support attracts more FDI.

Table 10.4 Residual estimation of MNE inward investment activity (estimates using political orientation variables)

Regressor	U(FACALL)	U(FACMAJ)	U(EMALL)	U(EMAJ)
			Regressand	
Constant	229.11	286.16	38050	62453
	(0.69)	(0.96)	(0.30)	(0.57)
CDAVE	–185.8	–154.06	–44764	–28280
	(1.17)	(1.07)	(0.69)	(0.53)
CDTR	3809.8	3428	1478100	1387100
	(2.98)**	(2.94)**	(3.22)**	(3.65)**
PCIAVE	–306.2	–293.7	–119630	–119850
	(4.00)**	(4.17)**	(3.63)**	(4.30)**
PCITR	–5183	–4724	–1908300	–1826900
	(3.58)**	(3.77)**	(3.69)**	(4.43)**
PSIAVE	552.03	523.06	179770	161520
	(1.78)	(1.92)	(1.59)	(1.62)
PSITR	–4295	–3605	–1097700	–816520
	(4.26)**	(4.14)**	(3.20)**	(2.65)*
INSTM	–4.529	–4.495	–1454.1	–1868.2
	(1.13)	(1.21)	(0.88)	(1.35)
ALFA	–90.676	–176.84	17654	–14799
	(0.21)	(0.45)	(0.10)	(0.10)
		Diagnostics		
Adj. R^2	0.1780	0.1673	0.1262	0.1383
F(8, 51)	2.60	2.48	2.07	2.18
Log-Likelihood	–315.6453	–309.4014	–671.4308	–663.7470
S.E. (residuals)	50.5557	45.5591	19012.1598	16726.8501
AIC	10.822	10.613	22.681	22.425
Breusch–Pagan Test	33.3249	32.1465	41.6703	39.4718
$\chi^2(8)$, ('p' value)	(0.000)	(0.000)	(0.000)	(0.000)

Notes

White's heteroskedasticity-consistent 't' statistics in parentheses.

* Estimate statistically significant at the 5% level.

** Estimate statistically significant at the 1% level.

The level of Center-left support does not appear to be significant. However, the trend of Center-left support is significant and inversely related to residual FDI. This seems to support the findings for the Center-right. The levels of Center-right and Center-left support do not seem to affect FDI, but changes in either of these levels seem to have an effect. If support swings from Center-left to Center-right, FDI is positively affected. The reverse occurs if supports swings from Center-right to Center-left. Support for the Far-left seems to have a uniformly negative effect.

We now turn to examining the competing merits of hypotheses H1 and H2. We do this by comparing the specifications of equations (10.1) and (10.2). This involves comparing the estimates presented in Table 10.2 with those presented in Table 10.3. We carry out this comparison using four separate measures. The first three are measures of fit, while the remaining one is a test of specification. These results are presented in Table 10.5.

We first note that fit as measured by adjusted R^2 deteriorates very slightly when we move from the estimates of equation (10.1) (Table 10.2) to the estimates of equation (10.2) (Table 10.3). However, it is generally accepted that adjusted R^2 does not adequately penalize the model for loss of degrees of freedom (Greene, 1993). Thus, we turn to more sensitive measures. The F statistic increases considerably, which suggests that equation (10.2) is the better specification. Further, the Akaike Information Criterion performs comparably in both estimations. On the basis of these three results, the principle of Occam's razor supports the use of the more parsimonious specification.

We also run a joint exclusion test on the political orientation regressors – a generalized F test. This tests whether including the political orientation variables, as in equation (10.1), results in a significant change in fit. This test fails to reject the null hypothesis of regressor exclusion. This suggests that including the political orientation variables in equation (10.1) is inappropriate. This is a powerful test, because as Davidson and MacKinnon (1993) note, for a linear model, the generalized F test contains all the information contained in the Lagrange multiplier, likelihood ratio and Wald tests.

We therefore conclude that we have uncovered strong evidence favoring H2 over H1. Government political orientation seems to function as an incremental variable, affecting MNE investment decisions at the margin. The primary determinants appear to be the location variables identified in the literature.

4. CONCLUDING REMARKS

We were interested in examining the effects of government political orientation on MNE investment. There is evidence in the literature that country risk,

Table 10.5 Exclusion tests on the political orientation variables

		FACALL	FACMAJ	EMALL	EMAJ
Estimates using all variables	Adj. R^2	0.9326	0.9218	0.8927	0.8765
	F(15, 44)	55.44	47.34	33.74	28.92
	AIC	10.828	10.676	22.745	22.529
Estimates using only location variables	Adj. R^2	0.8993	0.8909	0.8576	0.8404
	F(7, 52)	76.25	69.85	51.76	45.40
	AIC	11.130	10.909	22.928	22.686
Generalized ‘F’ test	SSE(U)	103845	89261.9	0.155×10^{11}	0.125×10^{11}
	SSE(R)	143457	121072	0.214×10^{11}	0.172×10^{11}
	F(8,44)	2.097992	1.960025	2.068825	2.022677
	‘p’ value	0.056403	0.074593	0.059846	0.065717

which is strongly affected by political orientation, is not a significant determinant of MNE investment decisions. It has been suggested that this is due to the endogeneity of the firm's rate of return and that it can adjust this rate of return in response to the level of country risk (Bettis and Mahajan, 1985).

Using political variables as regressors in a single-equation estimating framework, we obtain similar results, that is, political orientation has no significant effects on MNE investment. However, when we take account of the correlation between political orientation and location variables, we find that political variables have significant effects on residual FDI by MNEs. Further, a move towards a Center-right orientation has a positive influence on FDI whereas a move towards a Center-left orientation has a negative influence. A Far-left orientation has a uniformly negative influence on FDI.

Our results suggest an alternative explanation for the insignificance of country risk in studies of FDI. It is likely that country risk is highly correlated with location factors, that is, high-risk locations are likely to have inferior facilities while low-risk locations are likely to have superior ones. This means that a single-equation estimating methodology would be unable to disentangle the two effects. If location facilities are the primary determinants of FDI, then they would swamp country risk variables and drive them into insignificance. A two-step procedure, such as the one outlined in this chapter, could provide a means of taking a more incisive look at country risk.

The findings of our study, therefore, suggest that political traditions have a significant residual impact on FDI location decisions by MNEs. Our analysis, however, is limited to a single country. This approach does have the advantage of avoiding the problems associated with isolating the effects of political factors out of the many country factors that affect location decisions by MNEs. In the case of location decisions within a single country, given the homogeneity of political institutions, political traditions influence the way these institutions work. Thus, the manner in which rules are implemented may differ widely in the different regions of a given country. We believe that a relevant part of these differences are due to different political orientations that develop over time. We find that such observable differences in political traditions have a real impact on the MNE preferences regarding the location of investment. Our results suggest that MNEs are aware of and expect such systematic differences. However, such observable effects are only likely in countries with significant historical regional heterogeneity in political orientations.

However, the advantage of a single country study comes at the expense of raising important questions regarding the external validity of the results obtained. Can we generalize these results beyond Italy? Therefore the next step in this research agenda would be to extend this study to investigate the impact of political traditions on FDI location decisions by MNEs both within and across countries.

This possible extension should consider political tradition as one of the important elements that contribute to differences in the institutional environment and hence political risk across countries and over time. These differences in political orientation represent hazards and opportunities for MNEs in two respects. First, different political traditions can affect the actual implementation of policy at the national level and that in turn can impact key strategic conditions such as the regulations surrounding the acquisition of assets, licensing of new business and payment of taxes. Second, institutional differences between nations magnify the difficulties involved in collecting, interpreting and organizing the relevant information necessary to undertake successful entry. In other words, markets with similar political culture pose less uncertainty and therefore lower costs of entry and lower hurdle rates of return. When a foreign firm views a country whose political traditions are distant and dissimilar from any in its prior experience, it is likely to adopt a lower scale of entry (or desist from entry altogether), demand a higher rate of return or both.

REFERENCES

Amin, A. and A. Malmberg (1992), 'Competing structural and institutional influences on the geography of production in Europe', *Environmental Planning A*, **24**, 410–16.

Bettis, R.A. and V. Mahajan (1985), 'Risk/return performance of diversified firms', *Management Science*, **31** (7), 785–99.

Boddewyn, J.J. (1988), 'Political aspects of MNE theory', *Journal of International Business Studies*, **19** (3), 341–63.

Boddewyn, J.J. and T.L. Brewer (1994), 'International business political behavior: New theoretical directions', *Academy of Management Review*, **19** (1), 119–43.

Brewer, T.L. (1983), 'The instability of governments and the instability of controls on funds transfers by multinational corporations: Implications for political risk analysis', *Journal of International Business Studies*, **14** (3), 147–57.

Brewer, T.L. (1992), 'An issue-area approach to the analysis of MNE-government relations', *Journal of International Business Studies*, **23** (2), 295–309.

Buckley, P.J. and M.C. Casson (1976), *The Future of Multinational Enterprise*, London: Macmillan.

Cantwell, J. and R. Mudambi (2000), 'The Location of MNE R&D Activity: The role of investment incentives', *Management International Review*, **40** (1), special issue, 127–480.

Casson, M.C. (1991), *The Economics of Business Culture: Game theory, transaction costs and economic performance*, Oxford: Clarendon Press.

Coase, R. (1937), 'The nature of the firm', *Economica*, 4NS, 386–405.

Coates, J.B., E.W. Davis, C.R. Emmanuel, S.G. Longden and R.J. Stacey (1992), 'Multinational companies' performance measurement systems: International perspectives', *Management Accounting Research*, **3** (2), 133–50.

Cominotti, R. and S. Mariotti (eds) (1994), *Italia Multinazionale 1994: Le nouve e protagonisti dell'internazionalizzazone*, VI Rapport R&P al CNEL, Milano: Etaslibri.

Cominotti, R. and S. Mariotti (eds) (1997), *Italia Multinazionale 1996: Tendenze e protagonisti dell'internationalizzazione*, VI Rapporto R&P al CNEL, Milano: Franco Angeli.
Cubbin, J. and D. Leech (1983), 'The effect of shareholding dispersion on the degree of control in British companies: theory and measurement', *Economic Journal*, **93** (370), 351–70.
Czinkota, M.R., I.A. Ronkainen and M.H. Moffett (1998), *International Business*, 5th edn, New York: The Dryden Press.
Davidson, R. and J.G. MacKinnon (1993), *Estimation and Inference in Econometrics*, New York: Oxford University Press.
Davidson, W.H. (1980), 'The location of foreign direct investment activity: Country characteristics and experience effects', *Journal of International Business Studies*, **11** (2), 9–22.
Doz, Y. (1986), *Strategic Management of Multinational Companies*, New York: Pergamon.
Dunning, J.H. (1980), 'Toward an eclectic theory of international production: Some empirical tests', *Journal of International Business Studies*, **11** (1), 9–31.
Dunning, J.H. (1988), *Explaining International Production*, London: Unwin Hyman.
Greene, W.H. (1993), *Econometric Analysis*, New York: Macmillan.
Istituto Guglielmo Tagliacarne (1998), *La dotazione delle infrastrutture per la sviluppo delle imprese nelle 103 province*, Unpublished manuscript.
Kobrin, S.J. (1979), 'Political risk: A review and reconsideration', *Journal of International Business Studies*, **10** (1), 67–80.
Loree, D.W. and S.E. Guisinger (1995), 'Policy and non-policy determinants of US equity foreign direct investment', *Journal of International Business Studies*, **26** (2), 281–99.
Mariotti, S. and L. Piscitello (1995), 'Information costs and location of FDIs within the host country: Empirical evidence from Italy', *Journal of International Business Studies*, **26** (4), 815–41.
Miller, K.D. (1993), 'Industry and country effects on managers' perceptions of environmental risk', *Journal of International Business Studies*, **24** (4), 693–714.
Mudambi, R. (1995), 'The MNE investment location decision: Some empirical evidence', *Managerial and Decision Economics*, **16** (3), 249–57.
Mudambi, R. (1998), 'The role of duration in multinational investment strategies', *Journal of International Business Studies*, **29** (2), 239–62.
Poynter, T.A. (1985), *Multinational Enterprises and Government Intervention*, New York: St. Martin's Press.
Putnam, R.D., R. Leonardi and R.Y. Nanetti (1993), *Making Democracy Work: Civic Traditions in Modern Italy*, Princeton: Princeton University Press.
Simon, J.D. (1984), 'A theoretical perspective on political risk', *Journal of International Business Studies*, **15** (3), 123–43.
UNCTAD (1997), *World Investment Report: Transnational Corporations, Market Structure and Competition Policy*, Geneva: United Nations.
Young, S., N. Hood and E. Peters (1994), 'Multinational enterprises and regional economic development', *Regional Studies*, **28** (7), 657–77.

APPENDIX 10.1

Description of Variables

Variable	Description
FACALL	Region-wise number of MNE factories (including majority and minority interests) – 1992, 1994, 1996
FACMAJ	Region-wise number of MNE factories (including only majority non-Italian interest) – 1992, 1994, 1996
EMALL	Region-wise level of MNE employment (including majority and minority interests) – 1992, 1994, 1996
EMAJ	Region-wise level of MNE employment (including only majority non-Italian interest) – 1992, 1994, 1996
LTRANS	Quality of road and rail transportation links (index out of 200)
FTRANS	Quality of air and sea transportation links (index out of 200)
SERV	Quality of business services (index out of 100)
UTIL	Quality of electricity, gas and water services (index out of 300)
GDP	Regional GDP – 1990, 1992, 1994
URATE	Regional unemployment rate – 1990, 1992, 1994
EMIND	Size of regional industrial workforce – 1990, 1992, 1994
CDAVE	Average level of electoral support for the Center-right (1968–91)
CDTR	Trend of support for the Center-right (1968–91)
PCIAVE	Average level of electoral support for the Far-left (1968–91)
PCITR	Trend of support for the Far-left (1968–91)
PSIAVE	Average level of electoral support for the Center-left (1968–91)
PSITR	Trend of support for the Center-left (1968–91)
INSTM	Index which arrays regions according to Putnam's degree of institutional performance (1978–85)
ALFA	Cubbin–Leech power index for the regional upper house (1968–87)

APPENDIX 10.2

We have a dependent variable y and two sets of regressors, $\mathbf{X}$ and $\mathbf{Z}$. Initially we regress $\mathbf{y}$ on $\mathbf{X}$, that is, the system

$$\mathbf{y} = \mathbf{X}\beta + \mathbf{u} \tag{10A.1}$$

We then collect the estimated errors, which are denoted by $\mathbf{e}$. Therefore, we can write

$$\mathbf{e} = (\mathbf{y} - \hat{\mathbf{y}}) = (\mathbf{y} - \mathbf{X}(\mathbf{X}'\mathbf{X})^{-1}\mathbf{X}'\mathbf{y}) = (\mathbf{I} - \mathbf{X}(\mathbf{X}'\mathbf{X})^{-1}\mathbf{X}')\mathbf{y} = (\mathbf{I} - \mathbf{M})\mathbf{y}$$

where $\mathbf{M} = \mathbf{X}(\mathbf{X}\mathbf{X})^{-1}\mathbf{X}'$

We regress these on the second set of regressors, **Z**, estimating the system

$$\mathbf{e} = \mathbf{Z}\gamma + \mathbf{v} \tag{10A.2}$$

Collecting the equations (10A.1) and (10A.2), we have the system:

$$\begin{bmatrix} \mathbf{y} \\ \mathbf{e} \end{bmatrix} = \begin{bmatrix} \mathbf{X} & \mathbf{0} \\ \mathbf{0} & \mathbf{Z} \end{bmatrix} \begin{bmatrix} \beta \\ \gamma \end{bmatrix} + \begin{bmatrix} \mathbf{u} \\ \mathbf{v} \end{bmatrix}$$

Using the above information, the vector of regression estimators is

$$\Delta = \begin{bmatrix} \hat{\beta} \\ \hat{\gamma} \end{bmatrix} = \begin{bmatrix} (\mathbf{X}'\mathbf{X})^{-1}\mathbf{X}' \\ (\mathbf{Z}'\mathbf{Z})^{-1}\mathbf{Z}'(\mathbf{I}-\mathbf{M}) \end{bmatrix} \mathbf{y}$$

We may call these 'two-step' estimators, since the overall estimator is obtained in two steps.

Next, we regress **y** on **X** and **Z** together, estimating the system:

$$\mathbf{y} = \mathbf{X}\delta_1 + \mathbf{Z}\delta_2 + \mathbf{w} \tag{10A.3}$$

We can write this system as

$$\mathbf{y} = [\mathbf{X} \quad \mathbf{Z}] \begin{bmatrix} \delta_1 \\ \delta_2 \end{bmatrix} + \mathbf{w}$$

The vector of regression estimators is now:

$$\hat{\delta} = \begin{bmatrix} \hat{\delta}_1 \\ \hat{\delta}_2 \end{bmatrix} = \{[\mathbf{X} \quad \mathbf{Z}]'[\mathbf{X} \quad \mathbf{Z}]\}^{-1}[\mathbf{X} \quad \mathbf{Z}]'\mathbf{y} = \left\{ \begin{bmatrix} \mathbf{X}' \\ \mathbf{Z}' \end{bmatrix} [\mathbf{X} \quad \mathbf{Z}] \right\}^{-1} \begin{bmatrix} \mathbf{X}' \\ \mathbf{Z}' \end{bmatrix} \mathbf{y}$$

$$= \begin{bmatrix} \mathbf{X}'\mathbf{X} & \mathbf{X}'\mathbf{Z} \\ \mathbf{Z}'\mathbf{X} & \mathbf{Z}'\mathbf{Z} \end{bmatrix}^{-1} \begin{bmatrix} \mathbf{X}' \\ \mathbf{Z}' \end{bmatrix} \mathbf{y}$$

We can solve this equation in terms of **X** and **Z**, using results for partitioned inverses.

Define:

$$\begin{bmatrix} \mathbf{X'X} & \mathbf{X'Z} \\ \mathbf{Z'X} & \mathbf{Z'Z} \end{bmatrix}^{-1} = \begin{bmatrix} \mathbf{A_{11}} & \mathbf{A_{21}} \\ \mathbf{A_{12}} & \mathbf{A_{22}} \end{bmatrix}$$

The results for partitioned inverses yield the following results:

$$\begin{aligned}
\mathbf{A_{11}} &= \mathbf{(X'X)^{-1}[I + X'Z\,(Z'Z - Z'MZ)^{-1}\,Z'X\,(X'X)^{-1}]} \\
\mathbf{A_{12}} &= \mathbf{-(X'X)^{-1}\,X'Z\,(Z'Z - Z'MZ)^{-1}} \\
\mathbf{A_{21}} &= \mathbf{-(Z'Z - Z'MZ)^{-1}\,Z'X\,(X'X)^{-1}} \\
\mathbf{A_{22}} &= \mathbf{(Z'Z - Z'MZ)^{-1}}
\end{aligned}$$

It now follows that

$$\begin{aligned}
\hat{\delta}_1 &= \mathbf{A_{11}X' + A_{12}Z'} \\
\hat{\delta}_2 &= \mathbf{A_{21}X' + A_{22}Z'}
\end{aligned}$$

Substituting for $\mathbf{A_{ij}}$, we have

$$\hat{\delta} = \begin{bmatrix} \hat{\delta}_1 \\ \hat{\delta}_2 \end{bmatrix} = \begin{bmatrix} \mathbf{(X'X)^{-1}X' - (X'X)^{-1}X'Z(Z'Z - Z'MZ)^{-1}Z'(I - M)} \\ \mathbf{(Z'Z - Z'MZ)^{-1}Z'(I - M)} \end{bmatrix} \mathbf{y}$$

These estimators may be called 'one-step' estimators as they are obtained from a single estimation of (10A.1). It may be seen that they differ from the 'two-step' estimators in that they include interaction terms between the **X**s and the **Z**s.

PART III

Institutional Transition

11. The Glorious Revolution of 1688: successful constitutional and institutional adjustment in a period of rapid change

Charles K. Rowley and Matthew Dobra

1. INTRODUCTION

The English Glorious Revolution of 1688 was brief in duration and essentially bloodless in nature. On November 1, 1688, William, Prince of Orange, on the eve of his embarkation from Holland, gave his written reasons for invading England. The next day, James II of England imposed a ban on all public pronouncements made by the prince. On November 5 (Guy Fawkes Day) William's fleet, composed of 54 ships and 2040 guns driven by a Protestant wind, blowing first from the east and then from the south, landed at Torbay in Devon without any resistance by the poorly led and perhaps disaffected English fleet composed of 52 ships of the line, 17 fireships and 1876 guns (Ogg, 1955, p. 214).

Despite his signal failure to rouse English support in the western counties, William secured his military position in Exeter with a cosmopolitan army of between 12 000 and 14 000 men, less than half the size of the regular forces in the pay of James II. James marched to confront the invader, reaching Salisbury on November 19 at the head of a sullen though not necessarily malcontented army.

Warned of treachery among the high command, James hesitated to make arrests but rather, on November 24, ordered a retreat to London. His leading generals, Churchill (later the Duke of Marlborough), Grafton and Kirke, breached their oaths of office and deserted in favor of William leaving a demoralized army behind them. Simultanously, James's favorite daughter Anne, aided and assisted by the wife of the treacherous John Churchill, deserted her father and fled to Nottingham to join the Earl of Dorset, where a body of nobility and gentry issued a manifesto condemning the misdeeds of the king and calling for a free parliament.

William and his army left Exeter on his march to London, meeting little opposition on his route towards the capital. He arrived at Hungerford on December 7, and consulted with several English and Dutch ambassadors before announcing a set of conditions – papists must be removed from office, proclamations concerning himself must be recalled, the Tower and Tilbury fort must be entrusted to the City of London, and revenues must be assigned to him for the maintenance of his troops – that would be humiliating to James.

James, having received the report of the prince's conditions, sent his queen, Mary of Modena, and his son, James, to safety in France, then burned the writs for a parliament, ordered Feversham to disband the army and left Whitehall on the morning of December 11, throwing the Great Seal into the River Thames prior to embarking on a vessel bound for France. His vessel was captured by a group of fishermen and he was forcibly returned to London, where he arrived on December 16. Guarded laxly by William's troops in Rochester, and provided with easy access to the river, James escaped by boat on December 23 and arrived in France on December 25, his reign effectively at an end.

The Glorious Revolution is explained by Whig historians such as Macaulay (1888) and Trevelyan (1938) as one event in a natural tendency for English political institutions to improve over time. In this view, each adjustment in England's political system from the Norman invasion onwards is viewed as an advance over its predecessor.

In the view of many historians (Ogg, 1955; Prall, 1972), the Revolution is viewed as a consequence of irrational decision making on the part of James II whose religious beliefs allegedly set him on a disaster course that might have been avoided by a more rational decision maker.

In the view of economists such as North and Weingast (1989), the Glorious Revolution fundamentally redesigned political and fiscal institutions in a manner conducive to eliminating mercantilism and to fostering the Industrial Revolution. This chapter challenges each of these hypotheses and provides a radically different perspective on the causes and implications of the Glorious Revolution.

In response to the claims of modern historians, this chapter demonstrates that the path from the Restoration in 1660 to the Glorious Revolution in 1688 is better explained as the unforeseen (and unforeseeable) outcome of consistently rational decision making by all actors. It further demonstrates that the enduring nature of the Constitutional Settlement following the Revolution was a consequence of a discrete change in the level of transaction costs for constitutional change, from low, commencing with the three-week period of the constitutional settlement in 1689, to high, certainly once the Act of Settlement of 1701 secured the Protestant dynasty in England and eliminated the Jacobite threat. Finally, this chapter contests the conclusions of North and Weingast (1989) by clearly demonstrating that the political and institutional changes leading to the decline of mercantilism and to the onset of the Industrial

Revolution were not immediate outcomes of the Glorious Revolution but rather were the consequence of political changes ushered in during the twelve years following the Declaration of Rights.

2. THE PERSPECTIVE OF CONSTITUTIONAL POLITICAL ECONOMY

There is a categorical distinction to be made between constitutional and non-constitutional political economy, a distinction in the ultimate behavioral object of analytical attention (Buchanan, 1990, p. 2). Whereas political economy concerns itself with the varying and complex institutional arrangements within which individuals make choices, constitutional political economy directs analytical attention to the choice among constraints. It thus recognizes that individuals choose the constraints that will influence their future behavior, at least to a degree and within some limits (Buchanan, 1990, p. 3).

Constitutional political economy is a creature of the late twentieth century and has been developed primarily for application within the context of the United States of America. Associated as closely as it is with the contractarian approach of certain members of the Virginia School – most notably Brennan and Buchanan (1985) – constitutional political economy focusses on a process of reciprocity through which individuals choose to impose constraints upon themselves primarily, if not exclusively, as a part of an exchange in return for similarly imposed constraints on the behavior of others. In its extreme form, this process of reciprocity is advanced as a rule of unanimity that is deemed to govern all genuine constitutional settlements.

Allegories such as these are largely irrelevant, of course, for the real world (Rowley, 1990, 2001). The calculus of consent never remotely approaches the level of unanimity in constitutional settlements even in the most allegedly democratic of circumstances. Even in the case of the United States, a significantly divided minority of property-owning white males alone played any role in the process of constitutional settlement. Women, slaves and Native Americans, as well as all loyalists and white males without property were excluded entirely from this momentous determination. Yet this is the event most frequently referred to as an approximation to unanimity in the contractarian calculus (Buchanan and Tullock, 1962).

A constitution is defined for the purposes of this chapter as a set of rules that determine the political institutions of a society (Mueller, 1996, p. 43). Since a society is defined in terms of the existence of such a set of rules, every society, whether democratic, oligarchic or autocratic, has a constitution. All societies emerge from some pre-society that itself influences the behavior of individuals. In this sense, all constitutions evolve over time and are not justifiably to be viewed as rational constructs, established at one moment in time by some assembly of individuals.

Prior to the Glorious Revolution of 1688, the English constitution had evolved in a series of steps, some large and some small, over several centuries as a collection of disparate peoples, Celts, Angles, Saxons, Vikings and Normans, established a political community through a history of wars fought both among themselves and against common enemies. The English constitution, largely unwritten, but firmly embedded in custom and in the common law, is not the kind of constitution that has attracted the attention of constitutional political economy scholars. It is, nonetheless, a constitution in many ways more effective and more enduring than many of the worthless parchments that pass for such in less politically stable countries.

In the view of Hayek (1973), all authority derives from law. This law, which Hayek calls *Nomos*, is not the particular will of any ruler or legislature but rather reflects customs that have evolved over time on which the expectations and behavior of individuals come to be grounded. Such purpose-independent rules of conduct, categorized by Hayek (1973) as a spontaneous order, frequently evolve in direct conflict with the aims of specific rulers who may attempt to impose their own deliberate will upon their subjects in the form of legislated laws, categorized by Hayek (1973) as *Thesis*.

It is an undeniable fact that norms condition the behavior of individuals in society. What can be questioned from a normative standpoint is whether the existence of such norms requires that they should continue to be observed. On this issue, Hayek (1973) equivocates. Certainly, if some stability in expectations is to be inculcated, then it follows that members of a society must agree to adhere to certain rules of conduct. This does not imply that the law is rigid and incapable of development over time.

Customs and laws predictably will adjust in response to changes in society, but they will do so for the most part spontaneously and not as the result of the intention of any ruler or lawmaker. Legislators may codify the law from time to time, either to purge it of observed corruptions or to clarify it. However, prior to 1688 in England, it was not thought that they could make new laws, save in response to exceptional exigencies.

The law of the Roman Republic in all essentials was the law of *Nomos*, epitomized by Cicero in its most effective formulation of freedom under the law. Cicero fully understood that there was no conflict between law and freedom and that freedom is dependent upon certain attributes of the law, namely its generality, its certainty and the restrictions that it places on the discretion of authority (Hayek, 1960, p. 167).

England benefitted only briefly from exposure to classical Roman law, which was perverted during the Imperial period from as early as the second century AD, by a sequence of increasingly statist emperors who sought to impose their authority over the Empire unfettered by the barrier of law. By the time that Roman law was codified by the Emperor Justinian, the notion that the law should serve to protect the freedom of the individual was finally jettisoned.

The notion would never really be re-established in continental Europe where the code of Justinian with its conception of a prince who stands above the law would re-emerge as the dominant principle (Hayek, 1960, p. 167). However, in post-Roman England, vestiges of the classical law of Rome would survive through the Dark and the Mediaeval Ages, and the Renaissance, transmitted and consolidated in customary and common laws unique to the Anglo-Saxon tradition. In this manner, English laws and customs, facilitated perhaps unintentionally by such self-serving written instruments as the agreement between King John and the barons in 1215 AD (*Magna Carta*), provided limited protection for the individual against the state.

Magna Carta enumerated the fundamental rights of free Englishmen to trial by jury and to due process, rights that would frequently challenge the arbitrary use of royal prerogative through the following several centuries. Somehow these rights and processes would survive the collapse of stable government during the Wars of the Roses and the aggressive autocracies of Henry VIII and of his daughter, Mary I. Despite periodic setbacks, the customary and common laws of England slowly evolved to provide limited liberties even for the most lowly-ranked of free Englishmen and to establish albeit limited constraints against the unlimited exercise of the royal prerogative.

The most important attribute of this common law tradition is that the law consisted of purpose-independent rules that governed the conduct of individuals towards each other, that reached out to an unknown number of further instances, and that, by defining a protected domain for each individual, provided an order within which individuals could make feasible plans. In the words of the great eighteenth century judge, Lord Mansfield, this common law 'does not consist of particular cases, but of general principles, which are explained and illustrated by those cases'.

Only by understanding the deep-rooted adherence of the large majority of educated Englishmen to this order is it possible to understand the causes and consequences of the Glorious Revolution. It would be a grievous error of scholarship to evaluate the constitutional implications of the Glorious Revolution from the constructivist rationalist perspective almost universally adopted by scholars of constitutional political economy with respect to the forging of the Constitution of the United States.

3. A POLITICAL AND INSTITUTIONAL PERSPECTIVE ON THE RESTORATION OF 1660

From the Norman Conquest onwards, until the advent of the House of Stuart, the English for the most part had been devoted to the monarchy, had revered strong government and had been profoundly attached to the customary and the common law. They had willingly surrendered to the Crown a monopoly of violence in return for the maintenance of internal order and security against outside invasion (Johnson, 1972, p. 181). This close relationship between king and country reached its zenith during the reign of Elizabeth I.

Yet the outward consensus maintained by the majestic statesmanship of the Queen was accompanied by significant changes in the institutions of politics. Because the income of the Crown had failed to keep pace with inflation since the 1530s, Elizabeth had been increasingly forced to live off royal capital (by the sales of Crown land) and had become increasingly dependent on parliamentary provisions. Inevitably, this dependence reduced the dominance of the monarchy and increased the relative political powers of the House of Lords and the House of Commons.

Following Tudor policies of holding the nobility in check, Elizabeth deliberately kept the Lords small and encouraged the bulk of the landed wealth to pass into the Commons. The country gentry had begun to invade the borough seats early in the fifteenth century. By the end of Elizabeth's reign, the Commons had become a preserve of the gentry. The gentry had become the richest and the most influential class in the country (Johnson, 1972, p. 181). As such, its interest required careful nurturing if the unity of the kingdom was to be maintained.

Unfortunately for the Crown, the House of Stuart failed to match the statesmanship of Elizabeth Tudor. James VI of Scotland, who inherited the throne in 1603, although educated in Greek, Latin and Hebrew language and literature, was unskilled in the customs of a civilized court. His language was uncouth and his behavior in public was often obscene (Johnson, 1972, p. 182). He had no sympathy for Parliament, other than as a source of funding. Instead, he sought, albeit unsuccessfully, to rule as a Divine Right continental despot in an England that was in fact undergoing a social, religious and economic transformation hostile to that model (Prall, 1972, p. 6).

His son, Charles I, who inherited the throne in 1625, better-mannered than his father, with a more wholesome personal lifestyle, and with a much better command of the technical working of the English government, chose nevertheless to challenge the English political transformation and to consolidate Stuart despotism by abusing the royal prerogative. Within less than forty years, James and Charles demolished the Tudor legacy of politics by consent and drove the nation to armed rebellion pitting the court against the Commons in a struggle that would not be finally resolved until well after the Glorious Revolution of 1688.

As seen by James I and by Charles I, England was a true monarchy. The king was the symbol of the sovereign state in both its temporal and spiritual aspects. The royal prerogative was viewed generally as including the direct control of foreign and military policy, the power to call or not to call Parliament, the right to veto legislation, the right to coin money, the right to appoint the officers in Church and state who would administer the kingdom under the direction of the monarch, the responsibility for the administration of justice and the power to bestow honors and titles of nobility.

This was not sufficient for James and Charles who claimed in addition the Divine Right to set aside any or all the prescriptive or customary laws designed to limit the exercise of the prerogative on behalf of the ordinary English citizen. By their aggressive pursuit of this Right, James and Charles raised important constitutional issues concerning the relationship between the king and parliament and the relevance of the rule of law.

The first Civil War – 1642–46 – was fought between the king and his supporters (Cavaliers) and the parliamentary army (Puritans). The Puritans triumphed:

> In the main the middle class, being more solid for Parliament, had beaten the aristocracy and gentry, who were divided. The new money-power of the city had beaten the old loyalties. The townsfolk had mastered the countryside. What would some day be the 'Chapel' had beaten the Church. (Churchill, 1956, p. 226)

Yet, this victory was short-lived. The New Model Army, under the leadership of Cromwell, refused to hand over the reins of power either to king or to Parliament. In 1647, the second Civil War began.

The parts played by the principals in this war were significantly different. The king and his prerogatives were now viewed, 'not as obstacles to Parliamentary right, but as the repository of ordinary English freedom' (Churchill, 1956, p. 237). King, Lords and Commons, landlords and merchants, the City and the countryside, bishops and presbyters, the Scottish army, the Welsh people and the English fleet now turned against the New Model Army. The army defeated them all. By the end of 1648 all was over: 'Cromwell was Dictator. The royalists were crushed; Parliament was a tool; the Constitution was a figment' (Churchill, 1956, p. 238). On January 30, 1649 the regicides had their way and Charles I was executed.

On April 20, 1653, Cromwell entered the House of Commons with thirty musketeers, dismissed the Rump Parliament at gunpoint and seized the Mace, the symbol of the Speaker's authority. In one contemptuous gesture, he foreclosed on all the constitutional safeguards and processes that had slowly evolved in England since the Norman invasion. Thus it was that the Civil War, the Commonwealth and the Protectorate failed to resolve the evident crisis in the English body politic.

The fundamental problem was the inability to craft any new constitution that Cromwell and any parliament that he could devise could jointly live with. However much Cromwell tampered with the suffrage, Parliament was always dominated by the country gentry who were interested in nothing except the security of private property and low taxes (Johnson, 1972, p. 213). The gentry were opposed to any kind of reform; indeed they were really opposed to the principle of central government itself.

When the Lord Protector died on September 3, 1658, the Republic was already doomed. On May 25, 1660, Charles II returned to take up his Crown. The vast majority of his subjects welcomed his Restoration: 'Both Houses of Parliament acknowledged their devotion to his rights and person. And all around the masses, rich and poor, Cavalier and Roundhead, Episcopalian, Presbyterian, and Independent, framed a scene of reconciliation and rejoicing without compare in history' (Johnson, 1972, p. 285).

The Restoration settlement endorsed by the Convention of 1660 returned England to the constitution of 1641. All the laws of the Long Parliament, excepting those signed into law by Charles I in 1641 before he left London, were rendered invalid. All the statutes of the Commonwealth and the Protectorate were also removed. This does not imply that the English constitution was returned to that inherited by Charles I in 1625. For in 1641, Charles had been severely frightened and had signed into law major concessions to the Long Parliament. These concessions profoundly weakened the prerogative powers of the Crown.

The Triennial Act provided for the summoning of Parliament at least once in three years, if necessary without the consent of the Crown. The Court of Star Chamber, which had evolved to enable the Crown to evade the constraints of the common law, was abolished. The Court of High Commission, which had striven to impose religious uniformity, was also abolished. The principles of the Petition of Right, protecting individuals from arbitrary arrest, were also endorsed.

Although the Restoration appeared to endorse the doctrine of Divine Right, that of Absolute Power was not resurrected. The criminal jurisdiction of the Privy Council, the Star Chamber and the High Commission Court were gone. The idea of the Crown levying taxes without the consent of Parliament was history. All legislation, henceforth, required the majority support of legally elected Parliaments. The common law was returned in the form that the 1641 legislation had enhanced.

In these respects, the victory of Parliament in the Civil War would leave indelible marks on the English constitution. England was certainly not a democracy in the modern sense of that term. Equally, however, the Crown was not an unconstrained *Leviathan* in the sense of Thomas Hobbes (1651). Equally, as we shall demonstrate, a number of constitutional tensions between the Crown, Parliament and the common law remained unresolved.

4. THE LONG ROAD TO REVOLUTION: 1660–88: A RATIONAL CHOICE APPROACH

Although the relationship between King and country differed significantly under the rules of Charles II and James II, the fundamental constitutional tensions were invariant throughout the period 1660–88. A rational choice analysis focusses on the interplay of self-seeking actors across these constitutional divides, and downgrades, at least somewhat, the traditional historical emphasis on the personality differences of the two monarchs. It is necessary, therefore, for this study to merge the two rules for the purpose of evaluating the road from the Restoration Settlement of 1660 to the Glorious Revolution of 1688.

King and Parliament

The ultimate choice that was made in 1688 between royal absolutism and parliamentary government, fundamentally, was the same choice that had confronted Englishmen at the outset of the first civil war more than a quarter of a century earlier. Evidently, the Restoration Settlement of 1660 had failed fully to resolve this fundamental constitutional tension. The compromise system of the Restoration indeed fermented constant strife domestically and grave weakness in foreign affairs (Trevelyan, 1938, p. 245).

These weaknesses became apparent only through experience and were not perceived at all during the fever of royalist enthusiasm that accompanied the return of Charles II from exile. No more Strafford and no more Pym! That was judged in 1660 to be the final balance of the English Constitution.

Hypothesis 1: Rational self-seeking on the part of the Crown and Parliament fermented a fundamental discord that set the scene for the Glorious Revolution.

Episode 1: 1660–79: The Land Settlement and the Cavalier Parliament

In the Declaration of Breda, issued seven weeks before he embarked for Dover, Charles confirmed his willingness to allow a free Parliament to take the initiative in deciding the form of the Restoration. Furthermore, in a concession that was not well-received by many Royalists, Charles evinced his willingness to keep in being, until new elections could be called at the end of December, the Convention Parliament that had been established in April 1660. That Parliament, of 505 members, had returned a substantial minority of one hundred Presbyterians to elective office and yet would be authorized by Charles II to determine the details of the land settlement.

This decision was of immense constitutional significance. The sanctity of private property – most especially of landed property – ranked higher than the doctrines of the Church in the estimation of the aristocracy and gentry in 1660. During the Civil War, crown lands, church lands and the lands of many Royalists had been confiscated. Many other Royalists had been forced to sell land in order to pay fines to the victorious Parliament. Others had voluntarily disposed of land in order to contribute cash to the royal cause. A true Restoration would restore all such properties to their original owners.

The Act of Oblivion failed to make such a restoration. In order to secure national unity a compromise was effected. Lands were restored to the Crown and to the Church. Ordinary citizens had their lands returned only where the latter had been directly confiscated. Loyal Cavaliers were made to pay the price of reconciliation. The Act of Oblivion explains why the Cavaliers failed to become a political party in the service of the Crown. Instead, it made of them a Tory party, with both Crown and country elements. At the same time, the Crown would be rewarded with the support of many former Parliamentarians and moderate Puritans (Prall, 1972, p. 5).

The Convention Parliament was dissolved at the end of 1660 and a new Parliament was formed in 1661 in the first constitutional parliamentary election in twenty-one years. The new Parliament was decidedly more Cavalier in composition than the Convention had been. Fewer than 60 of its 505 members were Presbyterian. Approximately 100 members had sat in the 1640 Long Parliament. Except for land, the Restoration settlement was to be in their hands. Because of the land settlement, there was a strong urge to take revenge on the Puritan enemy in the area of religion and to take revenge on the Crown by weakening its control over the local authorities.

The Cavalier Parliament would prove to be the longest-lasting Parliament in English history, surviving for 18 years. By the time that it was dissolved, only 200 of its members remained in office. The remainder had been replaced at by-elections, many of them by Roundheads or their heirs. The Cavalier Parliament from the outset was unwilling to be governed by the King. The landed gentry had no intention of parting with parliamentary rights hard won in the Civil War. Charles and his Privy Council never succeeded in imposing their will on the Cavalier Parliament and in 1679 Parliament was dissolved, albeit not before it had tested its powers to the limits of the tolerance of the Crown.

The Cavalier Parliament proved itself to be loyal to the English

Constitution. It honored, within limits, the royal prerogative and the monarchical system of government. It confirmed parliamentary control of finance. It pressed for an increased responsibility of Ministers to the Lords and to the Commons, driving Charles's prime minister, Lord Clarendon, into exile in 1667 under the threat of impeachment and instituting capital proceedings against Clarendon's successor, the Earl of Danby, in 1678. It passed into law the Test Act of 1673; legislation that would later prove to be an important fulcrum for the Glorious Revolution. The parliamentary and the Protestant character of the English constitution were fundamental principles on which it had been established and to which it had remained loyal throughout its long existence.

Although the Long Parliament had continued without new elections for 18 years, its political balance had changed radically during that time from Tory to Whig as these opposing parties began to take form from their Cavalier and Roundhead roots. The Tory party, both in the Lords and in the Commons, was identifiable by 1679 by reference to a distinct set of characteristics. Tories were believers in hereditary monarchy and in the Anglican Church.

However, the Tories were also concerned to retain hegemony in their own bailiwicks, namely their country interests against the interests of the court. Their principal objective was to secure a constitutional monarchy in which the aristocracy and the gentry would hold sway on local matters and provide the personnel and the policies for the national government. In pursuit of this objective, the Tories naturally aligned themselves with the Anglican Church and looked to the Crown to support that Church. In essence, the emergent Tory ideology was grounded on economic self-interest, namely the preservation of property in the land and the securing of economic privileges from the Crown.

In a sense the Whig party at that time was identified less with an overt ideology as with resistance to the central principles advanced by the Tories. As we shall see, Whigs were less enamored with the Divine Right of Kings and less fully committed to the hereditary monarchy than the Tories, though few of them would openly advance republican sympathies after experiencing the dictatorship of Cromwell. Among them were the Dissenters, largely excluded from the privileges of the court, and those who eyed with jealousy the large estates of the aristocracy and the wealthy gentry. The Whigs were anxious to erode the central authority of the Crown and to narrow the scope of the royal prerogative in favor of parliamentary authority.

The Whigs, at this time, did not want Parliament to choose the ministers of the Crown. They did not want to be held responsible for any failures of policies initiated by those ministers (Prall, 1972, p. 60). They wanted to hold the Crown responsible for the behavior of its ministers. For this reason, the Whigs were less than enthusiastic about the policy of Charles II of co-opting Whigs into his Privy Council. The Whigs were especially irritated when their leader, the Earl of Shaftesbury, was co-opted by the King into his Privy Council as a means of countering the pressure of the Whigs in favor of excluding the Catholic Duke of York from inheriting the English Crown.

Despite concessions from the King offering to limit the ability of a Catholic king to influence the composition of the judiciary or to challenge the authority of the Church of England, a Whig Exclusion Bill passed the Commons over the opposition of Tory members. Before the Bill could reach the Lords, the King first prorogued and then dismissed his Parliament and called for a new election.

Episode 2: 1679–1681: The Collapse of Parliamentary Rule

In August 1679, despite attempts by the Court to forge a Tory majority, an overwhelmingly Whig House of Commons was elected. The trusty members of the Court, who hitherto had mustered 150, were diminished to only 30. The King now had to concentrate on protecting his brother James from a serious Exclusion threat in a political climate not dissimilar to that confronting his father in 1640.

Following repeated prorogations, the new Parliament opened in October 1680 in an atmosphere of anti-Catholic hysteria. Exclusion was the only subject on its mind. This time the bill passed the Commons and went to the Lords. The Earl of Shaftesbury, now no longer a member of the Privy Council, fought for the bill. The Marquis of Halifax, who had replaced Shaftesbury, fought against it. Halifax prevailed and the bill was defeated on first reading by a vote of 63–30. In January 1681, The King dissolved Parliament and once again called for new elections.

The new elections returned an overwhelming Whig majority to the House of Commons, many of them armed with specific instructions from their constituents in favor of Exclusion and for cleansing the realm of all papist influences. Shaftesbury was now openly aligned with Charles's bastard son, the Protestant Duke of Monmouth, and flirting with the notion that the Duke should succeed Charles to the throne. In order to avoid the potential violence of the London mob, this Parliament would meet in Oxford, a city favorably inclined to the interests of the Court.

On March 26, 1681, the King, armed with the open support of the Church and the Tory conscience as well as with widespread support of the citizenry, faced Shaftesbury down on the floor of the House of Lords under the threat of a new civil war (Prall, 1972, p. 71). Two days later he dissolved the Parliament. Despite the requirements of the Triennium Act that Parliament should meet no later than March 1684, Charles refused to call for new elections throughout the remainder of his reign.

Episode 3: 1681–85: The Descent into Dictatorship

Shortly after the dissolution of Parliament, in the wake of the conviction of Titus Oates on charges of treason, perjury and seditious libel in connection with the alleged Popish plot, Shaftesbury was arrested on a charge of high treason and sent to the Tower. He was released after a grand jury returned a verdict of 'no grounds for prosecution' and fled into exile in the United Provinces. The Exclusion crisis was over and Charles once again was firmly in control of the instruments of government.

In actions that ultimately would rebound to the detriment of his successor, Charles now sought revenge against those who had engineered the election of successive Whig dominated parliaments. He struck out at the vested rights of local authorities, attempting to restructure local authorities to the advantage of the court. To this end he relied on the authority of the royal prerogative supported deferentially by the judiciary. His principal targets were the enfranchised boroughs. He sought to diminish the electoral weight of the boroughs, and thus the Whigs, to the advantage of the gentry, and thus the Tories.

Until the reign of Charles II, the principal battlefield with respect to local government had been the administration of the Elizabethan poor law of 1601. The local justices of the peace sought autonomy from the Crown in its enforcement whereas the Privy Council sought to bind the justices to its centralizing will (Prall, 1972, p. 80). The Cavalier Parliament, in its Act of Settlement of 1662, had taken revenge on the Crown for the land settlement outlined above by freeing the justices of the peace from Privy Council control.

Charles realized that it would not be easy to reverse this decentralization given the large number of justices of the peace responsible for Poor Law policy. Instead, he exercised his prerogative by dismissing justices opposed to his interests and appointing new ones, while simultaneously strengthening the powers of the lord lieutenants at the expense of the justices. His objective was to create a series of semi-feudal fiefdoms under the control of the nobility. Those lord lieutenants who had opposed him over the Exclusion Bill were systematically removed and replaced by individuals presumed to be loyal to the interests of the court.

Charles was less concerned about who would be responsible for administering the Poor Laws than who would control elections to the House of Commons and who would control the use of the country militias and trained bands. By controlling the lord lieutenants, he hoped to insure the Crown against the election of any future Whig majority and to guarantee that the local militia would be loyal to the Crown.

Although of little immediate importance, since parliamentary elections were not contemplated in the foreseeable future (but of great long-term constitutional significance) was the institution by Charles of *quo warranto* proceedings to revoke borough and corporation charters. In this assault, more than patronage was involved. Rights enshrined both by law and by custom were at stake.

London was the first to be attacked and indeed was the only borough to fight, albeit unsuccessfully, for its rights. Many corporations and boroughs, in the wake of this defeat, voluntarily surrendered their charters in return for economic advantages such as the right to hold additional markets. The new charters, however, tightened central controls on how boroughs would be governed and by whom. They also centralized control over trading corporations, both domestic and international in nature.

The Court would not again allow itself to be embarrassed by hostile parliaments. Inevitably, this use and abuse of the royal prerogative exacerbated the underlying tension between Crown and Parliament over the division of spoils in a rent-seeking environment. Charles had taken advantage of the collapse of Whig credibility to rule by prerogative instead of by the classic mixture of King, Lords and Commons. In so doing he limited access to the economic rents and social privileges provided by government not only to the country party, the Whigs, but also to the court party, the Tories. This economic and social penalty served further to loosen the ties between the Tory party and the Crown, a development that would have serious political consequences for James II, and eventually would provide an important catalyst for the Glorious Revolution in 1688.

Charles II was a King with strictly limited objectives. His primary concern was to protect his own throne and to secure the inheritance for his brother. His religious beliefs, at most were skin deep. As long as he could secure sufficient revenues to run a limited government and to provide for 'his shoulder of mutton and his whore' (Johnson, 1972, p. 214), he was entirely content. Viewed from this perspective, his political actions throughout his reign were entirely rational.

Likewise, the Tory and Whig parties rationally pursued their respective objectives throughout Charles's reign. The one miscalculation was that of the Whigs in pursuing so relentlessly in 1681 the exclusion of James from the throne. This miscalculation was not irrational; indeed it was not surprising given the seemingly benign and politically careless nature of King Charles prior to 1681. No Whig could easily have foreseen the calculated revenge that the King would mete out during the last four years of his life against those who had threatened the future of the House of Stuart.

Episode 4: 1685: The Last Stuart Parliament

Charles II died on February 6, 1685. His brother, James II, a converted Catholic, acceded to the throne in a nation in which Catholics formed only 3 per cent of the population. In his accession speech, James swore to defend and support the Church of England. He was welcomed as King with widespread popular support.

James's first action as King was to summon a Parliament. Until a House of Commons had voted him the revenues for life that his predecessor had enjoyed, he could not effectively carry on government, even with help from the coffers of the King of France (Trevelyan, 1938, p. 45). The gerrymandering of the political constituencies by Charles II now reaped its intended consequences. The new House of Commons was packed in the Royal interest, returning only 40 out of 505 members who were neither Tories nor Courtiers.

The Tory-controlled House of Commons voted James the Customs revenues for life, providing him with a financial independence that it lived to regret since it encouraged the King to rule without Parliament for the final three years of his reign. The catalyst for this move to despotism was the unsuccessful rebellion launched in June 1685 by the Duke of Monmouth. Monmouth, without the consent of Stadtholder William, sailed from the United Provinces and landed at Lyme Regis in June 1685.

The Whig nobility and gentry lay low in their country seats surreptitiously encouraging some 6000 peasants from Somerset and Devon to flock to Monmouth's standard. The object of this rebellion was to overthrow not only the King but also the Anglican Church and to restore the Puritan Church to England. The militias of the two rebel counties stood by the King as did the regular troops. Stadtholder William lent his father-in-law three Scottish regiments in Dutch pay. The Tory establishment was enthusiastic in its support for the King; the Whigs were quiescent (Trevelyan, 1938, p. 50).

The rebellion was quickly suppressed and Monmouth was executed on Tower Hill. Many of the peasant supporters, and those who attempted to protect them were executed by the soldiers or by means of a suspect process of law; others were deported to Barbados. By autumn 1685, James was secure in his throne with a regular army of 30 000 men. He was now tempted to overreach his powers. In November 1685, he prorogued Parliament and in July 1687 he dismissed it fearing that it would not repeal the Test Act signed into law by his brother in 1673.

Episode 5: The Descent into Tyranny

The Test Act of 1673 required that anyone holding an office of trust under the Crown must (1) publicly partake of the sacraments of the Church of England, (2) take the oath of supremacy, and (3) subscribe to the declaration against transubstantiation. This removed all devout Roman Catholics and Dissenters from public office. James II was determined to override this statute by exercising, or by abusing, the royal prerogative.

Two distinct prerogative rights were to be deployed, namely the right to set aside the law in a particular case (the dispensing power) and the right to set aside the law in all cases (the suspending power). The dispensing power had been used on occasion in the past both in the Tudor and in the early Stuart eras and was widely viewed as a legitimate royal prerogative. The suspending power had not been an issue because of the ability of the Tudors and early Stuarts to work effectively with their parliaments. The frequent use of both powers by James II would undermine the English constitution (Prall, 1972, p. 121).

James's dispensing power was tested in the case of *Godden and Hales,* tried before the Court of the King's Bench in 1686. Godden brought suit against his master, Sir Edward Hales, for holding a commission in the army without having taken the required test. A court packed and cowed by James II and the Lord Chancellor (Bloody Jeffreys) ruled for the defendant.

Emboldened with his triumph, and in the knowledge that no Parliament that he could then gerrymander would endorse his policy of repealing the Test Act, James initiated a series of fateful steps. In 1686, in defiance of statute law, he revived the Court of High Commission and empowered it to govern the Church of England by virtue of the Royal supremacy, with the power of suspending and depriving recalcitrant clergymen.

In April 1687, recognizing that he could not attain his ends by relying on the Anglican churchmen, James issued his Declaration of Indulgence suspending both the Test Act and the penal laws, including trial by jury and the writ of *habeas corpus.* The English constitution was now in shreds and James was viewed as having declared war on the Church of England and on his original Tory coalition.

At first sight these actions may appear to have been politically irrational. Roman Catholics formed only a very small proportion of any electorate. James's 1685 Parliament had been favorably disposed towards him on all matters other than the repeal of the Test Act. Whig historians have concluded that James was driven irrationally by religion into the forfeiture of his throne (Macaulay, 1888; Trevelyan, 1938). As will be seen, however, the King behaved rationally from the relevant *ex ante* perspective.

Episode 6: James's Attempt to Forge a New Majority Coalition

James's first radical change of policy was initiated at the end of 1686 when he used his prerogative and patronage powers to provide Catholics with full religious freedom and a share of offices. These gains would not be secure, however, unless the Test Acts and penal laws were repealed by statute. Despite all his efforts to obtain Tory and Anglican concurrence, James had failed to achieve this end. Only by forging a completely new coalition of allies would it be possible to repeal these laws and to provide Catholics with permanent security from oppression (Jones, 1972, p. 99).

The shift in coalitions occurred between November 1686 and April 1687, during which period James purged his Privy Council of Tories and replaced them with Catholics. He reached out to Dissenters and former Whigs in the country at large with the Declaration of Indulgence in April 1687 before dissolving Parliament in July. The offer of toleration to Dissenters was an overtly political act preparing the ground for a campaign designed to create a Parliamentary majority in favor of his policies. There is no evidence that James was insincere in his offer of such a deal (Pinkham, 1969; Jones, 1972).

At first sight, James's bid to forge a majority coalition composed of Catholics and Dissenters appears implausible. An Episcopal census in 1676 suggested that Anglicans represented an overwhelming majority with a population of 2 477 254 as compared with 108 676 Dissenters and 13 856 Catholics (Jones, 1972, p. 107). However, James and his advisors believed that these figures were grossly misleading. They believed that under conditions of toleration, many professed Anglicans would reveal their true preferences either for Catholicism or dissent. Moreover, they were aware of the opportunities for manipulating electoral constituencies in order to pack Parliament with members of the new coalition (Jones, 1972, p. 128).

In this campaign, James was more sophisticated than his brother. Instead of relying on local interests to pursue his objectives, he established a network of paid professional agents under the centralized control of the Crown. Most of these agents were Whigs who understood the market that James was courting. Although the landowners and gentry in the counties remained largely impervious to their pressures, such was not the case within the municipalities and the towns where economic dependence upon the Crown was much more pronounced (Jones, 1972, p. 137).

In the late seventeenth century, electoral success and parliamentary majorities depended on the balance of power within these latter constituencies. The merchants and municipal officers of these constituencies were men of restricted ambitions and limited horizons. Those who complied with the wishes of the royal agents stood to benefit economically. Those who failed to do so stood to lose their offices or to forfeit their charters. Inevitably, therefore, the merchants and municipal officers manifested none of the political cohesion characteristic of the county landowners.

During the first phase of regulation, the agents focussed particular attention on towns with a corporation franchise. In these cases, control of the corporation would lead directly to control of elections. The first purges were made immediately after the regulating committee was established in November 1687. By March 1688, over 1200 persons judged to be unreliable had been removed from municipal offices. In 51 corporations this work involved only a single purge. In 14 others, a double purge was planned and executed (Jones, 1972, p. 149).

The second phase of the campaign began in April 1687, with further purges and the initiation of actions of *quo warranto* where progress proved to be difficult. In this phase, the agents collected electoral information, listing the names and describing the interests, prospects and opinions of intending candidates. A list of reliable collaborators was compiled and the Crown appointed many of these to positions of deputy lieutenants and justices of the peace (Jones, 1972, p. 150).

The third and final phase of the regulation began in August 1687 when James ordered writs to be issued for parliamentary elections. The principal business of this phase was issuing new charters. Only two had been issued in the whole of 1687, and a further two in the first half of 1688. Between July and September 1688, however, 31 charters were issued, 11 of which were major towns.

The Crown directed 33 individuals to stand for named constituencies and presented a long list of approved royal candidates for county and borough constituencies. The agents had identified several places as being entirely mercenary, willing to sell their votes to the highest bidder, but advised the Crown to await the election outcomes in these constituencies and then to approach the successful candidates with financial offers (Jones, 1972, p. 152).

London was dealt with as a separate unit during the campaign. Traditionally, it had been a center of political opposition to the Stuarts until Charles II shattered Whig control in 1681–84. James was able to displace the Tory party machine without difficulty, replacing the ejected aldermen and deputy lieutenants with a mixture of Catholics, Whigs and opportunists.

A new charter for London provided unlimited power for the King to displace dissidents, providing him with the prospect of winning prestigious elections in the city and in Middlesex. At Westminster, where the electorate was large and turbulent, James cut the number voting to one-tenth of those who had voted in previous elections (Jones, 1972, p. 164). By holding summer camps for the army on Blackheath and Hounslow Heath the Crown implicitly threatened military occupation and the billeting of troops on the local population should disorder occur.

By late August 1688, approximately 200 constituencies returning 400 out of 513 members of Parliament had been subjected to some kind of direct governmental intervention. A working majority supportive of James was certainly in reach (Jones, 1972, p. 173). James announced that writs for new parliamentary elections would be issued on September 5.

However, before James could put his strategy to the test, the threat of imminent invasion by William caused him to abandon all his plans. The writs were never issued. James determined instead that to protect his throne it was essential for him to rebuild his relationship with the Tory/Anglican establishment, to restore all charters and to allow free elections. It was already too late. William's invasion fleet waited only for a Protestant wind.

Although James's strategy ultimately failed, that does not mean that it was irrational. In the absence of an invasion most likely it would have succeeded. The rewards for James would have been immense. With the Test Acts repealed the Catholics would have been secured from discrimination and James's dynasty would have been guaranteed. Indeed, the principal factor leading the 'Immortal Seven' to invite William to invade in late June 1688 was the likely political success of James and his agents in constructing an electoral majority in Parliament capable of eliminating by statute the political and economic hegemony of the Church of England.

The Religious Factor

Despite the weight attached by historians to religious differences as a key factor leading to the Glorious Revolution, it is important to understand that Englishmen during the seventeenth century were much more careless about their religion than were their counterparts in continental Europe.

Hypothesis 2: The religious factor is driven more by considerations of political economy than by considerations of Faith.

The Anglican Church had played a major role in the Restoration and had closely allied itself with the Cavalier/Tory party interest. Despite concerns about the relationship between Charles II and Catholic France, the Church had remained supportive of the King through the sequence of Whig-dominated parliaments and the period of prerogative rule. In return the Church benefitted greatly from the patronage bestowed upon it by the Court.

The Test Acts and the Clarendon Code together locked in major economic privileges for the Anglican Church by denying Catholics and Dissenters the rights both to pursue openly their religious beliefs and to hold public office. The Anglican/Tory interest also benefitted from the maneuvers of Charles to pack Parliament as a basis for ensuring the succession for James II. In return, Anglicans and Tories had welcomed James II to his throne and had voted him financial independence in 1685. In retrospect, if James had been sufficiently flexible politically as to maintain that coalition, he could not have lost his throne.

However, the foremost objective of James II was the achievement of toleration for Catholics (and, if necessary, for Dissenters). In pursuit of this objective, he knew that he was bound to run counter to the Anglican Church, not particularly for reasons of religion but primarily because he was challenging that Church's economic rents. In this confrontation, James relied upon the established doctrine of the Anglican/Tory alliance: the doctrine of the divine hereditary right of kings and the doctrine of non-resistance in its extreme form to protect his throne from attacks by the Anglican Church (Trevelyan, 1938, p. 36).

According to this doctrine, no tyranny, however illegal or cruel, could ever justify a subject in resisting the hereditary monarch in arms, because hereditary monarchy was of divine origin. James II took this doctrine seriously. Initially, he expected the Anglican/Tory majority in Parliament to repeal the Test Acts and to allow him to populate the best places in the church with Catholics and High Anglicans. He would continue to apply the Clarendon Code against the Dissenters.

Primarily for economic reasons, the Anglican Church refused to endorse its own well-established doctrines. The Church recognized that a zealous Romanist King would control appointments to the cabinet, the Privy Council, the Army, the Navy, the Civil Service, the Bench of Judges and the Bench of Bishops, and that he would fill these positions to the limits of available individuals with Roman Catholics (Trevelyan, 1938, p. 58).

The concerns of the Church were validated when James proceeded to pursue just such policies under prerogative rule following the dismissal of Parliament in 1685. Ultimately, no Protestant would feel secure in office unless he was willing to apostatize.

The full vigor of James's attack on the Anglican Church manifested itself in his attack on Oxford University, one of the most influential bastions of the Anglican/Tory alliance. By a series of arbitrary and illegal acts, James placed three great Oxford colleges – Christchurch College, University College and Magdalen College – under Romanist rule. In particular, the expulsion of the Fellows of Magdalen College was viewed by the Anglican Church as an attack on the freehold rights of all ecclesiastical persons (Trevelyan, 1938, p. 72). More even than the trial of the Seven Bishops, in 1688, this act explains why the High Church bishops refused to pronounce against rebellion when William landed and why many of the most staunch Church laymen actually became rebels against the Crown.

In his attempt to forge a new religious coalition of Roman Catholics and Dissenters, James issued his famous Declaration of Indulgence in April 1687, suspending the Clarendon Code, the Test Acts and all laws injurious either to Catholic or Protestant Dissenters. Both groups could now worship freely and could assume public offices without renouncing their respective faiths. A minority of the Dissenters' leaders consented to become allies of the King. A majority refrained from so doing and responded to a counter-offer from the Anglican Church reinforced by promises from William of Orange.

The Anglican bishops and the leaders of the Tory party promised to support an Act of Toleration for Puritan worship as soon as a free Parliament should meet. William of Orange and his wife Mary (the heir presumptive) announced their opposition to James's policies. Instead, they favored freedom of religious worship for Catholics and Dissenters, while retaining the Test Acts and thereby the restriction of political rights for Catholics.

The game essentially played itself out as follows: James's actions constituted an offer both to the Dissenters and to Catholics, whereby both groups would receive freedom of worship and the ability to serve in public office in return for supporting him in Parliament. Separately, the Anglican Church and William of Orange made counter-offers. The Church offered freedom of worship to the Dissenters but not to the Catholics. The Church declined to offer members of either group the right to serve in public office. William offered both groups freedom of worship but declined to offer Catholics the right to serve in public office.

In terms of pure rationality the offer by James both to Dissenters and to Catholics looks attractive. Yet history tells us that both groups failed to take up arms vigorously to defend the Stuart dynasty from William's invading forces. Rationally, the Church sided with William and against James in order to protect its rents from Catholic competition. For the Dissenters, the deciding factor no doubt was the greater credibility of William's offer. William was a Dissenter himself. In this sense, William's offer constituted the Nash equilibrium. Although the Immortal Seven who invited William to invade were predominantly Tory/Anglican, they contained among them a minority of Whig/Dissenters, thus confirming the overall superiority of William's offer.

The very fact that James, William and the Anglican Church were competing with each other to sway Catholics and Dissenters into their respective camps is worth noting, since it vindicates in two ways the claim of this chapter. First, it demonstrates that both the Anglican Church and William shared James's belief that the true number of non-Anglicans was far greater than that reported in the 1676 Episcopal census. There would have been no reason for them to compete over only 4 per cent of the total population. This confirms the rationality of James's attempt to forge a new coalition based on religion.

Second, the competition strongly supports our contention that James's move to gerrymander a Whig/Dissenter majority in a new Parliament was entirely rational and was doomed only by the act of William's invasion. William's counter-offer to the Dissenters and his act of invasion was necessitated by the fact that James was on the point of controlling Parliament and securing the basis for the Stuart dynasty.

The dominant religious coalition against James was emboldened to invite William to invade by the birth of James's son (James III or the Old Pretender) in June 1688. This birth removed Mary as heir presumptive and promised to secure the Catholic dynasty in the absence of a revolution, at least for another generation. The Anglican/Tory alliance, in conjunction with a dismayed

William, spread a lie that James's second wife Mary of Modena had not been pregnant and that James's 'son' had been smuggled into the birth chamber in a bedpan.

How widely this convenient lie was genuinely believed among the politically relevant segment of the population it is now impossible to determine. The lie would certainly prove to be an invaluable fiction for an Anglican/Tory alliance in justifying the demise of the House of Stuart without overtly having to renounce its acknowledged belief in the Divine Right of Kings.

Fundamentally, all religious factors pursued rational self-interest throughout the period 1660 to 1688. The Anglican Church, ever fearful of the Puritans, placed its support behind the House of Stuart until the shift of policy by James II in favor of the Whig/Dissenter coalition. The Dissenters provided solid support for the Whig opposition again until James II pronounced in favor of the repeal of the Clarendon Code. Even as England moved towards tyranny and reeled towards revolution, all religious groups, and subgroups adhered to their own narrow economic interests, even to the evident corruption of their respective faiths.

The European Factor

William of Orange did not covet the throne of England because of any love for that country or its peoples. His affections, such as they were, were centered exclusively on Holland (Trevelyan, 1938, p. 101). Although his wife, Mary, loved England she would not have urged William to attack her father. In any event, William was not in the habit of forming policy in consultation with his wife.

In William's judgment, only by bringing England actively into the anti-France alliance that he had constructed in Europe could Protestant Holland be saved from ultimate conquest by Catholic France. Only as King of England could William achieve such an outcome. Like his brother before him, James II was in the pay of Louis XIV and would not have waged war against him. On the other hand, James was reluctant to enter into an alliance with France that would have wrecked his attempt to pack Parliament with Whigs and Dissenters and that might have led to widespread disaffection within the English army and navy (Jones, 1972, p. 177).

France was the European superpower in the late seventeenth century, and William could not rationally denude the United Provinces of their military defenses by launching an invasion of England while the United Provinces were under direct threat from France. Indeed, as *Stadtholder*, he had no authority so to do without obtaining the unanimous consent of each of the seven Provincial governments. A number of factors combined in 1688 to provide William with the authority to launch an invasion.

First, Louis XIV launched in 1688 a program of intimidation against the Dutch, including the seizure of all Dutch ships in French harbors, which was sufficiently venomous as to rally the Republican Peace Party to William's support. Second, he withdrew the French forces threatening Holland in order to plunge them into a campaign against the Emperor Leopold and the German Princes on the Rhine. Third, Pope Innocent XI had been deeply offended by the unwillingness of Louis XIV to respond to his appeals for a Crusade against the Turks and in response he offered tacit support for William's invasion. Fourth, the death of Elector Frederick William of Brandenburg in 1688 removed Brandenburg as the potential source of a Northern European coalition against the United Provinces. In these circumstances, the United Provinces reluctantly allowed William to launch his invasion of England.

The rational behavior of William of Orange and of the United Provinces with respect to the European factor underlying the invasion of England is evident from this account. He further secured himself from immediate Catholic repercussions by assuring Emperor Leopold and Pope Innocent that he was not seeking the English throne.

The behavior of James II and Louis XIV warrants further discussion since at first sight an alliance between the two and against William appears to trump the policies that each of them pursued separately with respect to the threatened invasion of England from Holland.

The behavior of James is easily explained as rational, given his objective of gaining parliamentary sanction for the elimination of the hated Test Acts. The non-Catholic English establishment dreaded the aggressive Catholicism of Louis XIV, especially after his repeal of the Edict of Nantes, which had offered safeguards against persecution to the French Huguenots. The English Dissenters in particular feared Catholic persecution should James ally himself to Louis XIV. James could not possibly hope for parliamentary support from the Whigs if there was any sign of such a deal. For, given the weakness of England in international affairs, James would have had little else to offer Louis in return for military support against William except for an aggressive policy in support of Catholicism in England.

The behavior of Louis XIV is a little more difficult to rationalize, but far from impossible. Louis was annoyed with James because the latter generally would not openly ally himself with the Catholic cause on the European continent and more specifically would not engage militarily against the United Provinces. As a supreme monarch in France, Louis had little understanding of or patience with James's difficulties with Parliament. He himself was entirely comfortable with a policy of ruling through the royal prerogative.

However, Louis in no sense was a slave of passion. He calculated that an invasion by William would result in a long and bloody civil war that would further neutralize England in international affairs and that would drain the

United Provinces of the resources to challenge France in continental Europe. In the meantime, Louis would be free to savage the Emperor Leopold in Germany and to bring Pope Innocent XI to heel, thus consolidating his position as the dominant figure on the European continent (Trevelyan, 1938, pp. 105–6).

These expectations would turn out to be unjustified, because the Glorious Revolution was so unexpectedly brief. Yet, the expectations were rational from an *ex ante* perspective. The Glorious Revolution in its brevity ran counter to all English precedents. James II, with a standing army of 30 000 men and a powerful navy, and with a dissolved Parliament incapable of raising an army against him, should have been invincible against any foreign invasion. Louis XIV was justifiably confident that William was making a grievous political error in invading such a substantial foe.

5. THE REVOLUTION SETTLEMENT

Whig historians view the Revolution Settlement of Church and State embodied in the 1689 Declaration of Rights as a major constitutional settlement that survived with little statutory change until the next era of English constitutional reform in the 1830s. This view is excessively optimistic. In significant respects, interventions over the period 1669 to 1701 proved to be arguably more important than the Declaration of Rights itself. Although these subsequent interventions were rendered more likely as a consequence of the Settlement, they were by no means assured implications of it.

Although James II had left England for France, he had not formally vacated his Crown. He fully expected to be restored to the throne once William of Orange returned to the United Provinces in accordance with his solemn promise to the Pope and to the Emperor. William, of course, had no intention of honoring that pledge and indeed controlled the constitutional settlement that followed his successful invasion (Prall, 1972, p. 247). From his powerful position at the Court of St. James, with his army available to quash political dissent, William held a winning hand throughout the period of interregnum.

The primary constitutional issue facing the country concerned the situation of the monarchy. The Tory/Anglican coalition responsible for bringing William to England now confronted a philosophical dilemma. The concept of the Divine Right of Kings allowed for no interregnum: *Le roi est mort. Vive le roi.*

If, indeed, James could be viewed as abdicating, his son James III was now King of England, since males held precedence over females in the line of succession. Even if James's son were to be excluded on supposititious grounds, itself a controversial judgment to say the least, William's wife, Mary, as the elder daughter of James was now monarch as Mary II. William of Orange himself, as grandson of James I, had only a remote claim to the throne, behind James, Mary and Anne.

William was not interested in the niceties of philosophy, but rather in the political realities of his successful invasion. He refused either to serve as Regent to James III or to act as usher to his wife. Inevitably the philosophical confusion of the Tory/Anglican coalition on the issue of succession allowed the Whig/Dissenter coalition to play the predominant role in the settlement proceedings. Whig philosophers such as John Locke at that time were arguing persuasively that the people had the right to overthrow and to replace any monarch who threatened their lives, liberties or property (Locke, 1690).

To resolve the constitutional crisis, a Convention Parliament was summoned by letters issued by William at the request of an unofficial assembly of peers and former members of the Commons. Elections for it took place during the Interregnum. In this sense, the Convention Parliament was unauthorized since only the King could serve writs for an election. The two Houses that met in January 1689 did not constitute a Parliament and their decisions had no legal authority at law. This fact allowed the Jacobites a legal standing to impugn the title of William and Mary as King and Queen in the post-settlement era. In this respect, the English constitutional settlement mirrored that of the United States since the Philadelphia convention also was not authorized at law to explore the dissolution of the Articles of Confederation or to propose an alternative constitution.

Because the Convention Parliament was elected and deliberated under abnormal conditions – the absence of a recognized monarch, internal upheaval and the threat of invasion by James II from Scotland and Ireland – it might be argued that a 'constitutional moment' existed. Certainly, Whigs and Tories for the most part suppressed their respective factional interests. Since the constituencies could not know for sure the outcome of the convention, there was little point in providing votes and influence in return for positions, pensions or royal favor. A sizeable proportion of those elected to the convention held no party affiliation and evidenced no significant constituency ties.

The outcome of the Convention's deliberations on the issue of the monarchy essentially was a victory for the Whigs, but with a significant concession to the Tories. James II was declared to have broken the original contract between King and people (a Whig victory) but to have abdicated the throne by his voluntary flight and not to have been deposed (the concession to Tory sentiment). The throne was declared to be vacant (a Whig victory of immense significance since use of the term conflicted with Divine Right philosophy). William and Mary were made joint sovereigns, reigning side by side (a Whig victory). The administration of the realm was vested solely in William during his life (a recognition of the reality of William's total dominance over his meek and loving spouse).

The Convention continued to acknowledge the hereditary principle, providing for a succession in favor first of heirs, if any, of Mary II, second of Princess Anne, third heirs of Princess Anne and fourth heirs (other than by Mary) of William III. Clearly, however, once the principle of Divine Right had been rejected, the monarchy would never be completely secure against parliamentary intervention on dynastic issues. The balance between King and Parliament, in this respect, had been significantly disturbed in favor of Parliament.

This outcome was not achieved without cost. Four hundred beneficed clergy, including five of the seven bishops who had been prosecuted by James, refused to take the oath of allegiance to William and Mary and instead relinquished their livings and their sees. Many other Tories became Jacobites and plotted in favor of the return of their divinely authorized monarch, James and his natural successors. This continuing opposition ironically played an important role in stabilizing the constitutional settlement.

The Convention Parliament did not invite William and Mary to assume the throne of England without conditions. The Declaration of Rights, in raising them to the throne, provided a lengthy recital of the illegal acts of James II, most especially his claim to suspend the rule of law by royal prerogative, and required their acceptance of the illegality of these aspects of royal power (Trevelyan, 1938, p. 149). In a solemn ceremony, at Whitehall on February 13, 1689, William and Mary accepted from the Houses of the Lords and Commons the Crown and the Declaration of Rights, thus acknowledging the limitations of their royal power.

The Declaration of Rights was a conservative document. Essentially, it restored ancient English liberties and rights that had been abused by James II. The Declaration prohibited: the pretended powers of suspending and dispensing with laws by regal authority; the levying of monies by the Crown without consent of Parliament; the jailing of subjects for the act of petitioning the Crown; and the raising or keeping of a standing army within the kingdom in time of peace without the consent of Parliament.

The Declaration further required: that Protestants should have the right to bear arms as allowed by law; that parliamentary elections should be free; that freedom of speech in Parliament should not be impeached or questioned in any court or place out of Parliament; that excessive bail, excessive fines and cruel and unusual punishment should not be inflicted; that jurors should be duly impaneled and returned and that jurors in trials for high treason should be freeholders; and that parliaments should be held frequently.

The Declaration was of immense constitutional significance in that it resolved a century-long struggle between royal prerogative and the rule of law decisively in favor of the latter principle (Trevelyan, 1938, p. 133). Henceforth, there would be no Court of the Star Chamber, no Court of High Commission and no Bloody Assize in England. Statutes would be altered only by the action of both Houses of Parliament with the consent of the monarch. At least in principle the English courts would be free from all governmental interference in their role of formulating and interpreting the common law. The first statute to which William and Mary consented, after acceding to the throne, was an Act converting the Convention into a Parliament. The Declaration of Rights was quickly re-enacted as a parliamentary statute.

The Declaration of Rights did not solve the problem of the responsibilities of ministers. William would choose his own Privy Council, and that Council would be responsible to him and not to Parliament. It did not solve the problem of the tenure of judges who would still serve with few exceptions at the will of the King. It did not solve the problem of religious comprehension or toleration. All of these issues would eventually be resolved by the now settled principles of interaction between Parliament and the Crown. These solutions, however, would be the outcome of politics-as-usual and not of any constitutional settlement. The constitutional settlement set in place a process of government compatible with those radical reforms that, within a period of twelve years would make England the first constitutional democracy.

6. WHY THE CONSTITUTIONAL SETTLEMENT ENDURED

It is generally agreed that the constitutional settlement provided by the Declaration of Rights in 1689 ushered in a system of constitutional democracy based on limited government, private property rights and the rule of law. Because this system proved to be incentive-compatible with capitalism, it provided fertile soil for the Industrial Revolution (Ekelund and Tollison, 1981, 1997; North and Weingast, 1989; Wells and Wills, 2000) and for the emergence of Great Britain in the nineteenth century as the greatest Empire that the world has ever known.

This system would survive for 150 years until a second era of constitutional reform based on the indiscriminate expansion of the suffrage ultimately destroyed the original constitution and stimulated a process that has culminated in the early twenty-first century in unlimited government, a pernicious violation of private property rights and the abrogation of the rule of law in favor of rule by parliamentary prerogative.

Fundamentally, the beneficial economic consequences of the Glorious Revolution were unintended consequences of the process through which William III replaced James II on the throne of England. Those who invited William to launch his invasion for the most part were Tory landowners and Anglican churchmen, individuals who prospered under mercantilism and who looked askance both at industrialization and international trade. Those who would benefit primarily from the Industrial Revolution were the businessmen and merchants who formed the major component of the Whig/dissenter opposition and whose interests James II was actively courting immediately prior to the invasion.

Why did the Revolution Settlement survive when all earlier attempts to resolve the tensions between the Crown and Parliament had failed? The answer lies in the peculiar transaction costs of constitutional reform. For reform to be feasible, the transaction costs surrounding such reform must be low. For reform to take on constitutional significance, the transaction costs must rise substantially and abruptly after the constitutional moment has been seized, thereby rendering reversal infeasible.

Such was the situation in 1689. James II had abused the royal prerogative to an extent that his more cautious brother had carefully avoided. Even his serious abuses in England paled into insignificance by comparison with the mass attainders and property confiscations that he endorsed on behalf of the Catholic Dublin Parliament in Ireland (Jones, 1972, p. 326). If the Revolution Settlement had failed, and if William had returned to Holland, the Restoration of James would imply for free Englishmen the acceptance of absolutism on the French model.

Once the constitutional settlement had been resolved, and the rights of free Englishmen had been re-established under a rule of law, the transaction cost scenario was fundamentally changed. Parliament must now work amicably with the Crown in order to stabilize the new dynasty. If it failed to do so and the Jacobite following in England expanded, Restoration of the House of Stuart would follow. Restoration would involve an Act of Oblivion eliminating all the statutory advances achieved since the flight of James II. Parliament and the nation could not countenance such a reversal of fortunes.

Thus it was that Crown and Parliament found themselves in fundamental agreement that the Declaration of Rights and its immediate legislative aftermath served their joint purposes over a period sufficiently lengthy as to establish the Protestant succession and to squeeze the Jacobite threat into oblivion. Thus it was that an entirely unpredictable sequence of events over the period 1660–89 culminated arguably in the best constitution that the world has ever known, albeit, unfortunately, one that would not survive into the late nineteenth century after the consequences of the Reform Act of 1832.

REFERENCES

Brennan, H.G. and J.M. Buchanan (1985), *The Reason of Rules*, Cambridge: Cambridge University Press.

Buchanan, J.M. (1990), 'The domain of constitutional economics', *Constitutional Political Economy*, **1** (1), 1–18.

Buchanan, J.M. and G. Tullock (1962), *The Calculus of Consent*, Ann Arbor: University of Michigan Press.

Churchill, W.S. (1956), *A History of the English Speaking Peoples*, Volume 2: *The New World*, 1992 Collectors Edition: Norwalk: The Easton Press.

Ekelund, R.B. and R.D. Tollison (1981), *Mercantilism as a Rent-Seeking Society: Economic Regulation in Historical Perspective*, College Station: Texas A&M University Press.

Ekelund, R.B. and R.D. Tollison (1997), *Politicized Economies*, College Station: Texas A&M Press.

Hayek, F.A. (1960), *The Constitution of Liberty*, London: Routledge & Kegan Paul.

Hayek, F.A. (1973), *Law, Legislation and Liberty*, Volume I, Chicago: University of Chicago Press.

Hobbes, T. (1651), 'Leviathan', in W. Molesworth (ed.), *The English Works of Thomas Hobbes*, volume 3, London: J. Bohn.

Johnson, P. (1972), *A History of the English People*, London: Harper & Row.

Jones, J.R. (1972), *The Revolution of 1688 in England*, New York: W.W. Norton & Co.

Locke, J. (1690), *Two Treatises of Government*, edited by P. Laslett, Cambridge: Cambridge University Press.

Macaulay, T.B. (1888), *The History of England from the Accession of James II*, 5 vols, Chicago: University of Chicago Press.

Mueller, D.C. (1996), *Constitutional Democracy*, Cambridge: Cambridge University Press.

North, D.C. and B.R. Weingast (1989), 'Constitution and commitment: the evolution of institutional governing public choice in seventeenth-century England', *Journal of Economic History*, **49** (4), 803–32.

Ogg, D. (1955), *England in the Reigns of James II and William III*, Oxford: Clarendon Press.

Pinkham, L. (1969), *William III and the Respectable Revolution*, Cambridge: Archon Books.

Prall, S.E. (1972), *The Bloodless Revolution: England 1688*, Madison: University of Michigan Press.

Rowley, C.K. (1990), 'The reason of rules: constitutional contract versus political market conflict', *Annual Review of Conflict Knowledge and Conflict Resolution*, **2**, 195–228.

Rowley, C.K. (2001), 'Constitutional political economy and civil society', in R. Mudambi, P. Navarra and G. Sobbrio (eds), *Rules and Reason: Perspectives on Constitutional Political Economy*, Cambridge: Cambridge University Press, pp. 69–96.

Trevelyan, G.M. (1938), *The English Revolution 1688–1689*, London: Oxford University Press.

Wells, J. and D. Wills (2000), 'Revolution, restoration and debt repudiation: the Jacobite threat to England's institutions and economic growth', *Journal of Economic History*.

12. The politics of poverty

Thráinn Eggertsson

1. INTRODUCTION

Although the complex causes of economic decline and economic backwardness probably defy generalization, I will attempt in this chapter to examine some of the political aspects of poor economic performance and distill basic themes from the new institutional economics and related fields concerning the interaction between politics and poverty. Static institutional analysis models the link between institutions and poor economic performance roughly in the following terms. A country is poor because its basic structure of formal and informal rules – its institutional environment – creates incentives that have perverse effects for economic progress. In the economic domain, the environment discourages capital formation, directs economic agents away from valuable economic opportunities, and encourages rent seeking. The citizens share norms that are hostile to economic progress and institutional reforms, and political actors prefer policies that undermine long-term growth.

In the new institutional analysis, static models take the preferences of actors as given and unchanging. Furthermore, the worldviews of actors are neutral rather than a force driving the analysis. For instance, in analyzing decisions about institutional policy, even in historical times, the investigator usually tacitly assumes that the decision maker shared his or her current social theories or social models. Competing social models or social technologies have no role in these studies, even when they analyze the behavior of actors who are attempting to make complex changes in the structure of their social systems, either for redistributive or remedial purposes. The assumption that rational selfish rulers and administrators have complete knowledge of social technologies usually leads to the conclusion that the spectacular economic failures of the twentieth century – the soviet experiment, various foreign aid programs, African socialism – either are unfortunate byproducts of redistributive policies or deadlocked political games.

The chief dependent variable in this chapter is economic performance and I have particular interest in the range of low values for the variable. In explaining economic performance, my interest is in the influence of political forces on the institutional environment of economic decision makers. As I have discussed elsewhere the role of norms in economic development, rules with decentralized enforcement, does not hold center stage in this chapter (Eggertsson, 2002).

Just as harmful exogenous events sometimes strike individuals and reduce them to poverty, so do harmful shocks hit nations and their economies. These impulses may be unavoidable, but for long-term growth the critical question is how nations cope with the shocks. The following section discusses two cases: the response by modem nations to the trade shocks of the 1970s, and responses by traditional agrarian societies to shocks emanating from nature. The subsection dealing with agrarian societies uses the social security systems of historical Iceland as an example of the institutional regimes used by traditional societies to cope with specific and general risks. Although traditional institutions often are relatively effective in their original context, they can act as breaks on economic development (Hoff, 2000). I make the case that the social security system of Iceland contributed to economic stagnation. The discussion of responses by nations worldwide to the trade shocks of the 1970s draws on Rodrik (1998). Until the 1970s the economic performance of the various regions of developing countries was roughly comparable. Many developing countries, however, were unable to adjust to the trade shocks of the 1970s, including the oil crises, with the result that their economic growth collapsed. According to Rodrik, other countries made the required adjustments in their macroeconomic policies and subsequently became associated with growth miracles, especially several Asian countries. I use the Rodrik (1998) study to introduce the reader to the strengths and weaknesses of the international cross-section growth regressions. Leaving statistical problems aside, the analytical level of these studies is close to the surface, because they usually relate economic outcomes to the strength of democratic rights and property rights. We also need to know why democratic rights and property rights vary from one country to another.

The third section discusses the political rationality of inefficient economic systems. I use Olson's (2000) recent work to discuss the impact of the 'horizon effect' on the decisions of autocratic rulers, and a study by Bueno de Mesquita and colleagues (2000) that introduces the 'coalition effect'. The 'horizon effect' explains why a ruler who takes the short view lacks the incentive to expand her tax base. The 'coalition effect' relates the size of a leader's winning coalition to her decisions about public policy. The third subsection goes on to discuss why support groups that enjoy government privileges race to dissipate their rents and also compete to be first to introduce reforms of the rent-seeking process. The third section concludes with a discussion of the problem of creating limited government and democratic stability, which I consider an unresolved issue in the literature. At the center of my discussion is a well-known model by Weingast (1997). In his study Weingast attempts to wrap the 'interest view' and the 'values view' in one parcel by presenting the problem of establishing limited government as a vast coordination game, in which elites attempt to coordinate the personal constitutional models of various groups. According to Weingast, if the coordination effort succeeds, it gives rise both to democratic stability and democratic values.

The chapter's fourth and last major section discusses the neglected role of competing social models in theories of economic performance. Olson (2000), for instance, in his recent analysis of the Soviet system, argues that Stalin and other creators of the system share our (recent view) of its efficiency properties – namely that it was grossly inefficient and, in the long run, doomed to failure. The section begins by discussing alternative explanations of why nations sometimes make sharp, discontinuous changes in their basic economic institutions. I make the case that coordinated shifts along an important policy axis of clusters of social models play an important role in regime changes. The following subsection examines the frequent long life of social technologies and social institutions that, in retrospect at least, failed to reach the desired goals. I suggest that lack of knowledge (incomplete social models) along with strategic factors are responsible for their longevity. The chapter concludes with a discussion of the complex set of factors that (roughly) in the 1780s initiated a centennial wave of liberal economic institutions, which in the 1880s was reversed by another centennial wave of state control of the economy that ebbed around 1980.

2. COPING WITH THE NATURAL ENVIRONMENT AND TRADE SHOCKS

When one is asked to explain why some countries are poor and others are rich, a natural response is to think of adverse external circumstances. Countries are poor because of hostile or changing climate (historical Iceland, sub-Saharan Africa); because of exploitation by colonial powers (India); because leaders in world trade have adversely manipulated a country's terms of international trade (Latin America); because the country lacks abundant natural resources (Japan while it was still relatively poor); because of an unfavorable geographic location (land-locked African countries); or because of epidemics and foreign invasions.

In social science the popularity of such external explanations wanes and rises with the times. Recent theoretical and empirical work, for instance, makes the case that abundant natural resources actually harm rather than help the long-term growth prospects of a country (Gylfason, 2000; Sachs and Warner, 1999). Of course, external events have devastated national economies, and poor countries employing primitive technologies usually are less prepared to deal with disastrous events than are rich and technologically advanced countries. In the case of unavoidable external events, it is relevant to ask whether a country, rich or poor, employed sound governance and effective institutional policy to cope with adverse impulses or whether poor policies aggravated a bad situation. In this section, I discuss how traditional societies, using decentralized institutional regimes, tried to cope with risks of natural origins, and how modern societies handled the foreign trade crises of the 1970s.

2.1 Responses to General and Specific Risks in Traditional Societies

Random environmental factors, such as climatic disturbance or disease, can cause large variation in the outputs of poor agrarian communities that operate with low levels of technology.[1] As lives may be at stake, traditional societies have a strong incentive to seek ways to reduce variability over time in their consumption, but high costs of transacting in these communities usually prevent or limit the use of insurance, credit, and other inter-temporal markets. Recent studies show, however, that traditional societies are able to stabilize their consumption and lower the cost of risks by relying on various non-market institutional arrangements and adjustment in production.[2] Usually, these studies do not explicitly examine the political problem of coordinating social responses to a risky environment, but it is often understood that these are local or decentralized decisions motivated by threats to the very existence of the community.

The literature on risk management distinguishes between covariate or *general risks* and uncorrelated or *specific risks*. If the risks faced by individual economic units have high positive covariance (misfortune strikes most of the units simultaneously), they are *general risks* and much of the gains from pooling and sharing risks are removed. Weather-related risks, for instance, have a positive correlation when all economic units in a community belong to the same climatic zone, and risks of disease are correlated when proximity exposes human or animal populations simultaneously to infection from contagious diseases. Consider a community of farmers on an island, all operating in the same climatic zone and facing a high positive yield variance for their crop. Although pooling their yield risks in the current activity would not help (even if transaction costs were low), the farmers possibly could reduce their risks by diversifying into new lines of production, for instance by reallocating some of their inputs to coastal fisheries. If the correlation between outcomes in the old and new activity is less than 1, each farmer has reduced his or her overall risk, but probably at a cost because of output losses from foregoing specialization.[3]

Specific risks are individual mishaps such as accidents, non-epidemic diseases, localized fires, or drowning of people and animals. The members of a social group can reduce the cost of specific risks by pooling and sharing the risks. Informal insurance systems may cover extended families, the labor force of a farm, the members of a village, a township or a whole nation. Informal insurance schemes in traditional societies tend to cover relatively small groups because primitive measurement techniques and weak formal enforcement mechanisms usually confine social networks of reciprocal obligations to small groups. However, the covariance of risks often falls when the size and geographic location of the insured group increases, and the choice of insurance groups involves a tradeoff between insurance costs and transaction costs.

Although the literature on non-market insurance arrangements in traditional societies usually assumes that, given the circumstances, these institutions are efficient, inefficient institutions are not unknown. As their knowledge is incomplete, societies may introduce imperfect institutions and then get locked into an unfavorable social equilibrium that precludes reforms. Institutions that are efficient at one point often become inappropriate when circumstances change, for instance with new markets or new technologies, and may prevent a required restructuring of the economy. I will now briefly illustrate these points with examples from my work on historical Iceland that (1) provides an empirical example of how poor farm communities cope with threatening external impulses, (2) how there may be flaws in such institutional arrangements, and (3) how traditional institutions can put breaks on economic development (Eggertsson, 1998).

The traditional system of social security in historical Iceland was based on relative sophisticated institutions for coping with risk (Eggertsson, 1998). Icelandic farmers cultivated grass to provide fodder for livestock in a climate that was extraordinarily marginal for farming. In the premodern period the major source of general risks in the farm community were random cold spells, although volcanic eruptions and epidemics also were important sources. To deal with general risks, farmers stored food, and diversified production by entering the country's rich coastal fisheries, but only on small open boats, on a part-time basis, and during the off-season in farming.[4] The polity supported the arrangement by enforcing a ban on specialization in the fisheries.

In traditional Iceland, *specific risks*, which could be pooled, included illness, accidents, fires, floods, avalanches, and local weather conditions, and, for coping with these risks, the community developed relatively sophisticated institutions. The social safety net that served the Icelandic community in the premodern age had its roots in the laws of the Commonwealth (930–1262), which are collected in *Grágás* and probably were first put in writing in the eleventh and twelfth centuries.[5] As is customary in traditional societies, the Icelanders were responsible for the welfare of their relatives, and 'kin' was defined broadly, but when family support failed, local governance units, some 160 communes, *hreppar*, became the centerpiece of the social safety net. The law required adjacent farms to form a *hreppur*, but these communes were fairly autonomous self-governing bodies. In historical Iceland the law provided each *hreppur* with tax revenue (a share in the tithe, which was introduced in 1096), and specified in detail the rights and duties of communes and their members in dealing with risks. The old Icelandic laws show sophisticated awareness of *moral hazard* in its stipulations, for instance, in compensating for fire damages on farmsteads.

In the labor market, general use of *linked* or *tied* long-term employment contracts was an important insurance mechanism whereby labor power was exchanged in return for a payment that links basic remuneration with credit and social security (Bardhan, 1983, 1989). Their responsibility for the welfare of all individuals in the communes gave rise to preoccupation among Icelandic farmers with potential abuse of the system. The farmers feared not only that lazy and irresponsible people might free-ride on their resources, but also that they would bear the cost of failed experiments in non-farming activities. They opposed independent fisheries and informally enforced population control by preventing most people from marrying before they could afford to rent or buy a farm. In 1703 some 44 per cent of all Icelandic women fifty years and older had never been married (Gunnarsson, 1983, p. 16).[6]

This decentralized system of hunger insurance, which generally worked well for *specific risks*, could not cope with major *general risks* (Eggertsson, 1998). The eighteenth century was Iceland's worst. One in nine Icelanders perished in the famine of 1756–57, some 24 per cent of the country's population perished in the famine of 1784–85 and even more people died in a smallpox epidemic of 1707–09. Vasey (1991, p. 344) reports that the excessive death rate in 1784–85 was double the size of most estimates of mortality from the Irish potato famine, and comparable to the worst local famines in early modern Europe.

The Icelandic case, with its disastrous outcomes, is introduced here because of its paradoxical quality. In terms of local capacities, and given the country's industrial organization and available technology, the country did not, it seems, suffer from poor (domestic) politics: the social security system was not obviously dysfunctional, and it was relatively egalitarian.[7] In his study of the famine of 1784–85, which is associated with one of the most massive volcanic eruptions in human history and belongs to the category of *general risks*, Vasey (1991, pp. 340–43) reports that servants and adopted children, and people on assistance, generally did not have lower survival rates than farmers and their immediate family. Modern information and transaction cost economics suggests, however, that institutional arrangements, which perhaps are efficient at one stage of development, sometimes create underdevelopment traps that prevent adjustment to more efficient institutional arrangements when circumstances change (Hoff, 2000).

> A very general insight of recent theoretical work is that while institutions may have, as their intention, the improvement in economic outcomes, there is no assurance that that will be the case. Institutions may be part of an equilibrium, and yet be disfunctional. For example, Arnott and Stiglitz (1991) consider the consequences of the social institutions that arise as a result of the incomplete insurance provided by markets because of moral hazard problems. They show that informal social insurance may crowd out market insurance and lower social welfare. Developing countries may be caught in a vicious circle in which low levels of market development result in high levels of information imperfections, and these information imperfections themselves give rise to institutions – for example informal, personalized networks of exchange relationships (Kranton, 1996) – that impede the development of markets. (Hoff, 2000, pp. 7–8)

The economic history of Iceland suggests that the ancient social policies and institutions, which were in place already in the eleventh century, in the long run placed the country in an underdevelopment trap. Elsewhere, I have argued that the norms of reciprocity, which supported the social security system, led to a dysfunctional equilibrium in the provision of fodder by creating incentives for farmers not to keep stores of fodder (hay) beyond the requirements of a normal year (Eggertsson, 1998; Eggertsson, 2002). In terms of fodder for livestock, the farm community was unprepared for cold spells and other random shocks. I also have argued that the country's formal and informal social security system was an important source of the ancient policy of discouraging specialization in production outside agriculture, particularly in the ocean fisheries. The anti-fisheries policy was one of two critical factors in maintaining an equilibrium trap that prevented the evolution of the country's industrial organization (Eggertsson, 1996). The other critical factor maintaining the underdevelopment trap was the policy of the Danish Kingdom from the early seventeenth century until the mid-nineteenth century to protect its interests in Iceland by isolating the remote and undefended colony from commercial contacts with the rest of the world. The ocean fisheries around Iceland are among the best in Europe. In premodern times vessels from various countries used state-of-the-art technology to exploit these fisheries. The Icelanders, however, were forbidden to cooperate with foreigners to develop a fishing industry and market the product internationally. They continued to operate the fisheries part-time, on a small scale, and with outdated technology. For exports (and imports) the Icelanders could only deal with a Danish royal monopoly. The interests of Icelandic farmers and their system of social security, and the defense interests of the Danish crown together blocked the development of the industry that in the twentieth century made Iceland a relatively wealthy country.

2.2 Modern Societies: Responding to Foreign Trade Shocks

Observing contemporary economic growth in medium-term periods of, say, thirty or forty years, economists have noted for countries worldwide that growth in the early part of the period is a poor predictor of growth in the later part. In other words, the growth performance of a country varies considerably from one period to another, even when there are no major changes in its domestic institutional environment or policy regime.[8] Easterly et al. (1993), who drew attention to this phenomenon, suggest it is caused by exogenous shocks such as wars or external trade impulses, which at times interrupt economic progress.

Although economic theory usually focusses on the technical economic issue of how to respond to trade shocks, the actual response is shaped by political institutions, political calculation and political bargaining. Depending on their severity, efficient adjustments to external trade shocks sometimes require only fiscal and monetary measures, but in other cases major structural changes also are needed, including the development of new industries and the shrinking of established and often politically powerful industries. Adverse trade impulses, such as a sharp fall in the value of a major export commodity, reduces a country's real income and attempts by the government to allocate the burden can initiate costly struggles among social groups. When old and established industries are undermined by developments in external markets, its owners, managers, workers, and even suppliers often seek protection and subsidies from the state. When macroeconomic adjustments are needed, some groups favor import controls over devaluation of the currency, while other groups prefer devaluation accompanied by wage controls (Rodrik, 1998, p. 2). When reduction in aggregate spending is required, organized groups often call for higher taxes on others than themselves or advocate cutting government spending in areas where they are not affected. The worst scenario for growth is created by governments that respond to these various pressures by allocating the cost of external shocks through inflation, and by protecting and subsidizing declining industries, without providing incentives for new industries to develop. Ineffective policy responses can magnify the economic cost of trade shocks and make adverse effects linger even long after the original external conditions have reversed themselves and become favorable again.

Easterly et al. (1993) draw the conclusion from their empirical evidence that, for the medium term, exogenous shocks are the chief cause of punctuated growth. Rodrik (1998, pp. 5–9) provides evidence indicating that different responses to trade shocks explain why growth in East Asia (excluding China) diverged in the mid-1970s from growth rates in Latin America, the Middle East and to some extent in Africa. From 1960 to 1973 the growth performance in all these regions, except Africa, was roughly comparable. The Middle East led with 4.7 per cent growth in GDP per capita, but even many countries in Africa did well. In Africa eight sub-Saharan countries had growth rates in GDP per capita that exceeded 3 per cent. The data show that during the years 1973–94 productivity growth collapsed in all these regions except East Asia, where growth continued at about the same rate as it had during 1960–73. Rodrik (1998) contends that in the 1970s terms-of-trade shocks triggered different developments in East Asia than in the other three regions. Rodrik's comparison of policy responses in South Korea, Turkey, and Brazil reveals that Korea, the country that changes in world prices during the 1970s hit harder than the other two countries, made efficient adjustments in its macroeconomic policy, whereas Brazil and Turkey failed to adjust. And only Korea kept growing at a rate comparable to the pre-1970s rate.

Why do some countries fail to absorb exogenous shocks? Rodrik (1998, pp. 9–13) uses a simple model of social conflict to develop the idea that countries fail to adjust to trade shocks because (a) they are constrained by latent social conflict and (b) they lack effective institutions for managing conflict. The model predicts that external shocks have the largest impact on growth when countries are plagued by serious social strife and also lack effective institutions of conflict management. Successful countries either have very little social strife or experience some social strife, which causes little harm because strong institutions of conflict management neutralize it.

The Rodrik (1998) model is in the spirit of the interest-group approach of public choice theory. The expectations, the incentives, and the behavior of organized pressure groups drive the story, but the state is in the background providing a playing field for these groups.[9] A simple equation roughly captures the essence of the model:

$$\Delta \text{ growth} = -\text{ external shocks} \times \frac{\text{latent social conflict}}{\text{institutions of conflict management}}$$

The recent availability of data sets containing comparable social, political and economic variables for a large number of countries has made it possible to test empirically various conjunctures about the general impact of both economic and non-economic variables on economic growth. These econometric tests involve high levels of aggregation, relatively crude proxies for social and political variables, potentially large measurement errors, and a range of doubtful statistical assumptions. The approach uses the assumption that we can derive general principles about the long-term development of economies by comparing countries at different levels of development at a fixed point in time.[10] Although we may doubt the ability of international cross-section regressions to give reliable answers, they are fruitful tools of discovery, insights, and for generating new hypotheses. The findings from cross-section regressions can be tested again later by other means such as time-series analysis for individual countries, statistical studies of individual industries in several countries or through deep case studies that rely on various methods of inquiry.

In Rodrik's (1998) empirical test of his social conflict theory, the dependent variable is the growth differential between 1960–75 and 1975–89 for each country. His proxies for latent social conflict are: (a) income inequality (measured by Gini coefficients), and (b) an index of the ethno-linguistic diversity in a country. The quality of institutions of conflict management is measured by the International Country Risk Guide index (ICRG), which, for each country covered, gives numerical values to factors such as rule of law, bureaucratic quality, corruption, expropriation risk, and government repudiation of contracts. The ICRG index, therefore, measures the quality of social outcomes – the security of economic property rights – rather than particular underlying rule structures or features of the economic environment. The other main proxy for measuring the quality of institutions of conflict management is the Freedom House index of democracy, which is composed of indicators of civil liberties and political rights. Again, the index is outcome oriented, but its emphasis on political outcomes provides a deeper explanation of growth than does the ICRG index. Presumably the nature of political outcomes influences expectations about secure property rights, which in turn influences economic behavior and the allocation of resources.[11]

The regression analysis seems to strongly support Rodrik's thesis about the link between social conflict and economic performance. In various versions of the regression model, key coefficients have the predicted sign and they are nearly always statistically significant. Many of the regressions explain (as indicated by adjusted R^2) about two-thirds of the country variation in growth performance. However, dummy variables for regions, such as Latin America and East Asia, remain significant after the social conflict and institutional variables have entered the regressions, which suggests that growth performance is influenced by region-specific factors.

When they enter the regressions, the social conflict and institutional variables usually render statistically insignificant the variable measuring the size of the trade turbulence that a country faced in the 1970s. The apparent lesson here is that external trade impulses are of secondary importance when latent social conflict is under control. The study also produces empirical evidence showing that trade shocks do not primarily affect growth by reducing a country's rate of investment, but by affecting the productivity of investments.

Finally, Rodrik (1998) creates an (outcome-oriented) index of macroeconomic mismanagement, which combines the increases between 1960–75 and 1975–89 in the rate of inflation and in the premium for foreign currency on the black market. The index of bad policy has a very strong negative correlation with economic growth, which suggests that social conflict and poor institutional arrangements influence medium-term growth by affecting the quality of macroeconomic policy (and presumably poor macroeconomic policy reduces productivity of investments).

Rodrik's (1998) brilliant and provocative study is a worthy representative of the new international cross-section literature. The study directs our attention to an important aspect of the pathology of economic decline, which the new institutional literature usually ignores: the interaction between the institutional environment and macroeconomic policy. A key assumption of the Rodrik study, which it shares with most other comparable work, concerns the information and knowledge available to macroeconomic policy makers (Rodrik, 1998, p. 2). The policy makers know exactly what economic measures must be taken to limit the effects of trade disturbances on the economy. But the study does not explicitly explain why rational politicians often choose not to use this knowledge. Why powerful rulers often conclude that bad macroeconomic (and institutional) policy is good politics. Admittedly, the study associates bad economics with uncertain property rights and insecure democratic rights, but these are the outcomes of the political process that we need to explain. My point here is not to criticize the Rodrik study, which sets itself another task than I have done. Rather I am trying to point out the direction in which we need to be looking if we want to understand the origins of poor economic and institutional policy.[12]

3. THE POLITICAL RATIONALITY OF INEFFICIENT ECONOMIC SYSTEMS

International cross-section growth regressions are an important link in our exploration of the politics of poverty, but they do not explain the circumstances that turn bad institutional policy into good politics. In this section of the chapter I discuss theories that model in simple terms the basic forces that lead rational selfish leaders to knowingly pursue politics of economic decline. These models in no way rely on limited knowledge or insufficient inexperience to explain economic failure, but find the roots of poor institutional policies in the circumstances of political leaders and elites, and in the political institutions that guide the selection of national leaders. I will identify three central themes that explain the choice of poor policies: (1) the leader's time horizon, (2) the size of the government's winning coalition and the size of the selector set (the group that selects heads of government), (3) the problem of neutralizing the divide-and-rule strategies of rulers.

The discussion below is based on certain assumptions about the nature of productive institutional environments. I assume that growth-friendly environments require that governments (1) credibly commit to protect capital assets and future earnings against appropriation by private or public actors; (2) aid in the creation of markets for goods, financial services, and insurance with measures that lower transaction costs; (3) maintain macroeconomic stability and facilitate international transactions, especially in new knowledge.

3.1 The Horizon Effect and Bad Economics

The rational choice story about political preferences for bad economics often begins by analyzing the decisions of an autocratic ruler in a simple setting that only contains two types of actors, rulers and citizens. Olson's (2000) account of roving and stationary bandits is perhaps the most colorful of these studies. Roving bandits behave like thieving armies on the march through a foreign territory, they steal everything of value that they can carry with them. If a roving bandit somehow acquires enough military power to claim an area for herself, she faces an important choice: whether to plunder the area or take the long view and expand her tax base by building a strong economy. The ruler's choice is comparable to the choice of economic actors before and after a natural resource, such as a fishery, becomes exclusive property. If the ruler is confident of her control of the area and expects to remain in power for many years to come, she is likely to take the long view. If the ruler sees her situation in some sense as temporary or immediately needs enormous amounts of resources, perhaps to defend her regime (and has no recourse to well-functioning capital markets), the ruler will heavily discount future tax revenues, and take the short view.

A ruler who intends to maximize (the present value of) her long-term tax revenues must attend to two issues: (1) Invest an appropriate amount of current tax revenue in growth-enhancing public goods. (2) Allow for negative supply effects of taxes when she selects her tax rates. The latter adjustment is required because the subjects of a powerful and voracious autocrat often avoid predatory confiscation of their resources by reducing the supply of productive inputs, by avoiding investments, or by selecting particular economic activities, often of little economic value, that are well suited for tax evasion. Olson's (2000) simple and elegant model shows how an autocrat will select a level of public expenditure and a rate of taxation that maximizes her revenue.

In equilibrium (ignoring discounting) an increase in rate of taxation beyond $1/s^*$ would through negative supply effects reduce the tax base (national income) by a larger proportion than $1/s^*$. Similarly, equilibrium is reached when a further increase of public goods expenditures by 1 dollar would not increase national income by an amount large enough to increase tax revenue by 1 dollar. If the equilibrium tax rate is 1/2, then the last dollar invested in public services must increase the national income by two dollars and yield one dollar in tax revenue. In short, self-interest makes an autocrat limit her taxation and invest in expanding the tax base (GDP), provided that the ruler is not plagued by emergencies and takes the long view.

Olson (2000) uses this simple model to demonstrate that a selfish majority in a democracy would invest more resources in growth-oriented public services than a growth-friendly autocrat would do. The autocrat stops at a relatively early point because she is interested only in the impact of growth on her tax revenues. A democratic majority is interested both in the impact of public services on tax revenues (which it controls) and on its own personal incomes. A democratic majority, therefore, receives more benefits from each dollar invested in public goods than does an autocrat and therefore is ready to invest more.

Although democratic majorities are more growth oriented than autocrats, Olson's stationary bandits do reasonably well in the growth game, if they take the long view. As far as growth is concerned, the problem with genuine autocrats is their ability to switch with changing circumstances from the long view to the short view. Their ability to enter a phase of outright predatory behavior is not constrained by laws or other social institutions, and the very thought of this possibility can dampen productive efforts by the citizens. A ruler may switch to short-run strategies in response to aging or problems with succession, because of costly changes in military technology or because of perceived domestic and foreign threats. And autocrats, like other people, sometimes lose their minds without losing their power.

The open access versus exclusive property rights analogy of the horizon model illustrates the fundamental political cause of inefficient economic policies. Actors whose property rights over resources are incomplete and uncertain have an incentive to use these resources uneconomically. In the case of open-access resources, the introduction of exclusive property rights constrains wasteful behavior. In politics the solution is more complex. The introduction of exclusive transferable property rights, which would make rulers the owners of their states and create a market for states, is not a practical solution for dealing with the horizon problem, but various forms of regulation are more practical. To make their own property rights secure, and to claim for themselves some of the ruler's private consumption, the citizens must create limited government and regulate the behavior of their leaders, but the regulatory problem is complex and also involves government support groups.

3.2 Winning Coalitions, Selector Sets, and Inefficient Policies

With only two sets of players, rulers and citizens, the basic bandit model lacks political detail, particularly because the story does not recognize that all rulers rely on supporters for staying in power. If rulers are to survive, their winning coalitions must keep rivals at bay. Political economy portrays the relationship between a leader and her winning coalition as economic exchange: governments buy support and pay for it with private and public goods. The particular nature of these political transactions influences government policy and the leader's choice between growth-oriented policies and cronyism. Put simply, leaders reward their winning coalitions in two ways: (1) With direct transfers from the state budget to specific supporters, by granting them rights of monopoly and the rights of bribe collection. Because these transfers benefit specific individuals we refer to them as 'private goods'. (2) By providing market-supporting infrastructure, the rule of law, and macroeconomic policies, all of which we (somewhat imprecisely) label 'public goods' (Bueno de Mesquita, 2000).

The relationship between rulers and their winning coalitions differs greatly from one country to another because of varying historical circumstances, expectations, and political institutions. Yet a few generalizations are possible. By definition, rational selfish rulers try to minimize the price they pay for support. Bueno de Mesquita et al. (2000) argue that the economic policy of a government is related to the size of its winning coalition, for instance whether the coalition is a democratic majority or a handful of military officers. The de Mesquita study provides evidence of a significant positive empirical relationship between economic growth and the size of winning coalitions for all countries in the Summers–Heston data set for the years 1961–81, The study also finds that the size of a winning coalition is positively related both to the efficiency of a country's trade policy and its human capital stock.

Two theoretical considerations explain why coalition size (holding population constant) affects government policy (Bueno de Mesquita et al., 2000). First, Olson's (1982) concept of encompassing and narrow interests suggests that even selfish demands of a very large winning coalition are more likely to coincide with the national interest than the demands of a small coalition. Democracies produce the largest winning coalitions, dictatorships often rely on a small number of cronies, and monarchies typically depend on a subset of the nobility. Second, the budget constraint of the government limits its ability to reward support groups. When the winning coalition includes one-half or more of the adults in a country, budget considerations severely restrict the amount of private goods that the average supporter can receive. Under these circumstances the supporters must make do primarily with public goods that contribute to general economic prosperity, which makes them relatively growth oriented. When winning coalitions are very small, which is true for instance of some monarchies or juntas, a ruler has enough resources to virtually make each supporter independently wealthy by passing out money, consumer goods, rights to monopolize industries and collect bribes. With small winning coalitions, the supporters of the government are relatively independent of the general economic state of the nation.

A rational selfish ruler does not provide her supporters with greater rewards than is needed to induce them not to defect from the coalition (Bueno de Mesquita et al., 2000). The minimum price for being loyal to the government depends directly on the following ratio

$$\frac{\text{size of winning coalition}}{\text{size of selector set}}$$

The selector set in this formulation includes all people who hold the political rights to participate in choosing a government. The winning coalition is a subset of the selection set.[13] When a government collapses, the model makes the strong assumptions that the members of the old winning coalition are assigned randomly to the new winning coalition. When the ratio of the winning coalition to the selector set approaches 1, which is its maximum value (a winning coalition can never be larger than the selector set), a defector from the current winning coalition becomes increasingly more certain that she will belong to the next winning coalition. A supporter defects if she expects to receive a better price from a prospective government than from the current one, and the temptation to defect increases as the offers become better and more credible. In short, a supporter defects when the expected net gain of defecting is positive.

When winning coalitions are large relative to the selector set, which makes successful defection relatively easy, it follows that (in comparison to small winning coalitions): (1) government leaders keep a small fraction of the budget for their personal consumption, (2) the supply of growth-friendly public goods is large, and (3) the government is unstable. Democracies have a large ratio of winning coalitions to selection sets, but in autocracies the ratio varies from large to small. According to the logic of the model, the regimes most likely to pursue politics of poverty are autocracies with small winning coalitions and rigged democratic elections. Here two bad things coincide: the relatively large selector set tends to stabilize such regimes and make them long lasting (because defection is risky), and the small winning coalition is likely to demand private rather than public goods. The relatively high cost of defecting, however, makes its possible for the ruler to keep a large share of the budget for her own needs.

3.3 The Race to be First and Destructive Winning Coalitions

The behavior of winning coalitions, especially small ones, can be puzzling. On the one hand, a winning coalition often acts, perhaps not surprisingly, as if its political good fortune will not be long lived and destructively pursues its political rents by depleting natural resources, weakening industries, and bankrupting firms. On the other hand, factions within such coalitions often create political crises by calling for economic reforms well before all their rents are depleted and a state of full-scale economic crisis has been reached. By instigating the measures, the factions frequently deprive themselves of privileges and make themselves worse off than prior to the reforms.

Tornell (1998) offers a rational choice explanation of both phenomena. The factions in a winning coalition usually have incomplete property rights to the various privileges that the state allocates to them. The privileges usually are tied to the life of the current regime, frequently they are not transferable, and the rights may be vulnerable to attempts by other groups to capture them. Again, the uncertain ownership of government privileges gives rise to behavior that is analogous to the strategy of fishermen in open access fishing grounds who race to be first to deplete the resource. To be ahead of other actors that might use their political influence to capture the resources, the cronies of a government hurry to deplete their rents, ignoring the costly consequences of such a race.

Why then do the beneficiaries of these uncertain economic privileges often instigate reforms before arriving at the final stage of their destructive race, making their immediate situation worse than it was prior to the reforms? Tornell (1998) explains the logic of such maneuvers as being attempts to control the agenda of unavoidable institutional reforms, which leads to a new race. The advantage of being first not only compels government supporters hurriedly to deplete their rents but it also drives them to be first to recognize and lead the call for the unavoidable reforms. By taking the reform initiative, a group hopes to influence the agenda, minimize its own costs of future reforms, and pass disproportionate burdens onto other groups. If several groups in a winning coalition recognize this possibility, the race will influence the timing of reforms. The race leads to reforms that come at an earlier time than in situations where the factions have solved their collective action problems and present a united front.

3.4 Constraining the Government and its Winning Coalition

Already we have encountered two rational explanations of the choice of destructive economic policies by governments, the horizon effect and coalition effect. Destructive policies make sense when leaders have short time horizons and when they must meet the demands of powerful support groups that have narrow interests. In spite of their surprising explanatory power, bare-bones models that make government behavior depend on the relative size of winning coalitions oversimplify and fail to account for variation in political behavior and economic results when coalition size is held constant. Also, the traditional categories of 'democratic government' and 'authoritarian government' are not very helpful for explaining economic performance. The growth performance of democratic countries varies considerably, and the growth record of authoritarian states with small winning coalitions varies from dismal to good, although on average democratic countries grow faster than authoritarian countries.

We need a new institutional analysis that specifies in some detail how growth-friendly political institutions emerge or, to be consistent with our theme, why such institutions fail to emerge. Ideally, the new theory also should provide potential reformers with blueprints for eliminating the politics of poverty by designing and installing political institutions for growth, or at least explain when such reforms are likely to succeed or fail. Our discussion of the ever-present possibility of shrinking horizons and narrow interests suggests that a reliable political framework for growth somehow must blunt the incentives associated with these perspectives. Such a task is not easy. Those who hold the reins of government usually possess overwhelming power, which suggests that only when it is in their personal interest will rulers exercise restraint. We have seen that rapid-growth equilibrium in authoritarian countries is unstable, and democratic growth calls for constitutional rules that effectively constrain special interests. I think it is fair to say, however, that the new institutional economics and related fields have not yet risen to the task of providing a general theory for analyzing these issues. We still lack a robust rational-choice theory that has the growth-friendliness of the political environment is the dependent variable, but it is fair to say that we have bits and fragments of such a theory.

If we ever develop a powerful general theory of limited government, it is unlikely that our new knowledge will provide social technology for installing growth-generating institutions with the same ease as knowledge of chemical engineering enables us to set up a chemical processing plant. Continuing this comparison of constitutions and production processes, we note that constitutional design relies on basic and applied social sciences and the design of production processes draws on basic and applied natural sciences. Scientific knowledge is a public good – its consumption is non-rival and in the long run its ownership cannot be limited to a small set of exclusive owners. In economics, growth theory disregards political and economic organization and, focussing on aggregate technical production functions, sees growth as driven by technical change – applications of new knowledge about the natural world. Traditionally the growth literature in economics assumes that all nations have access to the same production technology – according to the jargon, all countries are on the same production function. According to growth theory, differences in economic performance are due only to differences in the use of inputs in production. Why not take the next step and claim that all nations have access to the same technology for social organization, including constitutional technology?[14]

If the notion that all countries operate on the same technical production function is dubious, the idea that they all rely on the same social technology is even more unhelpful, for the following reason. Various interrelated factors distinguish physical and social technologies. Decision makers are much more likely to agree on what is the appropriate model in the natural sciences than in the social sciences. Genuine doubts about the effectiveness of social technologies are more common than doubts about physical technologies, partly because unambiguous tests of social technologies are rare. In addition, material self-interest and social beliefs color disputes about social organization to a greater degree than disagreements about technical production functions. Another factor that feeds disputes about social organization is the relatively large role that non-specialists have in choosing and installing institutional arrangements, compared, for instance, to the role of engineers in technical production processes.

The critical implication of disagreements about social technologies is that acceptance and expectations often profoundly affect the effectiveness of social organization. The response of individuals to institutional regimes depends on their beliefs concerning the effectiveness of the arrangements in reaching specific goals, and by the individual's preferences for the goals. In fact, individuals even have preferences for the alternative ways of reaching a particular goal. Some religious people find it morally unacceptable to use high interest rates to stabilize an economy. In sum, the purpose of social technologies is to coordinate and control social interactions and, therefore, the effectiveness of particular institutional regimes depends on people's perceptions about these arrangements. Great divergence of personal social models relating to some activity generally raises the cost of coordinating behavior in that sphere.

A well-known recent study by Weingast (1997) models the subtle relationship between personal social models and the effectiveness of institutions. The Weingast (1997) model attempts to explain the origins of limited government by focussing on the relationship between an autocratic ruler and two social groups, X and Y. The two groups are able to resist transgressions by the ruler when they act jointly, but at a cost to them all. Acting alone neither group can resist the ruler. If the ruler has a short horizon (or wants to keep her options open), the strategy of divide-and-rule is an attractive alternative. Under a divide-and-rule strategy, the ruler appropriates the assets of one group and buys off the other group by sharing with it some of the resources taken from the targetted group. In the Weingast model, the outcome is a stable equilibrium. Let us assume that the ruler acts first and decides to transgress against group X and share the booty with Y. Unless X and Y have coordinated their response, it is easy to show, using fairly general assumptions, that Y's best response is not to challenge the ruler. If Y challenges the ruler, it will suffer the cost of war, no matter whether X, the victim, fights back or not, and gain nothing. Note that the Weingast model assumes that X and Y will not profit from defeating the ruler – they are not allowed to appropriate the ruler's wealth. If Y does not challenge the ruler, X will lose, whether it fights back or not, but Y will not suffer the costs of war and receive part of X's assets in payment for acquiescing. Standing by is clearly a better strategy for Y than fighting the ruler when X is under attack.

In repeated games, the Folk Theorem tells us that a whole range of equilibrium outcomes is possible, but repeated games also create the possibility for the players to punish each other for non-cooperative behavior. X can make it clear that in future periods it will not support Y, if the ruler transgresses against it. In the long run, the best outcome for X and Y is one of freedom from aggression from the ruler. If X and Y can credibly commit to always support each other when one of them is under attack, a rational ruler will not attack them because together they are stronger than the ruler.

According to Weingast (1997) the asymmetric equilibrium, with the government transgressing against one group and buying the compliance of the other, is the most common political arrangement in history, because joint response requires that the members of X and Y (or social groups in general) solve a massive coordination problem. Furthermore, a divide-and-rule equilibrium is likely to be far more stable than the long-view equilibrium in autocracies, already mentioned. However, the developments leading to coordination equilibrium – limited-government equilibrium – pose one of the biggest puzzles in social science because it is not clear how societies overcome their huge coordination problem. The solution of the problem requires that members of major social groups and their leaders agree on the limits of legitimate government and also stand ready to punish government transgressions, no matter who is the victim. In terms of game theory, the players must agree on an appropriate trigger strategy. Consider these alternative solutions to the problem.

(1) Limited-government equilibrium emerges only when actors have developed and internalized democratic values and in that way overcome their coordination problem.
(2) Limited-government equilibrium is the result of a balance of power between divergent material interests. Values play no role in this process, except perhaps that over time the experience of limited-government may induce people to adopt democratic values. Values follow, they don't lead the process.
(3) Solution to the coordination problem gives rise both to limited-government equilibrium and corresponding mass values.

Weingast (1997), and North et al. (2000) attempt to wrap the interest and value approaches into the same parcel, as suggested by alternative (3). For creating convergence of interest, these formulations depend rather heavily on historical circumstances and they refer rather vaguely to a process of convergence of social models. Some groups, for instance, must give up their theory that the ruler takes her authority from god, and that resisting the ruler is comparable to resisting god. In history it appears that social upheaval, even civil war or other catastrophic events, precede pacts that cement agreements about limiting state power and defining duties of the citizens.

Weingast (1997) emphasizes that the various social groups and their leaders can agree on a self-enforcing trigger strategy although their social models, values and material interests differ in many ways. The groups only need to agree on limits on legitimate state action and the corresponding citizen's duty of responding to transgressions. The task of reaching agreements on limited government is more difficult in ethnically divided nations than in homogenous ones. Complex coordination problems require ingenious constitutional solutions, and the various groups may have to invent new social technologies that all sides trust and respect. North and Weingast (1989), for instance, emphasize that the invention of a central bank, the Bank of England, played a critical role in creating limited government in England.

Weingast (1997) portrays the process of agreeing on a trigger strategy as being comparable to a coordination game, but with a touch of the prisoner's dilemma. The process, however, requires far greater adjustments than when agreeing, for instance, on which side of the road one should drive. People usually are rather indifferent to the actual solution to such problems (whether cars drive on the left side or the right side of the road), but value the coordination itself. Even if we forget about conflicting social values, the transition to limited-government equilibrium involves choices between different constitutional solutions that have different wealth implications for the various groups. Furthermore, the actors may honestly differ on the effectiveness of alternative strategies.

So, how much do we know about the origins of limited government? Not very much, I am afraid. In terms of method, the novel aspect of the Weingast (1997) and North et al. (2000) approach is the role it gives to divergent models that self-interested rational actors rely on for interpreting and changing their social environment. But in these and similar studies social models are exogenous and usually no attempt is made to explain how they emerge or how they spread.

4. THE NEGLECTED ROLE OF COMPETING SOCIAL MODELS

Rational choice analysis of politics usually does not assign a critical role to uncertainty about social models and social technology.[15] Olson (2000, pp. 101–54) models the structure of the classic soviet system under Stalin as a novel mechanism explicitly designed by the dictator to maximize the surplus absorbed by him and his winning coalition. According to Olson, the novelty of Stalin's system was institutional arrangements for modifying the supply disincentives of exploited citizens, which allowed the rulers to reach higher levels of exploitation than prior forms of autarchy had reached. The Stalinist state overcame the usual disincentives of private investors that fear appropriation by taking over the ownership of physical assets and directly managing the entire economy, including investment decisions. Disincentives in the labor market were modified by setting wages and salaries for skilled and unskilled workers so low that the workers had to work overtime to meet their basic needs. Because low skill-differentials in wages for a normal workday discouraged people from acquiring human capital, the state made it up to educated workers by maintaining huge skill differentials for overtime work. Human capital also was rewarded with relatively easy access of those with valuable skills to durable consumer goods, and privileged groups could shop in special stores stocked with luxury goods and otherwise unavailable commodities.

According to Olson (2000), Stalin and his cronies had no illusions about their system and knew that gradually it would grind to a halt. Although early twentieth century production technologies enabled soviet rulers to run their economies (more or less) as one large factory, agency problems created a cumulative array of unsolvable problems. Stalin's relatively short horizon, however, made these problems irrelevant to him because he knew that the difficulties would not come to a head during his lifetime.

Although his insightful and clever retrospective analysis contains a good deal of truth, Olson reduces to ashes the biggest debate of the twentieth century, the intellectual struggle in all parts of the world between supporters of central management and decentralized markets. In Olson's analysis the soviet system simply is a modern version of Weingast's divide-and-rule equilibrium, except for advances in exploitation which modern technology had made possible.[16] Theft had become more efficient. The Olson story does not sit well with the beliefs of many leading intellectuals in the West and other parts of the world, including major figures in the economics profession, that soviet central management was an important advance in social technology. These scholars and intellectuals in various countries outside the soviet orbit, at least for a while, saw the soviet experiment as a vast improvement compared to the market as a mechanism for allocating resources and generating growth. These thinkers also left a long paper trail to prove their point.

Economists are reluctant to associate poor economic performance with uncertainty about social technologies. Bueno de Mesquita and Root (2000, p. 1) do concede that until late in the twentieth century poor economic performance sometimes was caused by uncertainty about the appropriate economic model, but at the end of the century:

> Substantial variation in economic performance can no longer be attributed to ignorance about what makes an economy grow; observers must look elsewhere than at competing economic theories to explain national economic failure. Today, the key to economic success or failure – indeed, to a broad array of policy successes or failures – lies within the political institutions of sovereign states. Political arrangements create incentives for political leaders to foster growth or steal their nation's prospects for prosperity. (2000, p. 1)

The future will tell whether the market model now has the world stage for itself or whether serious contenders will reemerge. In my view, modern history does not indicate that intellectual competition among social models has come to a happy end, with markets and democracy as the winners. In fact, the evidence reveals cyclical swings in the support for democracy and for free markets, involving both power politics and the rise and fall of ideas. The political science literature identifies three waves of democratic transitions: (1) from 1828 to 1926, (2) from 1943 to 1964, and (3) from 1974 to 1990, and between these waves of democracy we find reverse or anti-democratic waves (Diamond and Plattner, 1996). During roughly the same time period the world economy also has experienced long waves of pro-market and anti-market institutional arrangements, although the two types of waves are not fully synchronized. Finally, Siegmund (1996) finds empirical evidence for worldwide short-term nationalization–privatization cycles of enterprises in the twentieth century.

4.1 Why do Social Institutions Cycle?

Social institutions rise and fall because of (1) changes in the political balance, (2) new material circumstances, or (3) the changing fortunes of social models. These factors tend to be interrelated in a complex manner, an emerging social model, for instance, can affect the political balance. Scholars who are wedded to the basic economic approach (of rational choice and selfish motivation) usually take pride in demonstrating that social models are not a causal factor in economic and political development. Others scholars prefer to give the dominant role to ideas, but a compromise solution, which we discussed in the previous section, makes rational selfish actors rely on subjective social models in their decisions.

I will use this last major section of the chapter to discuss why governments of countries in various parts of the world have been known to suddenly reverse their institutional policy, sometimes in a synchronized fashion. According to the simple dichotomy introduced above, all states supply public goods for improving the economic system and private goods for the benefits of the rulers and their supporters. I begin by assuming that competing social models play no role in sudden reversals of institutional policy, because policy makers have complete knowledge of the nature of social systems. Consider now the factors that will make a polity change the direction of its institutional policies, and let us begin with institutions for improving the performance of the economy, and next consider institutions designed to reward support groups.

One would expect that adjustments in remedial institutions (institutions for supporting growth) usually tend to be gradual and piecemeal because the structural changes in an economy that might require institutional reforms tend to be gradual rather than lumpy, *natura non facit saltum.* It cannot be denied that innovations sometimes come in bundles, for instance when nations make massive investment in research and development to support a major war or prestige projects, such as space programs and high-speed transport. The fruits of such projects hit the general economy with a considerable lag and may create discontinuous structural changes, but on a relatively small scale. A large number of innovations clustered in World War III, and were commercialized 15–20 years later. These innovations lowered entry barriers in industries (microwave technology), increased capacity (wide-bodied aircraft), and changed economies of scope (electronic transfer of funds, automatic teller machines), and affected perceptions about the need for the state to correct market failures and adjust government control in particular industries (Vietor, 1990, p. 17). For instance Vietor (1994, pp. 18–20) discusses how in the late 1960s new technology began to undermine natural monopoly in telecommunications in the United States. These waves of new technology and new structures of business organization may affect perceptions about the role of government in the economy, but, assuming that policy makers have perfect knowledge, one would expect to see a series of marginal adjustments rather than radical changes of regime.

Next consider institutions of redistribution. In a world of complete social models redistributive institutions are more likely than remedial institutions to change rapidly. When governments sharply adjust their supply of private goods (commodities and rent-seeking regulations for their cronies) usually the adjustment is related to major political changes. Although the economic forces underlying changes in political power normally move slowly and smoothly, the political changes themselves tend to be discontinuous. Economic decline in an industry, a region, or a country, population growth, expansion of the urban working class, or an increase in the relative importance of service workers usually generate smooth time series, but the consequent political developments often have sharp turning points. Expansion of the franchise and other changes in electoral systems, revisions of internal procedures of legislatures, coups, and rebellions often produce rapid changes in the political balance and related swings of the public policy pendulum. The British iron and steel industry, which went through two rounds of nationalization and denationalization in the period after World War II, is a notable example of policy cycling

(Singleton, 1995). If we remove uncertainty about social technology, such rapid policy changes basically should be redistributive in nature.

In sum: if the players in the political game all rely on correct positive social models, massive changes in institutional regimes are more likely to involve the removal or installation of redistributive rather than remedial institutions, and be preceded by major shifts in the political balance.

If we relax the usual assumption of complete social knowledge, the complex role of social models in economic development comes to the fore. In a world like ours where knowledge is scarce, economic and institutional policy frequently is a walk in the dark. The intellectual history of the gold standard, which in the late nineteenth and early twentieth centuries linked the monetary system of several major countries with fixed exchange rates, illustrates well the walk in the dark metaphor. Specialists both at that time and later (UK Parliament, 1918; McCloskey and Zecher, 1976; Ford, 1989) offer different explanations of why the system worked well from 1870 to 1913.[17] The disastrous reintroduction of the gold standard in the interwar period is a good example of the frequent causal role of incomplete models in economic development (Moggridge, 1989). It is virtually impossible to argue that those responsible for reviving the system did so to serve the short-term interest of a support group, while knowing all along that the experiment would fail miserably.

Individuals with similar experience and interests tend to believe in similar social models and social technologies, and their models form a cluster. If we assume that social models are incomplete and changeable and that the various models favored by disparate groups sometimes shift all in the same direction along an important policy axis, the shift can result in discontinuous institutional change, irrespective of which political group is in power. If clusters of social models shift along a policy axis at about the same time in various countries and in several regions, global waves in institutional policy may emerge.

As we have seen, Bueno de Mesquita and Root (2000) contend that nonmarket solutions to the economic problem forever have lost their luster. In the years immediately prior to World War II it was the market model that was at a low ebb, and many people believed that the future belonged to central management. In the prewar era, even the British Conservative Party entertained a statist wing, which called for the introduction of various measures of central management. In his 1938 manifesto, *The Middle Way*, Harold Macmillan, a member of the party and later its prime minister, lists various services and industries that he sees as being ripe for nationalization. Singleton (1995, p. 19) remarks:

> Macmillan was concerned about the high levels of malnutrition in British cities. He thought that private wholesalers and shops were incapable of providing good food

at a price which working-class mothers could afford. Under Macmillan's plan, bread and margarine would have been delivered to the housewife's door by an organization resembling the Post Office. High technology National Bakeries would be built in order to secure economies of scale, although the production and distribution of scones and fancy cakes would remain in private hands.

In the social science literature, Albert Hirschman's study, *Shifting Involvement: Private Interest and Public Action* (1982) offers perhaps the best known explanation of medium-term private–public cycles. Hirschman draws on social psychology to explain how these cycles are caused by coordinated shifts in personal preferences. Hirschman's explanation is based on the notion that exposure to consumer goods, especially certain types of durables, creates more comfort than pleasure, and that comfort saturates and disappoints consumers, who then turn to other activities, especially to public life, to meet their need for pleasures. Similarly, frustrations of public life eventually discourage actors and send them back to private action and consumerism. According to Hirschman, these cycles are coordinated across nations that enter the phase of mass consumption about the same time.

Although there is a grain of truth in the Hirschman thesis, I do not consider his shifting consumer preferences as being the fundamental force driving the public–private cycles of the twentieth century (and probably neither did he). Hirschman began writing his fascinating and insightful study in 1978, stimulated by a puzzle: why the 'Spirit of 1968' turned into apathy ten years later. The study does not explicitly analyze whether these private–public cycles, driven by saturation, maintain constant amplitude, explode, or peter out, but there is a presumption of constancy. However, if society does not receive repeated impulses of a magnitude comparable to or greater than the initial entry into mass consumption, it is conceivable that people eventually learn to balance private and public action, which would dampen the cycles.[18]

4.2 A Note on the Long Life of Failed Social Models

The introduction of social models into the causal chain of economic analysis is not as decisive a break with the methods of economics as it may appear. In its early phase rational expectations macroeconomics modeled economic actors as having complete (accurate) models of the economy, enabling them to anticipate and often successfully avoid costs of public policy measures. These extreme assumptions were intended as simplification, particularly to ease the mathematical formulation of the models. However, the rational expectations hypothesis 'does not imply that all agents have the same information, or that all agents know the "true" economic model; it simply means that agents use available information in the best way and collect further information only if the expected benefit exceeds the cost' (Svensson, 1996, p. 3).

Incomplete or wrong social models need not have significant impact on economic development, provided that policy makers register almost immediately and unequivocally when their models produce undesirable results, discard the models and instead employ more reliable social technologies. In practice, imperfect institutions often lock in, persist, and become semi-permanent. I will consider three factors that possibly can explain the frequent long life of social models that *ex ante* turn out to be imperfect in the sense that institutions based on these models fail to produce the intended results.

The first point is that most social models lack the sophistication to predict or foresee the medium- and long-term dynamics of social institutions. Regulatory regimes frequently function relatively well at the outset, but sometimes they gradually deteriorate when the actors living under these regimes begin to adjust their models, expectations and strategies to their new institutional environment. These adjustments sometimes initiate cumulative processes that undermine the new order. Studies of the regulatory regime that governed the airline industry in the United States from 1938 to 1978 provide evidence for a negative cumulative process.[19] As the government compelled them to refrain from price competition, the airlines instead competed on various non-price margins, and gradually perverse competition spread from one margin to another. Toward the end of the period, attempts by the US Civil Aeronautics Board to control valuable margins of service provided by the industry involved 'writing regulations that defined the size of a coach class seat and the amount of meat that could be lawfully served on a sandwich' (Noll and Owen, 1983, p. 156). The regulatory path created an upward trend in operating costs and rent-seeking among employees and suppliers, and in the end there was broad political support for deregulation.

Second, in a complex world of random shocks it is often difficult to attribute negative outcomes to institutional failures rather than to some transient forces. Even when undesired outcomes are blamed on flaws in institutional arrangements, an unsatisfactory outcome either can be interpreted as a one-time blip or a repairable problem, rather than as a sign that the institutions should be discarded. Decisions are particularly difficult when the original choice of faltering institutions was not based on experiments and comparisons with alternative arrangements. In fact, once a community selects particular institutions, investment in additional knowledge usually centers on aspects of the existing arrangements rather than on finding out about alternatives.[20]

The third reason why policy makers do not discard institutions that fail to meet their goals is the following. Once rulers finally realize that their institutional regimes are imperfect and provide unacceptable results, they sometimes discover that they face an institutional lock-in (Killick, 1995). Winiecki's (1990) account of the inability of the last rulers of the Soviet Union to radically reform the system without destroying it belongs here. In the Soviet Union, successful reforms from the top down required whole-hearted cooperation from mid-level agents of the state who were needed to actually carry out the reforms. The human capital of these mid-level agents, however, was specific to soviet-type institutions. The agents had been selected for loyalty rather than competence and rewarded well with privileges and kickbacks, and the prospects in a market-oriented system for these functionaries were poor. The functionaries had strong incentives to sabotage the reforms, which they did while the top introduced one sequence of reforms after another, until eventually the whole system crashed.

4.3 Economic Institutions: The Modern History of Long Waves

The history of government control of the economy in Europe and the United States during the modern era indicates that discontinuous institutional change is driven by the confluence of technological change, power politics, and shifting beliefs in social models, which often are preceded by unexpected social developments. There is no evidence to indicate that the chaotic mixture of power politics, technology, and imperfect social models creates anything resembling mechanical cycles.[21] Yet looking back at two centuries of European and North American economic history, many scholars discern a long wave of decentralization and another of centralization, with each wave lasting approximately a century. These waves of institutional change are somewhat uneven and, although in the last twenty years we have entered a new phase of decentralisation, there is no reason to expect a repeat performance of centennial waves.

The various contributions in volume VIII of *The Cambridge Economic History of Europe* (Mathias and Pollard, 1989), which deals with the development of economic and social policies in the industrial economies, tend to support the idea of the two long waves of government control and decontrol. Schremmer (1989, p. 362) provides crude quantitative evidence in a figure showing changes in the share of central government expenditure in GNP. Series for Britain and France, which extend back to the 1780s, are U-shaped and bottom out somewhere around the middle of the nineteenth century, after decreasing by about one-half from the previous high of mercantilism and mutual warfare. The French, however, hit the low point earlier than the British, and in the 1910s, both series returned to the levels of the eighteenth century. In Prussia and in the German Reich the ratio of central government spending to GNP shows a sharp increase that begins in the last quarter of the nineteenth century.

The work of Adam Smith, Jean-Baptiste Say, James Mill, and David Ricardo, as well as the American Declaration of Independence in 1776, and the French Revolution of 1789 mark the emergence of dominant clusters of *laissez-faire* or liberal models (Bairoch, 1989, pp. 4–5). Yet, the long liberal wave contained much variety and more state intervention (especially at the local level) than many people assume. Britain moved toward free trade late in the eighteenth century, the trend was interrupted by the French wars, but culminated in the repeal of the Corn Laws in 1846, which marked the beginning of a free trade era in Britain that lasted until 1914 (Bairoch, 1989, p. 13). The other countries of Western Europe and the United States leaned more toward protectionism than Britain, the world's industrial leader. The phase of European free trade was short, lasting from 1846 to 1861 (Bairoch, 1989, pp. 36–50). Prior to World War II, the United States followed a policy of protectionism, except for a phase of liberalism or moderated protectionism that lasted from 1846 to 1861 (Bairoch, 1989, p. 140). Still, the historical evidence makes clear that the emerging industrial nations untied the knots of mercantilism, put fewer restraints on private property, released market forces, and encouraged competition – if not internationally, then domestically or within free-trade zones, such as the German *Zollverein*. The direct role of the state in production, distribution, and exchange was minimal compared with earlier and later periods, and, when the state was active, the activity generally was concentrated at the local rather than national level, which is particularly relevant for America (Letwin, 1989).

A strong move toward greater state control in the industrial countries began late in the nineteenth century and early in the twentieth. The turn reflected not only a shift in political power from the middle to the working class, which the state gradually enfranchised, but fundamental revision of social models as these nations grappled with new forms of industrial organization and unfamiliar economic realities.[22] Industrialization had brought new problems and new opportunities. Among new problems were rapid decline and dislocation in agriculture, industrial accidents, serious spillover effects such as pollution, and the dissolution of traditional rural social security networks. There also was concern about the role of women and children in industrial society, the low educational level of the labor force relative to the new production techniques, lack of infrastructure services for industry, and insufficient service utilities and housing for fast growing urban areas.

The opportunities of the industrial age included increase in wealth, and economies of scale in many of the new activities, which at this time of bewildering change gave credence to claims by political entrepreneurs and utopia peddlers that the end of scarcity was near. Improvements in communications and transportation, the concentration of economic activity in urban areas, and a huge increase in the scale of production suggested opportunities for central planning. It now seemed feasible that some form of central direction by the state could accelerate industrialization and, at the same time, bring the unruly process under control. Ronald Coase (1991) reports being perplexed in 1931 by the apparent conflict between a denial of the possibility of effective central planning and the current success of large corporations. Coase found it puzzling that in the industrial countries the corporation had in part taken over the coordination function of the price mechanism.

> The Russian Revolution had taken place only fourteen years earlier. We knew then very little about how planning would actually be carried out in a communist system. Lenin had said that the economic system in Russia would be run as one big factory. However, many economists in the West maintained that this was an impossibility. And yet there were factories in the West and some of them were extremely large. (Coase 1991, p. 7)

Rational actors with incomplete knowledge respond to new social structures by adjusting their social models and notions about available social technologies, but the structure of the emerging industrial society, an unprecedented phenomenon, was poorly understood. As the nineteenth century wore on, leaders of public opinion increasingly diverged in their views of the nature of social mechanisms. Early in the twentieth century, social models favored by leaders in Europe and America spanned a spectrum from a decentralized market economy with few restrictions on private actors, through a regulated market system with centralized industrial policy, to full state control of production and central planning. As we know, statist solutions emphasizing various degrees of central control won the day. America introduced extensive regulations of many of its industries, especially infrastructure service industries, whereas Europe nationalized many of these industries (Vietor, 1990). National governments in America and Western Europe assumed responsibility for the health and wellbeing of their citizens, with Europe taking a larger step toward a welfare state. And in 1928, following an intense industrialization debate, the leaders of the Soviet Union embarked on a massive centrally managed program of forced industrialization (Davies, 1989).

In the 1970s and 1980s a trend away from state control became apparent. Hopes for the effectiveness of central planning dwindled, and so did belief in state sponsored industrial policy. Even France disemboweled its once admired system of indicative planning, beginning in 1976 with the 7th Plan (Hall, 1986, p. 185). The United States entered a phase of deregulation of various infrastructure service industries, and in 1979 Britain under the Thatcher government began a move toward liberalism. By the 1980s, few people believed that state ownership of enterprises was an effective way to achieve economic efficiency, financial accountability, necessary restructuring, and pleasant work environments. History seemed to support the raw statement by a Tory pamphleteer who in 1949 wrote:

> The Socialists were never more wrong than when they believed that nationalization would send their miners sprinting to the pit-head and keep them slogging all day long as merrily as the Seven Dwarfs. (Singleton, 1995, p. 25)

As public ownership and various regulations of private industry increasingly lost their support because they were now perceived as flawed social technologies, the popularity of decentralized solutions and market-oriented systems increased. The collapse of the Soviet system in 1989 sealed these developments.

The discontinuity and reversal of government control of the economy in the last quarter of the twentieth century, which reminds some scholars of the move toward liberalization that began some 200 years ago, raises several questions.

(1) Does the discontinuity of the 1970s–1980s signify the beginning of a fundamental reversal of the previous century-long trend toward public control? Is the world economy headed toward a new century of liberalism, riding a downward curve of reduced public control?
(2) What forces brought about this new direction in social organization? In particular, does revision of personal social models play an important causal role in recent reversals of institutional policies or does the explanation entirely rest with shifts in political power, new technologies, and changes in industrial structure?

My response to these issues reflects the limits of my own social models. My hunch is that modern democracies, with their large winning coalitions and limited government, have rather strong incentives to promote economic growth. These countries in the near future are unlikely to reject recent liberal trends, as long as their leaders believe that a reversal of free-market policies is nearly certain to bring serious economic difficulties and sharp decline in growth rates. A major reversal of institutional policy, if it occurs, is likely to be preceded by a crisis that is perceived as catastrophic, creating fundamental uncertainty about social models. Such an event would be an opening for alternatives to the liberal market regime, alternative social models waiting in the wings for their turn.

We should also note that the current victory of *laissez faire is* not total. In a great many quarters, state regulations of worker and consumer safety is considered essential. But the greatest uncertainty about economic organization in the twenty-first century centers on conflicting social and technical models of the impact which modern industrial production has on the natural environment and the resources of the planet. At the beginning of the twenty-first century, the clusters of models concerning the environmental impact of production are just as scattered as were clusters of social models at the beginning of the twentieth century concerning the best institutional response to the new industrial age. In the environmental sphere, one cluster of models portrays the system as being roughly in balance and with no potentially catastrophic threats to the environment in sight. The optimism is often fueled by the belief that the market and also the political system spontaneously respond to serious and costly side-effects from the economy. At the other end of the spectrum are models that predict catastrophic (environmental) outcomes in the immediate future, if the world economy continues to grow at its current pace. Sometimes the damage is seen as irreversible. The logic of the pessimistic models suggests a return to older and simpler life styles, and an end to free international trade and economic growth as we know it, but instead redistribution from rich to poor countries. As for rapid institutional change, perhaps we have seen nothing yet.

NOTES

1. The discussion in this section draws on the first part of Eggertsson (1998).
2. For an introduction to the literature on traditional systems of social security in developing countries, see the various contributions in Ahmad et al. (1991). See also Janvry et al. (1991). Newberry (1989) combines the economics of risk and the information-transaction costs perspective in a lucid survey of the theory of agricultural institutions for insurance and stabilization. Also using the transaction-cost framework, Binswanger and Rosenzweig (1986) lay out a general theory of economic institutions in traditional rural areas; Binswanger and McIntire (1987) explore the structure of land abundant tropical agriculture, and Binswanger et al. (1989) analyze institutions in semi-arid African agriculture. Bromley and Chavas (1989) examine risk and transactions in semi-arid tropics, and Fafchamps (1992) studies mutual insurance networks in preindustrial societies in terms of information and transaction problems. Townsend (1992, 1993) applies general equilibrium analysis and contract economics in an empirical and theoretical study of Asian village communities, and Cheung (1969, 1970) pioneered the study of agricultural contracts in terms of risk and transaction costs.
3. If diversification of effort reduces expected wealth, risk-neutral actors or actors in a risk-free world would avoid output-reducing diversification. If actors diversify in spite of expected reduction in wealth, their action can be interpreted as willingness to pay an implicit premium for more security.
4. 'Although all studies find strong positive correlation between temperature and hay yield, there is only a weak correlation between temperature and output in the part-time fisheries (Ogilvie, 1981)' (Eggertsson, 1998, p. 7).
5. In 1281 the Icelandic parliament ratified a new law code, *Jónsbók,* which was modeled extensively on *Grágás* and was still in force in the nineteenth century.
6. In the census of 1703, some 90 per cent of all male heads of farm households, but only 2 per cent of male farm laborers, were married men or widowers. Illegitimacy was fairly low, and couples who had children out of wedlock often later married (Vasey, 1996, p. 377).
7. For centuries Iceland was under the Danish crown. If risk management had been extended to the Danish kingdom, *general risks* in Iceland caused by cold spells and volcanic activity would be *specific risks* in the Kingdom. If the royal administration in Copenhagen had operated a systematic relief system for Iceland, which it did not, poor communications with Iceland would have required supplies to be stored mostly in Iceland rather than in Denmark.

Storing the supplies in Iceland, however, would only have solved part of the problem because, within the country, poor communications would have hampered the distribution of supplies, especially in winter. During the crises of the eighteenth century, sporadic attempts by Copenhagen to send supplies to Iceland floundered because of bad communications (Eggertsson, 1998, p. 26).

8. Rodrik (1998, p. 4), using data for 110 countries regresses average growth rates in 1975–89 on average growth rates in 1960–75 and a constant term. The regression yields an R^2 of only 0.12 (and a coefficient on lagged growth of 0.39). When Rodrik excludes 11 East Asian countries and Botswana from his sample the coefficient on lagged growth becomes statistically insignificant and R^2 shrinks to 0.02.
9. Given the various assumptions of the model, the answer to the question whether a political system will magnify the negative impact of an external trade shock depends on the value of two variables. One, ø, measures the strength of institutions of conflict management, and the other, π, measures the expectations by each group that the other group will fight – their expectations about latent social conflict. Low ø (weak institutions) makes it the dominant strategy for both of the model's two groups, A and B, to fight, high ø makes cooperation a dominant strategy – in both cases regardless of the value of π. When ø takes on an intermediate value, the value of π, the indicator of latent social conflict, drives the outcome. Cooperation is dominant for low values of π, and fighting is dominant for high values of π (Rodrik, 1998, pp. 9–13).
10. Robert Solow (1994, p. 51) expresses doubts about international cross-section regressions using social variables. 'A particular style of empirical work seems to have sprung from the conjunction of growth theory and the immensely valuable body of comparative national-accounts data compiled by Summers and Heston (1991). It rests on international-cross section regressions with the average growth-rates of different countries as the dependent variable and various politico-economic factors on the right-hand side that might easily affect the growth rate if the growth rate were easily affected. I had better admit that I do not find this a confidence-inspiring project. It seems altogether too vulnerable to bias from omitted variables, to reverse causation, and above all to the recurrent suspicion that the experiences of very different national economies are not to be explained as if they represented different "points" on some well-defined surface.'
11. A reverse line of causation is possible, economic outcomes often affect political outcomes.
12. The study's two principal measures of latent social conflict, ethnic diversity and the income distribution, are not of much help to understand the political problem. For some governments ethnic diversity is a decision variable, and less so for other countries. The significant question here is why some and not all countries are able to live in peace with ethnic diversity. The model does not attempt to analyze this issue, but tells us that ethnic diversity does not slow economic growth in countries that have highly developed institutions of conflict management, but the empirical part of the study uses proxies for these institutions that essentially measure the degree of social stability. In other words, ethnic diversity does not slow economic growth, if diversity does not lead to social instability. Similar comments apply to the variable measuring the distribution of income.
13. Bueno de Mesquita et al. (2000) use the word 'selectorate' for what I call 'selector set'.
14. By its omission of political and economic organization, the traditional growth literature in economics is in effect saying that all countries have access to the same social technology.
15. In part, Section 4 draws on Eggertsson (1997).
16. The Weingast (1997) model actually focusses only on various forms of political equilibria and assumes explicitly that the country has set up appropriate economic structures (property rights) for economic growth, but faces a problem operating these structures because of political instability and predatory behavior by the government.
17. The system worked well 'in the sense of eliminating balance of payments imbalances without exchange rate changes in a rapidly changing world economy' (Ford, 1989, p. 197).
18. Attempts have been made to explain sequences of nationalization and privatization of enterprises in purely economic terms. Rosa (1993) assumes that governments nationalize firms to raise revenue through the profits of these firms. Governments have an incentive to combine various methods for raising funds in order to minimize the unpopularity and political costs

of such activities. Rosa assumes that private and public firms are equally efficient. Governments sell their family jewels, their public enterprises, when the political cost of raising taxes is high, as well as the rate of interest. Rosa (1993) finds empirical support for his hypothesis in European data.

19. Of course, regulatory regimes also can initiate virtuous circles.
20. When the opportunity arises, comparison frequently plays a large role in identifying imperfect institutions. In the United States, the performance of unregulated intrastate airlines in Texas and California helped convince rule-makers that the regime governing the national airlines should be abolished (Vietor, 1990, p. 19). Comparisons across countries, of varying degrees of accuracy, often help align social models across entire regions. The mainstream of the British Conservative Party used examples of state-owned industries abroad to fight nationalization at home. In 1928 a Tory publication noted that 'the state railways in Australia were reported to be at the mercy of voracious union leaders and their lazy overpaid members, while the government coal mines in Bulgaria were deemed to be hives of inefficiency' (as summarized by Singleton, 1995, p. 19).
21. Regular long-term business cycles conceivably could drive systematic cycles of institutional change. If we believed that market economies experience severe crashes regularly, say every fifty or one hundred years, these crashes conceivably could give rise to long private–public cycles. However, the case for long business cycles, as put forth by Kitchin, Juglar, Kondratieff and others, remains to be proven.
22. In Britain as late as 1831 the electorate was less than half a million in a population of 14 million. The Reform Act of 1832 opened Parliament to the business world, but the working class entered via a second Reform Act of 1867, which gave the vote to two-thirds of adult males. Finally, an act of 1918 opened the vote to males over 21 and women over 30 (Checkland, 1989, pp. 608–28).

REFERENCES

Ahmad, Ehtisham, Jean Drèze, John Hills and Amartya Sen (eds) (1991), *Social Security in Developing Countries*, Oxford: Clarendon.

Arnott, Richard and Joseph E. Stiglitz (1991), 'Moral hazard and nonmarket institutions: dysfunctional crowding out or peer monitoring?', *American Economic Review*, **81** (1), 179–90.

Bairoch, P. (1989), 'European Trade Policy, 1815–1914', in P. Mathias and S. Pollard (eds), *The Cambridge Economic History of Europe*, Vol. VIII, Cambridge: Cambridge University Press, pp. 1–160.

Bardhan, Pranab (1983), 'Labor tying in poor agrarian economy: a theoretical and empirical analysis', *Quarterly Journal of Economics*, **98** (3), 501–14.

Bardhan, Pranab (1989), 'A Note on Interlinked Rural Economic Arrangements', in Pranab Bardhan (ed.), *The Economic Theory of Agrarian Institutions*, New York: Oxford University Press.

Binswanger, Hans P. and John McIntire (1987), 'Behavioral and material determinants of production relations in land-abundant tropical agriculture', *Economic Development and Cultural Change*, **36** (1), 73–99.

Binswanger, Hans P. and Mark R. Rosenzweig (1986), 'Behavioral and material determinants of production relations in agriculture', *Journal of Development Studies*, **22** (3), 503–39.

Binswanger, Hans P., John McIntire and Chris Udry (1989), 'Production Relations in Semi-Arid Africa', in Pranab Bardhan (ed.), *The Economic Theory of Agrarian Institutions*, New York: Oxford University Press.

Bromley, Daniel W. and Jean Paul Chavas (1989), 'On risk, transactions, and economic development in semiarid tropics', *Economic Development and Cultural Change*, **37** (4), 719–36.

Bueno de Mesquita, Bruce (2000), *Principles of International Politics. People's Power, Preferences, and Perceptions*, Washington, DC: CQ Press.

Bueno de Mesquita, Bruce and Hilton L. Root (eds) (2000), *Governing for Prosperity*, New Haven: Yale University Press.

Checkland, S.G. (1989), 'British Public Policy, 1776–1939', in P. Mathias and S. Pollard (eds), *The Cambridge Economic History of Europe*, Vol. VIII, Cambridge: Cambridge University Press, pp. 607–40.

Cheung, Steven N.S. (1969), 'Transaction costs, risk aversion, and the choice of contractual arrangement', *Journal of Law and Economics*, **12** (1), 23–42.

Cheung, Steven N.S. (1970), 'The structure of a contract and the theory of a non-exclusive resource', *Journal of Law and Economics*, **13** (1), 23–42.

Coase, Ronald H. (1991), 'The Institutional Structure of Production', Nobel Memorial Prize Lecture. Reprinted in R.H. Coase (1994), *Essays on Economics and Economists*, Chicago: Chicago University Press.

Davies, R.W. (1989), 'Economic and Social Policy in the USSR, 1917–1941', in P. Mathias and S. Pollard (eds), *The Cambridge Economic History of Europe*, Vol. VIII, Cambridge: Cambridge University Press, pp. 984–1047.

Diamond, Larry J. and M.F. Plattner (eds) (1996), *The Global Resurgence of Democracy*, 2nd edition, Johns Hopkins University Press.

Easterly, William, Michael Kremer, Lant Prichett and Larry Summers (1993), 'Good policy or good luck? Country growth performance and temporary shocks', *Journal of Monetary Economics*, **32**, 459–83.

Eggertsson, Thráinn (1996), 'No experiments, monumental disasters. Why it took a thousand years to develop a specialized fishing industry in Iceland', *Journal of Economic Behavior and Organization*, **30** (1), 1–23.

Eggertsson, Thráinn (1997), 'When the State Changes its Mind: The Puzzle of Discontinuity in Government Control of Economic Activity', in Herbert Giersch (ed.), *Privatization at the Turn of the Century*, Berlin: Springer-Veriag.

Eggertsson, Thráinn (1998), 'Sources of risk, institutions for survival, and a game against nature in premodern Iceland', *Explorations in Economic History*, **35**, 1–30.

Eggertsson, Thráinn (2002), 'Norms in Economics with Special Reference to Economic Development', in Michael Hechter and Karl-Dieter Opp (eds), *Social Norms*, New York: Russell Sage.

Fafchamps, Marcel (1992), 'Solidarity networks in pre-industrial societies: rational peasants with a moral economy', *Economic Development and Cultural Change*, **41** (1), 147–74.

Ford, A.C. (1989), 'International Financial Policy and the Gold Standard 1870–1914', in P. Mathias and S. Pollard (eds), *The Cambridge Economic History of Europe*, Vol. VIII, Cambridge: Cambridge University Press, pp. 197–249.

Gunnarsson, Gísli (1983), *Monopoly Trade and Economic Stagnation. Studies in the Foreign Trade of Iceland 1602–1787*, Lund: Ekonomisk-Historiska Föreningen.

Gylfason, Thorvaldur (2000), 'Natural Resources, Education, and Economic Development', Working Paper: University of Iceland.

Hall, P.A. (1986), *Governing the Economy. The Politics of State Intervention in Britain and France*, Cambridge: Polity Press.

Hirschman, Albert O. (1982), *Shifting Involvements: Private Interest and Public Action*, Cambridge: Cambridge University Press.

Hoff, Karla (2000), 'Beyond Rosenstein-Rodan: The Modern Theory of Underdevelopment Traps', World Bank: Working Paper.
Janvry de, Alain, Marcel Fafchamps and Elisabeth Sadoulet (1991), 'Peasant household behavior with missing markets: some paradoxes explained', *Economic Journal*, **101**, 1400–1417.
Killick. T. (ed.) (1995), *The Flexible Economy. Causes and Consequences of the Adaptability of National Economies*, London: Routledge.
Kranton, Rachel E. (1996), 'Reciprocal exchange: a self-sustaining system', *American Economic Review*, **86** (4), 830–51.
Letwin, W. (1989), 'American Economic Policy 1865–1939', in P. Mathias and S. Pollard (eds), *The Cambridge Economic History of Europe*, Vol. VIII, Cambridge: Cambridge University Press, pp. 641–90.
Mathias, P. and S. Pollard (eds) (1989), *The Cambridge Economic History of Europe, Volume VIII. The Industrial Economies: The Development of Economic and Social Policies*, Cambridge: Cambridge University Press.
McCloskey, Donald N. and J.R. Zecher (1976), 'How the Gold Standard Worked 1880–1913', in J.A. Frenkel and H.G. Johnson (eds), *The Monetary Approach to the Balance of Payments*, London: Allen & Unwin.
Moggridge, D.E. (1989), 'The Gold Standard and National Financial Policies, 1913–1939', in P. Mathias and S. Pollard (eds), *The Cambridge Economic History of Europe*, Vol. VIII, Cambridge: Cambridge University Press, pp. 250–314.
Newbery, David M.G. (1989), 'Agrarian Institutions for Insurance and Stabilization', in Pranab Bardhan (ed.), *The Economic Theory of Agrarian Institutions*, New York: Oxford University Press.
Noll, Roger. G. and B.M. Owen (1983), 'Conclusions. Economics, Politics, and Deregulation', in Roger Noll and B.M. Owen (eds), *The Political Economy of Deregulation: Interest Groups in the Regulatory Process*, Washington, DC: American Enterprise Institute.
North, Douglass C. and Barry R. Weingast (1989), 'Constitutions and commitment: the institutions governing public choice in seventeenth century England', *Journal of Economic History*, **44**, 803–32.
North, Douglass C., William Summerhill and Barry R. Weingast (2000), 'Order, Disorder, and Economic Change: Latin America Versus North America', in Bruce Bueno de Mesquita and Hilton L. Root, *Governing for Prosperity*, New Haven: Yale University Press.
Ogilvie, Astrid E.J. (1981), 'Climate and Society in Iceland from the Medieval Period to the Late Eighteenth Century', Ph.D. Thesis, University of East Anglia, School of Environmental Science.
Olson, Mancur (1982), *The Rise and Decline of Nations*, New Haven: Yale University Press.
Olson, Mancur (2000), *Power and Prosperity. Outgrowing Communist and Capitalist Dictatorships*, New York: Basic Books.
Rodrik, Dani (1998), 'Where Did All the Growth Go? External Shocks, Social Conflict, and Growth Collapses', Working Paper, Harvard University.
Rosa, J.-J. (1993), 'Nationalization, privatization, and the allocation of financial property rights', *Public Choice*, **75**, 317–37.
Sachs, Jeffrey D. and Andrew M. Warner (1999), 'Natural Resource Intensity and Economic Growth', in Jörg Mayer, Brian Chambers and Ayisha Farooq (eds), *Development Policies in Natural Resource Economies*, Cheltenham, UK, and Northampton, MA, USA: Edward Elgar.

Schremmer, D.E. (1989), 'Taxation and Public Finance: Britain, France, and Germany', in P. Mathias and S. Pollard (eds), *The Cambridge Economic History of Europe*, Vol. VIII, Cambridge: Cambridge University Press, pp. 315–494.

Siegmund, Uwe (1996), 'Are there Nationalization–Privatization Cycles? A Theoretical-Survey and First Empirical Evidence', Working Paper No. 757, Kiel: Institute of World Economics.

Singleton, J. (1995), 'Labor, the Conservatives and Nationalization', in R. Millward and J. Singleton (eds), *The Political Economy of Nationalizalion in Britain 1920–1950*, Cambridge: Cambridge University Press.

Solow, Robert M. (1994), 'Perspectives on growth theory', *Journal of Economie Perspectives*, **8** (1), 45–54.

Summers, Robert and Allan Heston (1991), 'The Penn World Table (Mark 5: An Expanded Set of International Comparisons, 1950–1988)', *Quarterly Journal of Economics*, **106** (2), 327–68.

Svensson, L.E.O. (1996), 'The scientific contributions of Robert E. Lucas, Jr.', *Scandinavian Journal of Economics*, **98** (1), 1–10.

Tornell, Aaron (1998), 'Reform from Within', Working Paper 6497, National Bureau of Economic Research.

Townsend, Robert M. (1992), 'Understanding the Structure of Village and Regional Economies', in Lars Werin and Hans Wijkander (eds), *Contract Economics*, Oxford: Blackwell.

Townsend, Robert M. (1993), *The Medieval Village Economy: A Study of the Pareto Mapping in General Equilibrium Models*, Princeton, NJ: Princeton University Press.

United Kingdom Parliament (1918), *First Interim Report of the Committee on Currency and Foreign Exchange after the War*, Cmnd 9182 (The Cunliffe Report).

Vasey, Daniel E. (1991), 'Population, agriculture, famine: Iceland, 1784–1785', *Human Ecology*, **19** (3), 323–50.

Vasey, Daniel E. (1996), 'Population regulation, ecology, and political economy in preindustrial Iceland', *American Ethnologist*, **23** (2), 366–92.

Vietor, R.H.K. (1990), 'Regulation and Competition in America, 1920s–1980s', in M. Chick (ed.), *Government, Industries and Markets. Aspects of Government–Industry Relations in the UK, Japan, West Germany, and the USA since 1945*, Aldershot: Edward Elgar.

Vietor, R.H.K. (1994), 'Contrived competition: economic regulation and deregulation, 1920s–1980s', *Business History*, **36**, 1–32.

Weingast, Barry R. (1997), 'The political foundations of democracy and the rule of law', *American Political Science Review*, **91** (2), 245–63.

Winiecki, Jan (1990), 'Why Economic Reforms Fail in the Soviet System: A Property Rights-Based Approach', Reprinted in Lee. J. Alston, Thráinn Eggertsson and Douglass C. North (eds) (1996), *Empirical Studies in Institutional Change*, Cambridge: Cambridge University Press.

13. The role of international monetary institutions after the EMU and the Asian Crisis: some preliminary ideas using constitutional economics*

Friedrich Schneider

1. INTRODUCTION

After the Asian Crisis a new situation has arisen for the possible intervention of international financial institutions – especially due to the severe criticisms of many economists, politicians and other public officials in which they pointed out the ineffective or even contraproductive interventions of the IMF (regardless of whether such a criticism can be justified or not!). Also a lot of voices have been raised arguing that either one should abolish the IMF or give it some effective and powerful means in order to intervene with less difficulty. The international monetary institutions (like the IMF, the World Bank, and so on) will thus face new challenges and should react to this (compare Section 2). In Section 3 some theoretical ideas are put forward on how a new international monetary institution should operate. With the help of constitutional economics it will be shown what such a monetary institution could look like, in order to operate much more efficiently and react more properly to major financial economic crises like the Asian one. In Section 4 some elements of a 'new' institutional design of an international monetary system are developed, in which a new structure will be derived, for example what the major tasks should be and how this 'reformed' institution should operate. Section 5 gives a summary of the main results and draws some conclusions.

* This chapter was presented at the conference 'The Political Economy of Institutional Development: Institutional Design in Periods of Rapid Change', Messina, 14–17 September 2000. Earlier versions of this chapter were presented at the annual US Public Choice meetings, New Orleans, 1999, at the European Public Choice meeting in Lisbon, 1999 at the 55th IIPF congress in Moscow, Russia, 1999. The author thanks Keven Grier (University of Mexico), Bill Niskanen (Cato Institute), Zeljko Bogetic (IMF), Jorn Rattso (Norwegian University of Science and Technology), Vito Tanzi (Ministry of Finance, Rome, Italy) and Charles K. Rowley (George Mason University, Fairfax, Virginia) for critical and stimulating comments.

2. THE DIFFICULTIES OF CRISES PREVENTION BY INTERNATIONAL MONETARY INSTITUTIONS IN THE STATUS QUO SITUATION

The financial and economic crises of Asia are one of the best examples of an unexpected event, which had been foreseen neither by private rating agencies, nor by the international monetary organisations. The Asian financial and economic crises resulted in a contraction of output and employment, and in some countries poverty rose sharply. Negative spillover effects have affected numerous other countries. As a consequence of these crises, the growth in world output was projected at just 2.5 per cent for 1999, about 2 percentage points below the projection made before the outbreak of the Asian crises – a loss of some US$800 billion in 1999 alone. The question arises, what can be done better in the future and what can be done by the international monetary institutions? The latter will be discussed – as an example – with respect to the reaction of the IMF, so far the only international monetary institution which has some experience in dealing with financial crises.

During the past two decades the IMF's surveillance has relied on indicators, especially in the periods between consultations and/or discussions, to monitor economic developments and to draw conclusions from their likely future trends. While crises prevention is mentioned nowhere specifically as one of the IMF's main purposes,[1] there is an urgent need to undertake reforms, so that the IMF can react more quickly and properly to events like the Asian crises. Thus, while the aims of the IMF are clearly more ambitious than mere crises prevention, the latter can be said to be an indispensable prerequisite for the achievement of these objectives. Indeed, crises prevention should be a core function of the IMF, and surveillance should be the IMF's principal tool for crises prevention. Hence it is no surprise then, that surveillance activities, broadly defined, absorb the largest share of the IMF's human resources. Surveillance over the fund's 182 member countries is, however, a continuous process, and the executive board meets about once a month for informal country matters sessions, which aim to facilitate early identification of emerging financial tensions by focusing on potential problems and providing additional empirical material on a selective basis. The staff inform management monthly on important country developments, but also *ad hoc* when it is necessary. Beyond the usual annual consultation visits, formal financial arrangements, precautionary arrangements, informal staff-monitored programmes and enhanced surveillance provide additional channels for more intensive contact between the staff and country authorities. The closer monitoring in the context of a quantitative framework, which accompanies these modalities of the IMF's involvement, tends to reassure interested third parties, such as donors, creditors and financial markets, and thereby can contribute to crises prevention.[2]

It should be briefly mentioned that the IMF has also undertaken regional and multilateral surveillance. The former, which is increasingly becoming important in the surveillance of European economies, complements bilateral surveillance in areas where policy responsibilities have been shifted to the supranational level. Executive board discussions of regional surveillance reports provide guidance to the staff in conducting bilateral surveillance with the countries affected. In the future, this is expected to increase with respect to monetary policy in the euro area, for consultation missions to both EMU participants and countries that have close links with the euro area. The multilateral surveillance exercises provide valuable input for bilateral surveillance, for example in the form of projections for the growth of trading partner markets or market assessments of country financing prospects.

The eruption of the Mexican crises in late 1994 and especially the outbreak of the Asian crises 2.5 years later, raised severe questions about the effectiveness of the IMF's surveillance. The issue of relevance to today is not whether these crises could have been prevented, because of course they could have been avoided through better economic policies or subsequently mitigated by the readiness on the part of the government in the crises countries to deal swiftly and decisively with the emerging panics.

If one examines the record of surveillance in the Asian region, the IMF appeared to have been more aware of the risks in Thailand's economic policy course than were most market observers. In other cases in Asia, however, despite having identified critical weaknesses, particularly in the financial sector, the IMF had been taken by surprise, owing in part to lack of access to required information and also to an inability to see the full consequences of the combination of structural weaknesses in the economy and contagion effects.[3] In particular, in the case of Korea, the IMF had not attached sufficient urgency to the financial tensions that had begun developing in early 1997.

From these short remarks about the ability of the IMF to react to severe economic and financial crises, it can be seen that there is a need either to undertake major reforms of the IMF, so that the IMF is better able to fulfil its tasks, or to create a new international monetary institution.[4] Both steps require, however, much more far-reaching rights than the existing ones of the IMF. It will be shown, with the help of constitutional economics, that the new monetary institution will only be successful in handling financial crises if it can (re)act (at least for a certain time span) like an independent central bank with the additional rights to discipline governments and other actors in those countries. This new monetary institution can only act successfully if it is really independent; this means that no pressure from major donor countries can be put on it or it might be misused as a lender of last resort. An attempt to develop such a framework will be undertaken in the next two sections.

3. SOME THEORETICAL CONSIDERATIONS ABOUT A NEW INTERNATIONAL MONETARY INSTITUTION

3.1 The Economic and Political Independence of Monetary Institutions

The modern theory of financial institutions (like central banks or international monetary institutions) stresses the importance of the independence of these institutions and of the incentive structures of the decision makers responsible for monetary policy. According to Grilli et al. (1991), the monetary institutions can be described by their political and economic independence. Economic independence is defined as the ability of the monetary institutions to determine the use and choice of their monetary (and if necessary other) policy instruments to act autonomously and without interference from national governments (or donor countries) or national organisations.[5] Economic independence may be adversly affected by the monetary institutions' obligations to finance national governments, to supervise commercial banks and by a lack of freedom to set interest rates.[6]

Political independence is defined as the ability of the monetary institution to choose monetary policy goals autonomously and without interference from a government (or donor countries). The basic determinants for this ability are found in personal independence (for example procedures for appointing and dismissing the decisive managers of such an international monetary institution (and their terms of office)), in the national government's rights (or international institution's rights) to give instructions to the international monetary institution as well as the right to veto, to suspend or to fire the top executives (of such international monetary institutions).

The necessary precautions and arrangements for a 'new' IMF are shown in Table 13.1.

There are three areas of economic policy in which such an arrangement induces important institutional changes in the policy of the new IMF with respect to a country which wants help from the new IMF. These fields are:

1. no bail-out clause
2. monetary policy, and
3. fiscal policy.

Ad 1: No bail-out clause

In most cases this new institutional arrangement prevents a bail-out situation, because the addressee (under the old situation the IMF or the donor countries) is not allowed to act so by its statutes. Hence the moral hazard problem of the IMF is drastically diminished and if this no bail-out clause becomes credible

Table 13.1 Institutional precautions/arrangements for a 'new' IMF

Instititutional arrangements	
1. Statute of the new IMF	1.1 Commitment to stable currencies
	1.2 Commitment to price and fiscal stability
	1.3 Independence of the new IMF from donor countries
2. No bail-out clause	
3. Fiscal convergence criteria (pre-fixed limits) of	3.1 Government currencial budget deficit
	3.2 Government overall debt
4. Monetary structural convergence criteria	4.1 Inflation convergence
	4.2 Long-term interest rate convergence
	4.3 Exchange rate stabilization

it might already have some effects in advance of the financial behaviour of possible affected countries.

Ad 2: Monetary policy

Here, the statute of the new IMF is of particular relevance. In order to minimise the inflation risk and a weak currency, the IMF has been assigned a strong position. This can be seen in the following three aspects:

(i) commitment of the new IMF to price and currency stability as its main goal,

(ii) institutional independence of the new IMF and independence of its employees, and

(iii) strong influence with the help of fiscal convergence criteria on the countries' state deficit financing.

Ad 3: Fiscal policy

In the fiscal policy area two aspects are important:

(i) the 'no bail-out' clause, and

(ii) each country's specific set-up of the fiscal convergence criteria, which restrict the government budget deficit and the overall government debt to certain (politically accepted) levels.

3.2 Institutional Solutions to the Time Inconsistency Problem

A starting point for the theoretical foundations of the independence of a monetary institution can be that the behaviour of politicians is also greatly influenced by the existing rules of the political game.[7] Even for the simple case, that we have either benevolent policy makers (that is policy makers who behave like social planners) or we assume selfish policy makers who are opportunistic and have partisan preferences, the existing incentive constraints can lead to suboptimal policies. The fundamental reason for this is that policy makers operate in a discretionary regime, that is monetary policy decisions are taken sequentially over time in a second-best world and therefore a socially desirable monetary policy may suffer from a lack of credibility caused by time inconsistency (compare Persson and Tabellini, 1997; Wagner, 1997). According to Blanchard and Fischer (1989), a policy is time inconsistent when a future policy decision that forms part of an optimal plan, formulated at an initial date *ex ante*, is no longer optimal at the time the policy is implemented *ex post*, although there is no relevant *new* information (compare Schaling, 1995, p. 25).

Various economic decisions are based on agents' expectations of future monetary policy, if we assume that a monetary authority is able to influence the inflation rate. For instance, when deciding on labour supply, wage contracts, investments or portfolio allocation, agents have to form expectations of the future inflation rate. In a discretionary regime, policy makers can make revisions of *ex ante* announced policy decisions and therefore create more inflation than forward-looking agents expect. One possible way to deal with this 'credibility' problem consists in removing all discretionary power from the government – however, this is quite an unrealistic assumption. The establishment of an independent (international monetary) authority would then be unnecessary, if a strict, legally embedded simple x% money supply rule were used. Governments would then only have to pass a law requiring the government to fix the growth of money supply at a steady rate.

However, studies on the employment motive for monetary expansion show that when stochastic shocks are taken into account, the optimal monetary policy does not conform to a simple rule but also includes an optimal shock absorption mechanism (compare Rogoff, 1985; King, 1996). By following a simple rule the government might be able to eliminate the inflation bias, but would produce suboptimally high output fluctuations. On the other hand, statutory entrenchment of the optimal state contingent rule appears to be extremely difficult, because it is hard to imagine how all contingencies might be described *ex ante* and verified *ex post*. What remains is a choice between simple rules, which are inflexible, and discretionary policies which lead to an inflation bias. It is this trade-off between credibility and flexibility, which has led to a game-theoretic foundation of the independence of monetary institutions (like a central bank). In principle, two approaches can be differentiated: on the one hand, Rogoff's (1985) approach to delegate monetary policy to an independent 'central' banker and the contracting approach by Walsh (1995 a, b) on the other hand. What both theories have in common, is that they propose the establishment of monetary institution structures which permit monetary policy to react to economic disturbances independently, that is without interference from the government.

In the following some basic guidelines for a new monetary institution are developed using the contracting approaches, which seems more suitable for such a new framework.[8] However, they differ in their policy advice regarding the determination of central bankers' objectives and incentives. Starting from a principal–agent approach Walsh (1995a) and Persson and Tabellini (1993) come to the conclusion that even though the government should transfer the control of a monetary policy instrument to an independent monetary institution, the government should also provide this institution with incentives to optimise a social welfare function. This will be done in the form of a (performance) contract between the government (as the principal) and the monetary institution (as the agent). Under the assumption that the preferences of the government and the monetary institution coincide, Walsh (1995a) shows that a simple contract which makes the central bankers' remuneration linearly dependent on a realised rate of inflation, eliminates the inflation bias without any sacrifice in stabilisation efficiency. In addition he showed that the incentive structures of optimal performance contracts can also be generated through the implementation of inflation-dependent dismissal rules (Walsh, 1995b). Such dismissal rules come close to the corresponding rules of price targeting agreements practised, for example, in the New Zealand Central Bank System (Walsh, 1995b).

As incentives in the traditional approaches depend exclusively on deviations between realised inflation from the socially desirable rate of inflation, performance contracts are frequently interpreted in the sense of direct inflation targeting as well. Svensson (1997) shows that under conventional assumptions the result of an optimal monetary institution contract can also be achieved, when the government imposes an inflation target of the international monetary institution which is below the socially desirable inflation and other monetary targets.

However, an optimal monetary institution contract becomes considerably more complex if we consider 'distorted' or selfish preferences of the governments. If optimal contracts are very complex, problems with regard to their implementation are raised, because it becomes more difficult to review the compliance and the design in the incentive structures. Walsh (1995a) also shows, for example, that the incentive structures of an optimal monetary organisation contract are not solely dependent on inflation but also on output, if the managers of this international organisation try to maximise their income (Walsh, 1995a, pp. 158ff). Svensson (1997) highlights the importance of persistence in the labour market, which, among other things, leads to a discretionary monetary policy not only entailing an increased inflation bias but also a stabilisation bias. The reason for this is that surprise inflation also leads to real economic effects in subsequent periods.

In general these theoretical considerations show that it is quite difficult to achieve from the monetary theory an optimal framework under which an international monetary organisation should operate. However, some of the guidelines of the contract approach can be used for modelling an institutional design of an international monetary organisation.

4. SOME IDEAS ABOUT THE INSTITUTIONAL DESIGN OF A NEW INTERNATIONAL MONETARY INSTITUTION

After having experienced the Asian crises, the existing international monetary institutions were not able to deal adequately with these problems. Either they gave the wrong advice or they were under considerable pressure from the major donor governments to behave in a way which was in no way useful for the affected countries (like Indonesia or Korea). To lay down the right policies *ex ante*, so that such a major crisis can be overcome in the foreseeable future or may even be avoided in other countries, is an awfully difficult task. Under the current structure of the IMF and especially the powerless instruments this organisation has to achieve its goals, one should think of a completely different (new) institution with much more enforceable instruments.

The following suggestion may sound 'wild' and is to some extent normative, but on the other hand if one realises what happens in such major financial and economic crises, like those in Indonesia, Thailand or South Korea, it might be necessary to create a new monetary institution. If a financial crisis in a country emerges, and if this new institution is called upon for help by this country, it should be layed down in a contract between the country and the institution, that this organisation may act like a completely independent central bank but coming from outside. For a certain period of time (between one and three years) this new IMF will fulfil such a task, with all the influence and means of a central bank. The idea behind this contract is that on the one hand the moral hazard problem of the IMF (that is the IMF is a lender of last resort and bails out these countries) is considerably reduced,[9] and that this new monetary institution has a strong incentive to undertake the policies for the affected country which are best suited for it, because it now has full responsibility with respect to the monetary policy of this country so that it can act quickly. As the financial help from the donor countries depends on the success to overcome the crises in this country, there are strong incentives for this new institution to act accordingly. On the other hand, there are now considerably higher costs for affected countries, because the governments in these countries lose a considerable part of their (monetary and fiscal policy) power and autonomy. Hence, strong pressure can be put from this new IMF on the government to undertake necessary reforms, and (maybe the most important), the 'easy' bail-out option does not exist any more! When creating such an institutional design for the new international monetary organisation two aspects are very important:[10] the first is the institutional design and policy tasks of this new institution, and the second is the implementation problems.

4.1 The Institutional Design and Policy Tasks of a New Monetary Institution

4.1.1 A two-tier banking system

An important requirement of autonomous and successful central banking is the instalment of a two-tier banking system.[11] This means that there should be a strong and independent central bank and the new monetary institution should play this role for a certain time, until it has reformed or built up such an institution together with a number of competitive commercial (private) banks. Once we have such a type of banking system, where the central bank sets out clear policy guidelines to control the private banking system (with minimum reserves and other monetary policy guidelines) a certain stabilisation can be expected. But even when establishing such a two-tier banking system, the new international monetary organisation should be able to do more and to undertake a reform of the economic and financial environment of the affected state. In particular in the following fields major reforms are necessary: thorough restructuring of the banking system, a stable legal and administrative framework and the establishment of control mechanisms on the fiscal authority.

4.1.2 Thorough restructuring of the banking system

A main precondition for an efficient conduct of monetary policy is a well-functioning market-based banking system. It is not enough to commercialise state-owned banks and to give them new tasks and in addition let a number of new private banks emerge. In order to enable commercial banks to function effectively under market conditions, deregulation and sometimes privatisation of these institutions might be necessary and an adequate supervisory capacity is also absolutely necessary, because a weak and inefficient banking system hinders or even prevents a successful monetary policy: they distort the transmission mechanism of monetary policy, because unsound banks, which are not able to control the balance sheets, are less responsive to changes in reserve money or interest rates. In addition, the central bank (or the international monetary institution) may come under pressure to give credit for bailing out banks and to loosen monetary conditions thereby undermining their monetary control. Moreover, there are additional problems with unsound banks. There is a general consensus among economists that indirect instruments of monetary policy are more effective than direct instruments that promote more efficient financial intermediation (see, for example, Alexander et al., 1995, or Demelo and Denitzer, 1997). In the presence of unsound banks, however, introducing indirect instruments such as a credit auction or similar market-based facilities may induce adverse selection and moral hazard effects, because unsound banks may be willing to borrow at any cost to avoid illiquidity. What is needed are institutional innovations such as specific supervisory policies and bank restructuring schemes.[12]

4.1.3 A stable legal and administrative framework

A stable legal and administrative framework is extremely important for market economies to function, as we have seen in the financial crises of some of the Asian states, if such an institution is missing! The instalment of an independent legal system, however, usually takes a lot of time. During this period, the investment process in the real sector as well as in the financial sector is hampered by great uncertainty. As long as a stable legal framework has not been established, private investments are regarded as very risky by potential investors. Thus private domestic investments tend to be very low and urgently needed foreign investments are delayed. However, it is not only the legal environment that counts, the administrative and moral environments are important, too (compare Freyhold et al., 1995). Administrative inefficiency and corruption impose essential restrictions on the feasibility of projected monetary policy, rendering the assessment of the international monetary institution's performance very difficult.[13] During such a transition period this new financial institution can help to install confidence for domestic and foreign firms to invest in this 'crisis' country with a reliable monetary policy that brings back monetary stability.

4.1.4 Establishment of control mechanisms on the fiscal authority

The domestic monetary institutions are more or less permanently under the pressure of the fiscal authorities to ease their restrictive (anti-inflational) monetary policy. In the Public Choice literature, central banks are regarded as being exposed to strong political pressures to behave in accordance with government preferences.[14] The point is that restrictive monetary policy aggravates the budgetary position of the government. Since a (temporary) slowdown of economic activity, induced by restrictive monetary or disinflational policy, reduces tax income and receipts from seigniorage and since a short-term increase in interest rates means an additional burden on public debt, that worsens the deficit, the government may prefer 'easy money' and hence collect public support to push the central bank in this direction. Some evidence exists that the relatively independent US Federal Reserve and the German Bundesbank have often complied with such pressures (see, for instance, Allen, 1986; Alesina, 1989; Berger and Schneider, 1998). Hence it seems to be very likely that the relatively independent monetary institution will have difficulties in withstanding such pressure for a longer time. Such pressure from the fiscal policy side can make the commitment of the international monetary institution to follow a steady anti-inflationary policy incredible, since the sustainability of such a policy is doubted. This problem can only be overcome if some control mechanisms on the fiscal authority are established, like in the Maastricht treaty in the case of the European Monetary Union.

4.2 Implementation Problems

In a perfect world all of the above-mentioned institutional changes should be implemented instantly – and hence it would also be desirable to implement all reform elements simultaneously. This, however, is wishful thinking. The problem of sequencing and of making a wrong decision respecting the sequence of reform steps cannot be neglected. For example it is not sufficient to have formerly independent monetary institutions in such crisis countries, if they do not have the sufficient institutional and political support for such a step. In order to strengthen the position of the monetary institution and to enhance the credibility of its announcements, there are two ways to improve the situation. The first way is to implement the appropriate institutional control mechanism in order to control the inflation driving authorities or groups (such as the fiscal authority and wage price setting groups), or one could bring forward the idea of the introduction of constitutional restriction of government debt. The second way is to choose an appropriate nominal anchor in order to conduct monetary policy successfully. The question of nominal anchors is important, because the credibility of the monetary policy strategy eventually determines the success of the monetary institution. Credibility, however, is dependent not only on the classical time inconsistency aspects (namely the incentives of the monetary institution to deviate from its goal) but also upon the expected implementability of the strategy that is a function of the reform stage.

5. SUMMARY AND CONCLUSIONS

In this chapter it has been demonstrated that we have a new situation after having experienced the Asian crises. In the light of this new development a first attempt was made to put forward some ideas of a more powerful and effective new international monetary organisation. It is argued that the policies of this organisation will be successful only if it is really independent, especially from its major donors and hence can act independently if it is 'called' for help by certain countries. Then it was shown that various instruments should be developed for this new organisation giving it the status of an independent central bank in an affected country for a certain time period, so that the organisation can really control the monetary policy and has the appropriate instruments to interfere within the country's fiscal policy aspects, so that the goals of this institution can be achieved. In general this chapter should be seen as a first attempt at suggesting new international monetary institutions after having experienced the Asian financial and economic crises.

NOTES

1. Compare Frenkel (1999) and Mussa and Savastano (1999) for the traditional policies of the IMF for crisis intervention.
2. See here the contributions by Krueger (1998) and Gutmann (1995).
3. Compare the critical statements and general empirical results of the IMF policies by Edwards (1989), Khan (1990), Schadler et al. (1995) and Krueger (1998).
4. A third alternative would be to abolish international monetary institutions like the IMF because they are ineffective and cost a lot of money – with the consequence that 'the market' would solve such crises. Such a view is supported by some US economists like Charles K. Rowley from George Mason University in Fairfax (VA) or from some members of the US Congress.
5. This definition of economic independence is very similar to the meaning of instrument independence introduced, for example, by Debelle and Fischer (1994, p. 197), who distinguish between instrument independence and global independence.
6. Compare, for example, Alesina and Grilli (1992, p. 56).
7. In the Public Choice literature the selfish behaviour of politicians is extensively analysed and the importance of institutional arrangements is stressed. Compare Mueller (1987) and Schneider (1994).
8. Let me explicitly mention, that Rogoff's approach of a conservative central banker is also an attractive approach. Rogoff shows that social welfare can be improved if the government delegates monetary policy to a conservative central banker who agrees with the social preferences regarding the target values of inflation and output, but places a greater weight on the inflation targets than the government. Once appointed, the conservative central banker operates under discretion and is independent to pursue an activist policy. By appropriate choice of the degree of conservativeness a society realises a better equilibrium position than the government itself can achieve following inflexible rules or discretionary policy. For further elaborations see Rogoff (1985), Fischer (1994) and for an extension of this approach assuming a partisan interests of politicians, see Alesina and Gatti (1995). For a treatment in the context of the European Union, see Wagner (1997).
9. Due to this problem some economists (Vaubel, 1983) argue that it should be strictly forbidden for the IMF to give loans. For a general discussion see Sachs (1999) and Frenkel (1999).
10. Compare Eichengreen (1999) and Frenkel (1999) for general reform proposals.
11. Compare, for example, Frankel (1999), Romer and Romer (1997), Sahay and Vegh (1995) and IMF (1997).
12. For example Enoch and Breen (1997) demand this.
13. Compare here the work by Schneider and Enste (2000), who deal with corruption and the rise of a shadow or underground economy in developing states like those in Asia.

14. See for the US: Akhtar and Howe (1991) and Havrilesky (1995); for Germany: Frey and Schneider (1981) and Berger and Schneider (1998); for a survey see Cukierman (1996).

REFERENCES

Akhtar, M.A. and H. Howe (1991), 'The political and institutional independence of U.S. monetary policy', *Banca Nazionale del Lavoro, Quarterly Review*, **178** (3), 343–89.

Alesina, A. (1989), 'Politics and business cycles in industrial democracies', *Economic Policy*, **8** (1), 55–98.

Alesina, A. and R. Gatti (1995), 'Independent central banks: low inflation at no cost?', *American Economic Review*, **85** (1), 169–200.

Alesina, A. and V. Grilli (1992), 'The European Central Bank: Reshaping monetary politics in Europe', in M.B. Canzoneri, V. Grilli and P.R. Masson (eds), *Establishing a Central Bank: Issues in Europe and Lessons from the U.S.*, Cambridge, MA: Cambridge University Press, pp. 49–77.

Alexander, W., T. Balino and E. Enoch (1995), 'The Adoption of Indirect Instruments of Monetary Policy', IMF Occasional Paper 126, Washington, DC: International Monetary Fund.

Allen, S.D. (1986), 'The Federal Reserve and the electoral cycle', *Journal of Money, Credit and Banking*, **18** (1), 57–98.

Berger, H. and F. Schneider (1998), 'The Bundesbank's Reaction to Policy Conflicts: Evidence and Implications', Discussion Paper 9811, Linz: University of Linz, Department of Economics.

Blanchard, D. and S. Fischer (1989), *Lectures on Macroeconomics*, Cambridge, MA: MIT Press.

Cukierman, A. (1996), 'The Economics of Central Banking', Discussion Paper No. 3631, Center for Economic Research.

Debelle, G. and S. Fischer (1994), 'How Independent should a Central Bank be?', in J.C. Fuhrer (ed.), *Goals, Guidelines and Constraints Facing Monetary Policy Makers*, Boston: Federal Reserve Bank of Boston, Conference series No. 38, pp. 195–221.

Demelo, M. and C. Denitzer (1997), 'Monetary Policy During Transition: An overview', Washington, DC: World Bank, Policy Research Working Paper 1706.

Edwards, Samuel (1989), 'The International Monetary Fund and the developing countries: A critical evaluation', *Carnegie Rochester Conference Series on Public Policy*, **31** (1), 7–68.

Eichengreen, B. (1999), *To Award a New International Financial Architecture*, Washington, DC: Institute for International Economics.

Enoch, C. and J.H. Green (eds) (1997), *Banking Soundness and Monetary Policy: Issues and Experiences in the Global Economy*, Washington, DC: International Monetary Fund.

Fischer, S. (1994), 'Modern Central Banking', in F. Capie, G. Goodhart, C. Fischer and N. Schnadt (eds), *The Future of Central Banking*, Cambridge, MA: Cambridge University Press, pp. 162–208.

Frankel, Jeffrey A. (1999), 'International Lender of Last Resort: Discussion', in Jane S. Little and Giovanni P. Olivei (eds), *Re-thinking the International Monetary System*, Conference Series No. 43, June, Federal Reserve Bank of Boston.

Frenkel, Michael (1999), 'Der internationale währungsfonds – nothelfer oder krisenverschärfer?', List Forum für Wirtschafts- und Finanzpolitik, **25** (4), 382–400.

Frey, B.S. and F. Schneider (1981), 'Central bank behavior: a positive empirical analysis', *Journal of Monetary Economics*, **7** (3), 291–316.

Freyhold, H.V., V. Gessner, E.L. Vial and H. Wagner (1995), 'Cost of Judicial Barriers for Consumers in the Single Market', Brussels: A Report for the European Commission, DG XXIV.

Grilli, V., D. Masciandaro and G. Tabellini (1991), 'Political and monetary institutions and public financial policies in industrialized countries', *Economic Policy*, **13**, 341–92.

Gutmann, Michael (1995), 'Conditionality: past, present, future', *IMF Staff Papers*, **2** (4), 792–835.

Havrilesky, T. (1995), *The Pressures on American Monetary Policy*, Dordrecht, NL: Kluwer Academic Publishers.

International Monetary Fund (1997), 'Status of Market-Based Central Banking Reforms in the Countries of the former Soviet Union', Report prepared for the 10th Coordination Meeting of Cooperation Central Banks and International Institutions, Basel, Switzerland.

Khan, Michael S. (1990), 'The macroeconomic effects of fund-supported adjustment programs', *IMF Staff Papers*, **37** (1), 195–231.

King, M. (1996), 'Direct Inflation Targets', in Deutsche Bundesbank (ed.), *Monetary Policy Strategies in Europe*, München: Verlag Vahlen, pp. 45–74.

Krueger, Anne (1998), 'Whither the World bank and the IMF?', *Journal of Economic Literature*, **36** (3), 1983–2020.

Mueller, D. (1987), *Public Choice II*, Cambridge, MA: Cambridge University Press.

Mussa, Michael and Michael Savastano (1999), 'The IMF Approach to Economic Stabilization', IMF Working Paper, WP99/104, Washington, DC.

Persson, T. and G. Tabellini (1997), 'Political Economics and Macroeconomic Policy', NBER Working Paper, 6329, Cambridge, MA.

Rogoff, K. (1985), 'The optimal degree of commitment to an intermediate monetary target', *Quarterly Journal of Economics*, **100** (3), 1169–90.

Romer, C.D. and D.H. Romer (1997), 'Institutions for Monetary Stability', in C.D. Romer and D.H. Romer (eds), *Reducing Inflation: Motivation and Strategy*, Chicago: University of Chicago Press, pp. 307–34.

Sachs, Jeffrey D. (1999), 'The International Lender of Last Resort: What are the alternatives?', in Jane S. Little and Giovanni P. Olivei (eds), *Re-thinking the International Monetary System*, Federal Reserve Bank of Boston, Conference Series No. 43, June.

Sahay, R. and C. Vegh (1995), 'Dollarization in Transition Economies: Evidence and Policy Implications', IMF Working Paper 9596, Washington, DC International Monetary Fund.

Schadler, Samuel, Anton Bennett, Michael Carkovic, Luigi Dicks-Mireaux, M. Mecagni, J.H.J. Morsink and Michael A. Savastano (1995), 'The IMF conditionality: Experience under standby and extended arrangements', IMF Working Paper, Washington, DC.

Schaling, E. (1995), *Institution and Monetary Policy. Credibility, Flexibility and Central Bank Independence*, Aldershot: Edward Elger.

Schneider, F. (1994), 'Public Choice – Economic Theory of Politics: A Survey in Selected Areas', in H. Brandstätter and W. Güth (eds), *Essays on Economics Psychology*, Heidelberg: Springer Publishing Company, 243–69.

Schneider, F. and D. Enste (2000), 'Shadow economies: size, causes and consequences', *Journal of Economic Literature*, **38** (1), March, 78–120.
Svensson, L.E.O. (1997), 'Optimal inflation targets, conservative central banks and linear inflation contracts', *American Economic Review*, **87** (1), 98–114.
Vaubel, Roland (1983), 'The moral hazard of IMF landing', *The World Economy*, **6** (2), 291–303.
Wagner, A. (1997), *Geldpolitik in der Europäischen Wirtschafts- und Währungsunion*, Linz: Trauner.
Walsh, C.E. (1995a), 'Optimal contracts for central bankers', *American Economic Review*, **85** (1).
Walsh, C.E. (1995b), 'Is New Zealand's Reserve Bank Act of 1989 an optimal central bank contract?', *Journal of Money, Credit and Banking*, **27** (4), 1179–91.

14. On the delegation of powers – with special emphasis on Central and Eastern Europe*

Eli M. Salzberger and Stefan Voigt

1. INTRODUCTION

During the late 1980s and early 1990s, the countries of Central and Eastern Europe went through a peaceful transition to democracy, after half a century of communist rule. All of these countries adopted a new (or significantly amended an existing) written constitution. The vast majority of them based their new system of government on the continental model, two of whose main features are parliamentary democracy and a special constitutional court. However, there are significant differences in the specific details of their governmental structures. In this chapter, we try to determine the possible sources for the institutional differences in these regimes, which emerged in the same period of time and against a similar historical background. This is a very broad task, and obviously we will be able to address neither every possible feature that might be a viable explanatory factor for these institutional differences, nor every possible effect of such differences. The same limitation applies to the range of institutional components that will be scrutinized here. We will focus our analysis on the structure of the separation of powers and especially on the delegation of powers to domestic organizations, such as independent judiciaries and central banks, and to international bodies, such as international organizations.

This chapter is part of a more general project on the delegation of powers in which we attempt to explain why politicians delegate powers and their choice between international and domestic delegation (Voigt and Salzberger,

* This chapter was written while its authors were with the Institute for Advanced Study in Berlin. They would like to thank the Institute's staff for its immense hospitality. They would also like to thank the organizers and the participants of the Second Messina Workshop on 'The Political Economy of Institutional Development: Institutional Design in a Period of Rapid Change'. Others who discussed the chapter with us include Alexander Blankenagel, Laszlo Bruszt, and Gerald Rowe.

2002). In a companion paper to this one (Salzberger and Voigt, 2002a), more emphasis is on constitutional choices. Here, the focus is on post-constitutional choice. In yet another paper (Salzberger and Voigt, 2002b), the empirical development of Central and Eastern Europe is compared to that of Israel.

If one is interested in explaining the delegation of powers by politicians (see McCubbins and Page, 1987) and in distinguishing between domestic and international delegation, one is interested in nomological hypotheses, that is hypotheses that purport to be applicable everywhere and always. Thus, a chapter with a particular focus on a group of countries with particular characteristics might seem awkward. Yet, there are a couple of reasons why such a specific focus can be of importance.

On the one hand, there is a notion that there are special moments in which a group makes decisions not according to the standard self-interest rationale but according to special ones, only valid in that very moment. Ackerman (1991), for example, talks about 'constitutional moments'. Our chapter begs to differ. On the other hand, it has often been observed that shortly after radical regime changes, everything is up for grabs (see, for example, Hume 1777/1987, p. 474). To analyze constitutional and post-constitutional choices, we draw on rational choice broadly interpreted. We thus claim that this general framework should do. In times of radical constitutional changes, however, the identification of the constraints that the relevant actors are subject to might not be as clear-cut as in 'normal' times. In this chapter we will try to address some of these constraints.

Second, delegation of powers can be viewed usually as 'post-constitutional constitutional choice'. Basic choices are made on the basis of an existing constitution. In the case of the countries of Central and Eastern Europe, this sequential choice might have turned into a simultaneous one: decisions to delegate are taken at the same time as more basic decisions concerning who is to have the general competence to delegate power. It can be conjectured that this simultaneity will lead to different outcomes from sequential choices, because the post-constitutional choices will become part of more general package deals. This means that the analysis of decisions to delegate power will become more difficult because it will be more complicated to detect the relevant restrictions under which the actors operate.

If there is a broad consensus among the members of a constitutional convention regarding the need to apply for membership in specific international organizations (IOs), the statutes regulating these IOs could also constrain the framing of the constitution. This would be an unusual trait, because in our thinking about IOs we usually assume a number of nation-states with their respective constitutions as given, and that these form the basis for negotiating the founding of an IO. Here, the IO is already given and the constitution-makers can choose to comply with its rules in anticipation of subsequent membership. The procedural rules that a constitutional convention agrees upon (agenda-setting power, veto powers, voting rules, and so on) will, of course, also influence the content of the constitution.

Central and Eastern Europe might also be 'special' because of the pace of development of independent agencies. Independent agencies evolved very slowly in Western constitutional systems. In principle, the experiences that have been gained with various institutional arrangements in the West could be taken into account when deciding how to delegate powers in the newly passed constitutions.

We cover eight countries in this study, that is, those countries that the Freedom House Project found to be consolidated democracies and consolidated market economies: the Czech Republic, Estonia, Hungary and Poland; and four countries assessed to be transitional polities and transitional economies: Bulgaria, Romania, Russia, and Slovakia (Karatnycky et al., 1998, p. 4).[1] Eight countries are too many for doing serious case studies, but we wanted to provide the reader with varied information, also from countries which have so far been neglected. Eight countries are too few for doing regression analyses, so our conclusions are only tentative.

The chapter is organized as follows: In the next section, some theoretical conjectures concerning the delegation of powers will be presented after the key concepts have been defined. Section 3 offers an overview of the newly created institutional arrangements with regard to delegation – both domestic and international. The chapter concludes with an outlook in which some open questions are made explicit.

2. SOME THEORETICAL CONJECTURES

2.1 Delineating Domestic and International Delegation

Our general question is whether it is possible to explain the variance in the structure of agencies and their independence across the scrutinized countries, by analyzing the constitutional (and post-constitutional) competences and restrictions given to those organs that have the power to delegate power. The creation of an independent agency and the transfer of competence to that agency is thus to be explained, and it is our hypothesis that the modes of delegation chosen and the extent of powers transferred can be explained by constitutional structures, as well as by political considerations. Before spelling out some conjectures concerning delegation decisions, the term 'delegation of powers' needs to be defined. Post-constitutional delegation of powers is occurring 'whenever rule-making powers that are not constitutionally assigned to a body other than the legislature are in fact being exercised by such a body' (Salzberger, 1993, p. 359).

Special emphasis will be given to the distinction between domestic and international delegation. Domestic delegation occurs when the rule-making powers are exercised by a body created by the domestic legislature and is under the governance of the constitution. International delegation is a state where the rule-making powers are exercised by a body that is not entirely under the control of domestic constitutional organs. A government might participate in the creation of an international organization to which legislative power is delegated but it will not be the only actor having a 'say' in the modification and interpretation of its statutes. To qualify as 'international delegation', it is sufficient that the rule-making powers are not exercised by a body completely under the control of domestic constitutional organs. The involvement of an international body is, therefore, not necessary. This means that we would also talk of international delegation if rule-making powers are conferred to a constitutional organ of another nation-state. To be analyzable within a unified framework, domestic and international delegations have to be substitutes for each other. That means that international organizations that deal primarily with border-crossing externalities will not be taken into account here. The focus is, rather, on solutions that could, at least in principle, also be achieved domestically.

The most straightforward method of delegation of powers is when the legislature, by a statute, directs other bodies to create rules in a specific area, instead of creating them itself. Defined in such a way, delegation of power occurs on a different level from the separation of powers as envisioned by Montesquieu. The latter is usually interpreted as being confined to the separation of legislature, executive and judiciary, each being assigned a different governmental function.

We assume that the relevant actors maximize their expected utility. Rational legislators will only be ready to transfer competence if the benefits connected with delegation outweigh the corresponding costs. Put simply: among the three alternatives of (1) deciding for themselves, (2) delegating competence to a domestic agency, or (3) delegating competence to an international organization, rational legislators will always choose the alternative that promises the highest expected net gains. Notice, however, that our concept of benefits and costs is not restricted to monetary or power components. It is thus one of our tasks to identify costs and benefits connected with the relevant alternatives. In Voigt and Salzberger (2002), following Fiorina (1982 and 1986) and McCubbins et al. (1989), we identify a number of benefits from delegation. They include the following: legislators can secure influence beyond the end of the election cycle, delegation can be used as a tool to credibly commit, as a tool to reduce uncertainty, but also to reduce one's workload; it can be used to expand the public sector, and to remain in power or maintain legitimacy. These possible benefits have to be weighed against possible costs such as delegatee-drift, monitoring costs, reversal costs, coordination costs, and even legitimacy drift. In Voigt and Salzberger (2002), we conjecture that the type and extent of the observed delegation of powers can be explained by the constitutional structure underlying the delegation decision. As already pointed out, Central and Eastern Europe is 'special' in the sense that constitutional and post-constitutional choices have often occurred almost simultaneously. Due to space restrictions, constitutional choice cannot be analyzed here (but see Salzberger and Voigt, 2002a).

2.2 Explaining the Choice to Delegate

The general logic of choosing not to choose was spelled out above. We will confine ourselves here to the presentation of several conjectures and hypotheses related to this decision. The first one is that the costs of abolishing an independent agency or reneging on its decisions are higher if the existence and independence of this agency are regulated on the constitutional level and not by ordinary legislation. Thus, delegation of competence on the constitutional level may be an indicator of the 'seriousness' of the delegation, or the high level of benefits expected from it.

It has often been pointed out that it can be a disadvantage to be too strong (Weingast, 1993). A state that is strong enough to protect private property rights and to enforce private contracts is also strong enough to expropriate private wealth. Rational subjects know this and will therefore invest less than they would if they could be sure that the state would not misuse its strength. States that have not had the possibility to build up a reputation as being solely an impartial arbiter will be especially affected. In such cases – and we conjecture that the states of Central and Eastern Europe belong to this group – creation of post-constitutional domestic independent agencies will often not be a credible commitment because they can be abolished with relative ease. It might therefore be rational for these countries to delegate relatively more powers in the constitutional stage, and/or to delegate relatively more competence to international agencies. In both options, the resulting independent body cannot be easily influenced by the respective governments. But this is only one part of the story: many of those countries are independent for the first time ever. The popularity of the government in those countries might be (negatively) affected if competence that the society had hoped to achieve for a long time is freely delegated internationally. Domestic constitutional delegation, therefore might be preferred.

Taking the possible effects of international delegation into account, we hypothesize that the higher the prestige of an international organization among the electorate, the more likely it is that delegation to that organization will occur because domestic prestige will translate into votes, that is increased reelection probability. Making the hypothesis a little more elaborate, one could argue that the prestige of membership is not absolute, but relative, that is one wants to be in before the neighbors get in. In that case, we should observe a veritable race for membership.

Furthermore, the amount of international delegation chosen by a specific government could also be a function of its ideological position. If we assume that right-wing governments are more in favor of markets than left-wing governments, and further that international organizations are by and large in favor of markets, then we should expect right-wing governments to be more active in delegating to international bodies. A right-wing government, in order to ensure that the road towards a market economy will be pursued even after its own demise, might be more keen to delegate internationally. Closely connected is the conjecture that, at the beginning of the transition, old (communist) governments that expect to be outvoted soon might try to secure their influence beyond election date by quickly creating agencies and staffing them with ideological friends. Those governments are, therefore, more likely to delegate domestically rather than internationally. On the other hand, if right-wing governments are less keen on social rights, then we can expect left-wing governments to be more keen than right-wing governments to delegate internationally to certain organizations. One can even argue that since right-wing governments are *per se* more credible with regard to market reforms, it is the left-wing governments who will have to delegate more internationally to gain credibility.

We further expect the constitutions of those countries that early on expressed interest in membership in international organizations – and especially in the EU – to anticipate in their constitutions some of the rules that they would have to conform to later on. The statutes of a central bank could, for example, already be in conformity with the requirements of European Monetary Union.

3. SOME INSTITUTIONAL STOCK-TAKING

In this section, we aim at summarizing the various constitutional and post-constitutional rules that have been passed in our eight countries with regard to the delegation of powers. Of course, a complete overview is impossible. As to domestic delegation, we focus especially on the judiciaries and on central banks and allude to other independent agencies in a third subsection. Possible interdependencies will also be sketched in brief. With regard to international delegation, we focus on possible membership in the European Union, but membership in other organizations such as the WTO is also analyzed. The last step in this section consists in analyzing possible relationships between domestic and international delegation.

3.1 Domestic Delegation

Over the last couple of years, an entire cottage industry, which analyzes possible relationships between the independence of central banks and inflation rates, has evolved. Measuring such independence occupied a significant share of this literature, which we survey in Section 3.1.2. In Section 3.1.1, we offer an analogous analysis of the independence of constitutional courts, focussing on measuring the courts' independence. Basically, it would seem to make sense first to present the established literature (on central banks) and then proceed to our additions (on constitutional courts). We have decided to present our analysis in reversed order because in most cases, the independence of (constitutional) courts is provided for on the constitutional level whereas this is not always the case with regard to central banks. Moreover, the independence of central banks can be regarded as a function of the independence of courts. Thus, from a structural and substantive point of view, the discussion of the independence of constitutional courts ought to precede the discussion of the independence of central banks.

3.1.1 The constitutional courts

One can distinguish between two models used across the world: (1) Countries in which this task is assigned to the general courts system. The federal judiciary in the US may be encountered as the most significant example of this model, where every court can perform judicial review. (2) Countries in which this task is assigned to a special constitutional court separated from the general courts system and hierarchy. Most European countries subscribe to this model.

All the emerging democracies in our study, save Estonia, opted for the second model and established special constitutional courts. Estonia adopted a system which is closer to the American one. Indirect judicial review in Estonia can be performed by every court and direct judicial review or findings of unconstitutionality by lower courts are deliberated by the National Court which is the general Supreme Court of the land.[2] In what follows, we try to assess the various formal arrangements in the eight countries under scrutiny *vis-à-vis* the independence of the constitutional enforcement mechanism and its efficacy. We divide this assessment into several components, in each of which we give a score ranging from 1 (least independent) to 10 (most independent).

(a) Constitutional vs. post-constitutional arrangement The independence and efficacy of constitutional enforcement mechanisms and their ability to serve as a counterweight to the other branches of government, are dependent upon the stability and immunity of the definition of the court's powers, its procedures and the arrangements regarding its operators – the judges. If these

arrangements are specified in the constitution itself, we expect a greater degree of independence than in cases where these arrangements are fixed by ordinary law, which is subject to amendment by parliament whenever it is unsatisfied with the performance of the court. Thus, countries in which these arrangements are part of the constitution and in which constitutional amendment requires a referendum or a super majority will be given the highest score, whereas countries in which the arrangements are in regular statute will be given a lower one. Due to space restrictions, the reasoning behind the scores attributed to the various constitutional arrangements is not provided here (but see Salzberger and Voigt, 2002a). The scores themselves are listed in Table 14.1 of this chapter.

(b) The power to elect the judges The procedure of appointment of constitutional court judges and the identity of those who have the power to appoint them may have a notable effect on the independence of the court. The constitutional court is supposed to protect the citizens from illegitimate use of powers by the authorities, as well as to settle disputes between the branches of government. Thus, it ought to be as independent as possible from the other branches. The most independent procedure for judicial election is election by professionals (other judges or jurists). The least independent method is election by one powerful politician (prime minister or a minister of justice). In between, we may find combined arrangements, for example, appointments which are made by politicians but from different branches of government or representing different parties.

(c) Judicial tenure Judges are most independent if they are appointed for life (or up to a mandatory retirement age) and cannot be removed from office, save by legal procedure. Judges are least independent if they are appointed for a set period, where subsequent terms are optional, and removal from office is a fairly easy process. If judges can run for a second term, their independence in the first term is severely harmed and they will want to be popular among their nominators. Judges who are appointed for a set period and cannot be re-appointed are in between. They are more independent than judges who can run for a second term, but less independent than life-tenured judges, as they may seek another position contingent on those who elected them, subsequent to their end of term at the constitutional court. The following coding takes into account also the length of term, which ranges between seven years and life.

(d) The accessibility of the court Another component of judicial independence is the accessibility of the court and its ability to initiate proceedings. A court which is accessible only by a certain number of members of parliament

or other officials will be less effective than a court which is accessible by every citizen who claims that her rights are violated.

(e) The competence of the court The last aspect of the independence indicator of constitutional courts is the width of competence assigned to them. This is, however, a somewhat tricky variable. At a first glance, it might seem that extended competence enhances the independence of courts, or that there should be a direct correlation between the extent of powers assigned to a court and its impact. But, in fact, from a certain point, more competence can actually reduce the independence of the court, its perception by the public as a neutral and honest broker and, thus, its ability to counterbalance the other branches. In other words, a court which is drawn to participate in political power struggles can lose its reputation and thus its independence and effectiveness. This might have been the case with the Russian constitutional court, which took sides in the clash of powers between the president and parliament in the early 1990s.

Constitutional review of legislation is the core function of the constitutional court in all countries surveyed here. A second common power of the constitutional courts is to adjudicate conflicts of authorities between the different branches of central government and between federal and local authorities. A set of more problematic powers are, on the one hand, the power to review the compatibility of international treaties with the constitution, and, on the other hand, the power to review legislation against international law. The variance of the arrangements in this area is especially relevant to our study. It reflects, on the one hand, a component of international delegation – the normative position of international law within the municipal legal system – and on the other hand, domestic delegation – the extent of powers delegated to a constitutional court to review the suitability of domestic law to international law.

(f) Summary Table 14.1 summarizes our findings of *de jure* independence. What sort of conclusions can be drawn from this table, when we view it *vis-à-vis* the different constraints on constitution making and the actual processes of constitution making in the eight countries included in this study? First, it seems that those countries who were the first to enact a constitution – Bulgaria and Romania – resulted with less independent judiciaries. This is an interesting finding, as we concluded in the previous sections that these countries can be characterized by a relatively strong form of separation of powers. However, this form applies mainly to the division of powers between the political branches, rather than delegation to non-political ones. A more general lesson might be that one has to distinguish between delegation of powers to politicians and delegation of powers to non-politicians. Different reasons might apply to these two forms of delegation.

Table 14.1 De jure *independence of constitutional courts*

	Constitutional arrangement (a)	Judges election (b)	Tenure (c)	Access (d)	Competence (e)	Sum
Bulgaria	8	7	6	3	8	32
Czech Rep.	9	7	7	6	10	39
Estonia	6	8	10	9	8	41
Hungary	5	8	3	8	6	30
Poland	8	4	6	8	9	35
Romania	9	6	6	3	4	28
Russia	4	5	8	5	7	29
Slovakia	8	4	5	7	9	33

Second, it seems that in the case of the independence of the judiciary historical legacies can be viewed as an important explanatory factor. The two countries with no such legacy are ranked as sixth and seventh with regard to the *de jure* independence of their constitutional courts. Finally, it is interesting to note that the country in which we found the highest degree of judicial independence, or the most extensive delegation, is Estonia. Its constitution was enacted by an *ad hoc* constituent assembly.

3.1.2 Comparing the independence of central banks

Constitutional courts are in most cases regulated on the constitutional level and can thus be considered to be within the realm of constitutional choice. In many industrialized countries, central banks do not figure quite as prominently. They often operate on the basis of powers granted by regular legislation. Distinguishing precisely between these levels could prove important because the de facto independence of post-constitutional independent agencies (such as a central bank) could very well depend on the (de facto) independence of the independent agencies anchored on the constitutional level, such as the judiciary. One of the first steps in describing the role of the newly created central banks of Central and Eastern Europe, therefore, is to inquire whether they have constitutional or post-constitutional status.

The functions and the institutional structure of the central bank are specified in the constitution in the Czech Republic, Hungary, Estonia, Poland and Russia. The Romanian constitution does not mention the central bank. In Bulgaria and the Slovak Republic, the central bank is mentioned in the constitution, but there are no provisions regarding its functions or institutional setup, and thus, from a point of view of delegation of powers, we cannot view such delegation in those countries as on the constitutional level.

Historical legacies also played a role in the processes of writing central bank laws: the Hungarian central bank, for example, is organized as a joint-stock company. This can be explained by drawing on the founding of the bank in 1924 when this organizational set-up was common practice (Kobabe, 1999, p. 136). Similarly, central bank statutes in states which just regained sovereignty often took their historical predecessors as models, Estonia being a case in point. But historical legacy also played a role in exactly the reverse manner: Slovakia, for example, had never had a central bank, and thus it could be designed from scratch. An *ad hoc* hypothesis could read that in such cases, more modern statutes should be expected – at least in the books.

Summarizing his extensive study on central banks in Central and Eastern Europe, Kobabe (1999, chapter F) stresses that the safeguarding of the independence of central banks on a constitutional level can be important in case of conflicts with other constitutional organs. He notes that in case of conflicts, the Polish, the Hungarian, and the Estonian central banks do not have the right to take these conflicts to the constitutional court. In Bulgaria and Romania, there are no constitutional provisions concerning the central banks at all. Government participation in the nomination procedure of members of the decision-making organs of monetary policy is also evaluated critically. Governments do participate in this procedure in Hungary, Romania, and Slovakia (ibid.). The independence of a central bank is also shaped by its relationship to other state organs and the possibilities of those organs to influence monetary policy. Should the Czech central bank interpret its powers too extensively, this can lead to a reduction of its functional independence (ibid., p. 234). The independence of the Hungarian National Bank is ambivalent due to its being organized as a joint-stock company with the state as the only shareholder. In Poland, the annual report of the central bank needs to be approved by government. The budget of the bank is (co-) determined by the bank together with the government in the Czech Republic and Slovakia. In Estonia, parliament even has the function of settling disputes between the organs of the National Bank. Concerning the relevance of the price stability goal, Kobabe notes that this is the clearly dominating goal only in Slovakia.

Very few papers have attempted to apply the indicators designed to measure the independence of central banks to the countries in Central and Eastern Europe. The paper by Loungani and Sheets (1997) is one of them. The authors propose two measures: one is based on Debelle and Fischer (1995) who suggest that central bank independence is composed of 'goal independence' and 'instrument independence' to which Loungani and Sheets (1997) attribute equal weights. Goal independence is ascertained by the question whether the central bank law stipulates price stability as the central macroeconomic objective of the central bank. Instrument independence is ascertained by an equal weighting of four components: (1) Does the central bank control the 'instruments' of monetary policy? (2) Is there any binding legal limit imposed on the direct financing of the government by the central bank? (3) Is the government allowed to receive any direct financing from the central bank? (4) Is the central bank subject to government directives in the execution of monetary policy? The second index proposed by Loungani and Sheets (1997) is the 'similarity to the Bundesbank-Index (SIB)'. The Bundesbank is thus taken as the benchmark. The SIB-index is made up of nine components that not only include goal and instrument independence but also 'political independence'.[3]

The two indicators of Loungani and Sheets are used to rank the *de jure* independence of central banks (see Table 14.2). But we propose to add the components discussed above – whether the regulation of the bank is by regular legislation or by the constitution, and the substance of this arrangement *vis-à-vis* the procedure for appointment of its directors and the reversibility of their decisions (analysis which is based on Kobabe, 1999). The countries in which the fundamental issues regarding the central bank are in the constitution were given a score of 1, from which deductions were made if the substance of the arrangements allow easy reversal of the directors' decisions. The countries in which only partial regulation of the central bank is in the constitution started with a score of 0.7 from which the deductions were made accordingly. The one country (Romania) in which central bank regulation is only by statute started with a score of 0.5. The scores are presented in Table 14.2. The average of the two indices and our additional one results with the following ranking of *de jure* independence, from the most independent to the least independent: the Czech Republic, Bulgaria, Estonia, Poland, Russia, Hungary, Romania and Slovakia.

Table 14.2 specifies the indices for the eight countries of our study. The indices can take on any value between 0 and 1, with higher values representing higher degrees of independence.

Table 14.2 Central banks' independence

	DF-index	SIB-index	Constitutional arrangement	Inflation 1998	Inflation 1999
Bulgaria	0.875	1.000	0.7	22.3	0.3
Czech Rep.	0.875	1.000	0.9	10.6	2.1
Estonia	1.000	0.667	0.8	8.2	3.3
Hungary	0.312	0.722	0.7	14.3	10.0
Poland	0.500	0.611	0.8	11.8	7.3
Romania	0.500	0.556	0.4	59.1	45.8
Russia	0.375	0.500	1.0	27.7	85.9
Slovakia#	0.875	0.944	0.5	6.7	10.7

Note: # Slovakia is not included in Loungani and Sheets; we present our own calculations here.

Based on data from 26 formerly socialist economies, Cukierman et al. (2000) find that for the early stages of liberalization, central bank independence is unrelated to inflation. But as soon as sufficiently high and sustained levels of liberalization are reached and variables like price decontrols and wars are controlled for, central bank independence turns out to be negatively and significantly correlated with inflation. The authors ask what factors could possibly explain the variance in legal central bank independence and find that (a) being on the fast track toward EU (and EMU) membership and (b) passing a central bank law late in transition has a positive impact on the chosen level of independence. The problem with the first variable is that it could also reflect (i) geographical proximity to the West or – probably more important – (ii) cultural similarity.

So far, we have analyzed the independence of central banks as domestic delegation. However, the arrangements regarding central banks have also an international delegation dimension. The currency board introduced in Estonia (1992) and Bulgaria (1997), is a good example. The establishment of a currency board is almost equivalent to the abdication of a domestic monetary policy. Thus, monetary policy decisions are delegated internationally and taken by an organization beyond the immediate reach of domestic actors, namely those (foreign) central banks that serve as the anchor of the domestic currency. In addition, with most of the countries under scrutiny here wanting to join the EU, one could have expected that they anticipate EU standards in terms of their bank's independence and other structural and substantial components and that these countries pass central bank laws in accordance with those standards.

3.1.3 Other domestic delegatee bodies

Most previous studies in which independent agencies have been compared across countries have exclusively focussed on comparing central bank independence. This was simply because it was the only agency for which data that could be compared were available. In this chapter, we extended this limited view by offering a simple indicator for the independence of constitutional courts. The next step would be to develop indicators for other agencies such as antitrust offices and so on. Following the debate on central bank independence, it almost seems to suggest itself to conjecture that the more independent antitrust offices should be able to carry out better competition policies than dependent ones. Such a claim would, however, be very difficult to test empirically. With regard to the outcomes or consequences of competition policy, no unequivocal measure is readily available.

Empirically, we observe that antitrust offices are much less independent than many central banks. In the US, the (independent) Federal Trade Commission has to cooperate with the Antitrust Division within the

Department of Justice. In the EU, there is no antitrust office of its own. In Germany, which prides itself on having at its disposal an independent *Kartellamt*, the economics minister can override its decisions in the case of an overwhelming macroeconomic interest. It would still be interesting to have an indicator that evaluates quality and independence of the various antitrust offices.

In the course of a transition from centrally planned to de-centrally coordinated economies, competition authorities have a special role to play, at least potentially. Due to the legacies of the past, it is very likely that monopoly suppliers will dominate quite a few markets, and entry barriers for newcomers might be substantial. In such a situation, it seems quite likely that representatives of the ex-monopolists will lobby for special favors like subsidies, but also for being exempted from antitrust rules.[4] Normatively speaking, an independent antitrust office would thus appear to be especially important during transition. On the positive analysis level, the composition of the constituent assembly and the legislature can have a major influence on the substance of the institutional arrangement of antitrust authorities.

Five of the eight constitutions analyzed here make explicit mention of the term competition in its economic sense. These are the Bulgarian, the Hungarian, the Romanian, the Russian, and the Slovakian constitutions. It seems safe to argue that competition legislation in Central and Eastern Europe has been heavily influenced by the antitrust rules of the European Union.[5] The Agreements that some of the states of Central and Eastern Europe have concluded with the EU usually contain an article stipulating that EU competition policy should become the norm for the countries' internal legislation. This is quite different from monetary policy institutions, where EU influence was difficult to discern.

The quality of the various competition policies has been ascertained by the European Bank for Reconstruction and Development in its annual transition report. On a scale ranging from 1 to 4+, where 1 indicates the worst possible grade and 4+ means the standard of established Western market economies, the competition policies of our eight case countries have been ranked as follows: Bulgaria 2, Czech Republic 3, Estonia 3–, Hungary 3, Poland 3, Romania 2, Russian Federation 2+, Slovak Republic 3 (EBRD, 1999, p. 24f.).

It was mentioned in the introduction that we are using a broad concept of delegation of powers. It would therefore not only make sense to analyze other independent agencies, to which governments have possibly delegated some competence, such as environmental agencies but also to analyze direct-democratic elements (because the population at large becomes an actor in its own right), and even include the independent media. The more independent the media, the more likely it seems that it can play an important role in controlling the government; this could be framed within 'delegation' because the constitution-makers grant others the power to voice critical opinions. Such an analysis is, however, beyond the scope of the present chapter.

3.1.4 Interdependencies between domestic delegatee bodies

It is interesting to examine the relations between degrees of independence among various delegatee bodies in the same constituency. The possible interrelations between judicial independence and central bank independence are of particular interest. Three conflicting hypotheses can be mentioned in this context.

Based on the observation that judicial independence and central bank independence are usually regulated on different normative levels – the constitutional vs. the post-constitutional – it almost suggests itself to hypothesize that central bank independence is a function of judicial independence. In addition, one can hypothesize that the existence of one independent delegatee will decrease the costs involved in delegating powers to another independent delegatee. According to this assumption, if an independent constitutional court is provided for by the constitution, the costs for the government of delegating powers to an independent bank in the post-constitutional stage will be lower and, thus, greater independence is more likely to materialize.

A competing hypothesis is based on the benefits side of the theoretical analysis of delegation of powers, in particular responsibility shift (Fiorina, 1982, see also Salzberger, 1993). According to its rationale, different delegated bodies can be viewed as substitutes. As one can shift responsibility to various bodies, if there is already an independent delegatee, such as a constitutional court, the potential benefits from an additional body will be lower. This would point to a negative correlation between the degree of independence of the constitutional court and that of the central bank. However, since the substance matters dealt with by these two institutions are very different, this substitution effect might be marginal.

A third hypothesis would be that there is no correlation between the two, or that such correlation, if it exists, may be a result of a factor different from the delegation framework (for example cultural elements). According to this hypothesis, there might be yet another factor explaining both central bank independence and judicial independence. One hypothesis might be that the degrees of *de jure* independence of both the judiciary and the central bank are a function of the composition of the constitutional assembly, the preferences of the actors represented therein, as well as the rules of aggregating individual preferences into collective decisions.

Our study of only eight countries does not enable us to test rigorously the interrelations between central banks' independence and constitutional courts' independence. However, from looking at the results in Tables 14.1 and 14.2, a pattern of a positive correlation can be noticed between the two, which manifests itself by the fact that the differences in the ranking of the two does not exceed two slots. Countries that are ranked as having the more independent constitutional courts are ranked also as having the more independent central banks (the aggregation of the three indices) – the Czech Republic, Estonia and Poland. Countries that are ranked as having less independent constitutional courts also have less independent central banks – Hungary, Romania and Russia. The only exception seems to be Slovakia, which is ranked number 8 with regard to the independence of its central bank and number 4 with regard to constitutional court independence. Bulgaria is ranked number 2 in the central banks independence list and number 5 in the constitutional courts table. The indicator for the quality of competition policy, mentioned in the previous section, corresponds to the same pattern, that is, it tends to correlate positively with the other two independence measures, whereas Slovakia, again, stands as the odd one out.

3.2 International Delegation

3.2.1 The constitutional basis for delegating powers to international organizations

Before taking a look at the extent to which governments of Central and Eastern European countries have delegated actual power internationally, we propose to take a look at the constitutional basis of transferring sovereign rights or competence to a body external to the nation-state, and at the status of international law and international agreements within the municipal legal systems. The first indicator can tell us which domestic political institutions are assigned the power to delegate externally. Naturally, different delegating organs – parliament, executive or other – will have different incentives to delegate externally, but, more importantly, the identity of the delegator and the process of delegation can indicate how easy it is to delegate internationally. In countries where the government is empowered to bind the legal system by international treaties, the potential of delegation is greater than in countries where legislation or constitutional amendment is required to perform such delegation, or where such delegation is subject to a veto by another branch of government.

The second aspect – the normative status of international law within the municipal legal system – is a good indicator for the importance attributed to which international delegation.

Bulgaria, Estonia and Slovakia seem to have the highest potential of delegating internationally. In Bulgaria, the competence to delegate internationally is divided between the government and parliament. Some agreements require parliamentary ratification, and they include agreements concerning the Republic of Bulgaria's participation in international organizations or international adjudication, agreements containing obligations for the treasury, agreements on human rights and more. Likewise, in Estonia the parliament is empowered to ratify or denounce important treaties, among those are all the treaties by which the Republic of Estonia joins international organizations or leagues. In Slovakia, the president is empowered to conclude and ratify international treaties, but he is allowed to delegate this power to the government. In Hungary, the power to conclude international treaties is allocated to the president as well as to the government. But if the treaty is of outstanding importance to the foreign relations of Hungary, parliament has to ratify it according to article 19 of the constitution.

It is more difficult to delegate powers internationally in the Czech Republic, Poland, Russia and Romania. In Romania, international treaties are negotiated by the government, concluded by the President, and need to be ratified by parliament within 60 days. In the Czech Republic, all branches of government take part in the international delegation of powers. The Czech constitution attributes agenda-setting powers with regard to joining international organizations and signing international treaties to the President, but he may transfer the task of negotiation to the government or, with its approval, to its individual members, expressly specified in the constitution. Decisions of the President require a signature of the Prime Minister. He is, thus, endowed with a veto power. A greater share (than in the countries mentioned above) of international accords require ratification by parliament. They include accords on human rights and fundamental freedoms, political agreements, economic agreements of a general nature, as well as agreements for the implementation of which a law must be passed.

Art. 90 of the Polish constitution enables the transfer of certain sovereign rights to an international organization. The constitution mentions two possible procedures for ratification of international agreements: (1) a statute shall be passed by the House of Representatives (Sejm) and by the Senate by a two-thirds majority vote in the presence of at least half of the statutory number of deputies in each house respectively. (2) A referendum needs to be held. With regard to international treaties, the Polish President has the competence to ratify and renounce international agreements, and shall notify the House of Representatives (Sejm) and the Senate thereof. Before ratifying an international agreement, he may refer it to the Constitutional Tribunal with a request to adjudicate upon its conformity to the constitution. In other words, the court has the power to delay ratification and some veto power.

In Russia, international delegation is an exclusive jurisdiction of the Federation and the president is allocated the power to conduct negotiations and sign international treaties. The constitutional court has the power to examine whether the treaty does not contradict the constitution. Although there is no mention in the constitution of a ratification requirement by the Duma, article 106 holds that if ratification of such an agreement had been conducted by the Duma, the Federation Council has to consider it.

With regard to the status of international law within the municipal legal system, the Czech Republic, Bulgaria and Poland feature at the top of the table. The Czech constitutional court is empowered to invalidate laws that contradict international agreements and to give effect to decisions of international courts. Thus, the Czech constitution places international law as superior to domestic law. In addition, the court is also empowered to take 'measures necessary to effect a decision by an international court which is binding for the Czech Republic if it cannot be effected otherwise' (art. 87(I) of the Czech constitution). The far-reaching delegation implied in this article has already been stressed in the section on the competence of courts (3.1.1).

Article 85 of the Bulgarian constitution specifies that those 'treaties ratified by the National Assembly may be amended or denounced only by their built in procedure or in accordance with the universally acknowledged norms of international law'. This far-reaching clause could mean that the international delegation by ratification of parliament is irreversible, save by the terms of the treaty itself or international law. It also indicates that the normative status of international delegation is above regular legislation, and requires amendment to the constitution if the international agreement is in conflict with the constitution (as specified explicitly by the second part of the same article). Moreover, the constitutional court is granted the powers to strike down new legislation that contradicts international law or agreements that were ratified by Bulgaria. Thus, the infrastructure for international delegation is indeed very extensive.

In Poland, a ratified international agreement constitutes part of the domestic legal order and shall be applied directly, unless its application depends on the enactment of a statute. Moreover, although in the list of sources of the law in Poland (art. 87 of the constitution), international agreements are placed after legislation, article 91 specifies that international law has precedence over statutes if such an agreement cannot be reconciled with the provisions of such statutes.

According to the Estonian constitution (art. 123), all treaties are inferior to the constitution and if they contradict it they are not to be concluded. However, the same article holds that the treaties are superior to legislation and in case of conflict their provisions ought to be applied. The constitution also empowers the National Court to review the compatibility of international agreement with the constitution, but there is no explicit authority to review whether legislation is in conformity with international law.

In the Slovak Republic (according to art. 11 of the constitution), international agreements on human rights take precedence over statutes, provided that they guarantee a greater extent of liberties. It is not clear what is the relative normative status of other international agreements. The constitutional court has the jurisdiction to review the compatibility of laws with international treaties. Likewise, the Hungarian constitution states that 'The legal system of the Republic of Hungary accepts the generally recognized principles of international law and shall harmonize the country's domestic law with obligations assumed under international law' (art. 7). This can mean subjection of international legislation to international law and maybe also of the constitution itself. However, the constitution does not specify how this harmonization is to be conducted, save that the legislative procedures for that (harmonization) will require a two-thirds majority. It is also silent about the enforcement powers. In other words, there is nothing in the constitution with regard to jurisdiction of the constitutional court to strike down legislation contradicting international law.

Russia and Romania are ranked at the bottom of the list with regard to the status of international law within the municipal legal system. Article 15 of the Russian constitution provides that 'the commonly recognized principles and norms of the international law and the international treaties of the Russian Federation shall be a component part of its legal system' and 'if an international treaty of the Russian Federation stipulates other rules than those stipulated by the law the rules of the international treaty shall apply'. However, no enforcement mechanism is specified, and no explicit jurisdiction is given to the constitutional court on the matter, in contrast to its jurisdiction to review the conformity of international treaties with the constitution.

In Romania, treaties ratified by parliament become part of national law. This means that they are subject to the constitution and are also in the same normative level of legislation, that is, later legislation might take precedent over the international treaty. According to article 20 of the Romanian constitution, in case of inconsistencies between international treaties with regard to fundamental human rights, to which Romania is a member, and national law, international law prevails over national law. However, a possible interpretation of this article is that if the treaty does not concern fundamental human rights and is in conflict with municipal law, the latter takes precedent. Enforcement mechanisms, such as review of the constitutional court, are not specified by the constitution.

The left side of Table 14.4 presents the ranking of the structural foundations of delegation, which can also be viewed as the ranking of the *de jure* possibilities of international delegation, This ranking is composed of scores with regard to the two components scrutinized above: the constitutional capacity and flexibility of delegation, and the constitutional binding force or normative status (within the national legal systems) of such delegation.

3.2.2 The actual delegation of international powers, or: the de facto external delegation

When describing the sequence in which the countries of Central and Eastern Europe have become members of international organizations and have thereby delegated power, it has to be taken into account that this is not a unilateral decision. In order to become members, these countries do not only have to want to become members but the existing international organizations have to let them in. The basis on which they are admitted is often the similarity of their legal framework to those of 'more western' countries. In that sense, one should expect these countries first to ratify a post-communist constitution, and only subsequently to apply to the international organizations. If we look at membership of the Council of Europe – in which safeguarding of human rights plays a crucial role – there are two cases in which countries were let in before they had passed a new constitution: Hungary (admitted in November of 1990) and Poland (admitted in November of 1991). Bulgaria ratified the European Convention on Human Rights in 1992, accepting the optional protocol on civil and political rights. In October 1993, Romania became a member of the Council of Europe.

All of the countries here under scrutiny except Russia have signed so-called 'Europe Agreements' with the EU, providing for a transition period towards customs-free trade while also granting trade advantages over the general GATT standards. Cooperating states set up trade and diplomatic cooperation and prepare full membership. Russia and the EU have concluded a partnership and cooperation agreement, which does not envisage full membership in the near future. Three of the analyzed countries have become NATO members. All of them – except Russia which is negotiating membership – are members of the WTO. Some of the countries had been members of the GATT even before the transition started (Poland became a member in 1967, Romania in 1971, and Hungary in 1973). If one takes membership in various international organizations into account and ranks the countries of the region according to the degree of integration, the rank order from most to least integrated is the following: (1) Poland, (2) Hungary, (3) Czech Republic, (4) Romania, (5) Bulgaria, (6) Slovakia, (7) Estonia and (8) Russia (see Table 14.3).[6]

3.2.3 Summary

In Table 14.4, we summarize our findings with regard to international delegation in the eight countries covered in our study. As noted above the left side of the table presents the ranking of the structural foundations of delegation, which can also be viewed as the ranking of the *de jure* possibilities of international delegation. The right side of the table provides a ranking of the actual delegation, or the *de facto* extent of international delegation.

As can be noticed, there is no full correlation between the *de jure* delegation and the *de facto* one. While Hungary, Poland and the Czech Republic figure as having high levels of both *de jure* and *de facto* international delegation, other countries are ranked as having high *de jure*, but low *de facto* delegation (Bulgaria and Estonia) or as having low level of *de jure* delegation and

Table 14.3 Extent of integration

	EU timescore	Council of E timescore	NATO yes/no	GATT timescore	Sum	Integr. rank
Bulgaria	3	3	4	6	16	5
Czech Rep.	3	5	1	4	13	3
Estonia	7	4	4	7	22	7
Hungary	1	1	1	3	6	2
Poland	1	2	1	1	5	1
Romania	3	6	4	2	15	4
Russian Fed	8	7	4	8	27	8
Slovakia	3	8	4	4	19	6

Notes: EU timescore indicates the chronological order in which official applications for EU membership were filed (the fastest scoring one, the second two and so forth); Council of E timescore indicates the chronological order in which the countries became a member of the Council of Europe; NATO yes/no indicates whether the country is a NATO member or not (the coding is 1 for members, and 4 for non-members); GATT timescore indicates the chronological order of GATT (WTO) accession. The 'Sum' contains the addition of the four individual scores, from which the 'integration rank' is derived.

Table 14.4 Constitutional flexibility for international delegation

	Flexibility of delegation	Status of delegation	*De jure* delegation rank	Actual delegation*
Bulgaria	6	8	8	4
Czech Rep.	4	9	6	6
Estonia	6	7	6	2
Hungary	6	7	6	7
Poland	5	8	6	8
Romania	5	5	1	5
Russia	5	6	2	1
Slovakia	7	7	8	3

Note: *For coherence, we reversed the ranking: 8 is the highest delegator, 1 the lowest.

high level of *de facto* delegation (Romania); Russia has a low ranking in both indices. A possible and very tentative explanation for these results is that countries in which international delegation is binding domestically, and this delegation also has a high normative status within the domestic legal system as well as mechanisms of enforcement, will be more hesitant to join international organizations or bind themselves with international treaties. Be that as it may, one insight of this analysis is that the number of international organizations or treaties a country is a member of does not provide a full picture as to its level of integration to the international community, or the level of international delegation.

4. CONCLUSIONS AND OUTLOOK

In the introduction we justified our choice of countries by pointing to a study in which four of them are listed as consolidated democracies (Czech Republic, Estonia, Hungary, and Poland) and four others as countries in transition – both politically and economically (Bulgaria, Romania, Russia, and Slovakia). This division is partially reflected in our subject of analysis – the constitutional and post-constitutional delegation of powers. The Czech Republic and Estonia seem to have the highest level of both international and domestic delegation. Slovakia can be added to this group. Russia and Romania have the lowest levels of both domestic and international delegation. Our tentative findings categorize Hungary and Poland in a middle group, while Bulgaria seems to have a high level of *de jure* international delegation, as well as a high level of delegation to the central bank, but a low level of delegation to her constitutional court. An *ad hoc* hypothesis with regard to Bulgaria's central bank score could be that this is due to the currency board.

Piazolo (1999) observed that those countries that have been promised full EU membership have developed considerably better than the other transition countries. It is doubtful, however, whether this observation could be made policy-relevant in the sense that the EU only has to promise full membership and a boost in credibility will be the inevitable result. In other words, it is not clear whether EU membership promise was the cause or the result of 'better' development. Our findings also do not fully support the conjecture that the more the countries are located in the west, the more integrated (with the west) we can expect them to be. Geography might play a crucial role for institutional development – and political and economic development as well, but according to the findings it is certainly not the sole factor. The Transition Report of the EBRD recognizes regional patterns in development but insists that there are a range of historical and political factors such as the length of time under central planning that also play a role (EBRD, 1999, p. 27f.). We concur.

More than ten years into transition, many questions still appear to be unanswerable: we have focussed here on the newly passed *de jure* constitutions rather than on what they develop to be in reality, that is the *de facto* constitutions. To ascertain divergences between the two is probably too early still. Yet, it should be possible to come up with hypotheses on the various degrees of divergence: where constitutions are inherently contradictory, constitutional reality should diverge from the letter of the constitution. If one buys into the view that constitutions need to be backed by spontaneously arisen institutions (Voigt, 1999, chapter 5), one could try to predict divergence by looking at civil society ratings. The higher the ranking, the more costly it will be for the government to renege on the constitution and the less likely it is therefore to occur (*Nations in Transit* regularly reports civil society rankings).

This chapter has been interested in analysing the choice of rules, that is constitutional rules have been *explananda*. We have largely abstained from analyzing them as *explanans*. In other words, we have not asked for the welfare effects, the distributional consequences and so on of alternative constitutional arrangements. More than one paper needs to be written on this issue. We have also abstained from normative analysis. Surely, more than one paper deserves to be written with a normative focus in mind.

NOTES

1. The third category in this survey of 28 ex-communist countries is countries that are consolidated autocracies and statist economies. They include Tajikistan, Belarus, Bosnia, Uzbekistan and Turkmenistan.
2. The state ombudsman is the initiator of direct judicial review proceedings.
3. Political independence is ascertained by the following questions: (1) Can the governor of the central bank be dismissed by the executive branch or the parliament if there is conflict regarding monetary policy? (2) Does the term of office of the central bank governor exceed the election cycle? (3) Does the term of office of central bank board members exceed the election cycle? (4) Does a government official or representative sit on the central bank board with a vote? (5) Does a government official or representative sit on the central bank board with a veto?
4. They might also try to block the introduction of policy competition entirely.
5. With regard to the Czech Republic, this is argued by Bányaiová et al. (w.d.); with regard to Estonia by Sepp and Wrobel (2000), with regard to Poland by Posluszana and Wiercinski (w.d.).
6. The ranking is somewhat biassed against countries which were established only after 1989 (Estonia and Slovakia). This can be one reason for their poor ranking.

REFERENCES

Ackerman, B. (1991), *We the People, Vol.1: Foundations*, Cambridge, MA: Belknap.

Bányaiová, A. et al. (w.d.), 'Czech Republic – Current developments in competition legislation', http://www.global-competition.com/spl_rpts/ear/czech.htm.

Cukierman, A., G. Miller and B. Neyapti (2000), 'Central Bank Reform, Liberalization and Inflation in Transition Economies – An International Perspective', Tel Aviv University, Foerder Institute for Economic Research Working Paper No.19–2000.

Debelle, G. and S. Fischer (1995), 'How independent should a central bank be?', in J.C. Fuhrer (ed.), *Goals, Guidelines and Constraints Facing Monetary Policymakers*, Conference Series No. 38, Boston: Federal Reserve Bank of Boston, pp. 195–221.

European Bank for Reconstruction and Development (1999), *Transition Report 1999*, London.
Fiorina, M. (1982), 'Legislative choice of regulatory forms: legal process or administrative process', *Public Choice*, **38**, 33.
Fiorina, M. (1986), 'Legislator uncertainty, legislative control and the delegation of legislative powers', *Journal of Law, Economics and Organization*, **2**, 33.
Hume, D. (1777/1987), *Essays – Moral, Political, and Literary*, ed. and with a Foreword, Notes, and Glossary by Eugene F. Miller, Indianapolis: Liberty Classics.
Karatnycky, A., A. Motyl and B. Shor (1998), *Nations in Transit 1998*, New Brunswick et al.: Transaction Publishers.
Kobabe, Rolf (1999), *Zentralbanken in Osteuropa – Europäische Integration und rechtliche Konvergenz*, Baden-Baden: Nomos.
Loungani, Prakash and Nathan Sheets (1997), 'Central Bank independence, inflation, and growth in transition economies', *Journal of Money, Credit, and Banking*, **29** (3), 381–99.
McCubbins, M. and T. Page (1987), 'A Theory of Congressional Delegation', in M. McCubbins and T. Sulliva (eds), *Congress: Structure and Policy*, Cambridge: Cambridge University Press, p. 409.
McCubbins, M. and R. Noll and B. Weingast (1989), 'Structure and process, politics and policy: administrative arangements and the political control of agencies', *Virginia Law Review*, **75**, 431.
Piazolo, Daniel (1999), 'Growth effects of institutional change and European integration', *Economic Systems*, **23** (4), 305–30.
Posluszna, M. and A. Wiercinski (w.d.), 'Poland – protection of competition and consumers' interests in Poland', http://www.global-competition.com/spl_rpts/ear/poland.htm.
Salzberger, Eli M. (1993), 'A positive analysis of the doctrine of separation of powers, or: Why do we have an independent judiciary?', *International Review of Law and Economics*, **13**, 349–79.
Salzberger, Eli M. and Stefan Voigt (2002a), 'On the Delegation of Powers – With Special Emphasis on Central and Eastern Europe', S. Voigt and H.-J. Wagener (eds), *Constitutions, Markets, and the Law*, Cheltenham: Edward Elgar, pp. 221–85.
Salzberger, Eli M. and Stefan Voigt (2002b), 'On constitutional processes and the delegation of power, with special emphasis on Israel and Central and Eastern Europe', *Theoretical Inquiries in the Law*, **3** (1), 207–63.
Sepp, J. and M. Wrobel (2000), 'Besonderheiten der wettbewerbspolitik in einem transformationsland', *Wirtschaft und Wettbewerb*, **50** (1).
Voigt, S. (1999), *Explaining Constitutional Change – A Positive Economics Approach*, Cheltenham: Edward Elgar.
Voigt, S. and E.M. Salzberger (2002), 'Choosing Not to Choose: When Politicians Choose to Delegate Powers', Kyklos, **55** (2), 247–68.
Weingast, B. (1993), 'Constitutions as governance structures: the political foundations of secure markets', *Journal of Institutional and Theoretical Economics*, **149** (1), 286–311.

Index